# REYKJAVIK REVISITED

Steps Toward a World Free of Nuclear Weapons

Hoover Institution gratefully acknowledges

THE JOHN D. AND CATHERINE T. MACARTHUR FOUNDATION
and
THE WILLIAM AND FLORA HEWLETT FOUNDATION

for their generous support of the project that led to this book:
**Reykjavik Revisited: Steps Toward a World Free of Nuclear Weapons**.

# REYKJAVIK REVISITED

## Steps Toward a World Free of Nuclear Weapons

*Complete Report of 2007 Hoover Institution Conference*

*Conference Report Editors*

### George P. Shultz

### Steven P. Andreasen

### Sidney D. Drell

### James E. Goodby

*Conference Sponsored by the*
HOOVER INSTITUTION *and the* NUCLEAR THREAT INITIATIVE

HOOVER INSTITUTION PRESS
Stanford University   Stanford, California

The Hoover Institution on War, Revolution and Peace, founded
at Stanford University in 1919 by Herbert Hoover, who went on
to become the thirty-first president of the United States, is an
interdisciplinary research center for advanced study on domestic
and international affairs. The views expressed in its publications are
entirely those of the authors and do not necessarily reflect the views
of the staff, officers, or Board of Overseers of the Hoover Institution.

www.hoover.org

The Nuclear Threat Initiative (NTI) is a non-profit organization with a
mission to strengthen global security by reducing the risk of use and
preventing the spread of nuclear, biological and chemical weapons, and to
work to build the trust, transparency and security which are preconditions to
the ultimate fulfillment of the Non-Proliferation Treaty's goals and ambitions.

www.nti.org

Hoover Institution Press Publication No. 565
Hoover Institution at Leland Stanford Junior University,
Stanford, California, 94305-6010

First printing 2008
15   14   13   12   11   10   09   08      9   8   7   6   5   4   3   2   1

Manufactured in the United States of America

Library of Congress Cataloging-in-Publication Data
    Reykjavik revisited : steps toward a world free of nuclear
weapons / edited by George P. Shultz . . . [et al.].
        p.      cm. — (Hoover Institution Press publication series ; 565)
    Includes bibliographical references and index.
ISBN: 978-0-8179-4921-1 (hardback : alk. paper)
ISBN: 978-0-8179-4922-8 (pbk. : alk. paper)
    1. Nuclear proliferation—Congresses.   2. Nuclear arms control—
Congresses.   I. Shultz, George Pratt, 1920–     .
JZ5675.R49   2008
327.1'747—dc22                                        2008015427

# Contents

Preface
*George P. Shultz, Steven P. Andreasen, Sidney D. Drell, and
James E. Goodby*                                                    ix

Acknowledgments                                                     xiii

Introduction:
Closing the Gap Between the "Is" and the "Ought"
*Steven P. Andreasen*                                               xv

**1.** Further Reductions in Nuclear Forces
*David Holloway*                                                    1

**2.** De-alerting Strategic Forces
*Bruce G. Blair*                                                    47

**3.** Eliminating Short-Range Nuclear Weapons
Designed to Be Forward Deployed
*Rose Gottemoeller*                                                 107

**4.** Challenges of Verification and Compliance
within a State of Universal Latency
*Raymond J. Juzaitis and John E. McLaughlin*                        159

**5.** Transparent and Irreversible Dismantlement
of Nuclear Weapons
*Matthew Bunn*                                                      205

**6.** Monitoring Nuclear Warheads
*Edward Ifft*                                                       229

**7.** Securing Nuclear Stockpiles Worldwide
   *Matthew Bunn*                                                    243

**8.** Controlling Fissile Materials Worldwide:
   A Fissile Material Cutoff Treaty and Beyond
   *Robert J. Einhorn*                                              279

**9.** Preventing the Spread of Enrichment and Reprocessing
   *James Timbie*                                                   313

**10.** Internationalizing the Nuclear Fuel Cycle
   *James E. Goodby*                                                333

**11.** Comprehensive Nuclear-Test-Ban Treaty and U.S. Security
   *Raymond Jeanloz*                                                369

**12.** Regional Animosities and Nuclear Weapons Proliferation
   *Jack F. Matlock Jr.*                                            399

**13.** PART ONE
   A World Free of Nuclear Weapons
   *Max M. Kampelman*                                               425

   PART TWO
   Turning the Goal of a World without
   Nuclear Weapons into a Joint Enterprise
   *Max M. Kampelman and Steven P. Andreasen*                       436

**14.** Rethinking Nuclear Deterrence
   *James E. Goodby and Sidney D. Drell*                            449

**15.** Diplomacy for the Future
   *George P. Shultz and Henry S. Rowen*                            455

Appendix One:  Conference Agenda                                   465

Appendix Two:  List of Conference Participants                     467

Appendix Three:  A World Free of Nuclear Weapons
*George P. Shultz, William J. Perry, Henry A. Kissinger,*
*and Sam Nunn [*Wall Street Journal *op-ed, January 4, 2007]*       473

Appendix Four:  Toward a Nuclear-Free World
*George P. Shultz, William J. Perry, Henry A. Kissinger,*
*and Sam Nunn [*Wall Street Journal *op-ed, January 15, 2008]*      479

About the Authors                                                  487

Index                                                              493

# Preface

**George P. Shultz**
**Steven P. Andreasen**
**Sidney D. Drell**
**James E. Goodby**

This book is a report on an extraordinary conference.

The papers included here were presented at a conference held at Stanford University's Hoover Institution in collaboration with Sam Nunn's Nuclear Threat Initiative (NTI) on October 24–25, 2007. The topics emerged from discussions of a January 2007 essay in the *Wall Street Journal* in which the many signatories agreed to a central argument for rekindling the bold vision of a world free of nuclear weapons that Ronald Reagan and Mikhail Gorbachev brought to their 1986 meeting in Reykjavik. It is that a powerful synergy can be developed if the goal of a world without nuclear weapons is linked to the individual actions needed to move the world toward that goal. There is more political force in these ideas if they are considered as one program rather than as discrete entities. Without that vision, which has faded since that dramatic encounter in Reykjavik, measures that could provide greater safety to all the world's peoples have not been pursued with the intensity the times require. As recorded in this volume, the 2007 conference emphasized the importance of these measures.

The papers were prepared by highly qualified individuals, and they were reviewed and worked over by their colleagues and discussed in some detail at the conference. Each writer then had an opportunity to make whatever additions and revisions seemed appropriate. The result appears here.

Work continues to go forward on all of these steps toward a world free of nuclear weapons, steps which, in and of themselves, are vital to achieving a safer world. Many can—and should—be implemented or acted upon promptly.

The papers develop three main themes: practical ways to remove nuclear warheads from the world's inventories of ready-to-fire weapons and ultimately to eliminate them; methods to manage and control nuclear programs to ensure that nuclear materials are used only for peaceful purposes; and technical, political, and intelligence issues that must be considered in reducing incentives for acquiring nuclear arsenals and in creating a global coalition in support of a world free of nuclear weapons.

The number of nuclear warheads held by the United States and Russia has decreased significantly since 1986, and the number of states that have opted to develop nuclear weapons and maintain them in their arsenals still remains under ten. However, the international consensus that favored fewer, rather than more, nuclear weapons states has eroded. Some states that decided to forgo nuclear weapons, thinking that their national security could be protected without them, reportedly are reconsidering their positions, and more will do so, inevitably, if present trends persist. Moreover, with the global spread of technology, the threat that the world's most terrible weapons might fall into dangerous hands, including terrorist organizations, has grown.

In short, the situation that has developed in recent years is not favorable to nonproliferation efforts. Changing that will require nothing less than a new deal between the states that have nuclear weapons and those states that, for now, have volunteered to forgo their right to acquire them. It also has to be recognized that the path ahead is deeply entwined with, and dependent upon, political cooperation on a global scale and with nations of varying patterns of governance. The vision of Reykjavik is an essential part of the process. Unless this bold vision is embraced, individual steps along the way are unlikely to be perceived as fair or urgent. Rather, they would be seen as preserving the current situation of a two-tier system in which a small number of states possess nuclear weapons and all others must remain without them. This concept becomes less and less viable as nuclear technology and knowledge spread throughout the world.

Will this task be difficult? Yes, without a doubt. It will be especially daunting to eliminate all non-deployed warheads because the verification challenges are enormous. But with success in reducing operationally deployed warheads to zero on a global basis, the necessary experience and the mutual trust to proceed toward the elimination of all nuclear weapons should develop, making feasible the verification procedures that now appear to be so difficult.

As the world teeters on the edge of a new and more perilous nuclear era, it is crucial that world leaders work jointly to do everything within their power to free the world of the dangers of nuclear weapons. If a nuclear weapon were to be used in our future, it would symbolize a double failure: that we failed to resolve our differences peacefully and that we failed to address decisively the political, diplomatic, and security challenges associated with the most devastating instrument of annihilation ever invented, including keeping those weapons out of the hands of those who do not shrink from mass murder on an unprecedented scale.

Each of us found the conference highly educational and the discussions intense and satisfying. We hope that you will find these papers equally rewarding as reading and simultaneously stimulating as a guide to further work that is vital and necessary.

# Acknowledgments

The Hoover Institution and the editors of this volume gratefully acknowledge The John D. and Catherine T. MacArthur Foundation and The William and Flora Hewlett Foundation for their generous support of our project that led to this book: *Reykjavik Revisited: Steps Toward a World Free of Nuclear Weapons*.

This book contains papers prepared for a conference of the same name held at the Hoover Institution at Stanford University on October 24–25, 2007, co-sponsored by the Nuclear Threat Initiative (NTI). The editors thank the authors for writing excellent papers, and subsequently editing them in response to discussions at the conference.

Many individuals have made valuable contributions to the success of this project and the preparation of this book. In particular we want to recognize the Hoover Institution Press, Brooke Anderson and Joan Rohlfing at NTI, and Paige Mathes, Bonnie Rose, and Susan Southworth at Hoover.

# Introduction:
# Closing the Gap Between
# the "Is" and the "Ought"

## Steven P. Andreasen

Twenty years to the day of the 1986 Reykjavik summit meeting where President Ronald Reagan and Soviet President Mikhail Gorbachev came close to an agreement to eliminate all nuclear weapons, a small conference was held at the Hoover Institution to discuss whether the possibilities of a world without nuclear arms envisioned at Reykjavik could be brought to fruition. The outcome of this discussion was published three months later in a January 2007 Op-Ed in the *Wall Street Journal* signed by former Secretaries of State George Shultz and Henry Kissinger, former Secretary of Defense William Perry, and former Senator Sam Nunn.

Their conclusion—endorsed by almost all conference participants—is that in order to deal decisively with the tremendous dangers presented today by nuclear weapons, American leadership will be required to take the world to the next stage—"to a solid consensus for reversing reliance on nuclear weapons globally as a vital contribution to preventing their proliferation into potentially dangerous hands, and ultimately ending them as a threat to the world." Most important, the United States and other nations must embrace both the vision of a world free of nuclear weapons and pursue a balanced program of practical measures toward achieving that goal: "Without the bold vision, the actions will not be perceived as fair or urgent. Without the actions, the vision will not be perceived as realistic or possible."

The response to this January 2007 article, both in the United States and abroad, has been remarkable. Mikhail Gorbachev wrote that as someone who signed the first treaties on real reductions in nuclear weapons, he felt it was his duty to support the *Wall Street Journal* authors' call for urgent action. Soon after, then-Foreign Secretary of the United Kingdom, Margaret Beckett, gave a speech in Washington outlining a path forward for dealing with nuclear threats. Explicitly drawing on the views of the authors of the *Wall Street Journal* article, Beckett stated that while the conditions for the total elimination of nuclear arms do not exist today, that does not mean we should resign ourselves to the idea that nuclear weapons can never be abolished in the future. "What we need is both a vision—a scenario for a world free of nuclear weapons—and action—progressive steps to reduce warhead numbers and to limit the role of nuclear weapons in security policy. These two strands are separate but they are mutually reinforcing. Both are necessary, but at the moment too weak."

With both interest and momentum building, in October 2007, a second conference was convened at Hoover—jointly sponsored with the Nuclear Threat Initiative—to further examine how to advance the vision of a world free of nuclear weapons and to look in greater detail at a number of practical steps consistent with this goal. A central theme from that conference is that in order to reduce reliance on nuclear weapons globally and prevent their spread into dangerous hands, we must establish common objectives with other states. If a strong coalition of nations bands together on a set of practical steps, it can exert powerful pressures to prevent new nuclear weapon states and make it much less likely that terrorists can get the materials they need to build a nuclear weapon.

In this context, the October 2007 conference reviewed ten papers that had been prepared in advance for the meeting. They are included in this book after editing by the paper authors taking into consideration the discussions at the conference. They advocate urgent steps that can be taken now—and other steps that can build on the immediate priorities—to greatly reduce the nuclear threats that we face while enhancing global security and international stability. Those steps, many of which were summarized in a second *Wall Street Journal* Op-Ed that appeared in January 2008—include the following recommendations.

*Further Reductions in Nuclear Weapons*

According to published estimates, Russia now has about 15,000 nuclear weapons; the United States, 10,000; France, 350; and Britain and China about 200 each. The other nuclear weapons states—Israel, India, Pakistan, and North Korea—have smaller stockpiles, amounting to a total of about 200–350 warheads. The United States and Russia between them possess about 95 percent of all nuclear weapons, so that is where reductions should start. Our two countries should make further substantial reductions in their nuclear forces, making clear the expectation that the reductions process is moving forward. This could begin by lowering the number of operationally deployed strategic nuclear warheads permitted under the Moscow Treaty to 1000, followed by a second stage of reductions down to 500 (with another 500 in a responsive force). A third stage would limit the two countries to a strategic nuclear force with 500 warheads, all in a responsive force with zero operationally deployed. At some point, commitments will be required from other nuclear powers to limit their nuclear forces—including greater transparency and inclusion in a regime of monitoring and verification—in order to move beyond U.S. and Russian reductions toward a world with "zero" operationally deployed nuclear forces and—ultimately—a world without nuclear weapons.

*De-alerting Strategic Forces*

More than 15 years after the end of the Cold War, the United States and Russia continue to maintain thousands of nuclear weapons on ballistic missiles that can be launched and delivered to their target in minutes. Nuclear forces deployed this way run real risks—in particular, that of an accidental, mistaken, or unauthorized launch of a nuclear ballistic missile. Moreover, U.S. and Russian force postures lend legitimacy to the nuclear ambitions of other nations, and to those nations' adoption of launch-ready nuclear postures. Over time more states are likely to follow in our footsteps, and increase their own forces' combat readiness, resulting in growing worldwide dangers of accidental or unauthorized launch, or theft, of nuclear weapons.

Increasing warning and decision time for leaders in both nations should be a priority, so that we reduce the risk of a catastrophic nuclear accident to as close to "zero" as possible. Action on this front would also downgrade the role of nuclear weapons and convey a hopeful and serious message to the world that reliance on them is diminishing. Near-term steps could take the form of both procedural and physical modifications to existing nuclear force postures, such as dropping prompt launch and massive attack options from war plans, isolating missiles from outside launch signals (thus removing first-strike and launch on warning as attack options and eliminating the prospect of terrorists exploiting hair-trigger postures to cause a nuclear incident or actual firing), and separating warheads from delivery vehicles. Over the longer term, warheads removed from missiles might be stored and jointly monitored in ways that preserve survivability and stability. Ideally, the U.S. and Russia would undertake such steps in unison. The goal would be to establish a global norm against launch-ready nuclear postures.

### Missile Defense and Early Warning

Progress on these first two steps—further reductions in U.S.-Russian nuclear forces and changing Cold War era force postures—would be greatly facilitated by joint U.S. and Russian cooperation on missile defense, including an agreement on how to work together on joint early warning and European missile defense, a shared concern for Russia, the U.S., and NATO.

## Eliminating Short-Range Nuclear Weapons

Tactical nuclear bombs are the most likely targets for terrorists. This is an unacceptable security risk for all nations.

It is feasible that NATO could decide to recast its Strategic Concept during NATO's 60th anniversary celebration in 2009 to achieve the goal of ending NATO nuclear deployments in Europe. Russia's new dependence on nuclear weapons to compensate for its conventional weakness, however, will have to be dealt with—including resolving disagreements over the Conventional Forces in Europe Treaty. Confidence-building should be the first step and should be done now, taking advantage of cooperation that the U.S. and Russia have pursued in the past 15 years. Once mutual confidence grows, Russia, the U.S., and NATO can move to the next stage, beginning actual reduction measures, with the initial goal of banning tactical nuclear weapons in operational deployment. At some point, it may be best to place tactical nuclear weapons in the same "basket" as strategic nuclear weapons for elimination, acknowledging the difficulty of differentiating the two.

## Verification and Compliance

Reaffirming President Reagan's maxim of "trust but verify" would improve near-term security and contribute to achieving the vision of a world free of nuclear weapons. This effort—to include transparency and confidence-building measures—must be global in scope and involve all aspects of the nuclear fuel and weapons cycles while also encompassing actors ranging from established nuclear states to non-state entities.

In the near term, the U.S. and Russia must ensure the renewal of essential monitoring and verification provisions that otherwise will expire with the START I Treaty in 2009. They must also enter into discussions on non-deployed warheads. Second, diplomacy must focus on slowing and ultimately stopping the momentum toward nuclear armament in the non-nuclear weapon states. Third, to account for and globally secure nuclear explosive material, a number of initiatives—including a verifiable Fissile Material Cutoff Treaty (FMCT)—could be completed relatively soon and would help form a foundation for a more rigorous system of accounting and security. An international consensus must be built regarding ways to deter—or respond to—secret attempts by countries to "break out" of any agreements that are achieved.

*Securing Nuclear Stockpiles Worldwide*

Nuclear terrorism is a real and urgent threat. Al Qaeda and other groups have sought nuclear weapons and the materials to make them. If a terrorist group were able to obtain separated plutonium or highly enriched uranium (HEU), it is plausible they could make a crude nuclear explosive. The most effective tool for reducing this risk is to strengthen security for all nuclear weapons and weapons-usable nuclear materials worldwide. Preventing theft of nuclear weapons and materials would also block a major shortcut for states seeking nuclear weapons. Accurate and transparent accounting of nuclear weapons and materials stockpiles—a key part of a comprehensive nuclear security approach, and a prerequisite to verifiable and irreversible dismantlement of nuclear stockpiles—will also be an essential part of a verifiable path to deep reductions in, or prohibition of, nuclear weapons.

Although current efforts to improve security for nuclear weapons and materials have made substantial progress, particularly in Russia, unacceptable risks remain. Hundreds of buildings with HEU or, in some cases, plutonium in many countries around the world are demonstrably not secured against the kinds of outsider and insider threats that terrorists and criminals have shown they can pose. The most important ingredient for overcoming the obstacles to securing nuclear stockpiles is sustained leadership from the highest levels.

Also in the near term, the United States and Russia should seek to lead a global campaign to achieve effective and sustainable security for all nuclear weapons and weapons-usable nuclear materials worldwide as quickly as practicable, using all policy tools available. This campaign should pursue partnership-based approaches which respect national sovereignty and draw on ideas and resources from all participants—and which can be implemented while protecting nuclear secrets. The U.S. and Russia could play a key role in helping to implement United Nations Security Council Resolution 1540 relating to nuclear security by offering to jointly assist any nation in meeting its obligations under this resolution. The United States and other leading nuclear weapon and nuclear energy countries should seek to put in place best practices for global nuclear security to ensure that all nuclear weapons and every significant cache of plutonium or HEU has adequate protection from theft.

## Controlling Fissile Materials Worldwide: FMCT and Beyond

Over the last decade, the United States has viewed a Fissile Material Cutoff Treaty (FMCT) as a modest arms control measure of limited scope that could codify the existing de facto moratorium on fissile material production for nuclear weapons by the five NPT nuclear weapon states, and cap the fissile material weapons stocks of the three nuclear powers that never joined the NPT. Those goals remain valid, especially now that India and Pakistan appear poised to ramp up their bomb-making capabilities. Instead of only banning the production of fissile materials for use in nuclear weapons, an FMCT should also prohibit the production of HEU for civil purposes (which would reinforce ongoing efforts to convert research reactors to use low-enriched rather than HEU fuels) and either phase out or adopt a long-term moratorium on the production of HEU for naval propulsion. Moreover, while the scope of an FMCT itself should focus only on the production of fissile material after entry into force, the treaty should be accompanied by a voluntary, multilateral arrangement—a

"Fissile Material Control Initiative"—that would address the challenges posed by pre-existing fissile materials and, over time, would help monitor, secure, manage, and reduce existing stocks of fissile materials around the world.

### Preventing the Spread of Enrichment and Reprocessing

As countries consider nuclear energy, the potential spread of sensitive fuel cycle technologies—enrichment of uranium and reprocessing of spent fuel to separate plutonium—poses a serious non-proliferation challenge. Moreover, the latent potential to produce fissile material for weapons inherent in enrichment and reprocessing capabilities could be a substantial obstacle to further reductions or elimination of nuclear weapons.

Without prejudice to "whether" nuclear energy makes "economic sense" in any specific case, the most reliable and economical approach to nuclear energy is to rely on the international market for nuclear fuel services. That said, proponents of nuclear energy will advocate indigenous enrichment and reprocessing capabilities to promote energy security, to avoid falling behind regional peers technologically, and to gain security benefits, despite the economic and political costs and risks. As an alternative to indigenous development, advanced nuclear countries and the International Atomic Energy Agency (IAEA) could create a package of incentives that includes assurances of reliable supply of nuclear fuel, reserves of low-enriched uranium and spent fuel management. The purpose of this program would be to ensure that the means to make nuclear weapons materials is not spread around the globe.

### Nuclear Non-Proliferation Treaty (NPT) and the Comprehensive Test Ban Treaty (CTBT)

Near-term steps to strengthen the NPT are essential, and include ratification of the Additional Protocol that allows for enhanced monitoring of civilian nuclear power programs. Bringing the CTBT into force at an early date would also strengthen the NPT. The CTBT offers a significant opportunity toward implementing President Reagan's vision of establishing a global verification regime for nuclear weapons. A review of the past decade's development strengthens the argument that the CTBT is effectively verifiable; it does not undermine America's ability to sustain a nuclear deterrent; and its entry into force would enhance global security by constraining development of nuclear weapons. In the near term, leaders in the executive branch and Congress should undertake an informed bipartisan dialogue leading to ratification. The CTBT Organization is currently putting in place new monitoring stations to detect nuclear tests—an effort we should continue to support even prior to ratification. Enhancing international transparency and confidence-building measures associated with nuclear weapons and establishing a periodic review of the CTBT would assist in ratification.

*Regional Confrontations and Nuclear Weapons Proliferation*

As we look ahead to building the foundation for a world without nuclear weapons, we must recognize the reality that regional animosities can contribute to nuclear proliferation. An effective policy to prevent further proliferation will combine efforts to "de-legitimize" nuclear weapons as a source of national power with specific moves to defuse the most dangerous aspects of regional confrontations.

States that have terminated nuclear weapons programs (Brazil, South Africa, and Libya are examples) have done so when they deemed that possession of the weapons would create unacceptable dangers and that forgoing the program would actually make the ruling regime more secure, as well as provide tangible benefits to overall security. U.S. diplomacy in the 1980s, which led to an end of the Cold War, suggests that direct communication at the most senior levels of government is a useful—probably essential—tool to find peaceful ways to resolve disputes. In addition to dialogue and positive incentives, multilateral pressures will also be an essential component to successfully addressing regional proliferation.

## Turning the Goal of a World Without Nuclear Weapons into a Practical Enterprise Among Nations

Intensive work with leaders of non-nuclear as well as nuclear nations will be required to turn the goal of a world without nuclear weapons into a practical enterprise. While applying the necessary political will to build a consensus on priorities must be an international effort—one that incorporates the views of many nations—the U.S. and Russia, as the two leading nuclear powers, have a special role to play given their huge nuclear arsenals.

To facilitate progress on both near-term steps and achieving the vision of a world free of nuclear weapons, Washington and Moscow should enter into a broad "global security dialogue," designed to explore all aspects of security in the 21st century, including nuclear security. The process of nuclear diplomacy should also allow for early involvement of other key states, including, at some point, through the United Nations. Care should be taken not to "corner" nations that may lack enthusiasm for the vision or be averse to certain steps, as their positive involvement will be required. Most important, the process will also require the direct and sustained involvement of the president and other world leaders.

No one is under any illusion that progress on this complex nexus of nuclear issues can be achieved easily; however, one unavoidable fact is that we cannot wait to agree on every solution to every problem before we get started. Former Senator Sam Nunn has compared the goal of a world free of nuclear weapons to the top of a very tall mountain, noting that today, we are heading down—not up. In his words, "We can see that we must turn around, that we must take paths leading to higher ground and that we must get others to move with us. We must find trails leading upward." Achieving a world free from the threat of nuclear weapons will require a willingness to be idealistic and realistic at the same time, in order to find a way to move through practical, near-term steps from what "is"—a world with a risk of increasing global disaster—to what "ought" to be: a peaceful, civilized world free of the threat from weapons of mass destruction. Today, we have both a security and moral imperative to present and future generations to close the gap between what "is" and what "ought" to be.

# 1. Further Reductions in Nuclear Forces

## David Holloway

**Summary**

The United States and Russia have about 95 percent of all nuclear warheads. There is scope for further immediate reductions. Recent doctrinal statements by the United States and Russia suggest (i) that it should be possible to make substantial reductions in strategic nuclear weapons, and (ii) that there is no reason why their strategic nuclear forces should be "operationally deployed."[1]

The paper sets out four stages in the reduction of nuclear weapons to very low levels. Three criteria are used to assess those stages: strategic stability; monitoring and verification; contribution to the goal of eliminating nuclear weapons.

The reductions outlined here start with a feasible option (stage one) and end with a conceivable one (stage four). In stage one the United States and Russia could reduce the number of operationally deployed strategic nuclear warheads to 1000. That number could be inserted into the Moscow Treaty in place of the current target of 1700–

I have benefited enormously, in the writing of this paper, from discussions with Sidney Drell, James Goodby, and Edward Ifft. I am very grateful to Steve Andreasen, Bruce Blair, Malcolm Chalmers, Robert Einhorn, the late W. K. H. Panofsky, and Joan Rohlfing for comments on earlier drafts of the paper.

1. I follow convention by using "warhead" to include bombs as well as missile warheads, and "weapon" to include the delivery vehicle as well as the warhead.

2200. The parts of the START Treaty that are relevant to verification and monitoring should be maintained in one form or another beyond December 2009. An additional undefined number of warheads would remain in a responsive force.

In stage two the United States and Russia would each retain 500 operationally deployed strategic nuclear warheads plus 500 more in the responsive force. Stage three would be more radical, limiting the two countries to a strategic nuclear force with 500 warheads, all in a reserve force with zero operationally deployed.

Sooner rather than later, the other nuclear powers will need to be brought into the process of disarmament. Three commitments will be required from them: not to increase their nuclear forces; to agree to greater transparency; and not to have their nuclear forces operationally deployed.

Given the diminishing distinction between strategic and non-strategic weapons as numbers decrease, a conceivable stage four would be a configuration in which no state in the world has more than 500 (or 200 in a variant) nuclear warheads of any type with zero operationally deployed. As reductions are made, strategic stability becomes more complicated, while verification and monitoring become more difficult.

Reductions are complementary to other approaches; compared with de-alerting, they have the advantage, as long as the warheads are disassembled, of irreversibility. Missile defenses could be accommodated within the process of disarmament only if they were pursued cooperatively.

Some thoughts are offered on the transition to a world with no nuclear weapons.

**Introduction**

The number of nuclear warheads in the world reached its peak of about 70,000 in 1986, the year of the Reykjavik summit meeting. There has been a significant reduction since then, but the current total of over 20,000 is still high. Much remains to be done if the world is to be rid of nuclear weapons.

Nuclear weapons are distributed very unevenly. No government publishes detailed information about the numbers of nuclear warheads it possesses. According to careful estimates—which are, however, estimates—Russia now has about 15,000 nuclear warheads; the United States, 10,000; France, 350; and Britain and China about 200 each. The other nuclear weapons states—Israel, India, Pakistan, and North Korea—have smaller stockpiles, amounting to a total of about 200–350 warheads.[2]

These figures apparently include all nuclear warheads, those intended for deployment on long-range as well as short-range delivery vehicles. Not all of these nuclear warheads are deployed with armed forces. Some indeed are due to be disassembled in the coming years, but plans for disassembly have not been made public.

This paper takes as given—and desirable—the goal of a world without nuclear weapons. In that context it asks how the nuclear forces of all states that possess them could be substantially reduced. It looks first at the reduction of the strategic nuclear weapons of the United States and Russia and then asks how reductions in nuclear forces might be phased to involve all states that possess nuclear weapons. To what extent, and when, will these reductions require coordinated action and/or negotiated agreements? What arrangements for monitoring and verification need to be created to support such reductions? Finally it considers the steps that need to be taken to move from substantial reductions to the elimination of nuclear weapons.

---

2. I am much indebted to the work of Robert S. Norris and Hans M. Kristensen on nuclear stockpiles published in the Nuclear Notebook in the *Bulletin of the Atomic Scientists*. The sources for the figures in this paragraph are as follows: *Bulletin of the Atomic Scientists*, March/April 2007, p. 61 for Russia; *Bulletin*, January/February 2007, p. 79 for the United States; and *Bulletin*, July/August 2006, pp. 65–66 for the other countries. Unless otherwise stated I have relied on the Nuclear Notebook for the numbers in this paper.

## Current Plans for Reductions

The United States and Russia are committed to reducing the number of their strategic nuclear warheads to 1700–2200 by December 31, 2012, under the terms of the Strategic Offensive Reductions Treaty (SORT), which was signed in Moscow by Presidents Bush and Putin in May 2002.[3] On July 3, 2007, Secretary of State Rice and Foreign Minister Lavrov issued a joint statement: "The United States and Russia reiterate their intention to carry out strategic offensive reductions to the lowest possible level consistent with their national security requirements and alliance commitments."[4] This may—or may not—imply that further reductions are to be expected once the Moscow Treaty targets have been reached.

In its 2001 Nuclear Posture Review, the U.S. Department of Defense drew a distinction between "operationally deployed nuclear forces" and "responsive nuclear forces." It defined the former as those "required to meet the U.S. defense goals in the context of immediate, and unexpected contingencies." In other words, "a sufficient number of forces must be available on short notice to counter known threats while preserving a small, additional margin in the event of a surprise development." "Responsive forces," on the other hand, are "intended to provide a capability to augment the operationally deployed force to meet potential contingencies." The responsive force—essentially a reserve force—is intended to enable the United States to increase the number of operationally deployed forces in a crisis. "A responsive force," according to the Nuclear Posture Review, "need not be available in a matter of days, but in weeks, months, or even years. For

3. Text accessed at www.state.gov/t/ac/trt/18016.htm#1. The Treaty refers to reductions in strategic nuclear warheads, but the United States made it clear that it would reduce only "operationally deployed" strategic nuclear warheads. The United States and Russia did not agree on a definition of "operationally deployed warheads," nor did Russia at the time of the Treaty make clear how it understood that category.

4. Joint Statement by U.S. Secretary of State Condoleezza Rice and Minister for Foreign Affairs of the Russian Federation Sergey Lavrov, July 3, 2007. Accessed at www.state.gov/r/pa/prs/ps/2007/87638.htm.

example, additional bombs could be brought out of the non-deployed stockpile in days or weeks. By contrast, adding additional weapons to the ICBM force could take as long as a year for a squadron in a wing."[5]

In the Moscow Treaty the United States made the commitment to reduce its "operationally deployed strategic nuclear warheads" to 1700–2200 by the end of 2012. In the course of the negotiations, it defined "operationally deployed strategic nuclear warheads" as:

> Reentry vehicles on ICBMs in their launchers, reentry vehicles on SLBMs in their launchers onboard submarines, and nuclear armaments loaded on heavy bombers or stored in weapons storage areas of heavy bomber bases. The United States also made clear that a small number of spare strategic nuclear warheads (including spare ICBM warheads) would be located at heavy bomber bases and that the United States would not consider these warheads to be operationally deployed strategic nuclear warheads.[6]

Secretary of State Powell pointed out in Senate hearings that "this is a departure from the way in which warheads are counted under the START Treaty, but one that more accurately represents the real number of warheads available for use immediately or within days."[7] The START Treaty contains counting rules that attribute specific numbers of warheads to each type of ICBM, SLBM, or heavy bomber, regardless of the actual number of warheads on the missile or bomber. These numbers may be different from both the actual capacity of the specific system and the number actually carried by the system.

Under the Moscow Treaty, a warhead is counted if it is mated

---

5. These quotations are taken from p. 17 of the Nuclear Posture Review submitted to Congress on December 31, 2001. Excerpts from the Review were made public. Accessed at www.globalsecurity.org/wmd/library/policy/dod/npr.htm.

6. Letter of Transmittal from President Bush to the Senate, June 20, 2002. Accessed at www.state.gov/t/ac/trt/18016.htm#2.

7. "A New Way of Doing Business," Secretary of State Colin Powell, statement prepared for delivery to the Senate Foreign Relations Committee, July 9, 2002. Accessed at www.acronym.org.uk/docs/0207/doc01.htm.

with a missile or loaded on a bomber or stored at a bomber site. According to Powell, the United States and Russia did not agree on a detailed definition of "operationally deployed strategic nuclear warheads" during the SORT negotiations, but Russia too is committed to the goal of reducing its strategic nuclear warheads to the level of 1700–2200 by December 2012. As further cuts are made, agreement will be needed on the precise definition of "operationally deployed" and "responsive" strategic nuclear warheads.

The Moscow Treaty does not make explicit reference to verification, but the verification regime of the START Treaty will remain in effect at least until December 2009, when the Treaty expires.[8] In his letter transmitting the Moscow Treaty to the U.S. Senate for ratification in July 2002, President Bush wrote:

> It is important for there to be sufficient openness so that the United States and Russia can each be confident that the other is fulfilling its reductions commitment. The Parties will use the comprehensive verification regime of the Treaty on the Reduction and Limitation of Strategic Offensive Arms (the "START Treaty") to provide the foundation for confidence, transparency, and predictability in further strategic offensive reductions.[9]

In July 2007 Secretary of State Rice and Foreign Minister Lavrov announced that they had "discussed development of a post-START arrangement to provide continuity and predictability regarding strategic offensive forces."[10]

---

8. The Moscow Treaty did, however, establish a Bilateral Implementation Commission, where issues relating to the implementation of the Treaty can be discussed. In their Joint Declaration of May 24, 2002, Presidents Bush and Putin established a Consultative Group for Strategic Security, which is not part of the Treaty, to serve as the principal mechanism through which mutual confidence could be strengthened, transparency enhanced, and information and plans shared. "Joint Declaration on the New Strategic Relationship, May 24, 2002." Accessed at www.state.gov/t/ac/trt/18016.htm#13.

9. Letter of Transmittal (note 6).

10. Joint Statement (note 4).

On July 1, 2007, according to information exchanged by the two countries under the terms of the START Treaty, the United States had 550 ICBMs, 432 SLBMs, and 243 heavy bombers, while Russia had 509 ICBMs, 288 SLBMs, and 78 heavy bombers. Under the START counting rules, the United States had 5914 strategic nuclear warheads and Russia had 4237.[11] According to the estimates of Norris and Kristensen, however, the real numbers for early 2007 were 5236 deployed strategic nuclear warheads (including 215 spares) for the United States, while Russia had 3340 deployed strategic warheads. These latter figures are based on the counting rule outlined by Powell in the statement quoted above.

The START counting rules make the Treaty easier to monitor because the number of deployed warheads is a function of the number of delivery vehicles, but those counting rules also open up the possibility of a discrepancy between the number of warheads counted and the number actually deployed. For that reason, the Powell rule is more appropriate for counting nuclear warheads as nuclear forces are reduced, since discrepancies between counted and deployed warheads are likely to have greater significance at lower levels of forces.

The Moscow Treaty is innovative in a number of ways. It focuses exclusively on warheads, rather than on launchers, as SALT did, or on launchers and warheads, as START did. It does not define subceilings for different categories of forces; each side can decide on the composition of its own strategic forces. The Treaty contains no limitations on responsive or inactive forces, even on those that could be made operational in a relatively short time. That is not a matter of great consequence at the levels stipulated in the Moscow Treaty, but it will become more significant when substantial reductions are considered.

The Moscow Treaty is conservative in its goals. A much more

11. U.S. Department of State, *Fact Sheet: START Aggregate Numbers of Strategic Offensive Arms* (July 1, 2007). Accessed at www.state.gov/documents/organization/93342.pdf.

radical approach is needed if the world is to be rid of nuclear weapons. Several options for substantial reductions are examined below. The United States and Russia between them possess about 95 percent of all nuclear weapons, so that is where reductions should start. These two countries could reduce their strategic forces substantially before needing to bring the other nuclear powers into the process of disarmament.

## The Political and Doctrinal Context for Substantial Force Reductions

The end of the Cold War and the collapse of communist rule transformed the political and strategic relationship between the United States and Russia. Neither country now regards the other as posing a fundamental threat to its existence. In a Joint Statement issued on November 13, 2001, Presidents Bush and Putin declared: "The United States and Russia have overcome the legacy of the Cold War. Neither country regards the other as an enemy or threat."[12] Relations have worsened since then, but this deterioration does not presage a new cold war. There are serious conflicts of interest, but the fundamental enmity of the Cold War years is missing. An intentional nuclear war between the two countries is out of the question. As President Bush said on October 23, 2007, "Russia is not our enemy. . . . We no longer worry about a massive Soviet first strike."[13]

Neither country now regards the other as an imminent nuclear threat, or as the main source of nuclear danger. The 2001 U.S. Nuclear Posture Review declared that a nuclear strike contingency involving Russia "while plausible, is not expected."[14] In 2003 the Russian Min-

12. Joint Statement by President George W. Bush and President Vladimir V. Putin on a New Relationship Between the United States and Russia, November 11, 2001. Accessed at www.state.gov/t/ac/trt/18016.htm#6.

13. Speech to the National Defense University, October 23, 2007. Accessed at www.whitehouse.gov/news/releases/2007/10/20071023-3.html

14. Nuclear Posture Review (note 5), p. 17.

istry of Defense stated that global nuclear war and large-scale conventional wars with NATO or any other American-led coalition had been excluded from the category of likely conflicts for which the Armed Forces had to plan and prepare.[15]

Neither the United States nor Russia, however, is ready to dismiss completely the danger of a nuclear threat arising from the other in the future. According to the 2001 Nuclear Posture Review, "Russia's nuclear forces and programs . . . remain a concern. Russia faces many strategic problems around its periphery and its future course cannot be charted with certainty. U.S. planning must take this into account."[16] For their part, many Russians fear that the United States is seeking, and perhaps actually acquiring, the ability to deliver a disarming first strike against Russia.[17] As the current controversy over the deployment of elements of the U.S. missile defense system in Europe shows, Russia is determined to retain the capacity to retaliate in the event of a nuclear attack.

Both countries remain committed to the use of nuclear weapons for deterrence. The 2000 Military Doctrine of the Russian Federation, for example, states that Russia must possess nuclear forces capable of

15. Ministry of Defense of the Russian Federation, *Aktual'nye zadachi razvitiia vooruzhennykh sil rossiskoi federatsii* (Moscow, 2003), p. 8.

16. Nuclear Posture Review (note 5), p. 17.

17. Vladimir Dvorkin et al., "Iadernaia politika 'bol'shoi piaterki,'" in Aleksei Arbatov and Vladimir Dvorkin, eds., *Iadernoe oruzhie posle "kholodnoi voiny"* (Moscow: Moscow Carnegie Center, 2006), p. 47. See also Yegor Gaidar, "Nuclear Punditry Can Be a Dangerous Game," *Financial Times*, March 29, 2006. This was a response to an article in *Foreign Affairs* (March/April 2006) by Kier A. Lieber and Daryl. G. Press entitled "The Rise of Nuclear Primacy," which argued that the United States now stood on the verge of nuclear primacy and would soon—within ten years or so—be able to destroy Russian and Chinese nuclear arsenals with a first strike. The article caused considerable stir in Russia. Its basic thesis was dismissed by several prominent Russian specialists, including General Vladimir Dvorkin, former head of Central Research Institute No. 4 of the Ministry of Defense, which does research on strategic weapons and strategic weapons policy. For a discussion of these responses, see Nikolai Sokov, "Moscow Rejects U.S. Authors' Claim of U.S. First-Strike Capability," in *WMD Insights*, May 2006. Accessed at www.wmdinsights.com/I5/R1_MoscowRejects.htm.

inflicting assured destruction on an aggressor in any conditions.[18] The U.S. Department of Defense's 2001 Nuclear Posture Review refers to the:

> U.S. deterrence policy to hold at risk what opponents value, including their instruments of political control and military power, and to deny opponents their war aims. The types of targets to be held at risk for deterrence purposes include leadership and military capabilities, particularly WMD, military command facilities and other centers of control and infrastructure that support military forces.

This continuing commitment to deterrence is important, because deterrence has its own requirements, which need to be taken into account when considering reductions in strategic nuclear forces.

Both the United States and Russia see themselves as facing new nuclear threats for which deterrence is not necessarily the appropriate policy. The Bush administration, in its National Security Strategy of September 2002, claimed that deterrence could no longer play the role it had played in the Cold War and asserted its willingness to use force against "rogue states" and terrorist groups to prevent them from acquiring weapons of mass destruction, including nuclear weapons.[20] Russia too has begun to argue that deterrence is not an appropriate response to all threats and to stress the importance of using force preventively in certain circumstances. In the words of the 2006 Russian White Paper on Nonproliferation,

> For the foreseeable future, the greatest threat faced by Russia and other states in the area of nonproliferation will emanate from the

18. *Voennaia doktrina rossiskoi federatsii*, April 2000, Section II, point 17. Accessed at www.scrf.gov.ru/documents/33.html.

19. Nuclear Posture Review (note 5), p. 19. The United States now relies on both non-nuclear and nuclear weapons for "offensive deterrence." (Nuclear Posture Review (note 5), Foreword.) This affects the assessment of strategic balances in ways that might be important as the number of nuclear warheads is reduced, though conventional warheads are unlikely to pose a threat to hardened targets.

20. White House, *National Security Strategy of the United States of America*, September 17, 2002, p. 15. Accessed at www.whitehouse.gov/nsc/nss.html.

possible use by terrorists of some type of WMD. While the value of the doctrine of deterrence will remain as it relates to countries with WMD capabilities, where terrorists are concerned it will obviously not apply.[21]

Nuclear deterrence remains an important element in the policies of both the United States and Russia, but it no longer enjoys the central position it occupied during the Cold War. In particular, neither country regards it as the most effective instrument for dealing with the most urgent nuclear threats.

This changed context suggests two conclusions. First, even within the framework of nuclear deterrence it should be possible for the two countries to make further substantial reductions in strategic nuclear forces. Nuclear deterrence today, in the context of U.S.-Russian relations, hardly requires "operationally deployed nuclear forces" consisting of thousands of warheads. Drell and Goodby argue that, if both Russia and the United States were to reduce the number of their strategic nuclear warheads to a total of 1000 (half operationally deployed and half in the responsive force), the United States would be able to keep at risk 200–300 Russian military and military-support targets, and that that would be sufficient for deterrence.[22] A similar point could be made about Russian policy vis-à-vis the United States.

Second, to the extent that the United States and Russia are both concerned about what might happen in the future rather than about the current relationship, there is no reason why their strategic nuclear forces should be "operationally deployed" rather than held in a responsive mode. The "Russian contingency" as portrayed in the 2001 US Nuclear Posture Review does not require that U.S. forces be "op-

21. *The Russian Federation and the Nonproliferation of Weapons of Mass Destruction*, June 2006, chapter 1. Accessed at cns.miis.edu/pubs/other/rusfed.htm.

22. Sidney D. Drell and James E. Goodby, *What Are Nuclear Weapons For? Recommendations for Restructuring U.S. Strategic Nuclear Forces*, revised edition (Washington, D.C.: Arms Control Association, 2007), pp. 14–18. Accessed at www.armscontrol.org/pdf/20071104_drell_goodby_07_new.pdf.

erationally deployed." Nor do Russian fears that the United States is aiming for a disarming first-strike capability make it necessary for Russian forces be "operationally deployed" at present, because such a capability, even if it is possible, would not appear suddenly and will not materialize in the near future.

## Criteria for Assessing Reductions

The United States and Russia could each make substantial reductions in their strategic nuclear forces while still retaining an effective nuclear deterrent, the more so since mutual deterrence between them now serves as a hedge against a possible future danger rather than as protection against an immediate and pressing threat. Various options can be devised for substantial reductions in strategic nuclear forces, and some of these are considered below. By what criteria should these options be evaluated?

### Criterion I: Strategic stability

In order to move to a world without nuclear weapons it will be necessary to restrict and ultimately to eliminate the role of nuclear weapons in national security policy. The question to ask, therefore, is not "What role should nuclear weapons play in national security policy?" but rather "Is there an irreducible core role that nuclear weapons will play, even as nuclear forces are being reduced?" The answer, implicit in the paper so far, is that, if there is such a role, it is deterrence of a nuclear attack. As we have seen, that position is reflected in official statements by the United States and Russia. The first criterion to apply, therefore, in evaluating reductions is that they should not upset strategic stability. A balance should be maintained that is stable in terms of classic deterrence theory: The new balance should not offer incentives for the use of nuclear weapons in a crisis; nor should the new balance create incentives to acquire more nuclear weapons in the hope of achieving some kind of superiority for one's self or out of fear that the other side will gain superiority. What this means in practice is that each side should have survivable strategic forces that provide an assured capability to retaliate, under any circumstances, against an attacker. For the balance to be stable neither side should have the capability to destroy the other side's strategic forces in a first strike, and neither side should fear that the other side might be able to acquire such a capability. Each side needs to be confident that the other understands that it could not launch a nuclear strike without suffering retaliation. That is the first and most important criterion for assessing options within the framework of mutual deterrence. It is not essential that retaliation be immediate; the threat of delayed retaliation will be just as effective, as long as the potential aggressor is sure that retaliation will take place.

Strategic stability should not be viewed as a purely technical matter. The political context is crucial. Policymakers and planners have to make political assumptions as well as technical judgments. The level of destruction that a retaliatory strike needs to threaten, in order to deter, will vary according to political as well as military circumstances. The forces needed to deter a mortal enemy that has nuclear weapons are likely to be different from those needed to deter a country with which one has less hostile relations. (In the latter case the attacker is less likely to give his political goals a value that would outweigh the losses that even the smallest retaliatory nuclear strike could cause.) Mutual deterrence can thus exist at different levels of nuclear forces, and indeed it need not exist at all in relations between nuclear states, if those states have such good relations that war between them is inconceivable. There is no deterrence if neither side contemplates attacking or being attacked. The degree to which deterrence plays a role in relations among the nuclear powers can vary greatly over time; so too can the forces needed for deterrence.

The political context is relevant in other ways too. If policymakers and planners engage in worst-case planning, that may make stable deterrence at a low level of forces impossible. Worst-case planning was a common phenomenon during the Cold War, and there are two current examples: the U.S. is building a missile defense system to counter an Iranian ICBM that does not exist, and the Russians are developing systems to penetrate or overwhelm elements of the U.S. missile defense system that have not yet been deployed. Furthermore, if strategic nuclear weapons are regarded as important symbols of power and status, as they were during the Cold War, then it may prove difficult to bring the development and deployment of new weapons under control, because even marginal gains by one side will be seen to require a response from the other, if only for symbolic reasons. The present political context is different from that of the Cold War, however, offering some hope that a stable balance can be achieved by the United States and Russia at lower levels of forces, especially if those lower levels are seen to be steps on the path to a world without nuclear weapons.

## *Criterion II: Monitoring and Verification*

It is crucial that each side be able to monitor nuclear stockpiles and verify compliance with any agreement. This is important because deep reductions in nuclear forces will be possible only if each side is confident that the other is abiding by whatever agreement has been concluded. Confidence is important in two respects: operationally—each side needs to be sure the other cannot break out of an agreement in order to achieve a strategic advantage; and politically—each side needs to be sure of the good faith of the other in pursuing reductions.

The paper by Ray Juzaitis and John McLaughlin examines monitoring and verification in detail, but some comments are appropriate here.[23] [See Chapter 4.] There is variation in the degree to which nuclear warheads in different categories can be verified and monitored. There is a great deal of experience under the START Treaty with *deployed warheads* on both missiles and bombers. The problems and

23. My discussion of verification and monitoring in this paper relies very heavily on the advice of Edward Ifft, whose help I am very happy to acknowledge. [See Chapter 5.]

procedures are well understood. The procedures are good and would not need to change much for any level, including zero. Monitoring of *non-deployed warheads* would be much more difficult, and there might be opposition to even trying, but various methods could be adopted that would give some assurance about the number of warheads in a responsive force. One could require declarations of numbers and perhaps verify the data, but ultimately it might be difficult to ensure that absolutely no warheads had been concealed. Various attempts have been made, on both a bilateral and a multilateral basis, to develop mechanisms to ensure the transparency of *reductions in nuclear warheads and materials,* thereby making it possible to monitor the disassembly of nuclear warheads and to account for fissile material. One such effort was the Trilateral Initiative of the U.S., Russia, and the IAEA, launched in 1996. This went a long way to developing an international monitoring regime to verify permanent removals of both classified and unclassified weapons materials from the U.S. and Russian military programs. That initiative stalled some years ago over disputes about transparency, funding, and the length of time weapons material should be monitored by the IAEA, but it could be revived.[24]

## Criterion III: Contribution to the Elimination of Nuclear Weapons

In the context of this project this is the most important criterion. Reductions have to be judged in terms of the degree to which they help pave the way to the elimination of nuclear weapons. The first two criteria could be met with forces at their current levels. The argument for a world without nuclear weapons does not rest primarily on anx-

---

24. An important source on all these issues is National Academy of Sciences' Committee on International Security and Arms Control, *Monitoring Nuclear Weapons and Nuclear-Explosive Materials: An Assessment of Methods and Capabilities* (Washington, D.C.: National Academies Press, 2005). On the Trilateral Initiative, see pp. 140–141. See also Nuclear Threat Initiative, "Monitoring Stockpiles." Accessed at www.nti.org/e_research/cnwm/monitoring/trilateral.asp.

ieties about the stability of the nuclear relationship between the United States and Russia. It springs rather from the judgment that a nuclear order based on discrimination—with some countries possessing nuclear weapons and others denied the right to have them—will not work. It is not only that there will be additional states wanting to acquire nuclear weapons of their own. The nuclear regime will not be legitimate in the eyes even of those states that do not wish to have nuclear weapons. They may be less willing to sustain and enforce a discriminatory nuclear regime than a regime in which nuclear weapons are prohibited altogether.

This is not a simple criterion to apply. Elimination of nuclear weapons would not mean a return to the world before nuclear weapons. We would be entering a post-nuclear weapons world in which the knowledge of how to make nuclear weapons would exist, as well as fissile materials and the industrial technologies for producing them. New understandings and institutions would be needed to control and manage this condition of nuclear latency. Nuclear latency is generally regarded as undesirable from the point of view of proliferation, because it means that a number of states that do not now possess nuclear weapons could acquire them relatively quickly. From the point of view of elimination, however, latency can be regarded as a good thing, if it means that states that now have nuclear weapons get rid of those weapons, even while retaining some capacity to rebuild them. By the time the ultimate elimination of nuclear weapons becomes a practical matter, a great deal of progress will have to have been made on the other measures being examined in this project—elimination of non-strategic nuclear weapons, controls over fissile materials, and internationalization of the fuel cycle, for example—in order to ensure that nuclear latency cannot easily be converted into deployed forces. A greater measure of transparency and predictability concerning nuclear activities will be needed, as well as new and agreed arrangements for dealing with the danger of non-compliance with the non-nuclear weapons regime.

The reduction of nuclear forces is one of the essential paths to a world without nuclear weapons. It is only by reducing nuclear forces that we can approach the goal of zero nuclear weapons. Another, complementary, approach to the elimination of nuclear weapons is to remove nuclear weapons from operational deployment and to maintain them in a responsive mode as nuclear forces are being reduced. This latter approach would not merely lessen the risk of accidental or unauthorized launch of nuclear weapons. It would also signal a willingness to reduce the salience of nuclear weapons in international politics.

The rest of this paper uses these three criteria to examine the stages by which nuclear forces might be reduced. There are other criteria that could be applied in assessing the stages of nuclear force reductions. One is whether the reductions in strategic nuclear weapons do in fact reduce the danger of accidental nuclear war; another is whether they reduce the danger that terrorists might gain control of nuclear weapons or fissile material. These are extremely important criteria, but they are not discussed here, mainly because reductions in nuclear forces that meet the three criteria above should also reduce the risk of nuclear war, while having fewer deployed warheads would make it possible to reduce the nuclear danger from terrorists by storing warheads more securely and moving them less frequently.

The stages outlined below focus on two key parameters: the total number of warheads and the distinction between operationally deployed and responsive forces. Two points should be noted, however, before considering these stages. First, it will be very difficult to verify the numbers of non-deployed warheads. It is much easier to verify the number of delivery vehicles that could carry those warheads. Limits on delivery vehicles will therefore be required alongside limits on warheads. Those limits would cover ICBM launchers, SLBM launchers, and heavy bombers. The two sides have extensive experience under the START Treaty of monitoring non-deployed missile launchers, non-deployed missiles, and non-deployed bombers. Limits on the number of launchers and delivery vehicles would help to restrict the capacity of either side to break out of an agreement by reconstituting its forces rapidly.

The second is that the two categories—"operationally deployed" and "responsive"—contain within themselves further distinctions that are relevant to the process of disarmament. "Operationally deployed warheads" can be deployed in different states of alert. Many of the procedural and physical de-alerting measures outlined by Bruce Blair in his paper would not require removing the delivery systems from the category of "operationally deployed forces." [See Chapter 2.] Other measures discussed in Blair's paper—for example his Option 3—would automatically remove the strategic forces from the "operationally deployed" category to the responsive force. The responsive force itself—as was made clear above—can consist of delivery systems in various degrees of readiness, from those that could be made ready in a matter of days to those that might take more than a year to make operational. This latter point is important because it makes clear that the removal of forces from "operationally deployed" status can be reversed more or less quickly. Reductions have the advantage of irreversibility, as long as the warheads are disassembled, and this is an important consideration with respect to Criterion III above.

**Starting with Feasible Reductions: Stages 1 and 2**

How far can the United States and Russia reduce their strategic nuclear forces without having to take extraneous factors into account? There is little doubt that the two countries could reduce their forces to a level significantly lower than that set in the Moscow Treaty and still maintain a stable relationship within the framework of nuclear deterrence. Two recent studies have suggested that the United States and Russia could each reduce their strategic nuclear warheads to a level of about 1000.[25]

25. These two studies are not the only ones to have suggested 1000 as the target

Aleksei Arbatov and Vladimir Dvorkin have proposed that the United States and Russia could reduce their "operationally deployed strategic nuclear warheads" to 1000–1200 on each side, as long as the two sides can agree on definitions, counting rules, and verification. They argue that this is the lowest ceiling that the two countries could establish without taking into account the nuclear forces of other states, the counterforce capabilities of highly accurate conventional long-range systems, and the possible capabilities of air and missile defenses. They suggest 2017 as the target date for attaining the level of 1000–1200 nuclear warheads. Although they examine the strategic forces of both sides, Arbatov and Dvorkin do not propose any particular force structure for Russia or for the United States; nor do they discuss the idea of limits on the responsive force.[26]

Sidney Drell and James Goodby have proposed that the United States reduce its "operationally deployed strategic nuclear warheads" to 500 and set a ceiling of 500 warheads for the responsive force. The goal would be 500/500 within five years. They argue that an operationally deployed force of 500 nuclear warheads would be "more than adequate for deterrence." The responsive force would be configured in two parts, the first a Ready Responsive Force, able to respond to a crisis, and the second a Strategic Responsive Force that would be able to respond to warning signals of a year or so. They propose, for illustrative purposes, an operationally deployed force consisting of three Trident submarines on station at sea, each armed with 24 missiles and 96 warheads, 100 Minuteman III ICBMs in hardened silos, each with a single warhead, and 20–25 bombers. The Ready Responsive Force could consist of three Trident submarines, each with 96 warheads, in

for reductions by the United States and Russia before other nuclear powers are brought into the process of disarmament. See especially the report by the National Academy of Sciences' Committee on International Security and Arms Control, *The Future of US Nuclear Weapons Policy* (Washington, D.C.: National Academy of Sciences, 1997), pp. 77–78.

26. Aleksei Arbatov and Vladimir Dvorkin, "Otkhod ot vzaimnogo sderzhivaniia," in Arbatov and Dvorkin, eds., *Iadernoe oruzhie . . .* (note 15), pp. 107–110.

transit or in port, and 2–3 boats in overhaul; the Strategic Responsive Force would consist of 50–100 additional Minuteman missiles taken off alert and without warheads and 20–25 bombers, unarmed, in maintenance and training.[27] This is a more radical proposal than that offered by Arbatov and Dvorkin.

These two studies, by American and Russian experts, both focus on 1000 warheads as a level to which each country could reduce its strategic nuclear forces without taking into account the nuclear forces of third countries. They therefore provide a good starting point for a discussion of reductions in U.S. and Russian strategic nuclear forces. The two proposals can be considered as alternatives, but here they are presented as different stages in the process of nuclear disarmament.

***Stage 1:*** *The United States and Russia would each have 1,000 operationally deployed strategic nuclear warheads, with an additional undefined number of warheads in the responsive force.*

*Strategic stability:* The studies by Arbatov and Dvorkin, and by Drell and Goodby, indicate that it should be possible for both sides to deploy survivable forces capable of destroying a range of targets in response to a surprise nuclear attack. A stable deterrent balance could be constructed.

*Monitoring and verification:* Arrangements exist under the START Treaty for monitoring deployed warheads. The problem of monitoring non-deployed warheads would exist even if both sides said they did not have such warheads. The temptation to conceal warheads would not be great at this stage, however, because the benefit to be gained from secretly reconstituting additional strategic forces would be small, given that a surprise attack would not be able to prevent the other side from retaliating with a powerful nuclear strike. Each side could declare how many non-deployed warheads it had, without necessarily

27. Drell and Goodby (note 22), pp. 14–18.

making special arrangements to allow those declarations to be verified. It should be borne in mind, however, that cheating (in the sense of making false declarations) or suspicions of cheating could have serious political consequences, even if their operational consequences were minimal.

*Contribution to elimination:* This option would reduce the number of strategically deployed warheads on each side to about 50 percent of the Moscow Treaty target. This would be a significant indication of the willingness of the United States and Russia to reduce their strategic nuclear forces and, if framed in the right way, of their intention to eliminate nuclear weapons. This option could be an important step on the road to a world free of nuclear weapons. It does not, however, make that road any easier to travel because it suggests that it is essential to have operationally deployed strategic nuclear forces, thereby implying that each side believes that nuclear deterrence retains at least something of its former importance.

This stage could be implemented by taking two straightforward steps. First, as James Goodby has proposed, the United States and Russia could insert into the Moscow Treaty a new limit on the number of strategic nuclear warheads. They could replace the number 1700–2200 with the number 1000 or something close to it. They could extend by a year or two the date for achieving the new target, if that were deemed to be necessary. The second step is to ensure that the parts of the START Treaty that are relevant to verification and monitoring be incorporated—perhaps in a modified form—into a new agreement before START expires in December 2009. These two steps constitute a feasible starting point for substantial reductions in nuclear forces. If these steps were accompanied by a joint statement by the two countries' presidents to the effect that they shared the vision of a world without nuclear weapons, that would provide an even stronger impetus to the process of disarmament.

A logical second step would be to adopt the proposal made by

Drell and Goodby to reduce the number of operationally deployed warheads on each side to 500 and to set a limit of 500 or so on the size of the reserve force.

**Stage 2:** *The United States and Russia would each have 500 operationally deployed strategic warheads and 500 strategic nuclear warheads in the responsive force.*

*Strategic stability:* With a limit of 500 "operationally deployed strategic nuclear warheads," it should still be possible to maintain a strategic nuclear force capable of retaliating against a range of enemy targets in the event of a nuclear strike. The 500 warheads could be allocated to the three elements of the strategic triad. As noted above, Drell and Goodby propose a notional force structure for the United States, but alternatives should be considered.

*Monitoring and verification:*   Monitoring of the deployed force would certainly be possible, but monitoring and verification of the non-deployed force would be more difficult. It might not be possible to know with absolute assurance how many nuclear warheads there were in the responsive force. Relatively small uncertainties would not matter, because they would not be likely to upset the balance created by the deployed forces. But at this point the issue of monitoring and verification begins to become very significant for the whole project. As mentioned above, limits on launchers and delivery vehicles would be helpful in this respect.  ·

*Contribution to elimination:* This arrangement would be a further step on the path to eliminating nuclear weapons. It would make clearer than Stage 1 the possibility of taking nuclear weapons out of the current U.S.-Russian relationship and moving deterrence further into the background.

Stage 1 could be implemented by the United States and Russia without regard to the policies of the other nuclear powers. Before proceeding to Stage 2, however, it would be essential to begin to take into account a number of factors that will be discussed below.

## Going to Zero Deployed Warheads: Stage 3

The next step is the more radical one of limiting the size of each country's strategic nuclear force to 500 strategic warheads, none of which would be operationally deployed. This is the Zero Deployed Warheads option.

***Stage 3:*** *Zero Deployed Warheads: the United States and Russia would each have zero deployed strategic warheads and 500 strategic warheads in the responsive force.*

*Strategic stability:* The question of survivability does not arise for deployed forces (because there aren't any) but it does arise for non-deployed forces. Each country will want to retain the ability to reconstitute its strategic forces in case it should believe it needs to do so, but each will also fear the possibility that the other will breakout by means of a rapid reconstitution of strategic forces. Reconstitution of strategic forces by one side or the other is a key issue, and each side will have to take it into account in planning its own force structure—SSBNs in port, for example, are much more vulnerable than SSBNs on station. Careful planning will be needed to ensure that neither side can achieve the capability to destroy the other's strategic forces by clandestinely reconstituting its forces and launching a surprise attack. There are two approaches to dealing with this problem. The first is to provide effective monitoring and verification. The second is to ensure as far as possible the survivability of each side's forces, while recognizing that the goals of survivability and transparency may well come into conflict.

There has been a good deal of discussion, especially in the context of South Asia, of various forms of "virtual deterrence," exercised by forces that are not operationally deployed. Deterrence in such a case rests on the understanding that the other side could deploy operational forces in a crisis, if it decided to do so, or retaliate after an attack if it failed to deploy its forces in time. The Indian strategic thinker Jasjit Singh has proposed one variant of such "virtual deterrence," which he calls "recessed deterrence":

> All elements of the deterrent (warheads, delivery systems and infra-structure) are kept at a level of preparedness which allows for their rapid shift to a deployed status. This is not a doctrine of ambiguity, but one that seeks to define capabilities that can be rapidly trans-formed into an operational arsenal of a certain minimum level. This would provide an additional level of deterrence against escalation of tensions into a conflict since the adversary would know, and should be told, that India will move towards an operational arsenal if the security environment deteriorates.[28]

Singh characterized this as a policy of nuclear restraint, but one that would still have a deterrent effect. This would be different from "nuclear opacity," a term sometimes used to characterize Israeli nuclear policy, because "recessed deterrence" requires some degree of transparency, as well as restraint. The important point here is that nuclear weapons, even if not operationally deployed, can still exercise a deterrent effect.

*Monitoring and verification:* These are especially important at this stage. The total number of warheads held by the other side would not necessarily be the greatest concern. The crucial issue would be the ability to monitor the other side's state of readiness and to detect any moves it might take to reconstitute its strategic forces. It would be dangerous to have a situation in which one side could reconstitute its strategic forces before the other could do so, if those forces could then pose a serious threat to the other side's forces. That would create the danger of a mobilization race triggered by a political crisis. Mobili-

---

28. Jasjit Singh, "The challenges of strategic defence," *Frontline*, April 11–18, 1998. Accessed at www.hinduonnet.com/fline/fl1508/15080130.htm

zation, in those circumstances, could have an escalatory effect, adding to political tension.[29]

*Contribution to elimination:* This stage would move the world further along the path toward the elimination of nuclear weapons. By removing their forces from operational deployment, the United States and Russia would make clear their belief that nuclear weapons could be moved into the background of international politics. (This could be called a form of nuclear latency.) Zero Deployed Warheads has two other important advantages. The first is that, as Bruce Blair's paper argues, the danger of accidental nuclear war or nuclear launches would be greatly reduced if neither side kept its strategic nuclear forces on a high state of alert. [See Chapter 2.] Second, maintaining strategic nuclear forces in a responsive mode could reduce the danger of terrorists seizing nuclear warheads. The nuclear arsenals could be made more secure, and warheads would not need to be shuttled between launch sites and maintenance facilities, thus reducing the amount of time they spend in transit when they are most vulnerable to seizure.

Zero Deployed Warheads is clearly an advance on the other stages from the point of view of Criterion III, because it would do the most to move the world along the path to the elimination of nuclear weap-

29. According to the British White Paper on Trident, "any move from a dormant program towards an active one could be seen as escalatory, and thus potentially destabilizing, in a crisis." See *The Future of the United Kingdom's Nuclear Deterrent* Cm 6994 (London: HMSO, December 2006), p. 21. On the other hand, Rajesh Basrur, one of the shrewdest analysts of Indian nuclear policy, has written that the fact that both India and Pakistan kept their weapons in a non-deployed state (warheads unassembled and separate from delivery vehicles) contributed a "high degree of built-in stability" during the Kargil crisis of 1999 and the confrontation of 2001–02. "When tensions are high," he writes, "a fully deployed weapon system is extremely threatening, and also susceptible to early use in the event of misperception of the adversary's intentions." He does go on to say that a caveat is in order: "If nuclear weapons are deployed at some point in a crisis, this would constitute a sudden escalation that would also be destabilizing." Rajesh M. Basrur, *Minimum Deterrence and India Pakistan Nuclear Dialogue: Case Study on India* (Como, Italy: Landau Network—Centro Volta, March 2006), p. 12.

ons. From the point of view of Criteria I and II it is the most difficult, because it seems to contain the greatest danger of instability and because it puts the greatest demands on verification and monitoring. It might therefore be appropriate to consider a variant of Stage 3, whereby a relatively small number of warheads (say 50–100) remain operationally deployed until satisfactory arrangements are worked out for dealing with the reconstitution problem. (Measures could be taken to ensure these forces were not on high alert.) The United States and Russia would then have up to 100 deployed warheads each, and 400 non-deployed.

This variant would meet Criteria I and II more easily; it would not be the most desirable from the point of view of Criterion III, for reasons spelled out in the discussion of that criterion. In the context of the deterrent relationship between two nuclear powers, it might indeed make sense to keep a small number of strategic nuclear warheads operationally deployed, in order to provide an assured retaliatory capability. If, however, one accepts the argument that a discriminatory nuclear regime will not work, then zero deployment is likely to make a greater contribution to the elimination of nuclear weapons, because a policy of keeping some forces operationally deployed implies a greater need on the part of states for nuclear weapons in the face of strategic uncertainty—an argument that many states could invoke to justify the possession of nuclear weapons.

There are many technical and operational issues that would need to be resolved in passing through these stages toward the elimination of nuclear weapons. It is not clear how long that process would take, and it therefore does not appear to be useful to propose a timetable. It would, however, make a great deal of sense to move quickly—say within two years—to agree to implement Stage 1. In December 2009, START expires, and in 2010 another Nuclear Nonproliferation Treaty review conference will take place. It would be very desirable, from the point of view of further reductions, if the United States and Russia could implement Stage 1 before those dates. It might be appropriate to pause and take stock after each stage, as long as that did not weaken the commitment to further reductions.

Progress in disarmament should itself reinforce each side's confidence in the other's intentions, thereby making it easier to resolve the various issues that need to be dealt with. For example, as confidence grows, it should be possible for each side to reduce the number of warheads it estimates it needs for a retaliatory strike and the number of targets it calculates it needs to hold at risk. Even within the framework of deterrence theory, the answer to the question "How much is enough?" is not a fixed number; it changes as political and military circumstances change.

Or to take another example, the requirements for verification and monitoring become more stringent as the disarmament process moves from Stage 1 to Stage 3. Existing experience provides the means to monitor Stage 1, but careful analysis is needed to develop the appropriate approaches and methods for monitoring deeper reductions. The commitment to disarmament, and the process of disarmament itself, should encourage trust and openness in the area of nuclear weapons, reassuring each side about the intentions of the other and making both sides more willing to accept the verification provisions needed to monitor the path to the elimination of nuclear weapons.

## Verification and Monitoring

The Moscow Treaty contains no explicit provisions for verification. It relies on the verification and monitoring arrangements of the START Treaty, the most elaborate in the history of strategic arms control. As noted above, President Bush stressed the importance of the START provisions for monitoring and verification when he sent the Moscow Treaty to the Senate for ratification. START expires in December 2009. Secretary of State Rice and Foreign Minister Lavrov announced in July 2007 that they had begun to discuss the development of a post-START arrangement "to provide continuity and predictability" with respect to strategic offensive forces. It would be a great mistake to discard the START experience, to fail to make use of it as the basis for verifying further reductions.

The START provisions for verification and monitoring have worked well. They have created a high level of transparency, and each side has considerable confidence that it knows the nuclear weapons deployments, technical characteristics, and activities of the other. START has established a number of principles that are accepted by the United States and Russia: it forbids the two sides from interfering with each other's National Technical Means (NTM); it bans most forms of telemetry encryption, providing reassurance that ICBM and SLBM tests are not being used for illegal purposes; it establishes a system of on-site inspections and creates a special system of notifications and numerical and geographical constraints that control the numbers and locations of mobile ICBMs.

More generally, the United States and Russia have come to accept a number of well-understood verification tools, and these can be used in monitoring the different stages on the path to the elimination of nuclear weapons. These tools include National Technical Means; Data Exchange/Notifications; On-Site Inspection, both routine and challenge; Perimeter and Portal Continuous Monitoring; nuclear detection devices, both handheld and fixed; remote monitoring techniques developed by UNSCOM and UNMOVIC in Iraq. The paper by Ray Juzaitis and John McLaughlin examines the relationship of this experience to further reductions in nuclear forces. [See Chapter 4.]

The United States and Russia have considerable experience in monitoring warheads deployed on (or attributed to, in accordance with the START counting rules) missiles and bombers. They have not, however, attempted to monitor non-deployed warheads, which would be required by Stages 2 and 3 above. This presents a much greater challenge, because warheads are much smaller and easier to hide than bombers, submarines, or missile silos. Each side could make a declaration of the number of warheads it had in its responsive force, even perhaps including the kinds of warheads it has, e.g., for missiles or bombers. That would provide a total for the other side to monitor.

The two countries may not be willing, however, to say where their warheads are stored, because that would make the warheads more vulnerable to attack. Various approaches to monitoring will therefore need to be explored. It might be possible to monitor the perimeters of launch sites in order to provide warning of any effort to deploy warheads. It should also be possible to agree to limits on launchers, since the ability of one side or the other to violate an agreement would be bounded, to some degree at least, by the number of launchers it had available to it. Restrictions on force structure and delivery vehicles (e.g., a ban on MIRVs) would also be helpful in this respect. Controls on fissile materials, as discussed in Robert Einhorn's paper, would have an important role too. [See Chapter 8.] Finally, if arrangements could be made to monitor the production as well as the disassembly of strategic warheads, that also could be helpful in discouraging reconstitution of non-deployed strategic forces.

## Missile defenses

Is there a role for ballistic missile defenses in the process of nuclear disarmament? The answer depends on the context in which they are deployed. In a world of nuclear deterrence, even with deterrence becoming increasingly virtual or residual, missile defenses are likely to hinder the effort to reduce and eliminate nuclear weapons. If a state concerned about its ability to retaliate in the event of a surprise attack is confronted by missile defenses, it will be less willing to reduce its offensive forces and may indeed want to increase them. Even if the defenses are ineffective and can be overcome by countermeasures, the country against which they are aimed is likely to exaggerate their capability and to plan for the worst contingency. (The history of ballistic missile defense is rich in exaggerated claims, and exaggerated fears, of the effectiveness of these systems.) In that context missile defenses will be an obstacle to the reduction of strategic nuclear warheads.

In a world without nuclear weapons, missile defenses could *in principle* provide a partial safeguard against possible breakout from the non-nuclear-weapons regime. Whether it made sense to deploy them would depend on assessments of the effectiveness of the particular missile defense system against possible threats. It would also depend on the priority accorded to missile defenses as opposed to other defensive measures, given that ballistic missiles are not the only means by which nuclear weapons can be delivered. Nevertheless, it is conceivable that missile defenses might help to stabilize a world without nuclear weapons and to establish the condition of defense dominance. It is worth noting, however, that even in these circumstances missile defenses would have to be organized cooperatively, in such a way as to avoid creating the impression (or the reality) that the defenses were themselves part of a breakout strategy on the part of an individual state.

There is a third, and perhaps more immediately promising, option. The United States and Russia (and other countries too) could cooperate in the development of ballistic missile defenses even as they engage in the process of reducing their strategic warheads. The United States and Russia have more than once expressed an interest in such cooperation. (Ronald Reagan raised it at Reykjavik, though Mikhail Gorbachev responded skeptically.) Presidents Bush and Putin have supported the idea of missile defense cooperation.[30] The issue has come up recently in the context of the controversy over U.S. missile

30. For example, in their May 24, 2002, Joint Declaration on the New Strategic Relationship, Presidents Bush and Putin stated: "The United States and Russia have also agreed to study possible areas for missile defense cooperation, including the expansion of joint exercises related to missile defense, and the exploration of potential programs for the joint research and development of missile defense technologies, bearing in mind the importance of the mutual protection of classified information and the safeguarding of intellectual property rights." Accessed at www.state.gov/t/ac/trt/18016.htm#5.

defense installations in Europe.[31] Cooperation could cover such areas as early warning of ballistic missile attack, tracking and discrimination of warheads and decoys, and even interception; it could extend from R&D to the operation of the system. What form cooperation should take is a matter for joint study and analysis. This is not to say that cooperation will be easy: various obstacles—institutional, technical, strategic, and political—spring readily to mind. The important point to make here, however, is that only through cooperation will it be possible to ensure that missile defenses help, rather than hinder, nuclear disarmament. Without such cooperation missile defenses will lessen the likelihood of reductions in strategic nuclear forces. On the other hand, cooperation in this area, if it proved successful, would have considerable positive value in helping to create the trust necessary for moving along the path to the elimination of nuclear weapons.

For these reasons, the current controversy over missile defenses in Europe needs to be resolved in order to ensure that missile defenses do not constitute an obstacle to further reductions in nuclear forces.

## Bringing in the other nuclear powers:  Stage 4

This paper has focused so far on U.S. and Russian strategic nuclear warheads, i.e., on those systems covered by the START and Moscow treaties. Rose Gottemoeller's paper looks at non-strategic nuclear weapons. [See Chapter 3.] The distinction between strategic and non-strategic nuclear weapons is a matter of (sometimes disputed) convention, and warheads are strategic or non-strategic only by virtue of being loaded onto strategic or non-strategic delivery vehicles. As the United States and Russia move toward Zero Deployed Warheads, the distinction between the two kinds of warhead, which is based to a great extent on the range of their delivery vehicles, will make less and less sense. At some point in the process of disarmament, therefore,

31. See Theodore Postol, "A Ring Around Iran," *New York Times*, July 11, 2007; Henry A. Kissinger, "Don't Rule Out Putin's Initiative," *International Herald Tribune*, August 9, 2007.

that distinction should be dropped and each country's stockpile assessed in terms of all the warheads it contains. This should certainly be done before the nuclear forces of other countries are brought into the process of disarmament, since the definitions employed in the case of the United States and Russia cannot easily be applied to the nuclear forces of other countries.

The merging of strategic and non-strategic warheads into a single category has implications for the stages discussed above and would need to be managed carefully. The reductions set out in Stage 1 could be undertaken without taking non-strategic systems into account. For Stage 2 it would be desirable to have a clearer mutual understanding of the non-strategic nuclear warheads each side has, and perhaps to have agreed limits on those warheads. The merging of strategic and non-strategic warheads into one category should be completed—or at least well advanced—before the two sides have implemented the Zero Deployed Warheads option. This is an important issue that requires careful analysis. Important though it is, it cannot be addressed here. The paper now turns to the question of involving the other nuclear states in the process of disarmament. In the rest of this paper no distinction will be drawn between strategic and non-strategic nuclear warheads.

Seven countries besides the United States and Russia possess nuclear weapons. This number includes North Korea, but since specific negotiations are under way to de-nuclearize the Korean Peninsula, North Korea will not be discussed here. The three recognized nuclear weapons states—Britain, France, and China—first tested nuclear weapons in 1952, 1960, and 1964. They have possessed nuclear warheads for decades, but none has tried to match the United States and the Soviet Union in numbers of nuclear weapons. They have maintained relatively stable stockpiles consisting of hundreds, not thousands, of nuclear warheads. Britain and France have reduced their nuclear forces since the end of the Cold War. China has maintained a comparatively small nuclear force even as its economy has grown by leaps and bounds, though it is now modernizing its strategic forces, and it is not clear where that will lead.[32] None of these states has shown the desire, nor made the effort, to match the nuclear forces of the United States or the Soviet Union/Russia.

The second group of nuclear states—Israel, India, and Pakistan—acquired their nuclear weapons later, and their stockpiles are currently smaller than those of Britain, France, and China (though the upper limit of the estimate for Israel puts Israel on a par with Britain and China). Israel is believed to have built its first nuclear weapons in the late 1960s; India tested a nuclear device in 1974; and Pakistan is thought to have acquired nuclear weapons by the late 1980s. The Israeli nuclear force is estimated to consist of 100–200 weapons. The Indian and Pakistani nuclear forces are estimated to be smaller: 50–60 for India and 40–50 for Pakistan. The Indian and Pakistani nuclear stockpiles have been growing. It is not clear, however, how far, or how rapidly, they will grow in the future.

The deployment practices of the six nuclear states other than the United States and Russia differ from one country to another. Britain and France maintain operationally deployed strategic forces. Chinese strategic warheads are not mated with missiles and are reported to be stored separately from—but near—the delivery vehicles; that practice may change in the direction of greater operational readiness as China deploys new mobile missiles and SLBMs.[33] India and Pakistan appear

32. What the implications of this are for the size of the Chinese nuclear stockpile is not clear. The December 2006 Chinese White Paper on National Defense says: "China upholds the principles of counterattack in self-defense and limited development of nuclear weapons, and aims at building *a lean and effective nuclear force* capable of meeting national security needs. It endeavors to ensure the security and reliability of its nuclear weapons and maintains a credible nuclear deterrent force." [Emphasis added.] *China's National Defense in 2006* (Beijing: State Council of the PRC, December 2006), section II. According to a Pentagon report, "China is qualitatively and quantitatively improving its legacy strategic forces." *Annual Report to Congress: Military Power of the People's Republic of China 2007* (Washington, D.C.: Office of the Secretary of Defense), p. 18.

33. See Jeffrey Lewis, *The Minimum Means of Reprisal: China's Search for Se-*

to maintain their nuclear weapons in a non-deployed state, with warheads unassembled and at some distance from the delivery vehicles. No information is available on Israeli practice.

If nuclear weapons are to be eliminated, these six powers obviously must become involved in the process of disarmament. Before looking at the ways in which they can be brought into that process, there is an important point to be made about the political context. It is the end of the Cold War that has made it possible for the United States and Russia to make significant reductions in their enormous nuclear forces. In the section above on the political and doctrinal context for substantial force reductions, the argument was made that the changed political relationship between the United States and Russia has made it possible to contemplate substantial reductions in nuclear forces beyond those that have already taken place. In other words, the political changes caused by the end of the Cold War could be further exploited by the United States and Russia in the interests of disarmament. Britain and France have reduced their nuclear forces too since the end of the Cold War. Their forces are significantly smaller than those of the United States and Russia, and the opportunity for reductions short of elimination also smaller.

The end of the Cold War has not affected the nuclear policies of the other four nuclear powers in the same way. China has not reduced its small nuclear force, and has indeed embarked on a serious program of modernization, though it is not clear what the implications of that program are for the size of China's nuclear stockpile. Israel's nuclear policy can be understood only in the context of the Middle East, where Israel has confronted—and still confronts—hostile states that refuse to acknowledge its right to exist. The removal of nuclear weapons from the Middle East will require a transformation of the politics of

---

*curity in the Nuclear Age* (Cambridge, Mass.: The MIT Press, 2007), pp. 27, 165–166. For a deep analysis of China's approach to command and control, see John Wilson Lewis and Xue Litai, *Imagined Enemies: China Prepares for War* (Stanford, Calif.: Stanford University Press, 2006).

the region. Similarly, the nuclear forces and nuclear policies of India and Pakistan are, in great measure, rooted in the conflict between the two states over Kashmir, though China has had, and continues to have, an important impact on the nuclear policies of both states. Eliminating nuclear weapons from South Asia will depend, in part at least, on the normalization of relations between India and Pakistan. In other words, some resolution of the conflicts in South Asia and the Middle East will be necessary if nuclear weapons are to be eliminated from those regions.

The Stage 1 target of 1000 operationally deployed strategic warheads was chosen precisely so that the United States and Russia could reduce their forces to that level without taking the other nuclear powers into account. This indicates that the reduction of U.S. and Russian forces to the level of 1000 operationally deployed strategic nuclear warheads need not—and indeed should not—be made conditional on obtaining specific commitments from the other nuclear powers. If, however, further progress is to be made in reducing nuclear forces, several commitments will in time be required from the other nuclear powers:

1. The first is a commitment not to increase their nuclear warheads significantly beyond the levels they now have.

2. The second is to agree to greater transparency, and ultimately to inclusion in an international regime of monitoring and verification.

3. The third commitment is to maintain nuclear forces in a responsive mode rather than operationally deployed, according to some agreed definition of those terms.

Only when these commitments are forthcoming will it be possible to move to a world with zero deployed nuclear warheads and ultimately without nuclear weapons at all. It would make sense to begin official consultations on these points once the United States and Russia have initiated consultations on the Stage 1 reductions; unofficial consultations should begin as soon as possible.

How likely are the six nuclear powers to accept these three commitments?

*First*, only the United States and Russia have at present more than 500 nuclear warheads. The other nuclear powers have smaller arsenals and—apart perhaps from China, India and Pakistan—do not appear to be planning to increase their arsenals. They should, therefore, be willing to make the first commitment, namely, not to increase significantly the number of warheads they now have or are currently planning to have. They would presumably be all the more willing to do this if they thought that their *unwillingness* to make this commitment would discourage the United States and Russia from continuing with the process of nuclear disarmament. They might seek to ensure, however, that an equal ceiling—500 or even 200—be set for all nuclear forces. (A limit of 200 would require reductions by France, as well as by the United States and Russia, but apparently not by the other nuclear states.)

*Second*, apart from Britain and France, the other nuclear powers make public very little information about their current nuclear forces or about their force development plans. They would, of course, become more transparent if they were to adopt the practices that are now customary in U.S.-Russian relations. That might prove difficult for Israel and for India and Pakistan, in view of the political tensions in the Middle East and South Asia—though India and Pakistan have been pursuing confidence-building mechanisms for reducing the risk of nuclear war and avoiding an escalation of their nuclear rivalry.

Progress in nuclear disarmament will require movement toward a global verification and monitoring regime, perhaps including regional arrangements such as exist between Argentina and Brazil, which have created mechanisms for monitoring each other's nuclear programs. Otherwise it will not be possible to provide the assurances, or establish the confidence, necessary for substantial reductions. It should be pointed out that the closer the existing nuclear powers come to approaching a state of latency, the more the latent nuclear powers, which have never had nuclear weapons but have some capacity to make them, will have to be drawn into the monitoring and verification regime. Ultimately, in a non-nuclear-weapons world, all states would be subject to the same regime.

*Third*, apart from Britain and France, the other nuclear powers do not appear to have operationally deployed warheads. (China may change its practice when it deploys SLBMs and mobile ICBMs.) They should therefore be willing to accept the commitment to non-deployment. Britain and France, however, regard operationally deployed forces as an essential part of their deterrent. The British government does not think it advisable to remove all its strategic warheads from operationally deployed status. It rejects the idea of a "dormant" strategic force.[34] Britain's nuclear force is now based on one system, the submarine-launched ballistic missile, and the number of "operationally available warheads" is being reduced to fewer than 160 (the overall stockpile being somewhat larger). Normally only one Trident SSBN is on patrol at any given time, with up to 48 warheads on board. Britain has reduced the state of alert of its force since the end of the Cold War, with the submarine on patrol normally "on several days notice to fire."[35] France has a larger nuclear force, consisting of about 350 warheads, based on two systems: submarine-launched ballistic missiles and air-launched cruise missiles. Like Britain, France keeps at least one SSBN on patrol at any given time, each submarine capable of carrying 16 SLBMs with up to six warheads apiece. (British and French operationally deployed forces are very much smaller than the forces currently deployed by the United States and Russia (1–3 percent) and than the forces allowed in the Moscow Treaty (3–6 percent).) It is possible that Britain and France might change their position on deployment in the context of sharp reductions in U.S. and Russian forces, especially if the United States and Russia were ready

34. *The Future of the United Kingdom's Nuclear Deterrent* (note 24), p. 21.
35. *The Future of the United Kingdom's Nuclear Deterrent* (note 24), p. 13.

to go to zero deployed warheads, but this is an issue that would have to be dealt with at the time.

This discussion suggests that while there are serious obstacles to be overcome, it is not inconceivable that the other nuclear states would be willing to make commitments that would allow the United States and Russia to make far-reaching cuts in their nuclear warheads to the level of 500 or even lower, say to the level of 200.

If the six other nuclear powers besides the United States and Russia were to make the commitments outlined above, there would then be a nuclear regime in which no nuclear state had more than 500 (200) warheads, each nuclear state participated in a regime of verification and monitoring, and no state had operationally deployed strategic warheads.

How does this stage, Stage 4, measure up against the criteria set out earlier in the paper? Two variants should be considered, *Variant 1*, with no operationally deployed nuclear warheads, and *Variant 2*, with 50–100 operationally deployed warheads.

**Stage 4 (Variant 1):** *No state has more than 500 (200) nuclear warheads, and none of the nuclear warheads is operationally deployed.*

*Strategic stability:* The problem of stability in a multipolar nuclear world, in which each state possesses relatively small forces, presents novel problems and would need careful study. Force levels under this option appear to be sufficient to give each state the capacity to retaliate in the event of a surprise attack by an individual state. Complications might arise if two or more states were likely to act jointly against another state. Policymakers and military planners in each state would have to take account of that possibility. The U.S.-U.K. relationship would be brought into question: Could the two countries be treated as separate entities when they engage in joint planning and targeting? Would NATO count as a single entity? Would conventional forces—

especially long-range conventionally armed missiles—have to be taken into account? If the total number of nuclear warheads permitted to any state were reduced to 200 from 500, would that make a difference? These questions need to be looked at in a broad political context, with attention to new international security arrangements to allay some of the anxieties that reductions to this level might cause.

*Monitoring and verification:* These would be no less important in this case than in Stage 3. In fact the verification regime would by definition have to be more comprehensive, because it would include more states. The arrangements for monitoring the nuclear activities of states with a latent nuclear capacity would need to be strengthened.

*Contribution to elimination:* A world with zero operationally deployed nuclear weapons would mark a further significant step on the road to a world without nuclear weapons, as long as the dangers of instability and verification could be dealt with. This would be a very different nuclear world, and a good deal of consultation and analysis would be needed to understand what its dynamics might be. One of the crucial questions is whether the radical reduction in nuclear forces would discourage other states from acquiring nuclear weapons or encourage them to try to do so. This is a question that goes beyond the scope of this paper, but it is one that needs careful attention.

Given the British and French insistence on having some operationally deployed warheads, it makes sense to consider a separate variant that includes operationally deployed forces, as was done for Stage 3 above. As with Stage 3, a *Variant 2* that permits the operational deployment of up to 50–100 nuclear warheads (on reduced states of alert) might make it easier to meet Criteria I and II, though it would not do as much as *Variant 1* to move toward the elimination of nuclear weapons. This variant too would need careful study and analysis. It could perhaps be considered as an interim option before moving to zero deployed warheads. There are those who would argue that nuclear balances at low levels would be more stable if each nuclear power had some operationally deployed warheads. Even if that were the case—and it is by no means clear that it is—*Variant 2* carries the serious disadvantage, spelled out above, that insistence by the nuclear powers on having operationally deployed nuclear forces may provide non-nuclear weapons states with rationales for acquiring nuclear weapons of their own.[36]

At what point should the six nuclear powers be drawn into the process of disarmament? The United States and Russia would be more likely to begin to move from 1000 warheads to 500 warheads if they had agreements (even informal ones) on levels of forces and on transparency with the other nuclear powers. (Their incentive to reduce their nuclear forces would diminish if they thought that their reductions might lead to, or be matched by, an increase in the nuclear forces of other states.) It is possible, of course, that the other nuclear powers would make commitments about their own force levels conditional on continuing reductions in the strategic forces of the United States and Russia. This suggests that official consultations on these issues with all relevant countries should begin early in the process of disarmament—as soon as the United States and Russia have initiated discussions on Stage 1 reductions—so that potential obstacles can be identified as soon as possible. Unofficial consultations could start immediately for the same purpose.

## Making Deep Reductions

This paper has outlined four stages by which deep reductions could be made in nuclear forces. It has charted an overall approach to further reductions in nuclear forces, suggesting that there is a feasible starting point (Stage 1) and a transformed nuclear world that is at least conceivable (Stage 4). The paper has pointed to some of the most important issues that need to be resolved. Many of these issues—stabil-

---

36. For an acute analysis of this question, see Beatrice Heuser, "The British and French Nuclear Postures: Blair's and Chirac's Legacies" (unpublished paper).

ity, reconstitution, verification, and latency—are by and large familiar, but not less complex for that. There are, besides, many technical and operational questions that it has not been possible to discuss in detail here; for example, there has been no discussion of the relationship between nuclear and conventional balances as nuclear forces are reduced.

These issues notwithstanding, Stage 1 could be implemented—as was pointed out above—by taking two straightforward steps. The United States and Russia could insert into the Moscow Treaty a new limit on strategic nuclear warheads, replacing the number 1700–2200 with the number 1000. They could also ensure that the parts of the START Treaty that are relevant to verification and monitoring be incorporated—perhaps in a modified form—in a new agreement. Those two steps would give new impetus to the process of making substantial reductions in nuclear forces. If the alert status of the operationally deployed nuclear warheads were reduced at the same time in line with Bruce Blair's proposals, that would give these two steps added significance. [See Chapter 2.] Preparations could be made also for ratification of the Comprehensive Test Ban Treaty. If this group of measures were accompanied by a joint statement by the two countries' presidents to the effect that they shared the vision of a world without nuclear weapons, that would make the impetus even stronger. It is worth noting that public opinion in the United States and Russia is very largely in support of these measures.[37]

James Goodby has also proposed the Zero Option, under which no nuclear warheads would be operationally deployed anywhere in the world. This corresponds to Stage 4 (Variant 1) above. Goodby proposes four steps for achieving that goal. The first is a U.S.-Russian treaty gradually reducing operationally deployed warheads to zero; the

37. Steven Kull et al., *Americans and Russians on Nuclear Weapons and the Future of Disarmament: a Joint Study of WorldPublicOpinion.org and the Advanced Methods of Cooperative Security Program*, CISSM (University of Maryland: November 9, 2007).

second is the development of transparency measures and a commitment by each side not to have more than 500–1000 non-deployed warheads; the third is for the other nuclear weapons states to freeze their holdings and go to a non-deployed status by the time the United States and Russia had done so; the fourth is acceptance of verifiable measures to guard against clandestine or sudden reconstitution of nuclear forces. This process parallels the stages outlined in this paper, and it would raise the same issues. It puts more emphasis on de-alerting, and less on reductions, as a way of implementing the Zero Option, though reductions are of course an ineluctable part of the process of moving to a world without nuclear weapons. One benefit of the Zero Option is that it emphasizes how reductions and de-alerting can combine to form part of the strategy for ridding the world of nuclear weapons.

If all the parties involved accept the goal of a world without nuclear weapons, then they can focus collectively on the barriers to achieving that goal.[38] If the intermediate, but still radical, goal of zero deployed warheads is accepted as an interim target, then that goal can provide the basis for cooperation. Barriers can be of different kinds—strategic, legal, institutional, and psychological, for example. This paper has considered some of the barriers—the danger of breakout, for example—but there are others that have not been discussed here or have been mentioned only in passing. Among these are psychological barriers such as worst-case planning; historical and cultural barriers to do with the symbolic meaning of nuclear weapons for different societies; or institutional barriers arising out of traditions of military planning. The vision of a world without nuclear weapons is important precisely because it focuses attention on the barriers to achieving it; only in that context can those involved see what the barriers are and work jointly to overcome them.

---

38. On this approach, see Kenneth J. Arrow et al, eds., *Barriers to Conflict Resolution* (New York: W.W. Norton, 1995).

Should reductions be made through negotiated treaties or by unilateral steps that are then reciprocated by the other side? Both approaches can be employed, depending on the specific circumstances. The United States and Russia could reduce their strategic nuclear warheads to the level of 1000 by making parallel or unilateral statements of the kind that form the core of the Moscow Treaty, allowing each side to structure its forces as it wants.[39] Arbatov and Dvorkin argue that, before such a reduction is made, agreement should be reached on definitions, on counting rules, and on verification procedures. Whether or not all of those issues have to be resolved before reducing forces to 1000 may be an open question, but they will have to be resolved sooner rather than later. If they are not resolved, they will give rise to suspicion and loss of mutual confidence.

The advantage of reciprocal unilateral measures is that they make the process of reduction easier. A good example is President G. H. W. Bush's announcement on September 27, 1991, that the United States would take unilateral measures to limit and reduce its tactical nuclear weapons arsenal. On October 5 President Mikhail Gorbachev reciprocated with a series of Soviet measures. Those were important steps, and they were taken very quickly, although they did leave a residue of mistrust resulting from different interpretations of what each side had committed itself to do. This suggests that even if the warhead reductions themselves can be carried out through a series of reciprocal unilateral measures, the reductions should be codified in a treaty that clarifies definitions, counting rules, and verification procedures. That will make the agreement more salient politically as well as legally binding, thereby contributing to greater strategic predictability.

---

39. For a discussion of Reciprocal Unilateral Measures, see George Bunn and David Holloway, *Arms Control without Treaties? Rethinking U.S.-Russian Strategic Negotiations in Light of the Duma-Senate Slowdown in Treaty Approval*, CISAC Working Paper, February 1998.

**Moving to Abolition**

This paper has outlined some stages by which substantial reductions could be made in nuclear forces, but it has not specified how nuclear weapons could ultimately be eliminated. That omission is intentional. Making substantial reductions within the framework of mutual deterrence presents a number of familiar, even if complicated, issues. Moving to abolition, however, is to travel uncharted territory.[40]

There are some things we can say about a world without nuclear weapons, but how such a world would be organized—what its institutions and norms would be—is best left to be worked out as the process of nuclear disarmament is under way. We do know that it would be a post-nuclear-weapons world, not a pre-nuclear world, and that the knowledge that nuclear weapons could be built would remain, as well as the scientific knowledge and many of the engineering skills and industrial processes. There would inevitably be some degree of nuclear latency, and a world without nuclear weapons would require institutions and norms that would inhibit the use of that latent capacity to break out of the non-nuclear regime and enforce the regime against attempts to break out. What those institutions and norms might be is difficult to specify precisely, but they would surely involve the other elements being studied in this project—controls on fissile materials; internationalization of the fuel cycle; verification and compliance arrangements, etc. Cooperation in dealing with those issues—on both a bilateral and a multilateral basis—should provide the basis for moving beyond low levels of nuclear forces to the elimination of nuclear weapons. That final step to elimination would be taken in circumstances different from those in which we find ourselves today. But

40. For an extensive discussion see Jonathan Schell, *The Abolition* (New York: Knopf, 1984) and Schell, *The Gift of Time: The Case for Abolishing Nuclear Weapons Now* (New York: Metropolitan Books, 1998). See also the report of an independent commission established by the Australian government in 1995: *Report of the Canberra Commission on the Elimination of Nuclear Weapons* (Canberra: August 1995). Accessed at: dfat.gov.au/cc/cc_report_mnu.html.

even if the final shape of a post-nuclear weapons world cannot yet be clearly envisaged, it is important, for reasons given in this paper, to keep at the forefront of our minds the vision of a world without nuclear weapons.

# 2. De-alerting Strategic Forces

## Bruce G. Blair

### Key Findings and Judgments

*The end of the Cold War did not lead the United States and Russia to significantly change their nuclear strategies or the way they operate their nuclear forces.* Both sides maintain about one-third of their total strategic arsenals on launch-ready alert. Hundreds of missiles armed with thousands of nuclear warheads—the equivalent of about 100,000 Hiroshima bombs—can be launched within a very few minutes. The command and early warning systems are geared to launch on warning—firing friendly forces *en masse* before the arrival of incoming enemy missiles with flight times of 12–30 minutes.

The Russian early warning system has been decaying since the breakup of the Soviet Union and despite some recent upgrades it is more prone today to cause false alarms than it was during the Cold War. Despite this technical degradation, both the Russian and U.S. postures normally run a somewhat lower risk of launching on *false*

The author is grateful to James Goodby, Sid Drell, David Holloway, Henry Rowen, Gen. (ret.) George Lee Butler, Joan Rohlfing, Steve Andreasen, John Steinbruner, Frank von Hippel, and George Shultz for their keen observations and wise guidance during the preparation of this analysis. This report draws heavily upon previous research conducted by the author with the generous support of the John D. and Catherine T. MacArthur Foundation, the New-Land Foundation, Inc., the Ploughshares Fund, and Margaret R. Spanel. The author's current work on nuclear weapons de-alerting and elimination is generously supported by the Carnegie Corporation, Ploughshares, and Ms. Spanel.

*warning* due to their improved political relationship and higher propensity to discount tactical warning indications of enemy missile attack. But the *risk remains non-negligible in peacetime, and would spike upward in the unlikely event of a nuclear confrontation between them.*

Although both sides impose very strict safeguards on their strategic nuclear forces to prevent an unauthorized launch, the actual level of protection against unauthorized launch defies precise estimation due to the complexity of the nuclear command-control systems and of the threats to them. Serious deficiencies are routinely discovered. *There is reason to believe that state and non-state actors including terrorists may be able to exploit weaknesses in these systems of control by physical or informational means, heightening the risks of unauthorized or accidental launch.* Cyber-attack is a growing threat in these terms. The traditional two-man rule arguably is no longer an adequate safeguard in an era of information warfare.

*The traditional war-fighting postures keep nuclear weapons in constant motion and thereby create opportunities for terrorists to capture or steal them,* particularly in Russia where the number of weapons in transit or temporary storage is especially large. In precluding all weapons from being locked down in secure storage, the U.S. and Russian nuclear postures embody unnecessary risk and thwart the efforts of the Nunn-Lugar program.

*The U.S. and Russian force postures lend legitimacy to the nuclear ambitions of other nations, and to those nations' adoption of launch-ready nuclear postures.* Over time more states are likely to follow in our footsteps, and increase their own forces' combat readiness, resulting in growing worldwide dangers of accidental or unauthorized launch, or theft, of nuclear weapons.

*Major benefits would accrue from standing down ("de-alerting") the legacy postures.* Keeping thousands of weapons ready to fly upon their receipt of a short sequence of simple computer signals is inherently risky. De-alerting would increase warning and decision time far beyond the short fuse inherent in current command systems, thereby reducing the risk of mistaken launch to negligible proportions. De-alerting would greatly strengthen safeguards against unauthorized launch and terrorist exploitation.

*De-alerting could also strengthen crisis stability.* Driven by their current war-fighting strategies, a serious crisis today could spark an unstable re-alerting race between the two postures. Whereas de-alerting is often criticized on the grounds that it would contribute to instability during a crisis as forces race to return to launch-ready alert, the actual situation is the polar opposite. The current nuclear postures are prone to breakneck re-alerting during a crisis and would severely undermine crisis stability. De-alerted postures can be designed to alleviate this danger.

*Another major benefit of de-alerting is its contribution to curbing proliferation.* Standing down the forces would downgrade the role of nuclear weapons, and convey a hopeful and serious message to the world that reliance on them is diminishing. This would strengthen non-proliferation diplomacy, foster progress toward the global elimination of nuclear arsenals, and contain an otherwise growing worldwide risk of accidental or unauthorized use or theft of nuclear weapons.

*De-alerting is feasible.* Wholesale de-alerting happened once before, in 1991. There are many practical ways to extend the time needed to fire U.S. and Russian nuclear forces—by hours, days, weeks, months, and even years—while preserving stable deterrence during peacetime and in the remote event of a U.S.-Russian nuclear crisis. De-alerting options take the form of procedural or physical modifications, or both.

*Implementing such measures would nullify quick-launch options and* create an unmistakably second-strike posture geared to riding out an attack before retaliating. The traditional nuclear strategies of both nations would be transformed by this change; *the predominance of nuclear war-fighting would be ended.* Further, the demands on the command system required in this "launch after attack" posture would promote a salutary new focus on enhancing the survivability of present arrangements.

*Ideally, both U.S. and Russia would stand down in unison.* Reciprocal de-alerting would immediately yield major security and safety benefits to both sides. Because Russia's strategic forces today are vulnerable to a sudden surprise attack, U.S. de-alerting would allay Russian fear of a disarming U.S. first strike and justify Russia removing its own finger from the nuclear button. Reciprocal Russian de-alerting would bolster U.S. force survivability but would be especially welcome for lowering the risks of a mistaken or unauthorized Russian launch.

*This beneficial de-alerting dynamic could begin with U.S. unilateral steps that would preserve the survivability of its nuclear forces and give Russia confidence to follow suit.* Unilateral U.S. de-alerting would protect the United States if it causes Russia to begin to relax— physically or psychologically—its nuclear hair-trigger. Unilateral steps that jeopardize the survivability of nuclear forces obviously would not satisfy the criterion of maintaining stable deterrence and would thus not be recommended.

*The more deeply the postures are de-alerted—for instance, by separating warheads from delivery vehicles and consolidating the nuclear stockpiles in storage depots on land—the easier it becomes to verify their off-alert status, but the more critical this verification process becomes.* Strict monitoring becomes essential because the successful covert breakout of a small number of deliverable nuclear weapons could threaten the wholesale destruction of the concentrated stockpiles in depots on the other side.

*This report evaluates several of the most promising de-alerting options and finds many of them worthy of support.* Recommendations are made with varying degrees of enthusiasm and qualification.

*Procedural changes to extend the launch time line by dropping prompt launch and massive attack options from the emergency war plans.* These changes could lengthen the time line for both decision and execution, and preclude large-scale retaliatory strikes. By taking operationally meaningful, rather than cosmetic, steps to de-target the strategic missile forces, any move to bring them back to launch-ready status would incur significant delays in re-targeting. With some qualifications due to transparency and verification concerns, this report recommends these changes, which could readily be adopted, because they would reduce the risks of mistaken launch on false warning, *require significant time to reverse (many hours to re-target; many days to revert to former procedures),* preserve deterrence under the worst of plausible conditions, and build momentum toward a nuclear-free world. It is a qualified recommendation, however, because the degree of transparency and verifiability is low.

*Physical de-alerting measures that could be instituted immediately on the U.S. side by "safing" Minuteman missiles in their silos*—flipping a safety switch inside the silos that electronically isolates the missiles from outside launch signals—*and refraining from installing special electronic devices known as "inverters" on the tubes of Trident submarines going on patrol.* These simple, practical measures are stronger in all the respects noted above for the procedural changes, and have the added virtues of *extending the time to re-alert the bulk of the forces by approximately 24 hours* and of lending themselves to a modest degree of verification that would build confidence over time. Analogous or comparable measures can be effected in the Russian posture, resulting in a stable nuclear balance that removes sudden first strike and launch on warning completely from the array of response options available to decisionmakers, and that all but eliminates the prospect of unauthorized actors, including terrorists, exploiting hair-trigger postures to cause a nuclear incident or actual firing.

*Physical measures that could be instituted in 1–3 years by creating a reserve strategic nuclear force that entails separating warheads from their delivery vehicles (missiles) but widely dispersing both warheads and missiles in protected positions.* For a notional U.S.

strategic force utilizing the existing force of 14 Trident submarines and the planned force of 450 Minuteman silos, this de-alerting scheme calls for storing Minuteman warheads in 225 otherwise empty silos, adjacent to 225 silos housing the unarmed Minuteman missiles; and for storing Trident warheads on 11 boats in 11 otherwise empty tubes on each boat, adjacent to 11 tubes housing the unarmed Trident missiles. Supplemented by 143 bomber warheads in local base storage, this de-alerting scheme preserves a large margin of survivability under worst-case conditions of break-out and attack by opposing forces. Reciprocal Russian measures would produce a resilient 500-warhead reserve force on each side that further *extends the time to re-alert* (by re-mating warheads to adjacent silos/tubes) *by days to weeks*. This option is highly rated in terms of stable deterrence, re-alerting stability, depriving unauthorized actors of any opportunity to induce a launch, and eliminating the risk of mistaken launch on false warning. Furthermore, this option rates highly with respect to transparency and verification. It would both demand and benefit from U.S.-Russian monitoring cooperation that applies to the warheads as well as launchers and promote the creation of an auditable database of warheads that in turn would facilitate progressive disarmament. Most notably, this option would significantly reduce the relative importance of nuclear weapons in national security policies. It would provide a waypoint on the path toward storing the entire U.S. and Russian nuclear arsenals and inspire greater confidence regarding the path toward the long-term goal of total elimination.

*Physical measures for the medium-term future (4–6 years) that transfer nuclear warheads from their field deployment into warhead storage depots on land.* Such wholesale consolidation of nuclear stockpiles would mark the end of traditional nuclear war-fighting strategies. *Reconstitution times for the bulk of the arsenals would be measured in weeks and months, greatly marginalizing their role and significantly facilitating further steps toward* complete elimination. It would also put the stockpiles into a full "lock-down" status that would offer the optimal conditions for preventing accidental and unauthorized use, or theft, of nuclear weapons. However, this option must be implemented with great caution. Depots stocked with large numbers of warheads present a potentially lucrative target. The breakout of even a few weapons could pose an extreme threat if the opposing forces' nuclear ordnance is concentrated in only a few depots. Therefore *before any transition to this storage option is completed, a number of preconditions should be satisfied.*

*First,* monitoring and verification must be able to perform at a very high level with exact accounting of warheads in storage down to the single weapons unit. *Second,* all of the P-5 states and perhaps other nuclear states need to be involved in this option—even limited capabilities in the hands of third parties could pose a potentially severe threat to the locked-down forces of the U.S. and Russia. This de-alerting regime should thus be comprehensively multilateral with stringent and enforceable monitoring and verification provisions. *Third,* given the enhanced threat represented by a single nuclear weapon, a strict re-alerting protocol would be essential should any nuclear nation deem it necessary to take this highly momentous and potentially destabilizing step. *Fourth,* similar protocols and constraints may need to be devised for conventional forces. A party that covertly begins to reconstitute its nuclear forces could use conventional forces to degrade an ostensible opponent's ability to respond in kind. *Fifth* and last, storage depots on land can and should be designed to withstand a small-scale nuclear attack. With respect to the U.S., the 50 empty MX Peacekeeper silos and the 50 Minuteman silos slated for mothballing could be utilized to protect a stockpile of reserve warheads for submarines, land-based missiles, and bombers.

## Introduction

The inertia of almost half a century of maintaining the U.S. and Russian nuclear arsenals on launch-ready alert has proven difficult to wind down, even though the practice runs a host of dangerous risks and sustains a technical state of nuclear confrontation that is politically incongruent with the end of the Cold War. In the wake of the recent surge of terrorism and the growing danger of cascading nuclear proliferation around the world, however, estimates of the liabilities of maintaining the *status quo* are being revised upward. An array of new risks is coming to light. The war-ready nuclear postures perpetuate the danger of mistaken or unauthorized use, and may be susceptible to physical or cyber exploitation by terrorists. The war-footing postures keep nuclear weapons in constant motion and thereby create opportunities for terrorists to capture or steal them during the relatively exposed phase of their operation—transportation and temporary storage. They perpetuate a dynamic mutual reliance on nuclear weapons that lends legitimacy to the nuclear ambitions of other nations, whose proliferation makes intentional use more likely and whose deficiencies in nuclear command and warning systems multiply the global risk of accidental and unauthorized use, or terrorist theft.

In a new age of heightened nuclear danger, major benefits would accrue from standing down the legacy postures (called "de-alerting" herein), especially if it facilitates real progress toward the global elimination of nuclear weapons. This paper presents a set of feasible options to do that. They are designed to remove U.S. and Russian nuclear forces from launch-ready alert, reduce the risk of mistaken or unauthorized launch to negligible proportions, increase the time needed to re-alert them by hours, days, weeks, and months, and strengthen safeguards against terrorist exploitation, while preserving stable deterrence during a transition to a nuclear-free world.

The conditions favoring progress in de-alerting are numerous. The requirements of mutual deterrence between the United States and Russia are far less demanding today than they were during the Cold War. The end of the Cold War was an epochal event in U.S.-Russian relations that dramatically altered threat perceptions and the calculus of deterrence—e.g., the number of targets that need to be held at risk of destruction to deter an attack, and the promptness with which retaliatory strikes need to be delivered in order to underscore the threat of punitive retaliation. The former Cold War adversaries also share the view that while deterrent requirements have eased, the vexing challenge of preventing proliferation and nuclear terrorism has grown during the post-Cold War period. This ascendance is reflected in the high priority accorded the Nunn-Lugar program to secure "loose" fissile materials and nuclear weapons in the former Soviet Union. Many nuclear specialists believe that preventing the theft, illicit purchase, or capture of nuclear weapons by terrorists represents the single most important challenge of U.S. and Russian nuclear policy, and that it eclipses even nuclear deterrence as the overriding priority of our times.

Despite this strong mutual U.S.-Russian interest in cooperating in strengthening nuclear security, a number of obstacles impede progress on a de-alerting agenda in particular. Progressively reducing the alert status of nuclear forces demands commensurately more intrusive and cooperative verification in areas such as warhead monitoring for which the parties possess scant experience. Progress also depends upon addressing the conventional imbalance between them that puts Russia at a stark disadvantage with serious implications for Russia's ability to re-alert if necessary. Progressively deeper de-alerting—particularly if it involves the separation of warheads from delivery vehicles and their transfer to central storage depots—also cannot remain a strictly bilateral affair. Other nuclear states' arsenals become a major threat to warhead storage facilities and therefore new, complex multinational issues come to the fore. Lastly, their traditional nuclear strategies remain highly resistant to change in spite of the new deterrent climate and dramatic decline in the level of fear of a deliberate nuclear attack by either nation against the other. The drastic change of focus and concern away from U.S.-Russian deterrent relations and toward the urgent need to eliminate the threat of nuclear terrorism and arrest the danger of runaway proliferation has not yet altered the nuclear postures nearly as much as the objective situation warrants.

## Baseline Posture

The nuclear superpowers manage their strategic arsenals today in almost exactly the same manner as they did during the Cold War. Many hundreds of missiles on land and sea are fully armed, fueled, and targeted. The land-based missiles in silos will fly as soon as they receive a few short computer signals whose transmission is as simple as stroking a few keys on a keyboard, hitting "Enter," repeating the sequence once more, and then turning two keys in unison. The sea-based missiles on submarines will pop out of their tubes as soon as their gyroscopes are spun up, the onboard computer uploads their wartime targets and arms their warheads, and additional computer signals open the hatches and ignite the steam generators that propel the missiles to the surface.[1]

If the Kremlin and the White House ordered the launch of their alert strategic missiles right now, this minute, without any prior notice and advance preparation, the amount of firepower unleashed and the speed of its release would be astonishingly large and rapid. U.S. land-based launch crews would receive the order almost instantaneously, remove launch keys and codes from their safes, compare the authorization codes in the launch order with those in their safes, insert their launch keys, punch in the number of the selected war plan that automatically instructs their missiles which specific target file to pull from their computer files and what trajectory to fly, key in the "enabling code" contained in the launch order that arms the warheads on the missiles, and turn the launch keys that transmit the "Fire" command to the dispersed unmanned missiles in underground silos.

The time needed to execute all of these steps in the Minuteman fields of central plains America: one to two minutes. (They are called Minuteman for a reason.) At sea, analogous steps taken by submarine

---

1. For a complete step-by-step description of the launch procedures for Trident submarines, see Douglas C. Waller, *Big Red: Three Months On Board a Trident Nuclear Submarine* (New York: HarperCollins, 2001), pp. 203–237.

crews include retrieving a special firing key from a safe inside a safe, the access code to which is provided by the launch order from higher authority. From that point in time until missiles leave their tubes in quick succession only about 12 minutes would elapse.

Very similar procedures and timelines apply in Russia. Extremely high launch readiness for large numbers of alert missiles prevails on both sides. About one-third of their total strategic forces are poised for immediate launch under normal conditions. *The combined firepower that could be unleashed within these short time frames measured in minutes is approximately 2,654 high-yield nuclear warheads (1,382 U.S. and 1,272 Russian)—the equivalent of approximately 100,000 Hiroshima bombs* (assuming the Hiroshima bomb yielded 15 kilotons of explosive power).[2]

A high degree of vigilance suffuses the entire U.S. and Russian chains of nuclear command and warning, from the bottom all the way to the top. In the warning centers, such as the hub of the U.S. early warning network in Colorado, crews labor under the pressure of tight deadlines to assess and report whether a satellite or land radar sensor indicating a possible threat to North America is real or false. Events happen almost daily, sometimes more than once daily, which trigger this assessment drill that is supposed to yield a preliminary assessment within three minutes after the arrival of the initial sensor data.[3] Analogous drills take place under comparable deadlines in Russia. A rush

2. Assumptions for alert rates: U.S.: Minuteman III (95%); Trident (4 boats launch-ready); all others (0%); Russian: SS-18 (80%); SS-19 (66.6%); Delta IV (1 boat launch-ready at sea; 1 boat launch-ready on pierside alert); all others (0%). Other assumptions on payloads and yields are available from author.

3. These frequent occurrences involve diverse events—e.g., nations launching rockets to place satellites in space; developmental tests of military and civilian rockets; combat use of rockets of all kinds (including short- and medium-range rockets as well as intercontinental range); and airplanes using after-burners. Assessment drills are also triggered by natural phenomena—sunlight reflected from clouds, for instance, and even wildfires may be detected by infrared heat sensors on surveillance satellites designed to detect the hot plumes of rockets during their 2–4 minute first-stage burn.

of adrenalin and rote processing of checklists, often accompanied by confusion, characterize the process.[4]

If their early warning assessment determines that a nuclear missile attack is possibly underway, the entire chain of nuclear command in the United States or Russia would immediately kick into high gear with thousands of duty crews and nuclear support personnel involved. The same rush of adrenalin and rote decisionmaking by checklist drive a process whose intensity and deadlines practically rule out any chance for careful deliberation. An emergency conference involving the presidents and their top nuclear advisors would be convened, whereupon on the U.S. side the commanding duty officer at Strategic Command headquarters in Omaha would brief the U.S. president on the nature of the apparent attack, the wide array of response options, and their anticipated consequences for Russian physical and human resources. The time allocated for this briefing is about 30 seconds depending on the nature of the attack. The U.S. president then would come under intense pressure to absorb this complex set of data, weigh the consequences of the various options, and choose a course of action. His decision window is typically 12 minutes, although under certain extreme conditions it can be much shorter.

The extraordinarily brief time for such a momentous decision is driven by four factors: the 30-minute flight time for an intercontinental missile, and about one-half that for a submarine-launched missile; the time required to validate and characterize the attack, using two separate sources of warning data to ensure high confidence; the time required to convene a phone conference of the principals involved in the decision process, and the time required following presidential decision to encode and transmit that decision worldwide to the strategic

---

4. On the occasions of the two major false alarms in U.S. history (caused by human error and computer malfunction, respectively), it took the crews 8 minutes instead of 3 to resolve the confusing contradictory indications, resulting in their being immediately relieved of duty ("fired") both times. Cases in Russia were similarly fraught with confusion.

nuclear forces. The importance of the latter seemingly mundane factor cannot be overstated. Any delay in transmitting the response order runs the risk of losing retaliatory forces to the Russian attack, thus undermining the calculus of expected damage for the response option chosen by the president. This risk is compounded in the event of a so-called "decapitation strike," that is, an opening attack on the National Command Authority (the president and the secretary of defense), most likely mounted by Russian missile submarines operating close to U.S. shores. Under this circumstance, the integrity of the U.S. retaliatory response is greatly compromised, thus calling into question the very calculus upon which nuclear deterrence is based.

Given these acute conditions, it is no wonder that as much of the response process as possible is designed to be quasi-automatic. It can reasonably be described as going to war by checklist, enacting a prepared script, with little margin for human error or technical malfunction. The nuclear war machinery has a hair-trigger quality. And that quality has been a constant in the nuclear equation for decades. Comparable pressures and deadlines apply to Russia. Both of the traditional nuclear rivals still stand ready, despite the Cold War's end, to inflict apocalyptic devastation on one another in a first or second strike whose essential course would be run in less than one hour.

*Wartime Aims of the Nuclear Posture*

The main underlying cause for this continuing state of affairs is the undiminished commitment on both sides to traditional deterrent strategies of nuclear war-fighting. Both the Kremlin and the White House evidently continue to issue presidential nuclear guidance that requires their respective nuclear forces to be constantly prepared to fight a large-scale nuclear war with each other at a moment's notice. These forces are assigned long lists of targets, running into the thousands on each side, to strike in the event of war, and they are expected to inflict serious damage with high probability on all target categories—opposing nuclear forces, conventional forces, war-supporting industry, and leadership. The forces cannot achieve this wartime objective of high "damage expectancy" if the opposing forces destroy them first, and so both strategic arsenals are kept on hair-trigger alert, ready to launch on warning of incoming warheads launched by the opposing side.

The insidious role played by stringent (and arguably excessive) "damage expectancy" requirements in keeping warning and decision times so short can be demonstrated mathematically. Taking the mid-1980s as a point of reference, open sources indicate that the U.S. strategic war plan at that time called for attacks on up to 16,000 targets in the full-scale variant (major attack option 4).[5] Assuming an average damage requirement across the spectrum of targets of 80 percent[6]— that is, U.S. strategic forces had to be able to destroy 80 percent of the complete target base of 16,000 targets—U.S. forces had to be able to deliver some 12,800 weapons to those targets.[7]

Since the entire U.S. strategic arsenal in 1986 was comprised of around 12,314 warheads,[8] all of them would have been needed in wartime to ensure adequate coverage of the target base and to emerge from a nuclear exchange having fulfilled the mission successfully. All U.S. forces would have had to be brought to alert, and all launched before incoming Soviet weapons could inflict losses to them (or to the even more fragile U.S. command system whose ability to direct U.S. forces to coherent wartime missions depended heavily upon exercising

---

5. See Bruce G. Blair, *The Logic of Accidental Nuclear War*, Brookings, 1993.

6. Declassified documents describing the U.S. strategic war plan indicate that U.S. guidance prescribed a 90 percent probability of causing severe damage to the highest priority targets—the adversary's strategic nuclear forces. See *History of the Joint Strategic Target Planning Staff: Preparation of SIOP-63*; www.gwu.edu/nsarchiv/nukevault/ebb236/SIOP-63.pdf

7. Note that some single weapons could destroy multiple targets, while sometimes multiple weapons had to be assigned to destroy a single target—an example of the latter was the assignment into the 1990s of 69 strategic weapons to attack the Push-kino battle management radar in the Moscow suburbs which controlled the ballistic missile defense system ringing Moscow. Personal communications with SIOP planner, 1998.

8. NRDC: www.nrdc.org/nuclear/nudb/datab1.asp.

the option of launch on warning[9]). The stability of a nuclear crisis in 1986 would have been low and warning and decision time would have been short indeed. All the pressures worked to generate maximum forces to alert and to use them before suffering *any* losses to Soviet strikes, lest the damage expectancy requirement that defined "success" in a nuclear war with Russia should be unfulfilled. Launch on warning was essential to the success of the war plan.

Twenty years later, the situation is much the same. The number of targets in the U.S. strategic war plan declined drastically over those two decades—from an estimated 16,000 to 2,500 in 1995,[10] and leveling out at around 2,260 (plus a smaller number of China targets) in the year 2000.[11] *Assuming about 2,000 Russian and 400 Chinese targets in a notional 2007 strategic war plan, the U.S. strategic arsenal today must be able to destroy about 1,920 targets combined in Russia and China. That is well within the scope of current numbers (3,800 warheads) and capabilities of U.S. strategic forces, but the United States would still need to put more forces on alert in a crisis and launch them on warning or preemptively in order to meet the "damage expectancy" requirements of a successful wartime mission.[12]* **Russia's posture depends even more upon force generation during a crisis and upon launch on warning.**[13]

9. Bruce G. Blair, *Strategic Command and Control,* Brookings, 1985.

10. Bruce G. Blair, *Global Zero Alert for Nuclear Forces*, Brookings, 1995.

11. Bruce G. Blair, "Trapped in the Nuclear Math," *New York Times*, June 12, 2000.

12. It was earlier noted that the United States maintains about 1,382 strategic weapons on launch-ready alert today, which alone could cover only 58 percent of the total target base. All of these forces would have to be launched on warning or preemptively, and an additional contingent of 538 off-alert strategic weapons would need to be generated to alert, and launched before Soviet weapons could destroy any of them. (Chinese strategic weapons are too few in number to represent a counterforce threat to U.S. strategic forces.)

13. The pressures for generating and dispersing Russian forces during a crisis are even more intense than the pressures on the U.S. posture because Russia's day-to-day posture is highly vulnerable to sudden attack. On a typical day, no Russian deterrent submarine is patrolling at sea (compared to nine U.S. Trident subs armed

**In short, the mathematics of nuclear deterrence embedded in the current U.S. and Russian nuclear postures today offers practically no margin for extending warning and decision time.** *In the remote event of a U.S.-Russian nuclear confrontation that brings the two sides to the brink of conflict, there would be enormous pressure exerted on the respective nuclear command systems to raise the defense readiness conditions, rapidly bring the arsenals to full alert, and not to hesitate to launch them upon receiving indications of an apparent enemy nuclear missile attack. However ample the current amount of "overkill" may seem to reside in the arsenals from the perspective of an outside observer, the margin is actually razor-thin to the inside strategic planner, and the high damage requirements levied by the planners on the strategic nuclear forces creates conditions in which an unstable crisis alert dynamic is guaranteed to unfold unless extraordinary political will is exerted to moderate it.*

*In sum,* **the U.S. and Russian nuclear postures are still primed for an alerting race and for rapid launch during a crisis. These current pre-programmed processes are more unstable overall than the relatively slow re-alerting and reconstitution processes associated with the de-alerting options outlined later in this report.**

### Aligning the Postures with the Real Threats

The surrealism of the current nuclear war-fighting postures in the post-Cold War era is equaled only by their lack of efficacy in addressing the real nuclear threats that exist today. In the spirit of traditional deterrence, they are projecting a massive nuclear threat at potential contemporary adversaries that are scarcely in the same adversarial

---

with nearly 1,000 survivable warheads) and perhaps only one regiment of mobile land rockets—consisting of nine missiles and warheads—is operating covertly in the field away from home garrison. Practically the entire Russian arsenal depends on launch on warning and on crisis alerting to project a deterrent threat of severe punitive retaliation to attack. Similar rapid increases in command system readiness are planned on both sides to bolster their deterrent postures during a crisis.

league as the old Soviet Union. Meanwhile, this exercise in force projection not only wields no influence over transnational terrorist organizations, but also unintentionally legitimizes proliferation and increases a variety of immediate nuclear risks to ourselves. The operational postures reflect misplaced priorities driven by Cold War habits of mind, and what is worse, they are counterproductive in significant respects.

There are a host of reasons why removing forces from launch-ready alert and abandoning archaic nuclear war-fighting strategies are urgent priorities. *Beyond the familiar arguments about the danger of accidental nuclear attack triggered by false alarms, and unauthorized launches by unreliable personnel, lurk shadowy new threats stemming from terrorist scenarios and growing cybernetic threats to the nuclear command and warning systems.* In an era of terrorism and information warfare, staking the survival of humanity on the assumption that imperfect human and technical systems of nuclear command and control will forever prevent a disastrous breakdown of safeguards against mistaken or unauthorized use of nuclear weapons is simply imprudent in the extreme.

An in-depth discussion of the potential exploitable weaknesses in nuclear command systems is beyond the scope of this analysis, but a few general observations are pertinent. First, many of the deficiencies are unknown, some will never be found, and others will not be discovered until it is too late. The complexity of command systems prevents a full reckoning of the risks run by hair-trigger postures. Periodic investigations routinely discover glaring weaknesses, however. For instance, a Pentagon investigation conducted by an independent commission in the 1990s at the behest of then Sen. Sam Nunn to evaluate the effectiveness of U.S. nuclear safeguards against unauthorized launch found dozens of major deficiencies.[14] This commission

---

14. An especially noteworthy example is the discovery by the commission of an unprotected electronic back door into the naval broadcast communications network used to transmit launch orders by radio to the U.S. Trident deterrent submarine fleet.

recommended a multitude of remedies, including installing a special new safeguard on Trident subs—the inner safe described earlier—to create a technical barrier to unauthorized launch.

Second, many of the deficiencies that are identified and addressed turn out not to have been corrected. The introduction of "enable code" devices into Minuteman launch centers in the 1960s is a case in point. In theory, the devices required launch crews to receive an eight-digit code from higher authority in order to arm their missiles' warheads prior to launch. In practice, the Strategic Air Command, unbeknownst to higher authority (such as former Defense Secretary Robert McNamara, who initiated and pressed for this safeguard), configured the devices so that they were always set to all zeros—that was the secret password known to all launch crews. This circumvention persisted until 1976, when actual codes were finally introduced. In the interim, the posture ran a higher risk of unauthorized launch by crew members or others who might have gained access to the launch centers, including terrorists.[15]

Third, the nuclear command systems today operate in an intense information battleground on which more than 20 nations including Russia, China, and North Korea have developed dedicated computer attack programs.[16] These programs deploy viruses to disable, confuse, and delay nuclear command and warning processes in other nations. The U.S. Strategic Command is no exception. Information warfare is

---

Unauthorized persons, including terrorists, may have been able to seize electronic control of shore-based radio transmitters such as the very low frequency facility at Cutler, Maine, and actually inject a launch order into the network. The deficiency was taken so seriously that new launch order validation protocols had to be devised and Trident crews had to undergo special training to learn them.

15. During the mid-1970s this author personally pressed for the activation of these codes as a way to prevent the exploitation of Minuteman systems by terrorists. See Bruce G. Blair and Garry D. Brewer, "The Terrorist Threat to World Nuclear Programs," *Journal of Conflict Resolution*, 1977.

16. Estimates based upon Adam J. Hebert, "Information Battleground," *Air Force Magazine*, Vol. 88, No. 12, December 2005. www.afa.org/magazine/Dec2005/1205info.html.

now one of its core missions. *At the brink of conflict, nuclear command and warning networks around the world may be besieged by electronic intruders whose onslaught degrades the coherence and rationality of nuclear decisionmaking. The potential for perverse consequences with computer-launched weapons on hair-trigger is clear.*

Other information warfare programs are designed to infiltrate and collect information on, for example, the schedule of the movement of nuclear warheads during peacetime. Hacking operations of these sorts are increasing exponentially as the militaries of the world increasingly depend on computer and communications networks. *The number of attempts by outside hostile actors to break into Defense Department networks has surged by tenfold in the past couple of years.* Hostile intrusion attempts against Pentagon computer systems now run in the neighborhood of 1,000 per day. (China is especially active.)

What is worse, some of this expanding illicit penetration involves insiders, creating a whole new dimension to the "insider" threat to nuclear systems. If insiders with knowledge of special passwords or other sensitive information related to nuclear weapons activities collude with outsiders, the integrity of nuclear command and control systems and safeguards against the unauthorized launch of nuclear weapons on launch-trigger alert may well be compromised. *The guiding principle of nuclear safeguards during the past 50 years—the two-man rule—may be obsolete in the age of information warfare.* The notion that having a second person present during any sensitive nuclear operation would prevent an accidental or intentional nuclear incident may have been sound during the labor-intensive and analog-dominated era of nuclear command and control, but in the modern age of information warfare, new safeguards may be needed to prevent the electronic compromise of missiles on hair-trigger alert.

*Adding terrorists to this equation gives further reason to believe that the Cold War nuclear postures are counterproductive*—they exacerbate rather than alleviate nuclear problems, and they are an accident waiting to happen. There is a possibility that terrorists could spoof early warning sensors and thereby engender false alarms that precipitate nuclear overreactions. The possibility also exists that terrorists, possibly with insider help, may get inside the command and communications networks controlling nuclear forces. They might gain information useful to interdicting and capturing weapons, or unauthorized actors might discover ways to inject messages into the circuits.[17] Again, the wisdom of keeping nuclear forces ready to fly instantaneously upon receipt of a short stream of computer signals is dubious.

The more likely scenario is one in which nuclear weapons fall into the hands of terrorists because of intrinsic fault lines in the nuclear postures. The simple fact that maintaining war-ready nuclear postures requires many hundreds of nuclear bombs to be moving around on alert or going back and forth between the field and bomb refurbishment facilities means that they are exposed to terrorist capture or theft during the most vulnerable phase of their operating cycle: transportation, the Achilles Heel of security.[18] *As long as traditional deterrent practices continue, it will be impossible to truly "lock down" the arsenals to protect them from terrorist theft.* Sooner or later, the Nunn-Lugar program will fail unless the day-to-day adversarial nuclear relationship is ended.

*One can also readily imagine the rampant problems of these kinds that afflict, or will afflict, the nuclear command, control, and early warning systems of nuclear proliferators who lack the technical sophistication, experience, and resources of the United States and Russia.*

17. Recall the findings reported earlier concerning the Trident communications deficiency.

18. This is an especially acute concern for the Russian posture because of its relatively greater reliance on mobile nuclear forces, and also because of its need to transport large numbers of plutonium pits from the field to remanufacturing facilities and back to the field. Russian pits have a short shelf life—8–12 years (compared to 50–80 years for U.S. pits) and thus on average 10 percent of the Russian arsenal needs to be refurbished each year. At any given time in Russia, hundreds to thousands of nuclear devices are in transit or temporary storage.

Undoubtedly the global nuclear threshold will become steadily lower and easier to cross if, say, Pakistan and India follow in the footsteps of the nuclear superpowers by mating nuclear weapons to delivery vehicles and preparing to launch them on warning. Although this analysis focuses on the U.S.-Russian case, it is important to recognize that the second nuclear age involves a normal process of force "modernization" that leads militaries from other countries to increase the launch readiness of their forces. Arresting this trend on a global basis is essential to avert the mistaken or unauthorized, as well as the intentional, use of nuclear weapons by one or another of the nine nuclear nations, or by some future new proliferator.

On the face of it, *establishing a universal norm that prevents any nation from adopting a hair-trigger alert posture has considerable merit.*[19] Britain, France, and China ought to be formally engaged and assume obligations for verification. Their transparent adherence to a de-alerting regime would help bring Russia into full compliance with it. Russia may insist on maintaining at least a small portion of their current arsenals on high alert until all of the other major declared its nuclear-weapons states join the regime and adopt comparable restrictions on readiness.

---

19. By some indications, Britain, France, and China have already assumed a de facto de-alerted posture. China has traditionally maintained a low state of nuclear readiness, with warheads stored separately from their delivery vehicles. France has kept its missile submarines at sea on modified alert, and Britain has declared that its strategic monad of missile submarines are now routinely at a "'notice to fire' measured in days rather than the few minutes' quick reaction alert sustained throughout the Cold War." British Ministry of Defense, *Strategic Defense Review*, Supporting Essay Five: Deterrence, Arms Control, and Proliferation, June 1998. The information on the French SSBN modified alert posture is based on personal communications with a French military official. The Chinese nuclear posture is discussed in Hans M. Kristensen, Robert S. Norris, and Matthew G. McKinzie, *Chinese Nuclear Forces and U.S. Nuclear War Planning*, FAS/NRDC, Nov. 2006; www.nukestrat.com/china/chinareport.htm. Nevertheless, the operational postures of these nations as well as India, Pakistan, Israel, and North Korea are opaque and ought to become more transparent.

*Precedents for De-Alerting*

President George H. W. Bush led boldly to de-alert nuclear weapons at the end of September 1991, when the Soviet Union began to crumble in the wake of the August coup attempt, and as the Soviet nuclear weapons complex quaked along with it. On the advice of his advisors including Gen. George L. Butler, then commander of the Strategic Air Command, Bush ordered an immediate stand-down of U.S. strategic bombers that for decades had stood ready for takeoff within 15 minutes. Nuclear weapons on them were unloaded and placed in storage at the bomber bases. In addition, Bush took off alert a large number of land- and sea-based strategic missiles slated for elimination under START I—450 Minuteman II missiles along with the missiles in 10 Poseidon submarines. These measures, removing about 3,000 strategic warheads from high alert, were implemented in a matter of days, and they encouraged comparable actions by Russia.[20]

President Gorbachev followed suit a week later by ordering the deactivation of more than 500 land-based rockets and six strategic submarines, by promising to keep strategic bombers at a low level of readiness, and by consigning Russia's rail-based missiles to their home garrisons. These reciprocal steps would entail removing about 2,000 strategic warheads from high alert.

In subsequent months, both countries de-mated the nuclear warheads from the de-alerted missile forces. Furthermore, they withdrew many thousands of shorter-range tactical nuclear weapons deployed with their far-flung armies and surface navies and placed these weapons in central storage depots on their home territories.

Presidents Clinton and Yeltsin took a further step together in 1994, when they pledged to stop aiming strategic missiles at each other's country. The gyroscopes on U.S. land-based missiles were ori-

---

20. The de-alerting measures introduced initially for land-based strategic missiles were procedural and minor physical modifications similar to those discussed under *Option 2* below. The warheads were de-mated later on.

ented to ocean areas in the far northern latitudes, and Russia switched its land-based rockets to a "zero flight plan." These adjustments of the primary target settings, though a welcome gesture, can be reversed in seconds and had negligible military significance.[21]

## De-alerting Options and Criteria for Evaluating Them

This paper presents and evaluates several de-alerting options for the immediate-, near-, and medium-term future that show promise in satisfying the basic criteria outlined below. Our aim is mainly to *illustrate rather than prescribe* a blueprint for de-alerting. Military and technical experts will bear responsibility for devising steps that pass muster in practical operational terms and that meet the essential criteria. No claims are made that the plan outlined below represents an optimal course of action. This caveat especially applies to the illustrative Russian de-alerting steps, which are presented below with less detail and texture.

Having offered this disclaimer, it should be noted that the options described below survived the author's winnowing of a multitude of

21. Pre-programmed wartime target coordinates remained in the computer memories of the missiles, and missile commanders could activate these target files within seconds. In other words, the Clinton-Yeltsin "de-targeting" agreement could and can still be reversed by either side in seconds. Selecting targets in this fashion is in fact a standard procedure for launching missiles in wartime (see earlier discussion of launch procedures) and hence the accord did not extend the launch preparation time by even a single solitary second. In the United States, local launch crews in the missile fields perform this standard procedure in accordance with the target plan designated by their launch orders. In the case of Russia, the local crews can perform the procedure or the General Staff, from their wartime command bunkers in the Moscow vicinity, can use a computer network called Signal-A to override the agreement and re-aim all their silo-based missiles at the United States in ten seconds. In fact, if the General Staff transmits a launch order directly to the missiles over Signal-A in the mode called "automatic regime," then the missiles automatically switch over to their primary wartime target. For detailed discussions of all aspects of "de-targeting," see Bruce Blair, "Where Would All the Missiles Go?" *Washington Post*, October 15, 1996, p. A15; Bruce Blair, *Global Zero Alert for Nuclear Forces* (Brookings, 1995); and Bruce Blair, "Russian Nuclear Policy and the Status of De-targeting," Testimony before the House Committee on National Security, March 13, 1997.

possibilities. Furthermore, they have been reviewed by a cadre of knowledgeable U.S. and Russian military experts with experience in the operational arena of all three legs of the strategic triad—land- and sea-based missiles, and bombers. Without question *feasible de-alerting schemes that satisfy the basic criteria exist and can be defined.*[22] *Moreover, the number and variety of possible de-alerting schemes create an opportunity to fashion agreements that impose equitable constraints on asymmetrical force structures and operational practices.* The basic criteria are:

**Criterion A:** *time to re-alert*, which measures how long it would take to reverse de-alerting and restore forces to their original launch-ready configuration. The longer the time needed to re-alert the forces, the greater the merit of the option. It is important to recognize that the time to re-alert a given weapon may vary greatly depending upon its position in the queue of the larger force of similar weapons. Thus while it may take several hours or days to re-alert one or a handful of nuclear forces, such as Minuteman missiles, it may take many weeks or months to re-alert all of the weapons in the same category of forces. *This paper generally gauges both the time needed to re-alert the first batch of weapons and the time needed to re-alert the bulk or all of the weapons.*

**Criterion B:** *impact on strategic stability*, which for de-alerted postures places special emphasis on the stability of dynamic re-alert-

---

22. For additional reading of work to devise de-alerting options, see Bruce G. Blair, "De-alerting Strategic Nuclear Forces," in Harold A Feiveson, ed., *The Nuclear Turning Point: A Blueprint for Deep Cuts and De-alerting of Nuclear Weapons.* Brookings, 1999; Bruce Blair, Hal Feiveson, and Frank von Hippel, "Taking Nuclear Weapons off Hair-Trigger Alert." *Scientific American*, Vol 277, No. 5, Nov. 1997; David Mosher, David Howell, Lowell Schwartz, and Lynn Davis, *Beyond the Nuclear Shadow: A Phased Approach for Improving Nuclear Safety and U.S.-Russian Relations.* Rand, 2003; Bruce Blair, "Command, Control, and Warning for Virtual Arsenals," in Michael J. Mazaar, ed., *Nuclear Weapons in a Transformed World: The Challenge of Virtual Nuclear Arsenals*, St. Martin's Press, 1997; Thomas Karas, *De-alerting and De-activating Strategic Nuclear Weapons*, Sandia National Laboratories, Report 2001-0835, April 2001.

ing. De-alerting should not create exploitable advantages from break-ing out and re-alerting. It especially should not be possible to seize a disarming first-strike advantage by reconstituting faster than an op-ponent can. Retaliatory forces need to be sufficiently survivable under normal peacetime circumstances as well as during a crisis period in which restraint may break down. *It is assumed that the certainty of retaliation is far more important to deterrence than is the timing of retaliation, and that stable deterrence would not be adversely affected by delays in retaliation.*

**Criterion C:** *degree of transparency/verifiability.* This refers to *monitoring the operational status* of nuclear weapons, placing em-phasis on monitoring non-deployed forces as the importance of reserve forces increases during the transition to a nuclear-free world. Moni-toring and verification should support the goal of preserving strategic stability (Criterion B) as well as help pave the way to the elimination of nuclear weapons (Criterion D).

**Criterion D:** *foster progress toward a nuclear-free world.* De-alerting options should serve to downgrade the role of nuclear weap-ons in national security policy and strengthen diplomatic efforts to curb and reverse proliferation. They should also serve the technical purpose of bringing reserve as well as operationally deployed war-heads under surveillance in order to establish a baseline database of warhead numbers and types. An accurate global audit of warhead in-ventories is a precondition for the eventual verifiable elimination of nuclear weapons.

**Criterion E:** *impact on today's risk of accidental, mistaken, or unauthorized launch or theft.* Measures that reduce these risks and strengthen safeguards against terrorist exploitation of U.S. and Russian nuclear postures are critical today. Widening the margin of safety in these areas is arguably the overriding priority of the post-Cold War era. De-alerting options should above all enhance nuclear safety.[23]

23. For an elaboration of this thesis, see Sam Nunn and Bruce Blair, "From Nu-clear Deterrence to Mutual Safety," *Washington Post,* June 22, 1997, p. C1.

## De-alerting Option 1:  Procedural Modifications (Present-term) to Eliminate Prompt Large-Scale Launch

The basic immediate aim of increasing warning and decision time, and reducing reliance on prompt launch procedures, can be achieved by modifying command and control practices. Two straightforward approaches involve changing Emergency War Orders, and substituting real de-targeting measures for the symbolic measures of the Clinton-Yeltsin agreement on nuclear de-targeting.

*Dropping Prompt Launch from Emergency War Orders.* A great deal of progress toward preventing hastily executed launch procedures can be made simply by altering the nuclear war plans and their implementing procedures. In U.S. military circles, these procedures are called Emergency War Orders, or EWO. All nuclear wartime operations are strictly governed by EWO, the mastery of which represents the crux of all nuclear war training. U.S. and Russian planners could readily revise EWO to ensure that none of their respective strategic forces could be launched on warning. Simple changes of EWO would suffice.[24]

Additional EWO changes could be made to increase the time needed to reach a launch decision as well as the time needed to carry out the decision. Top-level deliberations could be prolonged to preclude a hasty decision and enhance the quality of attack information.[25]

24. To illustrate, EWO could introduce an automatic, built-in delay for firing the forces, increasing the response time of the launch crews from the current period of a few minutes to a period of, say, one hour. According to the new procedures, launch crews would simply wait that long after receiving the authorization to fire before completing the launch sequence that unleashes the forces. As long as the crews followed their standing instructions under EWO, and there is every reason to expect them to comply, then no missiles would leave their silos or submarine tubes for an hour, during which time the validity of missile attack indications may be ascertained.

25. The timelines would be lengthened so that the president and his top nuclear advisors received more attack information before conferring in an emergency conference. This conference would be convened later than currently planned, and the period of consultation and deliberation among the top leaders would be lengthened.

In short, EWO procedures for organizing the launch decision process could be designed to discourage a quick decision.

*Dropping Massive Attack Options from the Strategic War Plans.* To excise massive attack options from the strategic war plans of the United States and Russia would mean the end of the practice of pre-programming large-scale strikes. The form this practice takes in the United States is a Single Integrated Operational Plan (SIOP). Specifically, the Major Attack Options (MAOs) in the SIOP and Russian war plans would be scrubbed, as would many if not the vast majority of the Limited Attack Options (LAOs) in their respective plans.[26] Pre-programmed, large-scale (MAOs) and medium-scale (LAOs) options would be replaced by EWO procedures designed for adaptive planning, targeting, and execution of small numbers of nuclear sorties.

In eliminating preprogrammed options from the strategic war plans, the wartime targets currently assigned to the forces would lose their priority. Their coordinates and related targeting information could be downloaded from the computers onboard the delivery vehicles or collocated at the launcher.

*Keeping Submarines Out of Range of Targets.* This oft-proposed option is essentially a procedural change that warrants a closer examination. Both U.S. and Russian submarine patrol areas would be moved as far south as the Southern Hemisphere, putting them far out of range and requiring many days to weeks of transit time to reach their launch stations. Patrol restrictions could thus establish a built-in delay for launching submarine missiles, an especially significant constraint for Trident D-5 missiles armed with W-88 warheads in the Atlantic that pose a potential first-strike counterforce threat. Departing from current practice, these hard-target-kill weapons assigned to Atlantic-based U.S. Trident boats could stop transiting to forward launch stations in the North Atlantic. Specifically, they could refrain from patrolling north of an imaginary line stretching from Kings Bay to

---

26. U.S. LAOs may unleash between 2 and 120 weapons; author's estimate.

Liberia in West Africa. Boats armed with the heavier W-88 warheads would be far out of range (by approximately 2,000 miles) of a wide spectrum of critical Russian targets—notably, the four Russian SS-18 missile fields in southern Russia.[27]

Trident boats armed with lighter and/or fewer warheads would be in firing range well south of this imaginary line, and thus it would need to be drawn much farther toward the equator. If Trident missiles were armed with four W-88 warheads, their range would extend another 2,000 miles, just close enough to deliver a counterforce blow against the SS-18 fields despite adhering to the proposed demarcation line restricting Trident patrols. Drawing the line farther south, indeed restricting the patrols of all Trident boats regardless of payload to the Southern Hemisphere, should solve the general problem.

It is true that as the number of warheads carried by a submarine missile decreases, as is the current trend, the range of these forces theoretically increases to a point where the missiles achieve infinite range around the globe. For example, a Trident missile carrying only two warheads could launch those warheads into orbit—i.e., infinite range. Deployment, even in the Southern Hemisphere, would not necessarily preclude strikes against very distant targets in Russia. As a practical matter, however, the range of Trident missiles appears to be limited to about 6,000 miles for various reasons having to do with speed limits on warhead fuzing during reentry, and on reentry vehicle stability and accuracy. The longer the range, the faster the speed and the shallower the angle of reentry. Warhead fuzing using altimeter readings during the final stage of reentry would be problematic at excessive speed and thereby degrade the capability to achieve the proper height of burst. Reentry vehicle stability would also suffer at excessive speeds and longer exposure to the atmosphere caused by a shallower reentry angle. If the vehicle goes too fast and shallow, it

27. Note that SSBNs in the Atlantic typically carry a heterogeneous mix of Mk-4 and Mk-5 armed missiles, and that any given D-5 missile carries a homogeneous load of either Mk-4 or Mk-5 warheads.

could actually skim off the atmosphere (the way a rock can be skimmed along the surface of a lake) resulting in a substantial degradation of accuracy. In any case, missile ranges of 6,000 miles or longer would at least provide longer tactical warning time—equal to the warning time for U.S. land-based missiles—for Russia to disperse its mobile ICBMs and command posts.

Verifying adherence to patrol restrictions should be adequate if special provisions are made. U.S. boats could be required to report their locations on a regular basis, and submit to visual or electronic identification by various means employed by joint monitoring stations such as surface ships. Boats could surface, or release buoys, to transmit position coordinates (as well as data from the electronic seals on the inverters and guidance sets) once a day, or less frequently depending upon their previously reported location. They would do so one at a time with intervals between them, in order to minimize the fleet's exposure. Submarines that operate well south of the demarcation line, even as far south as the Southern Hemisphere, could report at longer intervals of several days in view of their long transit times to launch stations. For instance, if their last report fixing their location established that it would take them a week to move within range of Russian targets, then in principle their next report would not be due for upwards of a week.

Assigning Russian submarines to patrol out of range of U.S. territory is much more problematic because of their vulnerability to U.S. anti-submarine warfare. Patrol areas for Russia's deterrent boats are close to home territory where they can be actively defended from the lethal forays of Western anti-sub forces. Russia historically sent them to patrol off the U.S. coasts but gravitated to home water patrols during the 1970s and 1980s. It would be justifiably reluctant to disperse them to far-flung regions of the ocean, and doubtless would strongly prefer other de-alerting measures for its fleet.

Furthermore, Russian submarine reactor safety would be a real problem while transiting the equator en route to the Southern Hemisphere. According to a Russian admiral interviewed by the author, Russian sub reactors need to operate in cool seas for safety reasons; ocean temperatures that exceed 20 degrees Celsius would pose a hazard. He noted that the water temperature at 200 meters depth at the equator was approximately 25 degrees Celsius, well above the safe limit.

This de-alerting option is not further considered in this report for two reasons. First, it is very unlikely to be adopted by the Russian posture, and therefore it would be an entirely asymmetrical obligation. Second, and more importantly, this option scarcely advances the goal of a nuclear-free world. It represents a diversionary rather than a progressive step.

An evaluation of the other candidate options—dropping prompt launch and massive attack options from current launch procedures—follows next.

*Evaluation*

Criterion A: (*time to re-alert*). *Hours to days.*

These changes to the emergency war plans would require significant time to reverse—many hours to re-target;[28] many days to change procedures back to their original form.

Criterion B: (impact on strategic stability). *Positive.*

Reasonable requirements of deterrence would be met under the worst of plausible circumstances.

Procedural modifications eliminating prompt large-scale launch

---

28. By stripping such targets out of the local computers that are integral to land- and sea-based missiles and associated launchers and fire control systems, any move to bring forces back to high alert status would incur lengthy delays in re-targeting. For Minuteman missiles, for instance, it would take 30 minutes to re-target 10 missiles, and 25 hours to re-target the entire force of 500 missiles. See Bruce G. Blair, *Global Zero Alert for Nuclear Forces*, Brookings, 1995, pp. 79–80.

would generally require the strategic postures to absorb an attack and suffer substantially greater losses than would occur if prompt launch remained in place. Reciprocal modifications of this sort, however, would preclude a full-scale coordinated first strike by either side. In the worst case of a covertly prepared large-scale Russian attack, a potent U.S. second-strike retaliatory force would still survive at sea, and depending upon the circumstances, substantial numbers of U.S. land-based missiles and bombers could also survive.

The procedural changes would prevent U.S. strategic forces from mounting a sudden coordinated and large-scale attack against vulnerable Russian forces in their normal peacetime configuration. Russian forces, especially land mobile rockets and submarines that surge out of garrison and port during a crisis warning period, would also be expected to constitute a bedrock of deterrence under virtually all plausible circumstances leading to nuclear conflict.

Criterion C: (degree of transparency/verifiability). *Low/Weak.*

Monitoring of the new wartime nuclear procedures and response timelines would be possible by monitoring nuclear exercises by communications intelligence gathering. The procedures could be covertly changed back to the earlier form, however, and go undetected for a prolonged period of time.

Criterion D: (foster nuclear-free world). *Positive.*

These procedural and targeting modifications would substantially alter the nuclear superpowers' postures and their underlying war-fighting strategies. This option would reduce their mutual reliance on nuclear weapons and demonstrate a genuine commitment to moving down the path toward zero weapons.

Criterion E: (impact on today's risk of accidental/unauthorized/ theft). *Positive.*

Removing prompt and large-scale launch from the repertoire of war options would extend warning and decision time well beyond the timeframe required to resolve false alarms in early warning systems, and would thus be a salutary move in reducing the risks of mistaken launch. The deprogramming of large-scale orchestrated attacks would also greatly reduce the amount of damage that an unauthorized or accidental launch could inflict, including terrorist-abetted launches.

### De-alerting Option 2: Physical Modifications (Present-term) to Eliminate Prompt Large-Scale Launch

*Overview of Illustrative U.S. Measures.* The United States could immediately adopt measures that would align its nuclear alert posture with the Pentagon's 2002 Nuclear Posture Review, whose key provision pertinent to de-alerting is the determination that Russia does not pose today an immediate nuclear threat.

*Land-based Missile Force.* The key step for Minuteman missiles, whose wartime targeting is presumably concentrated almost entirely on Russia,[29] is that they be "safed" in their silos—a safety switch in each silo is flipped to isolate the missiles from remote launch control. This "safing" measure was taken to de-alert older Minuteman missiles in 1991 in accordance with the Bush-Gorbachev initiative. (The launch keys and authentication codes were also removed from the manned launch control centers that controlled the older missiles.) "Safing" involves actuating a safety switch in each missile silo to open the circuit used for first-stage missile motor ignition. When the circuit is open, any launch commands sent to the missile would fail to cause motor

---

29. U.S. nuclear planners avoid overflying Russia to strike China targets. Therefore, Minuteman forces would be expected to have primary wartime targets in Russia, while Trident submarines and strategic bombers would be expected to cover the China target set as well as Russia targets.

ignition. In 1991, maintenance crews went around from silo to silo and "safed" the older missiles (450 of them) almost overnight. A "safed" missile cannot be fired by ground or airborne launch crews unless and until maintenance teams return to the silo and deactivate the safety switch.

*Trident Submarine Force.* The key step for Trident submarines is to remain on "modified" alert throughout their sea patrol, during which time the electronic "inverters" remain off the missile tubes.[30] U.S. submarines in transit on modified alert have not reached their assigned launch stations and their weapons systems are technically unprepared for launch. When a submarine departs home port, the crew needs to perform numerous procedures to reach launch-ready ("hard") alert, such as installing the "inverters" on the launch tubes that bring the missiles to a high state of launch readiness.[31] Also, U.S. submarines on modified alert only periodically listen for messages transmitted from shore. By contrast, boats on full alert release a long wire with a communications buoy at the end, which floats a few feet below the ocean's surface, to listen continuously for emergency war orders that would be sent over very-low-frequency radio. Boats on full alert remain capable of firing within 15 minutes after receiving the order, while those on modified alert would need almost a day just to install the inverters.

As an alternative or supplementary measure, missiles onboard the submarine could leave port without their guidance sets installed, and those sets could be kept detached from the submarine for the duration of the patrol. This step would greatly increase the time needed to reconstitute the force.[32]

30. The guidance set of each missile could also be removed prior to patrol and kept off for the duration. See discussion below.

31. The inverters convert DC to AC to deliver a 2,800-volt charge to the pyrotechnics of the Westinghouse steam generator that when fired, propels the missile out of the tube under pressurized steam. These electrical boxes are always removed from the tubes and stored in a special compartment at the end of a patrol as a safeguard against accidental or unauthorized launch.

32. Normally a Trident boat carries 24 intact missiles with their guidance sets

*Strategic Bomber Force.* The bomber force would remain in its current unarmed disposition at several bases with warheads kept at local storage bunkers.

*Overview of Illustrative Russian Measures*[33]

*Silo-Based Missiles.* To de-alert these forces, Russian experts have proposed removing the gas generators that produce the explosive charges that blow the lids off the missile silos. Maintenance crews would open the silo lid, remove the generator, close the lid, and move the generator to a nearby storage location or main base. It is possible to remove the generator but store it inside the silo.

*Road-Mobile Missiles.* Russia operates mobile land-based missiles fitted on trucks called transporter-erector launchers. The United States has none. The road-mobile SS-25 and SS-27 missile force will eventually form the backbone of the Russian strategic arsenal. Devising measures to de-alert the road-mobile force is therefore an especially pertinent task. A menu of options for standing them down is available. It appears likely that re-alerting these forces would involve observable procedures and take substantial time—at least several

---

attached. It also carries a small number of spare guidance sets, each about half the size of an oil drum, to replace sets that malfunction during patrol. The maintenance crew onboard is well-trained in this replacement procedure, though it is seldom practiced due to the very high reliability of the sets. Under this blueprint, all 24 guidance sets would be detached at the time of departure from port, and would remain detached throughout a patrol. In an emergency that requires the re-alerting of this force, the onboard crew would take about 3 hours to install 1 guidance unit into 1 missile, or about 3 days per submarine to re-alert all 24 missiles, assuming the guidance systems were reloaded 1 at a time. Many additional hours would be required for electronic testing after installation.

33. This analysis draws heavily upon interviews conducted by the author with a dozen top Russian experts, and upon the best published sources of information about Russian nuclear force operations and de-alerting possibilities: Col. (ret.) Valery E. Yarynich, *Nuclear Command Control Cooperation*, Center for Defense Information, May 2003; Alexei Arbatov and Vladimir Dvorkin, *Beyond Nuclear Deterrence: Transforming the U.S.-Russian Equation*, Carnegie Endowment for International Peace, 2006.

hours to several days depending on the exact details of the de-alerting scheme adopted.[34]

*Submarine Missiles.* Russian submarines undoubtedly have critical components similar to the "inverters" used in U.S. boats, or other components that could be kept off the weapons systems during their sea patrols or pierside alerts in order to de-alert them. One of the key aims of this option would be to terminate the Russian practice of keeping one or more of its submarines on quick-launch alert while stationed on the surface in port. Special measures to de-alert these boats in particular could be taken. One of the leading deactivation techniques for submarines proposed by A. Arbatov and V. Dvorkin is to weld shut the hatches on submarine launch tubes. Any boat so configured obviously could not fire its payload without first restoring the combat readiness of the hatch.

---

34. One approach is to keep the missiles in their garages and to block their launch path. The one or two regiments of nine missiles that typically deploy out of garrison into the field would be confined to their garrisons in this scheme, and their garage shelters would be modified to prevent quick launch. Currently, the roofs of these shelters are designed to slide open, allowing the launcher inside to be erected and the missile fired. Metal beams or other obstacles built over the sliding roofs could either prevent the roofs from opening or obstruct the raising and launching of the missiles inside. To impede the rapid dispersal of mobile missiles from their garages, heavy obstacles could be placed at the garage exits. The removal of impediments would be time-consuming and require heavy equipment that provides a detectable signature. Another approach is to incapacitate the launcher itself in ways that would take a long time to reverse. Candidate methods for doing so include (1) emptying the hydraulic fluid from the erector mechanism of the launcher and storing the fluid in liquid-container trucks; (2) removing the large gas canister at the base of the missile and storing it in a local depot—the missile cannot be ejected from the launcher without the gas canister, thereby preventing liftoff; and (3) removing the struts and related mechanisms that erect and then support the missile after raising it to the vertical position.

*Evaluation*

Criterion A: (time to re-alert). *Hours for individual weapons; days to weeks for entire force.*

Reversing these de-alerting steps would take hours to days. For example, re-alerting Minuteman missiles would entail dispatching maintenance troops to the missile fields to reenter each individual silo to flip the "safing" switch back on, a process requiring many hours to complete. Re-alerting all 500 Minuteman III missiles at the three U.S. ICBM bases[35] on an emergency basis prior to enemy nuclear attack would take approximately 10 hours.[36] A group of 100 missiles could be re-alerted about 2.5 hours after the decision was made. The remainder would be re-alerted at a rate of about 100 every 2 hours. Reconstitution thus involves maintenance teams going from silo to silo. Full reconstitution of the U.S. silo-based force would take about one-half day.

For Trident submarines, the installation of "inverters" to re-alert

35. Malmstrom Air Force Base in Montana; Minot Air Force Base in North Dakota; and F.E. Warren Air Force Base in Wyoming.

36. This is best-case analysis. Maintenance teams dispatched to the silos would need about 1 hour travel time to reach the missile fields. Upon their arrival, a given team authenticates with the local launch control center over dedicated telephone links, receives the combination to open the entry hatch, waits 1 hour for the security plug on the hatch to open, descends into the silo, deactivates the safety switch, notifies the local launch center, and departs for the next silo. Since the silos in a given flight of ten missiles are located within a few miles of each other, the travel time between silos would be short. The time needed to re-alert the entire force in this manner would depend mainly on the availability of maintenance teams. We assume that 2 teams would be available for each flight of 10 missiles. There are 45 flights of Minuteman III ICBMs in the current arsenal. Based on an initial preparation and travel time of 1 hour, plus 1.5 hours at each silo, plus travel time between silos (.15 hours), the maintenance teams would return 100 ICBMs to full alert status in 2.5 hours. Additional ICBMs could be re-alerted at a rate of 100 every 2 hours. All 450 ICBMs (764 warheads) would be launch-ready about 10 hours after the decision to re-alert them. This process could be accelerated by several hours if advance penetration teams move from silo to silo to begin lowering the security plug prior to the arrival of maintenance teams.

all 24 missiles on a given Trident boat would take about 1 day. Maintenance teams normally need about 90 minutes to 2 hours per pair of launch tubes, and the pairs are processed sequentially. For a 24-tube Trident submarine ordered to re-alert during a crisis or reconstitute after an attack, the team would need 18 hours to 1 day to install all the inverters.

Russian forces appear to require somewhat more time to re-alert. For example, the reinstallation of gas generators for fixed silos takes about 1 hour once inside the silo with the device in hand. Counting travel time to a silo and several additional hours to raise its lid, the re-alerting time per missile would run in the neighborhood of 10 hours. Assuming the availability of 1 maintenance team for each regiment of missiles (6 to 10 missiles each), the silo-based force could be reconstituted fully within about 1 week.

It appears likely that re-alerting the Russian road-mobile rockets in garages or in the field would involve observable procedures and take substantial time—at least several hours to weeks depending on the exact details of the de-alerting scheme adopted.[37]

Russian submarines with launch tubes welded shut could be restored at a rate of about 2 hours per hatch, or about 1 day for each boat to reconstitute.

Criterion B: (impact on strategic stability). *Positive.*

This option is a modest but significant confidence-building measure that bolsters strategic stability by removing the capacity of either U.S.

37. One of the most time-consuming re-alerting procedures would be to reinstall struts on the truck erectors. This maintenance would almost certainly take place at the main maintenance facilities at each SS-25/SS-27 base. In our estimation, the depots could modify only 2 launchers (TELs) at a time, and would spend about 1 or 2 days working on each launcher. At this rate, the depots could re-alert 1 regiment (9 TELs) in 5 to 9 days. Using the conservative estimate of 5 days for re-alerting a regiment at each of the main mobile missile bases, a total of 10 regiments (90 missiles) would be returned to alert in 5 days, 20 regiments (180 missiles) in 10 days, 28 regiments (252 missiles) in 15 days, and 36 regiments (324 missiles) in 20 days.

or Russian strategic forces to initiate a bolt-from-the-blue surprise attack for as long as the de-alerting measures remain in place.

A U.S. de-alerting initiative along these lines would establish the nation's clear intention not to pose a first-strike threat to Russia while preserving ample capacity to satisfy reasonable requirements of deterrence. With almost 1,000 U.S. warheads remaining invulnerable at sea, each capable of destroying the heart of a large city, the United States would deter any potential nuclear aggressor with any hold on rationality. At the same time, the U.S. daily alert force would relinquish enough of its day-to-day counterforce threat to warrant a reciprocal relaxation of the Russian nuclear posture. This forfeiture would help persuade Russia to emulate the example by taking its missiles off hair-trigger alert. The net effect on force survival under static peacetime conditions would be positive overall given the constraint on the initiation of sudden attacks.

A breakout or re-alerting race during a crisis could confer significant attack advantages for the United States in particular, but considerably less advantage than it would enjoy under the *status quo ante* in which Russia's survivable forces would be counted in single digits or tens of warheads because of their low operational tempo. And if detected in a timely fashion, such U.S. reconstitution would give Russia enough time to disperse its submarines and land-mobile rockets into more survivable positions. The rates of reconstitution are roughly the same on each side, and could be calibrated to be more equivalent, which would work to bolster mutual deterrence and stabilize any crisis re-alerting dynamics that may ensue.

In the event of the preemptive use of nuclear weapons against the land-based missiles and bomber bases on either side, the rates of reconstitution would be slowed considerably due to radiation dangers. This degradation, as well as any degradation from preemptive strikes by conventional weapons, represents a much larger complication for Russian than for U.S. reconstitution, given Russia's greater dependence on land-based strategic forces and given the far greater capabilities of U.S. conventional weapons. However, the net assessment of re-alerting stability under this option is that it compares very favorably with the present-day postures in which the amount of latent instability is actually very large as shown mathematically in an earlier section.

Criterion C: (degree of transparency/verifiability). *Positive; builds mutual confidence over time.*

Monitoring and verification would certainly be possible. The considerable amount of time required to re-alert and the scale of reconstitution necessary to effect a significant shift in the strategic balance would increase the likelihood of timely detection. Periodic on-site inspections could confirm the status of "safing" switches, and special sensors for visual monitoring (like webcams) could be installed at the individual silos and linked to a monitoring agency. These video cameras could detect manned entry into silos and thus identify candidate sites for on-site inspection. However, the level of confidence that some electronic bypass does not exist would probably not be high.

To verify that inverters are not installed on U.S. submarines, special seals could be placed on the missile compartments where the inverters are normally attached. At minimum, the seals could be checked by Russian inspectors in port at the end of a typical 78-day patrol, proving that the boat never moved up this ladder of alert. The possibility that all U.S. Trident boats could re-alert fully within one day and escape detection in the process cannot be ruled out unless very frequent interrogation of the special seals were possible. Their reconstitution would take several days longer if guidance sets were kept off the missiles. Like inverters, the status of the guidance sets is not verifiable without special provisions, such as the use of seals on the missiles that could periodically report their status through burst satellite communications or buoys. Alternatively, as a confidence-building measure the U.S. could permit Russian inspectors to examine the guidance seals along with the inverter seals at the end of a 2-plus

month patrol to reassure them that the submarine never went on full
alert.

A thorough set of inspection procedures to verify Russian compliance with its de-alerting measures has been outlined by A. Arbatov
and V. Dvorkin.[38] Restoration work on submarine hatches, for instance, would likely be visible to satellite observation and to on-site
inspection. Other analyses by U.S. agencies suggest reliable methods
of monitoring the obstruction of Russian garaged missile launches and
the incapacitation of road-mobile missile launchers.[39]

Criterion D: (fostering a nuclear-free world). *Positive.*

This plan would mark a notable step on the path to nuclear latency
and reduce the salience of nuclear weapons in ways that promote their
ultimate elimination. It would still sanction arsenals whose size exceeds the threshold number estimated to cause mass social destruction
and it would not repudiate traditional war-fighting strategy. However,
it would contest the standard assumption that deterrence depends upon
the capacity for instant retaliation and would thus represent a significant challenge to the primacy of traditional nuclear planning. On bal-

---

38. Arbatov and Dvorkin, *Beyond Nuclear Deterrence*, op.cit., esp. pp. 114–126.

39. Regarding the former measure—obstructing the launch path of missiles in
garages—a JCS review of this option as presented by Nunn and Blair notes that "the
metal beams could be verified through imagery. Emplacement of the beams would
be monitored to ensure no explosive bolts were embedded to allow rapid removal.
U.S. forces could even construct the beams." The latter measure—removing the support mechanisms—has been analyzed by Sandia National Laboratories. Sandia suggests substituting a "tamper-proof" surrogate for the original mechanism in order to
ensure the timely detection of activities to restore the latter. ["This surrogate would
be properly instrumented and configured to broadcast a message to a satellite if an
attempt were made to remove it. Receipt of this message would in turn cue a challenge, on-site inspection team to take a closer look at the suspect TEL. In addition
to these "Case-Tamper-Event" (CTE) messages, periodic "State-of-Health" (SOH)
messages would also be transmitted indicating that all is well. Of course, each broadcast would require a unique or message-dependent password be appended to the end
of each message to guarantee authenticity. The technology to rapidly implement such
a device exists today in prototype form."]

ance it would convey an impression of growing commitment to nuclear disarmament and strengthen the non-proliferation diplomacy of both states.

Criterion E (impact on today's risk of accidental/unauthorized/theft). *Very positive.*

The de-alerting steps taken in this realignment would physically eliminate the hair-trigger and remove sudden first-strike and launch on warning from the repertoire of response options available to nuclear decisionmakers. This option would also effectively prevent unauthorized actors, including terrorists, from exploiting hair-trigger postures to cause a nuclear incident or actual firing. For these reasons the implementation of this option on both sides would represent a major accomplishment.

### De-alerting Option 3: Physical Modifications (Near-term 1–3 years)

*Responsive Warhead Force with On-site De-mating*

In this option, the United States and Russia would relinquish all operationally deployed forces and rely instead on an off-alert reserve force. The de-alerting steps undertaken would be in unison with functionally equivalent Russian steps. A key feature of this suggested method of de-alerting is that it would preserve the survivability of the strategic forces by widely dispersing the responsive reserve force into protected positions.

For the United States, the transition to "zero alert" under this option would entail separating nuclear warheads from their delivery vehicles. The key step for the *Minuteman land-based missile force* (450 currently planned for silo deployment) is to keep the separated warheads nearby and protected from attack. *The novel twist in this recommendation is that the warheads would be stored individually in 225 otherwise empty silos, adjacent to 225 silos housing the unarmed*

*Minuteman missiles.* This highly dispersed and protected force could survive any plausible breakout attack by opposing forces that may covertly re-alert and fire at the Minuteman sites.

The key de-alerting step for the *Trident submarine fleet* consisting in this option of 14 boats, of which 2 are normally in overhaul, 9 are normally at sea, and 3 are normally undergoing short- to extended-maintenance of days to weeks before they could surge to sea, is also to separate the warheads from the missiles. *Rather than store the warheads on land, a possible way to reduce vulnerability problems is to store individual warheads on the boats in 11 otherwise empty tubes on each boat,* adjacent to 11 tubes housing the unarmed Trident missiles.

If force reductions down to a level of, say, 500 reserve warheads were negotiated with Russia, then 20 B-2 and B-52 heavy *strategic bombers could be deployed under this option.* The 143 warheads for these bombers would continue to reside in local base storage, i.e., bunkers at the primary bomber base. In this case, it would take 12 hours to upload the first group of bombers and 30 hours to upload the entire bomber force. Alternatively, the warheads could be stored at a different base and flown to the primary base in an emergency. This arrangement would increase the time to reconstitute the bomber force by an additional day.

The total U.S. strategic force would thus consist of 225 Minuteman warheads, 132 Trident warheads, and 143 bomber warheads (in local base storage for one wing of strategic bombers) for a grand total of 500 warheads on 357 strategic missile delivery vehicles and 20 bombers.

For Russia, it should be possible to adopt a similar de-mating approach to its silo-based force of about 229 missiles. A portion of the silos would house missiles and a portion would store the warheads in containers. In the Russian case, the missiles would have to be equipped with special devices that substitute electronically for the warheads in order to properly maintain the missile's internal environment.

A variety of measures that de-alert Russia's road-mobile launchers could be effective. Missiles could be removed from the launchers and put in base storage. Alternatively, warheads (or perhaps flight batteries) could be removed from the missiles and put in local storage.

Russian submarine crews do not have access to the onboard missiles in their tubes, and thus at-sea re-mating procedures of the sort described for U.S. submarines would not be possible. The feasible alternative would be for Russian submarines to download their warheads to nearby port storage, as described in the section below on Option 4.

*Evaluation*

Criterion A: (time to re-alert). *Days to many weeks.*

These measures would substantially delay launch preparations. To illustrate, in an emergency, re-alerting this Minuteman force would entail dispatching warhead transport vans to retrieve the warheads in silos and transport them to the individual missile silos for installation. This reconstitution would under plausible assumptions take about 1 full day to re-alert 18 missiles at each of the 3 Minuteman bases, and 2 full weeks to bring the entire Minuteman force back to launch-ready status.[40] For Trident submarines, it would take about one-half day to

---

40. Re-mating warheads to Minuteman missiles under crisis conditions could be accomplished at a rate of approximately 18 per day. This schedule assumes that each of the 3 Minuteman bases have 6 special warhead vans and corresponding maintenance support. A Minuteman base normally has 3 warhead vans but the consolidation of bases, equipment, and support teams increases the number to 6. Each van and team would each day retrieve a single warhead from a storage silo (or other storage site) and install it on a Minuteman missile in a different silo. A team drives to a storage silo; raises the silo lid using a hydraulic instrument (the size of a big snow blower); positions the van over the silo opening; retrieves a warhead using a winch/pulley; places it in the van; drives to a nearby silo housing a Minuteman missile; repeats the procedure for opening the lid; pulls up the nosecone using a winch; puts the nosecone

fully reload the 11 missiles on a given boat after it had surfaced and stabilized in calm waters.[41] Many additional hours would be required for electronic testing of the weapons system.

Russian experts estimate that re-alerting a silo-based missile would take at least 20 hours. Several hours are required for each of several tasks including opening the silo lid, removing the special devices, and installing the reentry vehicle containing the warhead. For road-mobile missiles, the normal reconstitution time would be lengthy—upwards of 30 hours for a single missile although the re-mating of the warhead to the missile itself can be accomplished within 5 hours. For Russian submarines, returning warheads to missiles onboard would take about 3 hours per warhead, which means that upwards of 2 days would be needed to fully re-arm a Russian submarine.

Criterion B: (impact on strategic stability). *Very Positive.*

*This arrangement allows for extensive dispersion, position location uncertainty, and hardness of the force—thus avoiding common-mode failure and buying a large margin of survivability under worst-case conditions of breakout and attack by opposing forces.* Some vulnerabilities would be present, particularly on the Russian side, where

---

aside; lowers the warhead onto the platform; restores the nosecone; closes the silo lid; and special maintenance teams conduct electronic tests. At this rate, which probably could not be sustained over a long period without resting the teams, the entire force of 225 Minuteman missiles could be re-alerted within a few weeks. This procedure would clearly be transparent to Russian surveillance.

41. The 12th pair of tubes on each boat would hold a 5-ton capable crane in one and other equipment in the other, which could be elevated after surfacing to transfer warheads one at a time between the adjacent hatches to the waiting missile if emergency circumstances would require the re-mating of weapons. This re-mating would have to take place in fairly calm waters, and depending upon engineering details might involve the submarine leaning for stability on another ship, pier, oil rig, or other stable fixture for maximum safety. The option to surface and re-mate the warheads (which only weigh about 500 pounds in their reentry vehicles) without outside stabilization does appear to be quite feasible, however.

various bottlenecks at maintenance depots and ports would exist. One Russian expert has determined that for road-mobile forces the warheads (but not missiles) could be placed on trucks before or during re-alerting, and then reinstalled after a rendezvous with the missiles in the field.[42] This approach, among others, could mitigate the vulnerability of warheads and service bottlenecks while preserving leeway for verification.

In general, reconstitution would involve elaborate and time-consuming operations on both sides, and force generation would proceed at roughly the same pace on both sides. In my estimation, sufficient weapons would survive even under worst-case conditions—i.e., a large differential in the technical pace of re-alerting favoring one side over the other, and a failure to detect covert re-alerting for a long time—that stability could be sustained even during an irrational re-alerting race. *A case can be made that today's nuclear postures are substantially more unstable in these terms than this posture.*

The end result would be a resilient reserve force on each side that removes any incentives for rushing to re-alert forces during a U.S.-Russian crisis, the likelihood of which is remote in any case. The amount of dynamic stability would be high.

Criterion C: (degree of transparency/verifiability). *Very high for large-scale breakout. Very high for small-scale breakout if intrusive, cooperative monitoring is arranged.*

This transition to "zero alert" would demand and benefit from a degree of cooperation, and transparency comparable to that required for the START I warhead inspections, in which each country is allowed to carry out a considerable number of short-notice inspections of randomly selected missiles in order to verify the number of warheads affixed to them. It is essential for the monitoring and verification of warheads and launchers in this de-alerting option that the START I

42. V. Dvorkin personal communications with author, 1998.

verification provisions in the expiring treaty be renewed by the parties. Preserving this transparency would contribute to the aim of ensuring that no party could gain a decisive preemptive advantage by breaking out of a zero-alert commitment.

Verification would involve on-site inspections, use of electronic seals that could be remotely electronically interrogated, and national technical means of verification. Since re-alerting tens of warheads would take at least tens of hours, and re-alerting the entire arsenals would take many weeks to months for each side to complete, even small-scale re-alerting would be relatively easy to detect in a timely manner, providing all parties with time to respond. As emphasized earlier, however, this posture is designed to ensure successful reconstitution even if an egregious failure of verification occurred and warning of a breakout was not provided.

Since monitoring and verification procedures would address warheads as well as their launchers, *this option would advance the cause of building an auditable database that in turn would facilitate progressive disarmament* (Criterion D).

Criterion D: (foster a nuclear-free world). *Very Positive.*

This down-scaled posture featuring de-mated warheads would transform the traditional war-fighting nuclear strategies. *The overall affect is to deeply downgrade the salience of nuclear weapons in national security, and to move further down the road toward total elimination.*

Criterion E: (impact on today's risk of accidental/unauthorized/ theft). *Very Positive.*

Removing all warheads (or, alternatively, separating other critical components from missiles) from all missiles would end the hazardous rapid-reaction postures of the strategic forces under normal circumstances. With de-mating, no strategic weapon could be fired quickly, and re-alerting would be fairly slow as a general rule. Since it would take at least a day to put any significant number of forces back on launch-ready alert, unauthorized actors—including terrorists—would be deprived of any opportunity to induce a launch, false alarms of any consequence, or other untoward events. Authorized actors would function within a command system that precludes mistaken launch on warning. *For these reasons, this option earns very high marks along this critical dimension of security and safety.*

## De-alerting Option 4: Physical Modifications (Medium-term 4–6+ years)

*Responsive Warhead Force in Warhead Storage Depots*

*Overview of Illustrative U.S. and Russian Measures.* This posture consigns warheads to warhead storage facilities on their respective territories. This entails a large expansion of secure storage space that Russia and the United States evidently lack at the present time. Warheads in depots also require a controlled environment and, in the case of Russian missiles, special electronic monitoring equipment must be substituted for warheads in order to maintain the missiles within proper environmental (e.g., temperature, humidity) tolerances.

*Land-Based Rocket Weapons De-mating.* The normal destination for U.S. warheads taken off land-based missiles and placed in long-term storage is a large facility near Albuquerque, New Mexico. From that point of origin, the time needed to re-mate warheads to Minuteman missiles located in the plains states would be an average of one day per missile. Additional storage bunkers at the three main missile bases could be constructed, however, to provide some protective dispersion and to locate the warhead stocks closer to missiles in their silos. However, this configuration still concentrates hundreds of warheads in a small number of storage depots, creating a potential acute vulnerability to attack not only by Russian forces but also by other nations with large or small nuclear arsenals. An adversary might be tempted to attack them (along with warheads for bombers and submarines at other storage sites) preemptively.

Comparable arrangements would be established for de-mating Russian warheads and storing them in monitored storage depots (large central facilities or local weapons storage depots at missile division headquarters).

Russian experts argue that their country does not have adequate facilities to store such a large number of warheads taken from missiles and maintain them in good condition. They are therefore now considering other options, such as removing the battery that operates the missile-guidance system during flight.[43]

*Download Submarine Warheads to Storage Depots.* Both countries could remove all of their warheads, or all their warheads and missiles, from their submarines and place the warheads in storage. For Russia, this would involve removing warheads from its launch-ready boats surfaced in port on pierside alert as well as from its submarines deployed at sea. (The United States, by contrast, does not maintain submarines on alert in port and cannot launch its missiles from a surfaced Trident boat.)

*Relocate Bomber Warheads.* Strategic bombers could be further de-alerted by transferring their weapons to off-base locations. The arsenals could be distributed to depots at former bomber bases, achieving greater dispersion of warheads and improving their survivability. This adjustment is especially recommended for the B-2 bomber force

43. Russian experts have proposed that they remove the in-flight guidance batteries located under the nosecone and warheads of the top stage of their missiles. Reinstalling the batteries would require the use of a large crane to open the silo lids and would take as long to reverse as reinstalling warheads, according to these experts. Russian experts claim that the reinstallation of a battery into a missile would actually take longer to complete than the reinstallation of a warhead. As a result, no more than a few missiles per day per base could be re-alerted in either case, and the extensive re-alerting procedures would be readily observed from space. In addition, a battery's absence could be confirmed by inspectors conducting START I spot checks of warheads because it sits just below the warheads. Once confirmed, spot checks would not be necessary for lengthy periods because silo-based missiles normally require minimal maintenance; the lid of a particular silo may not be raised for up to three years.

and its warheads because of its potential for penetrating Russian territory undetected and delivering B-61 earth-penetrating bombs, which
are designed to destroy underground command posts. Russian bombers should also conform to the same principle of removing their weapons to off-base locations.

*Evaluation*

Criterion A: (time to re-alert). *Days for small numbers; weeks to
many months for arsenals of hundreds.*

For the U.S., re-mating warheads to Minuteman missiles under crisis
conditions could be accomplished at a rate that is considerably slower
than the rate for re-mating warheads stored in silos as described above
under Option 3. The long distances between the main base depots and
the far-flung silos would increase the reconstitution time by several
times: about six warheads per day, or two to three months to restore
a notional arsenal of 500 warheads to their missiles.

Regarding U.S. submarines, the return of U.S. payloads would
happen slowly and lend itself to observation. Trident missiles could
be installed in tubes at a rate of two missiles every three hours (one
installation per port).[44] The installation of warheads onto the missiles
could be accomplished at a rate of about two warheads per hour (one
warhead per hour per port).

Regarding U.S. bombers, during a crisis the weapons could be
transported back to the three primary bomber bases or the bombers
could fly to the depots. In either case the initial re-alerting of U.S.
bombers to launch-ready status would require at least several extra
hours compared with the current arrangements. Thus the first several
American bombers, each with 16 or 20 warheads, would achieve full
alert perhaps 16–24 hours or so after the decision to re-alert was made.

Comparable reconstitution time lines apply to Russia. Due to the

44. Currently this procedure uses special cranes and nuclear-certified crane operators at the home ports at Kings Bay, Georgia, and Bangor, Washington.

small number of warhead-transportation vans, cranes for opening and closing silo lids, and crews to operate this equipment, reversing this step would be time-consuming and readily observable by satellite surveillance. Russia could take as long as one day per missile per base to reload its warheads, and as long as two to three months to reconstitute its entire silo-based force. At a breakneck pace in emergency conditions of reconstitution, this rate of re-alerting might be doubled or tripled.

Regarding Russian boats, due to the extensive procedures and heavy equipment needed to reinstall submarine warheads (and probably needed to reinstall batteries too), reversing this step would be slow and transparent. It would take approximately two to three days per boat per port for Russia to re-alert its fleet.[45]

Criterion B: (impact on strategic stability). *Very Negative to Positive: Tipping Point Danger.*

Due to the relative concentration of warheads, missiles, and submarines under this option, and the laborious and time-consuming process involved in reconstitution, the strategic deterrent postures could be severely degraded, and perhaps neutralized, by a relatively small-scale nuclear or even conventional attack.

This vulnerability would be most acute for submarine forces. The warhead and missile stockpiles in storage would be concentrated at a small number of depots and would be uploaded at a small number of ports. The off-alert submarines themselves would be exposed at these ports, as would the extensive support infrastructure that would be used to re-arm any of the boats. Boats would enter a queue for re-arming and those at the front of the line would sit on the surface for many days. The installation of the missiles and the mating of warheads

45. Re-mating warheads and/or missiles would be performed at two or three ports, two in the Northern Fleet—Nerpichya and Yagelnaya on the Kola Peninsula—and one in the Pacific Fleet at Rybachi, just south of Petropavlovsk on the Kamchatka Peninsula.

would require the use of cranes and could be accomplished only on calm seas. The entire delicate sequence of submarine re-alerting would be overt and readily detectable. The armada in either its static or re-generating disposition would be extremely vulnerable to attack by a very small nuclear force.

In principle, any forces covertly reconstituted to stage such a sneak strike would have difficulty circumventing the severe restrictions placed on their own readiness and operation without being detected. Strict monitoring and verification would have been essential and surely applied to these postures, and the wholesale reconstitution of forces would doubtless be readily detectable at an early stage.

*But the stealthy re-alerting of a small number of strategic forces could be far more likely to escape detection, and even a small-scale breakout could be significant.* It potentially could pose an extreme threat—a single weapon could destroy an entire depot consisting of hundreds of stored warheads. *Thus the initial breakout phase could be very volatile and probably more dangerous than any subsequent re-alerting race during a crisis.* A lopsided advantage might be seized by stealth and duplicity if the opening gambit goes unnoticed or unanswered during the initial stage, whereas a re-alerting race could quickly disperse enough weapons to stabilize the reconstitution process.

The role of conventional forces could be important and double-edged. On one hand they could be used as part of an opening gambit to degrade the opponent's ability to reconstitute. On the other hand they could be used to respond quickly to an opponent's breakout to prevent the latter from gaining the upper hand in a re-alerting contest. On both scores, U.S. conventional forces have far superior capabilities over Russian forces and thus represent an aggravating factor in re-alerting dynamics from a Russian perspective, and a mitigating factor from a U.S. perspective. Deep de-alerting with all warheads placed in storage depots may call for negotiated constraints on the use conventional weapons for offensive missions.

A gradual transition from Option 3 to Option 4 is recommended due to these questions about the stability of deterrence and the consequences of breakout. It seems imprudent to make the transition to depot storage too rapidly and completely. *A small force of de-mated reserve weapons deployed in silos and submarine tubes would provide an insurance policy during the transition to land-based storage until the breakout problem can be solved.*

In a similar vein, storage depots on land can and should be designed to withstand at least a small-scale nuclear breakout and attack in order to protect a minimum deterrent capability. On the U.S. side, for example, the 50 empty MX Peacekeeper silos and the 50 Minuteman silos slated for mothballing (along with additional mothballed silos over time) could be utilized for this purpose—they could well protect a stockpile of reserve warheads for submarines and bombers as well as land-based missiles.[46]

Lastly, the need for involving at least all of the P-5 nuclear states in this option is also clear. All of them have sufficient numbers of weapons in their arsenals to be significant under these buttoned-down arrangements for the U.S. and Russia.

*Summary Recommendation:* Before any transition to Option 4 is completed, a number of preconditions should be satisfied. First, monitoring and verification must be able to perform at a very high level with exact accounting of warheads in storage down to the single weapons unit. Second, all of the P-5 states and perhaps other nuclear states

---

46. It is even possible to relocate the operational reserve plutonium pits now stored or slated for storage at the Texas Pantex complex into the spare storage space in the headworks of the 225 Minuteman silos earmarked in Option 3 to store the reserve warheads (and/or the 100 empty MX and Minuteman silos to be mothballed). By my estimation, we can easily store the reserve pits (about 6,000 of them in drums) in 40 silo headworks. Furthermore, we could store the 34 tons of excess plutonium slated for eventual elimination in 50 silos, and if we want to store the pits from the ~5,000 warheads to be dismantled over the next 10 years, we can put them into 33 silos. In other words, U.S. missile silos could easily accommodate all of the current and planned inventory of pits from retired nuclear weapons in the U.S. inventory—upward of 20,000 pits in total. Author's estimates.

need to be involved in this option. All of them have sufficient arsenals to pose potentially severe threats under these buttoned-down arrangements for the U.S. and Russia. This de-alerting regime should thus be comprehensively multilateral with stringent monitoring and verification provisions to enforce it. Third, since even a single nuclear weapon is significant in this de-alerting scheme, protocols for re-alerting nuclear forces would have to be devised to provide adequate reassurance and stability if one nation decides that it must take this step to protect its national security. Fourth, similar protocols and constraints may need to be devised for conventional forces. A party that covertly begins to reconstitute its nuclear forces could use conventional forces to degrade the opponent's ability to respond in kind. On this score the United States would possess vastly superior capabilities and therefore conventional offensive missions may need to be regulated and constrained in order to allay Russian concerns. Fifth and last, storage depots on land can and should be designed to withstand at least a small-scale nuclear breakout and attack.

Criterion C: (degree of transparency/verifiability). *High, but adequate only under certain conditions. Adequate verification demands extremely high transparency achievable only through close cooperation on a multilateral basis.*

Monitoring and verification must be able to achieve very high levels of performance, for reasons made clear in the previous discussion. *The accounting of weapons would need to be exact, providing a reliable determination of the number of deployable weapons in storage down to the single weapons unit.*

The implication is that surveillance of both the warheads and delivery vehicles will require full declarations of warhead stocks and locations, and associated delivery vehicles, by all P-5 nations, and development of a sophisticated regime of international identification and continuous monitoring for accurate accounting. This will entail an extensive set of monitoring tools and unprecedented cooperation

for intrusive inspections of both warhead depots and launchers belonging to the United States, Russia, China, France, and the United
Kingdom. One upside to this otherwise daunting proposition is that
the delivery vehicles are key to any breakout and reconstitution, and
they do lend themselves fairly readily to continuous monitoring, especially if the historical START inspection regime for strategic forces
can be extended through negotiation. The United States and Russia
also have numerous other surveillance means to detect a large-scale
reconstitution effort that would be extremely difficult to conduct
stealthily for very long, given the elaborate and extensive operations
that would need to be executed. It is only the stealthy leading edge
of this process that is worrisome because of the extreme threat it could
present.

The overall assessment of prospects for adequate verification for
this option of placing all weapons in storage depots is that it faces
serious obstacles but that they can be surmounted if the necessary
political will can be mustered. This challenge must be squarely confronted sooner rather than later if the groundwork is to be laid for
serious progress toward the complete elimination of nuclear weapons.

Criterion D: (foster a nuclear-free world). *Extremely Positive.*

Getting all U.S. and Russian, not to mention the other P-5 nations',
nuclear weapons into storage sites, putting them and their potential
delivery systems under continuous surveillance for purposes of monitoring and verification, and providing access to all pertinent areas of
the nuclear weapons complexes to insure against breakout, would constitute a giant stride down the path toward complete elimination. Under this plan, strategic planners would also tend to phase nuclear
weapons in storage out of contingency war plans and basically discount their utility to such a degree that their phaseout would become
self-reinforcing. Dismantlement of the stockpiles would move inexo-
rably forward, marking more strides toward a nuclear-free world.

Criterion E: (impact on today's risk of accidental/unauthorized/ theft). *Extremely Positive.*

The transition to de-mated weapons consigned completely to storage depots would vastly simplify and reduce the nuclear dangers and risks associated with the current nuclear postures. The declining utility attached to the stored reserve weapons and the ensuing atrophy of war-fighting postures would also stanch the flow of weapons in the maintenance pipeline. The decline in the tempo and scale of weapons "circulation" would raise the barriers against terrorist theft or capture during weapons transportation. In general, this option receives the highest marks possible along this criterion.

## Implications and Concluding Thoughts

The de-alerting options described in this paper represent alternative approaches to achieving the same goal of lengthening the fuse on strategic nuclear forces, which is currently timed to fire them within minutes and seconds. Taken as a sequence of de-alerting steps, these options chart a course for lengthening the fuse by progressively longer periods of time. The reconstitution time of a coherent force would be initially extended by hours and days (Options 1, 2), then by days and weeks (Option 3), and finally by weeks and months (Option 4).

Getting U.S. and Russian strategic weapons into warhead storage depots under strict surveillance (Option 4) would be a milestone of great significance. Not only would "locking down" the arsenals allow for the maximum degree of security and safeguards to be imposed, but it would also so demote the military role and utility of nuclear weapons that the process of force deactivation would only accelerate. This path of de-alerting thus appears to offer the single most promising route to rapidly reducing a host of immediate and growing nuclear dangers and to moving the world closer to its ultimate destination of zero nuclear weapons.

The path of zero nuclear alert culminating in "locked down" storage under Option 4 needs to be cleared of a multitude of thorny preconditions. A zero-alert regimen at this fourth stage could be exploited by even small launch-capable arsenals and thus needs to be adopted multilaterally by the major nuclear weapons powers, and instituted with unprecedented transparency and rigorous verification, demanding an abnormal amount of multinational cooperation. Conventional forces which can severely interfere with a nation's ability to reconstitute nuclear force for legitimate reasons will need to be addressed, and probably regulated in order to reassure the weaker parties. Ballistic missile defenses likewise will need to be considered and possibly regulated for the same reason.[47] Zero alert will require the command and warning systems to be redesigned to allow for riding out an attack instead of merely for launching on warning, and therefore the systems will need to be afforded far better protection than they currently receive. To relieve pressures on national decisionmakers to make quick execution decisions, they must have confidence in the continuity of command-control while under attack.[48]

Perhaps the thorniest of the preconditions concerns the core determinants of the U.S. and Russian nuclear postures. De-alerting implicitly contests the axioms of nuclear strategy that have shaped the operational character of the deterrent forces for nearly 50 years. Implementing any of the four options presented in this report will hinge

---

47. As a former senior general put it in commenting upon our de-alerting article (Nunn and Blair, "From Nuclear Deterrence to Mutual Safety," op. cit.): "The impact of one side having an asymmetric advantage in missile defenses could become significant at reduced alert rates." VCJCS Talking Paper, July 8, 1997, p. 8.

48. This is one of the dominant concerns of the U.S. military about de-alerting. As a former senior general said about our de-alerting article (Nunn and Blair, "From Nuclear Deterrence to Mutual Safety," op.cit.): "De-alerting forces does not necessarily eliminate the need to make quick execution decisions . . . De-alerting extends launch time, but does not reduce need to "launch on warning" since the C3 for launch execution become much less reliable after absorbing a first strike, i.e., there would still be strong pressures to get an execution order out before impact and degradation of the C3I system (which may include "incapacitation" of the key decisionmakers authorized to execute nuclear weapons)." VCJCS Talking Paper, July 8, 1997, p. 7.

on reconceptualizing deterrence and transforming the traditional war-fighting strategies. De-alerting presents more than a mere technical challenge of devising verifiable ways to reduce reliance on prompt-launch capabilities. It so challenges traditional deterrent concepts and operational practices that it must be grounded upon a visionary and enlightened conception of national and international security.

The core premise of that new conception is that the Cold War between the United States and Russia is finished and done, and that non-proliferation, the prevention of nuclear terrorism, and safeguards against accidental and unauthorized use of nuclear weapons now lie at the core of their national security interests, and head the list of urgent nuclear priorities. The leaders of the United States and Russia have but to assert in their nuclear guidance that U.S.-Russian mutual nuclear deterrence no longer demands launch-ready forces servicing war-fighting objectives and the cosmic risks that hair-trigger forces carry are no longer justifiable in the name of deterrence.

Such guidance would overturn the longstanding view that deterrence demands real-time coverage of a comprehensive and long list of military, economic, and leadership targets in Russia and China, a readiness to rapidly generate the full U.S. strategic arsenal to maximum alert during a crisis, and a predisposition to launch on warning of an enemy attack in progress. De-alerting, as well as reductions of weapons below a certain floor measured in units of thousands, would violate the traditional tenets of strategic planning.[49] Five hundred weapons at the upper limit of available forces, as an earlier notional strategic force was constituted under de-alerting Options 3 and 4, would clearly fall short of meeting the conservative standard of deterrence vis-à-vis Russia.

One variant of this conservative judgment was expressed by a

---

49. One longstanding conservative estimate holds that deterrence requires levels of damage involving 40 percent of populations and 75 percent of industrial floor space and would require attacks on 1,000 to 2,000 targets. Key military targets including nuclear forces lengthen the target list by another 1,000.

senior general in conversations with this author and Sam Nunn during his review of our joint article on de-alerting.[50] He said that "Finally, as we remove counterforce weapons from alert . . . virtually eliminat[ing] war-fighting capability in a day-to-day scenario . . . we must philosophically address the desirability of returning to a strategy of mutual assured destruction, since deterrence will then rest on the capability to destroy the 'soft' targets an enemy would value."[51] The general's point is well taken and deserves to be debated and resolved by national leaders. One pertinent datum based on computer modeling is that only a few tens to low hundreds of warheads could wreak havoc on such a scale as to meet a common-sense standard of deterrence based on mass destruction.[52] That a survivable and reconstitutable arsenal of 500 U.S. weapons, or even a relatively small portion of it, would project a threat of retaliation sufficient to deter an actor with any hold on rationality seems difficult to refute. That is also the judgment of S. Drell and J. Goodby, who argue that 200–300 would suffice.[53] Regardless of the actual targeting assignments given to these forces—counterforce or countervalue—the deterrent effect of their raw numbers would be sufficient to claim that stable mutual deterrence can be established at this level if the de-alerted forces are survivable in peacetime and during reconstitution.

50. Nunn and Blair, "From Nuclear Deterrence to Mutual Safety," op. cit.

51. VCJCS Talking Paper, July 8, 1997, pp. 7–8.

52. Recent modeling work shows that damage worthy of the term "mass destruction" can be accomplished with targets in the tens or low hundreds. Scientifically rigorous simulations of nuclear attacks find that 51 weapons (475 kiloton each) could kill 25 percent of the Russian population (~38 million people); and 124 such weapons could kill 25 percent of the U.S. population. The model indicates that a total of only 500 such weapons would inflict this level of damage (25 percent population fatalities) on the U.S., all other NATO member countries, Russia, and China. Matthew G. McKinzie, Thomas B. Cochran, Robert S. Norris, and William M. Arkin. *The U.S. Nuclear War Plan: A Time for Change*, Natural Resources Defense Council, June 2001, p. 126, Table 5.7 (www.nrdc.org/nuclear/warplan/warplan_ch5.pdf).

53. Sidney D. Drell and James E. Goodby, *What Are Nuclear Weapons For? Recommendations for Restructuring U.S. Strategic Nuclear Forces* (Washington, D.C.: Arms Control Association, April 2005).

As long as this debate remains unsettled and the default position is the traditional one, the path to standing down the Cold War postures will be obstructed. The default position, moreover, will create further barriers to de-alerting as it confronts China's nuclear modernization and general economic rise. The growing emphasis on China in U.S. threat perceptions, deterrence thinking, and actual nuclear planning since it was reinstated in the U.S. strategic war plan in 1998 is a trend that needs to be arrested, lest China become the next "designated enemy" for U.S. military planners and the rationale for maintaining a large U.S. nuclear arsenal on high alert.[54] The 2002 Nuclear Posture Review designated China as an "immediate nuclear contingency" and that designation appears to have led to steadily increasing U.S. nuclear operations aimed at a growing list of Chinese targets. This growing pressure on China may well induce it to adopt the traditional countermeasures that decrease warning and decision time and thus heighten the risk of inadvertent or unauthorized launch against the United States. Shortening the Chinese fuse and adding a third nation to the launch-ready alert club would scarcely represent progress in the quest for mutual nuclear safety.

The lesson suggested by the China complication is that a vision of nuclear de-alerting and force reduction ought to cast a wide net that brings all of the nuclear weapons states into the discussion, negotiation, regulation, and elimination. After all, that is the only path to a nuclear-free world.

---

54. China thus reappeared in the plan after a hiatus of nearly two decades, having been removed in the early 1980s by President Reagan following normalization of U.S.-China relations. Limited attack options for China were created by Strategic Command in January 1998 in response to President Clinton's nuclear guidance issued in November 1997 (NSDD-60). See Elaine Grossman, "Nuclear Weapons Expert Says U.S. Warfighting Plan Now Targets China," *Inside the Pentagon*, January 14, 1998; Bruce Blair, "Trapped in the Nuclear Math," op. cit.

# 3. Eliminating Short-Range Nuclear Weapons Designed to Be Forward Deployed

## Rose Gottemoeller

### Summary of Conclusions

This analysis proceeds from the assumption that *until the United States and Russian Federation, along with NATO countries, are able to eliminate short-range nuclear weapons from Europe, efforts to eliminate them anywhere else in the world will be stymied.* For that reason, the major focus of this paper is on what it will take to get NATO and Russia talking about the weapons, understanding the problem from each other's perspective, building up confidence, and moving into controlling and eventually reducing and eliminating the weapons from Europe. While that goal is being accomplished, the other states deploying short-range nuclear weapons—India, Pakistan, China, and Israel—should be brought into the discussion and into confidence-building activities. However, these countries will be very unlikely to move to control and reduce their own short-range weapons if the problem in Europe is not on its way to being resolved.

*Russia's new dependence on nuclear weapons to compensate for its conventional weakness is one of the key issues that will have to be dealt with in order to begin the process of control and reduction.* Working toward resolution of differences over the Conventional Forces in Europe (CFE) Treaty will be one major way to do so. So Russia, in this regard, is the difficult side of the policy equation.

At the same time, it is worth emphasizing how far NATO and the United States have come in transforming themselves into the easier side of this policy equation. As recently as 1999, NATO was not in a position to move beyond a traditional statement of the importance of nuclear weapons in its Strategic Concept. By 2005, however, politicians in Europe became ready to move the issue out of the closet and debate it openly. Also throughout this period, nuclear readiness levels in NATO Europe steadily declined and in one case—Greece in 2001—nuclear weapons were completely withdrawn from a NATO country. On the other side of the Atlantic, U.S. strategy became more and more focused on centralizing nuclear planning and operations at Strategic Command in Omaha. This move was consonant with a trend in the direction of centralized capabilities to attack targets worldwide under the "Global Strike" concept. Global Strike became synonymous with long-range, highly accurate, deep-strike conventional missions, which also supported the notion of deemphasizing nuclear weapons in U.S. and NATO policy.

*Thus, the environment for ending NATO nuclear deployments in Europe is much more welcoming than it was less than a decade ago, and it is feasible that NATO could decide to recast its Strategic Concept to achieve this goal in the context of its 60th anniversary celebrations in 2009.* The key question for NATO policymakers, however, is whether they wish to lead on this issue without requiring a major change in Russian policy at the same time. There are arguments that may be made about the exemplary effect that unilateral action would have in this case, as well as benefits for the NATO allies' defense budgets (including that of the United States). But it is realistic to assume that Russia will not be willing to move so quickly to temper its dependence on nuclear weapons in its military strategy.

Therefore, NATO would probably want to maintain an insurance policy while work with the Russians moves forward. The alliance, for example, could agree to remove short-range nuclear weapons from Europe while leaving the infrastructure for deploying the weapons in place. The alliance could continue to train and certify personnel for nuclear operations, and could continue some specific exercise activities to ensure that command and control capabilities remain intact and that nuclear weapons could be quickly reintroduced into Europe if necessary. These steps could then be phased out as mutual confidence builds between NATO and Russia, and particularly if Russia were willing early on to address NATO concerns about possible continuing deployment of nuclear weapons in Kaliningrad.

*This issue of a disconnect between Russia and the United States/ NATO on the importance of nuclear weapons is the most difficult one to grapple with in any effort to eliminate short-range nuclear weapons. The disconnect will take time and patience to address, and this paper recommends an "inch-by-inch, step-by-step" approach.*

*Confidence-building should be the first step,* but we need not be satisfied with superficial site visits and other slow steps that characterized confidence-building during the Cold War era. Instead, *confidence-building should take advantage of the intensive cooperation that the United States and Russia have pursued in the past 15 years to have some practical effect on real problems being encountered in each side's nuclear forces.* For example, in the context of the Warhead Safety and Security Agreement (WSSX), the U.S. and Russia have been working intensively on measures to improve the safety of nuclear weapons against threats of fire and lightning. Bringing such measures to bear on nuclear weapons in Europe would help to solve real problems that both sides have encountered, and also build confidence in the nature of the deployments. Confidence-building, therefore, should be linked to intensive problem-solving for both sides, which in turn will have a rapid impact on the growth in confidence—a confidence feedback loop, in other words.

*Once mutual confidence is growing, Russia and the United States/ NATO can move to the next stage, beginning arms control and reduction measures. Initially, finding a way to exchange data should be the focus of these efforts,* for two reasons. First, differences over how to exchange data under the Presidential Nuclear Initiatives has been a persistent irritant between Russia and NATO practically since the PNIs were agreed in the early 1990s. The resulting damage has made it difficult for the two sides to imagine how they might sit down with each other at the negotiating table. Thus, figuring out a judicious way to do data exchanges by itself would play a vital confidence-building role.

Second, an agreed baseline of weapons systems has always been a necessary and significant precursor to success in arms reduction negotiations. Only once the parties have agreed to the number and nature of deployments can they agree on how much and in what way to reduce them. Either side might begin by trying unilaterally to spur movement, for example through declassification of deployment numbers. The United States has established procedures to do so, and could agree on such steps with its NATO allies. However, there should be no expectation of a quick response from the Russian side, as procedures for declassification are not routinely established and the political environment in Moscow is difficult. Nevertheless, the Russians might be willing to share some data on a confidential government-to-government basis if the United States comes forward with an initiative.

*Several larger policy steps will be required before the two sides will be willing to sit down to significant arms reduction negotiations— NATO will have to decide what it wants to do about short-range nuclear weapons deployed in allied countries, and Russia and NATO will have to be on the road to resolving their differences over the CFE Treaty.* As these solutions are in train, arms reduction negotiations can begin. Even before that point, however, the two sides could pursue further unilateral measures to convince each other that nuclear-capable bases have been or are being closed down—and here, Russian willingness to shed more light on the situation in Kaliningrad would be very important. Another interim measure with some risks attached to it would be to recommit to the PNIs. Uncertainties over implementation of the PNIs have added up to some serious mistrust between

Moscow and Washington, and for that reason an initiative to recommit could stir up old frustrations. Bringing high-level authority to bear—and particularly President George H. W. Bush and President Gorbachev, who launched the PNIs originally—could be an important way to overcome such irritation.

*The unquestionable goal should be a ban on short-range nuclear weapons in operational deployment, linked to a continuing campaign to eliminate nuclear warheads and dispose of their nuclear materials—with accompanying transparency measures.* Efforts to negotiate this ban, which should first engage Russia and the NATO countries, should come to engage the other nuclear weapon states. This could be done through development of a step-by-step confidence-building process that would lead to more comprehensive control and reduction measures, and eventually in the long-term future to a broader ban. The configuration of this group is complicated: It should certainly involve the nuclear weapons states under the Non-Proliferation Treaty—the United States, France, and the United Kingdom (which are NATO countries) plus Russia, China—and also the other states in possession of nuclear weapons—India, Pakistan, and Israel.

*In theory, because China, India, and Pakistan do not maintain their nuclear weapons at a high level of operational readiness, negotiating with them a ban on operational deployments would be straightforward.* Ironically, the accompanying transparency into their programs, which would be necessary for a negotiated ban, is likely to be much more difficult. The United States and Russia, after 30 years of negotiated nuclear arms reductions, are accustomed to mutual monitoring and verification—but these countries are not. Moreover, Israel does not publicly admit to a nuclear weapons program. Therefore, no area of short-range nuclear arms control will be simple. However, confidence-building measures with all the relevant countries could start early, and should be the focus of immediate policy efforts.

Strategic arms will also be a target for further arms reductions, and as David Holloway argues in his paper for this project, these should be considered in four stages, beginning in the near term with reductions between Russia and the United States but proceeding toward the eventual elimination of nuclear weapons. [See Chapter 10] *As these stages advance, short-range weapons should be placed in the same basket with strategic arms for negotiating actual elimination of the weapons.* This approach would acknowledge the reality that nuclear weapons are impossible to differentiate when they are divorced from their launch vehicles, and would also anticipate deep reductions, when the difference between short- and long-range systems becomes steadily less relevant.

*Short-range nuclear weapons designed to be forward deployed have the potential, in fact, to serve as a special harbinger for later stages of the strategic arms reduction process.* In the early 1990s, the Presidential Nuclear Initiatives were early expressions of the concept that warheads should be moved out of operational deployment and into secure status, not ready for immediate launch. The PNIs may be revivified and lead to a ban on short-range weapons in operational deployment, or a ban may be negotiated on its own. In either case, implementation of the ban would be a type of "pilot project" for zero deployed warheads in the strategic forces. The transparency, verification, and monitoring measures applied to short-range weapons would serve well in the strategic case, and certainly as strategic and short-range weapons begin to fall into the same basket for elimination.

*The agenda for eliminating short-range nuclear weapons is potentially an exciting one, taking full advantage of the lessons learned over the past 15 years,* and particularly the practical ways in which Russia and the United States have learned to work together to enhance the safety and security of nuclear weapons. This mutual interest should help to overcome the frustration, anger, and disconnects that have hampered Russian cooperation with the United States and NATO. *But patience and attention to multiple problems—including the CFE Treaty—will have to be the watchwords of the effort. Efforts to engage*

*Russia on the nuclear front cannot be divorced from attempts to solve these other problems.*

## Introduction

Short-range nuclear weapons designed to be forward deployed generate complex problems in the world not only of arms reduction and control, but also in the world of nuclear strategy and policy. Such weapons have historically drawn the most attention in the relationship between the United States and its NATO allies—they were supposed to form a kind of "glue" to ensure the survival and strength of the trans-Atlantic alliance. "Nuclear burden-sharing" was the expression of that glue, meaning that NATO countries in Europe would help to pay for the nuclear weapons deployed in Europe, and would also share the risks of deploying, and if necessary, delivering them. Thus, of the approximately 480 nuclear weapons deployed in NATO Europe, some 180 are to be released to the control of the European countries hosting them should it ever become necessary to deliver them.[1]

In addition to these challenges, short-range nuclear weapons have also not fit easily into defined categories for analysis and control. The Russians have complained since the dawn of the nuclear age that what looks tactical to NATO looks strategic to them, since geopolitics has placed them exactly adjacent to Europe. They worried consistently that they might expect an attack from a NATO base in Europe on one of their strategic targets—say, Moscow—at any time. Indeed, this ar-

---

1. For the U.S. and NATO, this analysis depends on the data provided in Hans M. Kristensen, "U.S. Nuclear Weapons in Europe: A Review of Post-Cold War Policy, Force Levels, and War Planning," Natural Resources Defense Council, February 2005. Kristensen's table summarizing the numbers of U.S. nuclear weapons in Europe appears as Appendix B of this chapter (p. 156). For Russian data, this analysis depends on Alexei Arbatov's figures, as reproduced in Gunnar Arbman and Charles Thornton, "Russia's Tactical Nuclear Weapons; Part I: Background and Policy Issues," Systems Technology, SE-172 90 Stockholm, FOI-R-1057-SE, November 2003, ISSN 1650–1942, pp. 24–34. A table summarizing the numbers of Russian nuclear weapons appears as Appendix C of this chapter (p. 157).

gument was one of the drivers for the Khrushchev-era decision to deploy medium-range nuclear missiles in Cuba—the reasoning being that if NATO Europe could menace Moscow with very little warning, then the Soviet Union should be able to menace Washington in the same way. The outcome of the Cuban missile crisis forced the Soviets to climb down from that goal, but the asymmetry continued to trouble them. And as the types of dual-use weapon systems have continued to expand, the problem has been further exacerbated.

And although they have mistrusted short-range nuclear weapons in NATO hands, the Russians have come to depend on them to compensate for the perceived weakness and disarray of their conventional forces. Russian military doctrinal statements and exercise activities have focused on nuclear weapons as the ultimate way to defend Russian territory against enemy incursions. It was in this context that Russia abandoned its Soviet-era "no-first-use" strategy in 1991, coming closer and closer to the nuclear policies that NATO had pursued through the years of the Cold War, when it was vulnerable to much more powerful Soviet conventional forces.[2] The Russians treat short-range nuclear weapons, therefore, as a critical capability, one that they would be hard-pressed to do without. On that basis, as one Russian analyst recently put it, short-range nuclear weapons designed to be forward deployed are "the most sensitive military-strategic topic" among the Russian military.[3]

Because today Russia and NATO are no closer to addressing these nuclear conundrums than they were at the end of the Cold War, this analysis will focus on eliminating short-range nuclear weapons from Europe.[4] It is assumed that the other states deploying short-range nu-

2. For a thorough discussion of the evolution of Russian military doctrine during this period, see Gunnar Arbman and Charles Thornton, "Russia's Tactical Nuclear Weapons, Part I: Background and Policy Issues," Systems Technology, SE-172 90 Stockholm, FOI-R—1057—SE, November 2003, ISSN 1650–1942, pp. 24–34.

3. Private conversation with the author.

4. For purposes of this analysis, "tactical nuclear weapons," "non-strategic nuclear weapons," and "short-range nuclear weapons" are treated as synonymous. A

clear weapons—India, Pakistan, China, Israel—will not be willing to engage on the issue of reductions in their own stockpiles until the weapons are dealt with in Europe. They should be encouraged to join early in nuclear confidence-building, however, which will be discussed further below.

### Returning to the Reduction Agenda

So why pull the issue off its back shelf? Could it not remain there indefinitely? There is no question that the issue is quiescent at the moment, not attracting public attention and not preoccupying policymakers, most of whom, if they think about nuclear weapons at all, are focused on the problems of potential proliferation in Iran and North Korea.

There are two compelling reasons. First and most important remains the reality that policymakers confronted when START II was signed in 1993: reductions in launch vehicles can only proceed so far. Deeper nuclear reductions, and those that involve systems that can launch both conventional and nuclear weapons, will have to focus on reducing the nuclear weapons themselves. Thus, to pursue a policy agenda of moving toward a world free of nuclear weapons, nuclear weapons will have to become again the focus of reductions. They may not pose an immediate threat to the United States or its allies, but they are clearly a barrier to achieving eventual zero.

Second, they remain a vestige of the Cold War that continues to cause real worry. The United States, working together with the Russian Federation, has spent over $1.6 billion on warhead protection, control, and accounting in Russia from FY92 through FY06.[5] These

---

good summary of the problem of defining such weapons may be found in Amy F. Woolf, "Nonstrategic Nuclear Weapons," CRS Report for Congress, Order Code RL 32572, updated January 9, 2007, pp. 4–6.

5. See "Securing the Bomb: Overview Funding Summary," Nuclear Threat Initiative, www.nti.org/e_research/cnwm/overview/funding.asp#historical, accessed August 2, 2007.

funds have gone to improve the physical security of weapons storage and handling sites and transportation capabilities in Russia, and also control and accounting procedures. This massive effort was undertaken out of concern that Russian nuclear weapons might be stolen or lost, ending up on the nuclear black market and ultimately in the wrong hands. As long as nuclear weapon reductions remain on the back shelf of policy, the ultimate terrorist threat to international security will never be definitely addressed. Eliminating the weapons and disposing of the fissile material that comes out of them are the only ways to address this threat once and for all.

A third reason, related to both of the proceeding two, is less compelling but might, in the end, be more important in terms of moving policy forward. Although reductions in nuclear weapons have been off the public agenda for some time, they are a coin of policy that is well understood by the man and woman on the street, and will be appealing to people around the world. Thus, if the United States and Russia are able to move quickly in the direction of controlling nuclear weapons, especially those designed to be forward deployed, they will earn an immediate policy "bounce." Their own publics will understand that the two countries have reengaged in a serious way on the issue, and countries where the weapons have been forward deployed, especially in Europe, are also likely to respond well. The U.S. and Russia will look to be again on the road, decisively, to implementing their commitments under Article VI of the Non-Proliferation Treaty.

The two countries will also be seen as taking steps to at last address vestiges of the Cold War that have posed a profound proliferation risk not only to themselves, but also to all countries around the world concerned about nuclear terrorism. This is a threat that affects countries individually, but also poses a danger of profound and wider instability in political environments and economic markets. Therefore, if Russia and the United States are at last moving decisively to eliminate such weapons, the world will breathe easier.

Thus, early momentum in controlling and reducing short-range nuclear weapons will be an indicator that the United States and Russia are again serious about containing and eventually eliminating the nuclear threat. This paper begins by exploring a spectrum of confidence-building and arms control approaches that would work well, and quickly, to move Russia and the United States back onto this agenda.

## Toward Eliminating Short-Range Nuclear Weapons

### NATO to the Table

The uncertainties that flow from the contradictory environment in Europe require some careful thinking about the best policy options to pursue to control and eventually eliminate short-range nuclear weapons deployed there. Given the current mood among NATO countries deploying nuclear weapons, the notion of a total ban on short-range nuclear weapons in Europe would seem easy to negotiate. The NATO nuclear countries no longer place the same priority on nuclear weapons in their military strategy; relatively few nuclear weapons remain deployed in NATO Europe; and interest is growing among political actors—even ruling parties—to withdraw the weapons from Europe.[6]

However, NATO operates according to consensus, so all members of the alliance, including the new countries that view Russia as a threat, would have to be brought along to pursue a ban. That effort alone would be at least a two-step process: negotiating a change in NATO nuclear policy that would allow for a withdrawal of the weapons, and a process of confidence-building with Russia that would eventually bring all parties to the negotiating table for a more ambitious negotiation toward a ban.

The first step would specifically involve changing NATO's Strategic Concept, which dates from 1999 and was clear in its support of nuclear weapons in the alliance: "solidarity and common commitment to war prevention continue to require widespread participation by Eur-

6. A more extensive discussion of these trends in Europe is contained in Appendix A of this chapter (pp. 147–148).

opean Allies involved in collective defence planning in nuclear roles, in peacetime basing of nuclear forces on their territory and in command, control and consultation arrangements."[7] An opportunity for change is coming up in 2009, the 60th anniversary of NATO and also the 10th anniversary of the current Strategic Concept.

But the decisive impetus is unlikely to come from NATO European countries. According to Robert Bell, who was NATO Assistant Secretary-General from 1999 to 2003, there is little enthusiasm among the member states in Europe to do the heavy lifting required to craft a consensus in this area. The initiative, he believes, will have to come from Washington. However, Bell said, "were this or were a new administration to decide to end the program, I do not believe the participating NATO allies would seriously try to stop it."[8]

Thus, step one is in the hands of Washington, but step two, confidence-building, would extend to a broader range of NATO countries. Here the foundation laid by the activities of the NATO-Russia Council would be a solid place to start. The NATO-Russia Council has agreed to a work plan that embraces arms control and reductions, including short-range nuclear weapons. However, that portion of the work plan has lain rather fallow in the years since it was agreed. Interestingly, cooperation on missile defense in the European theater has been among the most active areas of work plan implementation, which might bode well for the future of missile defense cooperation as a whole—if the current political tensions can be addressed.

Nevertheless, there is a project area of more direct application to nuclear weapons confidence-building: accident and emergency response involving weapons of mass destruction. NATO and the Russian Federation have held a successful series of exercises under this rubric, including "Avaria (Accident)-2004," which was held near Murmansk in August 2004, with NATO observers present. This nuclear emer-

---

7. Cited in Oliver Meier, *Arms Control Today*, July-August 2006.
8. Meier, *Arms Control Today*, July-August 2006; and author's conversation with Bell.

gency response exercise simulated a terrorist attack on a truck and a rail convoy with the aim of capturing the nuclear weapons being transported. Russian response teams included helicopters and armored vehicles to back up the convoy guard forces.[9]

Unlike the arms control-related tasks under the work plan, emergency response seems to have been blessed by the Russian Ministry of Defense and General Staff and to enjoy wide support in the Russian government, including the Kremlin. In discussing how to avoid nuclear emergencies, the task group could be a venue for discussing such basic arms control measures as consolidation of weapons under better protection and tighter control and accounting. These topics have long been priority topics between the United States and Russia in the context of the warhead protection, control, and accounting programs run by the Departments of Defense and Energy, so pursuing them in the NATO-Russia emergency response context would not be an innovation.

Eventually, as the scope and success of certain NATO-Russia work plan tasks expands and grows, energizing moribund areas such as arms control and reduction should be possible. But for the meantime, confidence-building will have to take place in a slightly different, although complementary venue.

Tasks one and two could take place in parallel over the next two years, with the goal of arriving at the NATO 60th anniversary celebration in spring 2009 with a consensus position on deemphasizing nuclear weapons in NATO, and an agenda and proposal for pursuing short-range nuclear arms talks with Russia.

This first example illustrated what it would take to get the United States and NATO to the negotiating table with Russia to talk about short-range nuclear weapons—with confidence-building, of course, being relevant to both sets of negotiators. Let us now consider more

9. NATO Update, "Nuclear weapons accident response exercise held in Murmansk region," August 11, 2004.

explicitly what it would take to get Russia to the negotiating table with NATO.

## Russia to the Table

Russia clearly threw down a number of gauntlets in 2007, such as an angry reaction to U.S. missile defense deployments in the NATO countries, especially on the territories of new members Poland and the Czech Republic. Russia has threatened to target extra nuclear missiles toward Europe in response to these deployments, and it has also threatened to withdraw from the INF Treaty. At the same time, however, it has offered some interesting ideas about missile defense cooperation with the United States and NATO, and the seeds of a negotiation seem to be in place. For that reason, this crisis seems to be self-contained and not necessarily relevant to the problem of short-range nuclear weapons.

Not so the case with the CFE Treaty. President Putin first threatened to withdraw from CFE during his February 2007 speech in Munich, then announced a moratorium on Russian implementation of the treaty during his State of the Nation speech in April. In July 2007, he signed a presidential decree that confirmed the moratorium: if the other CFE signatory states in NATO did not ratify the treaty within 150 days, then Russia would institute a full moratorium on fulfilling its obligations under the treaty. And in November 2007, addressing top Russian military officers for the last time before his presidential term was due to end in May 2008, Putin declared that suspending participation in the CFE Treaty was part of an "adequate response" to NATO "muscle-flexing" on Russia's borders.[10]

Russia's complaints about CFE relate to NATO's unwillingness to be more flexible with regard to the "frozen conflicts" in Georgia and Moldova, and to flank limits imposed on the deployment of Rus-

10. Simon Saradzhyan, "Putin Talking Adequate Response to NATO," *The Moscow Times*, November 21, 2007.

sian troops inside Russia. Therefore, they would seem to have little relevance to negotiating constraints on short-range nuclear weapons. Russia's complaints, however, reflect a broader malaise in Moscow that is linked to concerns about the weakness of Russian conventional forces. Perceived NATO inflexibility in responding to these concerns has heightened the Russian suspicion and anger. Russia itself has built up political barriers to working with NATO, although it has had many constructive engagements in recent years—not only the work plan tasks mentioned above, but also actual military exercises in the Black Sea and even at NORAD in Colorado Springs. Nevertheless, the idea that NATO-Russian cooperation is a good thing is currently off-limits for Russian politicians, a sure source of opprobrium among peers in the Moscow establishment.

Therefore, to engage Russia successfully on short-range nuclear weapons will require some progress on the Conventional Forces in Europe Treaty. By December 2007, when Russia threatened to cease implementing the treaty, NATO and the United States had made a number of proposals to Russia, and Russia too had made some proposals, thus the seeds of a negotiation finally seemed to be falling into place. The most important negotiating goal should be to restore Russian confidence in the predictability that the CFE Treaty can provide, thus addressing—at least with regard to the European theater—Russia's concerns about its conventional weakness. There is no objective reason today why Russia should see a military threat emanating from Europe, although that is the gist of current Russian discourse about NATO.

Of course, observers of the Putin administration suspected that much of the anti-NATO rhetoric and scaremongering was associated with the Russian Duma and presidential elections, the first in December 2007, the second in March 2008. In that period, the time indeed was not ripe for successful negotiations on CFE. Europe should nevertheless be persistent in making the case clearly that it poses no threat to Russia and in fact would like to expand cooperation under the NATO-Russia Council.

Although positive momentum on solving the CFE problem is an important factor in engaging the Russians on short-range nuclear weapons, NATO should consider some more explicit nuclear discussions with the Russians. Such discussions would be in the interest of reiterating the message that NATO is not a threat to Russia; they would also lay the groundwork for eventual nuclear negotiations, and could add to general confidence-building in the context of the NATO-Russia Council.

NATO might brief the Russians, for example, on plans to update the Strategic Concept in 2009. NATO might even ask Russia formally to comment. Less ambitious but also useful might be a discussion of the history and intentions behind the 1997 statement that NATO has no intentions, plans, or reasons to deploy nuclear weapons on the territory of new member states—and how that statement has had an impact on NATO policy and force deployments. If carefully managed, this discussion could also engage the new nuclear member states— recognizing, however, the great tensions that would color the environment.

Thus, getting Russia to the table to negotiate constraints on short-range nuclear weapons involves at least a two-step process—one to address the problems with the CFE Treaty, and one to engage in serious confidence-building. Some ideas have already been discussed in the context of the NATO-Russia Council, but others might involve some explicit discussions of NATO nuclear policy with Russia.

## Options for Pursuing Controls and Reductions: Inch by Inch, Then Step by Step

The preceding discussion has underscored that major political and policy issues have to be addressed before NATO and the Russian Federation will be ready to move to a negotiated arrangement that would lead to the elimination of short-range nuclear weapons from

Europe, as a precursor to their total elimination worldwide. Despite these barriers, there is no reason why the United States, Russia, and European NATO countries cannot begin now to build confidence toward achieving this goal.

This section, therefore, considers some confidence-building measures specific to nuclear arms control and reduction processes. In other words, in contrast to the political confidence-building described above, these nuclear confidence-building ideas could progressively be fitted into control and reduction measures—including verification—and eventually into a negotiated ban on the weapons. Although many ideas are available, this analysis places high value on ideas that already have some grounding in joint cooperation with the Russians, and might therefore be able to grow and develop rapidly, even in the troubled political environment that currently exists between Russia and NATO.

*Ways to Do Confidence-Building*

There are many directions that nuclear confidence-building could take in the near term. "Confidence-building" in this context is defined as general activities to enable each side to gain some understanding of the other's nuclear weapons in Europe, including their day-to-day deployment status, and the challenges inherent therein. For the purposes of this discussion, other means of confidence-building such as data exchanges are discussed separately, as a distinct prelude to arms control and reduction measures.

- Cooperation on nuclear weapon safety. In a similar category to nuclear emergency response, nuclear weapon safety has long been a mutual concern of the United States and Russia, and the two countries have pursued some extensive cooperation on technical and operational aspects of safety in their bilateral Nuclear Weapons Safety and Security Agreement (WSSX). Both Russia and NATO European countries have reportedly experienced difficult situations where their deployed nuclear weapons might be affected

by fire or lightning strikes.[11] Cooperation to mitigate fire and lightning effects has already been a major agenda item in U.S.-Russian
bilateral cooperation under the WSSX Agreement. Although as
nuclear weapon states they would not want to share technical details concerning the warheads, they could share some results of
their research, including training measures for troops on both the
NATO and Russian sides, enabling them better to handle fire and
lightning situations.

- "Close-out" activities at old bases. Both Russia and NATO countries have been consolidating nuclear weapons and in some cases
  removing them altogether from base facilities. These close-out activities have involved specific procedures, but also adjustments to
  command and control, operations, maintenance, and personnel
  policies at the bases affected. Ideally, Russia and the NATO countries would be willing to allow reciprocal site visits during close-
  out activities, but that might be too challenging a step for early
  stages of confidence-building. If that is the case, then the two sides
  might begin by simply meeting to provide mutual briefings and
  discuss what procedures are followed to close out ("decertify") a
  facility's nuclear status.

- Site visits to compare nuclear and non-nuclear bases. This would
  be a site visit designed to provide information on specific aspects
  of a non-nuclear base that differentiate it from a nuclear base.
  Russia and NATO are accustomed to reconnaissance of each
  other's bases and understand much about the "tattle-tales" of a
  nuclear base, but this measure could be helpful in building confidence that non-nuclear bases are in fact "clean" and could not
  hold nuclear weapons according to national or alliance policy.

11. For lightning problems on the NATO side, see Kristensen, p. 50–52; and for
fire and lightning problems on the Russian side, see Gunnar Arbman and Charles
Thornton, "Russia's Tactical Nuclear Weapons, Part II: Technical Issues and Policy
Recommendations," Systems Technology, SE-172 90 Stockholm, FOI-R—1588—SE,
February 2005, ISSN 1650–1942, p. 42.

Another important advantage might be to ensure confidence that new bases, such as those being constructed in Bulgaria or Rumania, are not acquiring new nuclear capabilities. This advantage could also apply to bases being refurbished, as for example the Russian naval base at Novorossiysk. The Russian Navy began refurbishing it in accordance with presidential orders to upgrade the base, but the MOD's Twelfth Main Directorate responsible for safety and security of weapons decided that it could not be brought up to their standards. According to Russian reports, the MOD consequently removed all nuclear weapons from Novorossiysk.[12]

- Observation of personnel training, including certification activities. Both Russia and the NATO European countries have been experiencing difficulties training and retaining sufficient personnel to serve at nuclear bases.[13] Although clearly some aspects of operational training and command and control would have to remain off-limits, observing training in certain aspects could build confidence, and might serve the additional beneficial effect of providing each side with some new ideas about personnel training and retention. The two sides might initiate a discussion, for example, of personnel recruitments, including educational, health, and personal profile requirements, as well as incentives offered during the recruitment process. They might also emphasize particular aspects of training that would not only be mutually beneficial, but would dovetail with other confidence-building being pursued—for example, in the realm of weapon safety and mitigation of fire and lightning risks.

Each of these confidence-building ideas draws on cooperation that has already developed in other settings—the WSSX Agreement, the Cooperative Threat Reduction program, the NATO-Russia Council

12. Arbman and Thornton, Part I, p. 22.
13. Kristensen, p. 34–36; and Arbman and Thornton, Part II, pp. 52–53.

work plan, and even the grand world of START verification. Therefore, they should be backed by enough bureaucratic precedents that they could be supported in both Moscow and NATO capitals. Once momentum is growing toward negotiations, then the next phase could be started: exchanges of information and data.

### Ways to Do Data Exchange

Data exchange has had a troubled history during the era of the Presidential Nuclear Initiatives (PNIs). Both sides agreed informally to exchange data pursuant to the PNIs, but the Soviet Union and later the Russian Federation have not so far agreed to exchange data on short-range nuclear weapons in any detail. Instead, Russian spokesmen have issued general statements that entire classes of weapons have been moved or destroyed, or they have used percentages rather than providing absolute numbers of weapons. The Russians state that since the details of a data exchange were never agreed in a legally binding treaty, they are justified in providing data in the form they see fit. This point of view has been frustrating for the United States and NATO countries, which have considered the Russian position to be in bad faith.

NATO and Russia will therefore have to build up a fair amount of mutual confidence to get to the step of exchanging data. Nevertheless, moving in this direction will be an important precursor to entering into more formal processes of weapons reduction and elimination. And of course, establishing an agreed baseline of data will be a necessary condition for a formal, legally binding arms reduction process.

Data exchange can also usefully be thought of in stages, however, beginning with some unilateral actions and then developing in more formal and detailed directions:

- Declassification/unilateral declarations. The United States might decide to declassify certain nuclear weapons information, such as the total number of weapons operationally deployed or in storage at a particular time, or the total number eliminated during a certain period. In cooperation with European allies, the U.S. might also formally declassify information such as the number of weapons withdrawn from bases over time—although this would have to be done carefully to take account of public sentiment. This information could then be provided in a unilateral declaration, a kind of "weapons status report," to the Russian Federation. For Russia, such declassification is likely to be challenging politically, since there do not appear to be such routine procedures for declassification in place as there are in the United States. However, Russia and the United States now have considerable joint experience in releasing sensitive information to each other's governments under CTR, WSSX, the HEU agreement, etc., so such a Russian declaration might be "releasable to the United States only" or "releasable to NATO countries only," rather than a public declaration.

- Renew the PNIs. A number of analysts have also seen renewal or revival of the Presidential Nuclear Initiatives as a relatively straightforward way to undertake a data exchange. The goals are already laid out and well understood by the parties involved. Renewing these commitments would almost certainly have to involve the U.S. and Russian presidents agreeing to make a clear restatement of the PNIs. Because of the mutual frustration that has been experienced over the years in their implementation, only reassertion of the commitments at the highest level is likely to have some effect—and even then, the effect is not guaranteed.

- Negotiate a new data exchange agreement. The frustration surrounding the PNIs might make it necessary to negotiate a new agreement on data exchange as a confidence- and security-building measure. Such an agreement could only come on the heels of considerable confidence-building between NATO and Russia regarding short-range nuclear weapons. However, the concept of such an agreement might develop out of confidence-building cooperation in other areas—as a logical progression from examining together the nuclear/non-nuclear status of bases, for example. Thus, it need not necessarily become trapped in the bad memories of the PNI experience, but might naturally flow from more positive confidence-building related to CTR and other successful joint efforts.

## *Ways to Do Arms Control and Reductions*

Once NATO and Russia are on the way to resolving differences over CFE, once NATO develops a consensus internally on what it wants to do about nuclear weapons, and once the two sides have engaged in some specific confidence-building regarding short-range nuclear weapons, then they can proceed to actual control and reductions. In each of the approaches outlined below, the goal of elimination of the weapons would be explicit.

- New unilateral steps. Russia and the NATO countries could agree to take certain steps in parallel, but essentially on a unilateral basis. Again, because of past tensions over the PNIs, and because of recent tensions over security in Europe, both sides would doubtless want to have some transparency measures explicitly tied to the implementation of the new steps. In other words, the steps would have to be implemented with a certain level of transparency agreed in advance. For example, NATO could announce a unilateral withdrawal of the remaining short-range nuclear weapons from European member states back to the United States. The alliance could agree with Russia, based on prior confidence-building activities involving bases, that Russia could visit the former nuclear deployment sites after the warheads had been removed, to assure itself that the nuclear activities at the bases had been closed out. Likewise, Russia could recommit itself to storing short-range nuclear weapons in central storage facilities on Russian territory, and could provide opportunities to NATO observers to visit bases that had been closed out of nuclear operations. For NATO, it would doubtless be most important to see such a development in Kaliningrad; the suspected nuclear deployments there have been a source of considerable concern to NATO. Major improvements in the NATO-Russian relationship will have to come about, however, before a nuclear close-out visit in Kaliningrad would be possible.

- Transform the PNIs into a legally binding arrangement. Renewing the PNIs with a handshake has been one approach that arms control experts have considered, but another would be to use them as the basis for a new legally binding agreement that would focus on consolidating short-range nuclear weapons to central storage facilities. In the case of NATO, these central storage facilities would be in the United States. In the case of Russia, the storage facilities would be a limited number of sites deep within Russia. However, as noted above, the frustrations with the PNIs have been considerable, so perhaps they are not the most encouraging basis for a new initiative on short-range nuclear reductions. Nevertheless, high-level attention might be enough to transform the situation. One idea would be to appeal to President George H. W. Bush and President Gorbachev to help re-launch the PNIs as a basis for negotiation, with perhaps the endorsement of Mrs. Yeltsin in memory of her husband. If these eminent figures made a recommendation to the next presidents of the United States and Russia, their action might effectively shake off the malaise that has surrounded the PNIs and lead to new and significant nuclear reduction negotiations.

- A ban on short-range nuclear weapons in operational deployment. Weapons would be consolidated to central storage facilities in the United States and Russia and permanently stored there; according to an agreed schedule, they would be slated for elimination. Given Russia's stated dependence on short-range nuclear weapons to ensure national security, a ban on operational deployment of such weapons is unlikely to tempt the Kremlin for a long time. The confidence of the Russian leadership in instruments such as the CFE Treaty would have to be fully restored, and Russia, the United States, and NATO would have had to enter into an unprecedented era of cooperation. At the moment, it is difficult to see it. Nevertheless, Russia itself has suggested proposals that would seem to herald such an era—particularly the proposals to join with the United States and NATO countries to provide a missile defense for Eurasia. Here is one area where missile defense developments could have a significant impact on the short-range nuclear weapon problem. If Russia and the United States are able rapidly to enter negotiations to cooperate on missile defenses, and those negotiations rapidly produce results, then the environment might emerge to begin exploring a ban on short-range nuclear weapons in operational deployment. In addition to the extant Russian proposals, the possibility of rapid progress on missile defense cooperation is supported by two other relevant policy developments: First, as mentioned above, Russia and the United States, with NATO, have cooperated very well in joint exercises and other joint activities involving missile defenses under the NATO-Russia Council. Second, Russia and the United States now have more than a decade of experience cooperating on manned space flight, which has produced clear evidence that the two countries can work successfully together in former Cold War bastions such as their respective space programs.

The crossover to strategic arms reductions is a point that must be emphasized. Strategic arms will be a target for further arms reductions, and as David Holloway argues in his paper for this project, these should be considered in four stages, beginning in the near term with reductions between Russia and the United States but proceeding through stages toward the eventual elimination of nuclear weapons. [See Chapter 1.] As these stages advance, short-range weapons will naturally fall into the same basket with strategic arms for negotiating actual *elimination* of the weapons.[14] This approach would acknowledge the reality that nuclear weapons are impossible to differentiate when they are divorced from their launch vehicles, and would also anticipate deep reductions, when the difference between short- and long-range systems becomes steadily less relevant.

The difficulty of distinguishing between short-range and strategic nuclear weapons has been identified earlier in this analysis; nowhere does it become more evident than when operational deployments are moving lower and lower, and greater and greater emphasis is being placed on dual-capable systems or, in fact, on conventional strike missions at longer and longer ranges. The United States is probably already at that point today, having deemphasized nuclear weapons in its military strategy and put greater stock into highly capable conventional weapons accurate at long range. The U.S. might very well be ready, therefore, to place long-range and short-range nuclear weapons in a basket together, to try to maximize flexibility in the dreaded case that nuclear operations would be necessary, but also in the positive case that negotiations could begin on reducing and eliminating nuclear weapons. The Russians, however, are not close to this point in terms of military strategy—in fact, they have been heading in the opposite direction. Nevertheless, bringing short- and strategic-range weapons together will be necessary once arsenals grow smaller, if only to smooth out at the negotiating table asymmetries that have appeared in the evolution of the nuclear arsenals of the nuclear weapons states. As numbers of nuclear weapons decrease, "strategic" and "short-range" will eventually lose their meaning.

And the crossover creates a special benefit for strategic nuclear reductions. Short-range nuclear weapons designed to be forward deployed have the potential, in fact, to serve as a special harbinger for

14. I am indebted to Jim Timbie for the clear expression of this point during the Reykjavik II Conference at the Hoover Institution, October 24, 2007.

later stages of the strategic arms reduction process. In 1991–92, the Presidential Nuclear Initiatives were early expressions of the concept that warheads should be moved out of operational deployment and into secure storage, not ready for immediate launch. The PNIs may be revivified and lead to a ban on short-range weapons in operational deployment, or such a ban may be negotiated on its own. In either case, implementation of the ban would be a type of "pilot project" for zero deployed warheads in the strategic forces. The transparency, verification, and monitoring measures applied to short-range weapons would serve well in the strategic case, and certainly as strategic and short-range weapons begin to fall into the same basket for elimination.

*The European complication*

One might argue that the U.K. and France have also already reached the point of a crossover between strategic and short-range weapons, since they have undertaken significant unilateral reductions and retain relatively small nuclear arsenals.[15] After significant downsizing of their nuclear forces during the 1990s, both countries tend to describe their remaining nuclear weapons as "strategic" in nature. However, from time to time both have also noted that their "strategic'" nuclear forces can cover theater targets if necessary.[16] While these arguments

15. In 2005, France was thought to have 350 total nuclear warheads in its indigenous arsenal and the United Kingdom 200; China had approximately 410. See "Nuclear Weapon Status 2005," *Deadly Arsenals*, Second Edition (Joseph Cirincione, Jon B. Wolfsthal, Miriam Rajkumar, eds.), Carnegie Endowment for International Peace, 2005, p. 55. In a March 2008 speech, French president Nicolas Sarkozy announced that France would take unilateral reductions in its nuclear arsenal that would bring its number of warheads to "fewer than 300." See "Speech by Nicolas Sarkozy, President of the French Republic, Presentation of Le Terrible in Cherbourg," 21 March 2008, found at www.acronym.org.uk/docs/0803/doc09.htm.

16. The U.K. advanced this argument in 1997, for example, when it was considering downsizing its nuclear arsenal. The remaining weapons based on Trident submarines, it was argued, could cover both "strategic" and "theater" targets. Conversation with Professor John Simpson, Mountbatten Centre for International Studies, University of Southampton, United Kingdom, on September 15, 2007.

reinforce the long-standing conundrum regarding nuclear weapons in Europe—Are they strategic or not?—they also bespeak difficult budget and policy decisions that have had to be made in Paris and London. Both countries, over time, have cut steadily back on the variety and numbers of their indigenous nuclear weapons.

Thus, explicit control and reduction steps for short-range nuclear weapons deployed by NATO can only be undertaken if there is a degree of support for them among the European NATO allies, which is why a NATO consensus regarding the withdrawal of NATO nuclear weapons from Europe will be vital. The nuclear forces controlled wholly by the U.K. and France might be a complicating factor, however, since those two countries would likely want to have them folded into strategic reduction talks involving all of the nuclear weapons states. The long-standing position of these two countries, and also China, has been that until the United States and Russia reduce to 1000 nuclear weapons on each side, then it makes no sense for them to become engaged in the talks.

The Russians, for their part, historically have demanded that the U.K. and French nuclear forces be on the table during key arms control negotiations, including both INF and START. The British and the French have always strongly resisted those efforts, backed fully by the United States, which had the seat at the negotiating table. In August 2007, General Vladimir Verkhovtsev, the head of the 12th Main Directorate of the Russian Ministry of Defense, the guardians of Russia's warheads, offered to begin negotiations with the United States to reduce stocks of tactical nuclear weapons. However, he insisted that such negotiations must take place "with the participation in the process of other countries, above all Britain and France."[17]

This demand could give rise to speculation that the Russian Federation was returning to an old argument, which it had never won, to

17. See, for example, "Britain, France must be included in weapons talks: Russian General," Agence France Presse, 3 September 2007. See also www.armscontrol.org/ act/2005_07–08/US_Russian_NuclearReductions.asp.

ensure that negotiations on weapons in Europe would not begin any-
time soon. There is another possibility, however: Verkhovtsev's for-
mulation actually represents a slight softening of the recent Russian
position, which had held that NATO nuclear weapons would have to
leave Europe before Russia would come to the negotiating table. Verkhovtsev's comment, in short, might represent an opening to talk with
the Russians and the Europeans, including the U.K. and France, precisely about a process—one that would involve at the first stage confidence-building, and later reduction and elimination measures. But
this possibility is by no means certain, and needs exploring.

The ban on operational deployments outlined above would essentially bypass the issue of geography by focusing on consolidation to
central storage facilities.[18] The weapons would be consolidated to central storage facilities inside U.S. and Russian territory, the number and
location of which would be designated in a negotiation. This approach
would correct the tensions and disagreements that grew up under the
PNIs, when each side was able to determine for itself what the term
"central storage" meant. The Russians tended to define it as storage
in the vicinity of operational bases; for the United States, it meant
returning the weapons to the continental United States. However, the
Russian Federation has centralized storage facilities in the heart of
Russia and not adjacent to operational bases, which could readily be
used to satisfy the definition of "central storage."

*Complicating factors: new regional views and developments*

Although the established NATO powers seem politically and strategically ready to consider an exit of nuclear weapons from their
territory in Europe, their new partners to the east might be more reluctant. The Baltic states and Poland in particular have been engaged
in some sharp exchanges with Russia and may consider NATO's nu-

18. I am grateful for this insight to Robert Einhorn, who emphasized in his comments the importance and effectiveness of consolidation to central storage facilities
regardless of the strategic direction—Europe or Asia.

clear weapons to be an extra insurance policy as they try to establish a new *modus vivendi* with Russia. Much will depend on the strength of leadership from the United States in this case, in terms of reinforcing the NATO security guarantee and, perhaps, maintaining vestigial capacity in Europe for some period of time—that is, the nuclear base structure and training activities mentioned above. The confidence of these states will only be raised over time, of course, and as part of a comprehensive process of establishing a healthy relationship between NATO and Russia. Nevertheless, the willingness of Washington to play down the utility of the NATO nuclear weapons remaining in Europe will be important.

Another complicating regional factor comes from far to the south—the nascent nuclear program in Iran. Where NATO is concerned, the reaction of Turkey will be all-important. Opinion polls in recent years have found Turks to be the NATO public most opposed to continuing deployments of nuclear weapons on their territory.[19] Nevertheless, if Iraq continues to be unstable and Iran continues to insist on accelerating its nuclear enrichment program, the Turkish public might become more concerned about Iranian regional hegemony and less interested in de-nuclearization. Already Turkey has stated its claim to an indigenous nuclear energy program—which can in some circumstances be the precursor to a military nuclear program. Here again, much will depend on how attentive other NATO capitals are to Turkey's security concerns, and how willing to continue the process of integrating Turkey into Europe. The United States can again play a reassuring role, but Europe's role will be preeminent.

It is worth emphasizing that if the Iranian nuclear program continues apace and creates more and more momentum for indigenous nuclear programs throughout the Middle East, then NATO countries will require enormous energy and leadership to shift from the status

19. See, for example, "Nuclear Weapons in Europe: Survey Results in Six European Countries," A Study Coordinated by Strategic Communications for Greenpeace International, May 25, 2006.

quo. In other words, they will be loath to change the Strategic Concept and dispense entirely with nuclear weapons in NATO Europe if nuclear weapons in the Middle East are a rising threat. The current NATO position is a hedging strategy, and the Iranians would essentially give the Europeans a continuing reason to hedge. Under such circumstances, only a strong NATO leader or coalition of leaders could make the case that the small number of nuclear weapons in Europe would make no earthly difference to the strategic situation in the Middle East.

Each of the issues raised in these last pages argues for early involvement of other countries in the confidence-building process regarding nuclear weapons designed to be forward deployed. A confidence-building process will likely be needed among NATO countries in preparation for making changes in the Strategic Concept; this could focus on the contemporary nature of the U.S. security guarantee and maintenance of vestigial nuclear capacity in NATO Europe. Another confidence-building process would involve NATO and Russia, including the new NATO countries, and would focus on laying the ground to come to the table to negotiate first controls, and then a ban leading to total elimination of nuclear weapons from operational deployment. Yet another would bring the nuclear weapon states together to prepare for more comprehensive control and reduction measures, leading in the long-term future to a broader ban. The configuration of this group is tricky: it should certainly involve the nuclear weapons states under the Non-Proliferation Treaty—the United States, Russia, China, France, and the United Kingdom—but it should also involve the other states in possession of nuclear weapons—India, Pakistan, and Israel.

In theory, because China, India, and Pakistan do not maintain their nuclear weapons at a high level of operational readiness, negotiating with them a ban on operational deployments should be straightforward. Ironically, the accompanying transparency into their programs, which would be necessary for a negotiated ban, is likely to be much more difficult. The United States and Russia, after 30 years of negotiated nuclear arms reductions, are accustomed to mutual monitoring and verification—but these countries are not. Moreover, Israel does not publicly admit to having a nuclear weapons program. Therefore, no area of short-range nuclear arms control will be simple. However, confidence-building measures with all the relevant countries could start early, and should be the focus of immediate policy efforts.

Whether such confidence-building activities come into the orbit of the NATO-Russia talks or remain in another regional basket is a major question to decide, and this paper does not attempt an answer. Most important is the recognition that a "step-by-step, inch-by-inch" approach such as that outlined here has the potential to draw a number of regional nuclear issues into its orbit—or else create intersecting orbits. Multiple confidence-building venues, with care, can create more rational and consistent nuclear arms control policies, but the effort to maintain focus will be complicated.

## Concluding Recommendations: The Road to Eliminating Short-Range Nuclear Weapons

This analysis proceeds from the assumption that until the United States and Russian Federation, along with NATO countries, are able to eliminate short-range nuclear weapons from Europe, efforts to eliminate them anywhere else in the world will be stymied. For that reason, the entire focus of this paper is on what it will take to get NATO and Russia talking about the weapons, understanding the problem from each other's perspective, building up confidence, and moving into controlling and eventually reducing and eliminating the weapons from Europe. While that goal is being accomplished, the other states deploying short-range nuclear weapons—India and Pakistan, Israel, China—should be brought into the discussion and into confidence-building activities. However, these countries will be very unlikely to move to control and reduce their own short-range weapons if the problem in Europe is not solved.

Russia's new dependence on nuclear weapons to compensate for its conventional weapons receives much attention in this discussion, and it is one of the key issues that will have to be dealt with in order to begin the process of control and reduction. Working toward resolution of differences over the CFE Treaty will be one major way to do so. So Russia, in this regard, is the difficult side of the policy equation.

At the same time, it is worth emphasizing how far NATO and the United States have come in transforming themselves into the easier side of this policy equation. As recently as 1999, NATO was not in a position to move beyond a traditional statement of the importance of nuclear weapons in its Strategic Concept. By 2005, however, politicians in Europe became ready to move the issue out of the closet and debate it openly. Also throughout this period, nuclear readiness levels in NATO Europe steadily declined and in one case—Greece in 2001—nuclear weapons were completely withdrawn from a NATO country.

On the other side of the Atlantic, U.S. strategy became more and more focused on centralizing nuclear planning and operations at Strategic Command in Omaha. This move was consonant with a trend in the direction of centralized capabilities to attack targets worldwide under the "Global Strike" concept. Global Strike became synonymous with long-range, highly accurate, deep-strike conventional missions, which also supported the notion of deemphasizing nuclear weapons in U.S. and NATO policy.

Thus, the environment for ending NATO nuclear deployments in Europe is much more welcoming than it was less than a decade ago, and it is feasible that NATO could decide to recast its Strategic Concept to achieve this goal in the context of its 60th anniversary celebrations in 2009. The key question for NATO policymakers, however, is whether they wish to lead on this issue without requiring a major change in Russian policy at the same time. There are arguments that may be made about the exemplary effect that unilateral action would have in this case, as well as benefits for the NATO allies' defense budgets (including that of the United States). But it is realistic to assume that Russia will not be willing to move so quickly to reverse its dependence on nuclear weapons in its military strategy.

Therefore, NATO would probably want to maintain an insurance policy while work with the Russians moves forward. The alliance, for example, could agree to remove short-range nuclear weapons from Europe while leaving the infrastructure for deploying the weapons in place. The alliance could continue to train and certify personnel for nuclear operations, and could continue some specific exercise activities to ensure that command and control capabilities remain intact and that nuclear weapons could be quickly reintroduced into Europe if necessary. These steps could then be phased out as mutual confidence builds between NATO and Russia, and as the two sides move toward agreeing on reductions and an eventual ban.

This issue of a disconnect between Russia and the United States/ NATO on the importance of nuclear weapons is the most difficult one to grapple with in any effort to eliminate short-range nuclear weapons. The disconnect will take time and patience to address, and this paper recommends an "inch by inch, step by step" approach.

Confidence-building should be the first step, but we need not be satisfied with superficial site visits and other slow steps that characterized confidence-building during the Cold War era. Instead, confidence-building should take advantage of the intensive cooperation that the United States and Russia have pursued in the past 15 years to have some practical effect on real problems being encountered in each side's nuclear forces. For example, in the context of the Warhead Safety and Security Agreement (WSSX), the U.S. and Russia have been working intensively on measures to improve the safety of nuclear weapons against threats of fire and lightning.

Bringing such measures to bear on nuclear weapons in Europe would help to solve real problems that both sides have encountered, and also build confidence in the nature of the deployments. Confidence-building, therefore, should be linked to intensive problem-solving for both sides, which in turn will have a rapid impact on the growth in confidence—a confidence feedback loop, in other words.

Once mutual confidence is growing, Russia and the United States/ NATO can move to the next stage, beginning arms control and reduction measures. Initially, finding a way to exchange data should be the focus of these efforts, for two reasons. First, differences over how to exchange data under the Presidential Nuclear Initiatives has been a persistent irritant between Russia and NATO practically since the PNIs were agreed to in the early 1990s. The resulting damage has made it difficult for the two sides to imagine how they might sit down with each other at the negotiating table. Thus, figuring out a judicious way to do data exchanges by itself would play a vital confidence-building role.

Second, an agreed baseline of weapons systems has always been a necessary and significant precursor to success in arms reduction negotiations. Only once the parties have agreed to the number and nature of deployments can they agree on how much and in what way to reduce them. Either side might begin by trying unilaterally to spur movement, for example through declassification of deployment numbers. The United States has established procedures to do so, and could agree on such steps with its NATO allies. However, there should be no expectation of a quick response from the Russian side, as procedures for declassification are not routinely established and the political environment in Moscow is difficult. Nevertheless, the Russians might be willing to share some data on a confidential government-to-government basis if the United States comes forward with an initiative.

Several larger policy steps will be required before the two sides will be willing to sit down to significant arms reduction negotiations— NATO will have to decide what it wants to do about short-range nuclear weapons deployed in allied countries, and Russia and NATO will have to be on the road to resolving their differences over the CFE Treaty. As these solutions are in train, arms reduction negotiations can begin. Even before that point, however, the two sides could pursue further unilateral measures to convince each other that nuclear-capable bases have been or are being closed down—and here, Russian willingness to shed more light on the situation in Kaliningrad would be very important. Another interim measure with some risks attached to it would be to recommit to the PNIs. Uncertainties over implementation of the PNIs have added up to some serious mistrust between Moscow and Washington, and for that reason an initiative to recommit could stir up old frustrations. Bringing high-level authority to bear—and particularly President George H. W. Bush and President Gorbachev, who launched the PNIs originally—could be an important way to overcome such irritation.

The unquestionable goal should be a worldwide ban on short-range nuclear weapons in operational deployment, linked to a continuing campaign to eliminate nuclear warheads and dispose of their nuclear materials—with accompanying transparency measures. Efforts to negotiate this ban, which should first engage Russia and the NATO countries, should come to engage the other nuclear weapon states. This could be done through development of a step-by-step confidence-building process that would lead to more comprehensive control and reduction measures, and eventually in the future to a broader ban. The configuration of this group is complicated: it should certainly involve the nuclear weapons states under the Non-Proliferation Treaty—the United States, France, and the United Kingdom (which are NATO countries) plus Russia, China—and also the other states in possession of nuclear weapons—India, Pakistan, and Israel. Because of the complexity involved in engaging these different countries, decisive progress will not come quickly. However, thoughtful confidence-building could start quickly, and should be the focus of immediate policy efforts.

As strategic nuclear arms reductions advance through several phases, from reductions in operationally deployed warheads to eventual warhead elimination, strategic and short-range weapons should be placed in the same basket for negotiating the actual elimination process. This approach would acknowledge the reality that nuclear weapons are impossible to differentiate when they are divorced from their launch vehicles, and would also anticipate deep reductions, when the difference between short- and long-range systems becomes steadily less relevant. In fact, implementation of a ban on operationally deployed short-range weapons will be a type of "pilot project" for zero deployed warheads in the strategic forces. The transparency, verification, and monitoring measures applied to short-range weapons will serve well in the strategic case, and certainly as strategic and short-range weapons begin to fall into the same basket for elimination.

The agenda for eliminating short-range nuclear weapons is potentially an exciting one, taking full advantage of the lessons learned over the past 15 years, and particularly the practical ways in which Russia and the United States have learned to work together to enhance the safety and security of nuclear weapons. We have essentially proven to each other that we can together solve vexing problems with regard to our nuclear forces. This mutual interest should help to overcome the frustration, anger, and disconnects that have hampered Russian cooperation with the United States and NATO in Europe. But patience and attention to multiple problems will have to be the watchwords of the effort. Efforts to engage Russia on the nuclear front cannot be divorced from attempts to solve other problems.

## Appendix A:  Background Materials

*A Small History of the Problem*

When START II was signed in January 1993, control and reduction of nuclear weapons were seen as the next Everest to be essayed. For the first time, START III would attempt to constrain not only weapon launch systems, but also the weapons themselves. This process would require more daring verification measures, both technically and politically, than had ever before been tried. Nevertheless, Washington and Moscow agreed that shifting the focus of reductions to nuclear weapons was important, since it would open the pathway to steadily deeper reductions in nuclear capability.

Although the progression in strategic arms reductions attracted the most attention, a new frontier also seemed to be opening for constraints on short-range nuclear weapons. The United States, with its allies, had deployed short-range nuclear weapons in the European and Asian theaters for decades. They figured in U.S. war plans against both the Soviet Union and China. The Soviets also deployed many types of short-range nuclear systems in Europe and Asia—mines, artillery shells, aviation bombs, short-range missiles. History tells us that they actually came close to using them against the Chinese in 1968. Many of these weapons, in both NATO and the Warsaw Pact, cohabited with conventional weapons in dual-use launch systems.

The ambitious new agenda to constrain nuclear weapons persisted through the 1990s, last receiving presidential endorsement in March 1997, when Russian President Yeltsin and U.S. President Clinton met in Helsinki, Finland. Their "Helsinki Summit Statement" reaffirmed that Russia and the United States were intent on controlling and reducing nuclear weapons not only at the strategic level, but also those short-range systems designed to be forward deployed in European and Asia theaters.[20]

20.  See "Joint Statement on Parameters on Future Reductions in Nuclear Forces,"

At the end of the 1990s, a different trend was developing, however. Some analysts concluded that the game was not worth the candle: the Soviet threat had collapsed, and the old Soviet nuclear arsenal, whether at the strategic or non-strategic level, posed no threat to the United States or NATO. Furthermore, tough and legally binding arms control measures, especially intrusive verification, would sharply constrain the flexibility that the United States had to plan and deploy its forces.[21] If the United States interacted with Russia at all on nuclear matters, it should be to constrain the threat that Russian nuclear weapons might go missing and fall into the hands of terrorists or rogue leaders who could use them against the United States.

Furthermore, governments in NATO Europe were not particularly keen to pursue the issue. They had been buffeted by public opposition to NATO nuclear deployments in the 1970s and 1980s. At that time, the United States had advanced proposals for a new neutron bomb that was supposed to be especially efficient for urban warfare. The U.S. with its NATO allies had also successfully deployed intermediate-range nuclear missiles (INF) in Europe to counter new Soviet INF systems. Both initiatives had aroused strong and sometimes violent public protests in Europe, and the European governments of the 1990s, many of them relatively weak coalitions, did not welcome the idea of bringing nuclear weapons again into the public eye. Nuclear weapons could remain deployed in Europe, only quietly so.

These trends were complemented on the Russian side as strategists in Moscow became more and more fixated on nuclear weapons as a way to compensate for the weakness and disarray of the Russian armed forces. Russian military doctrinal statements focused increas-

---

("Helsinki Summit Statement"), found at www.armscontrol.org/act/1997_03/js.asp, accessed August 2, 2007.

21. Robert Joseph, "Nuclear Weapons and Regional Deterrence," in Jeffrey A. Larson and Kurt J. Klingenberger, eds., *Controlling Non-Strategic Nuclear Weapons: Obstacles and Opportunities*, United States Air Force, Institute for National Security Studies, July 2001, pp. 90–92.

ingly on nuclear weapons as the ultimate way to defend Russia against enemy incursions. The doctrine foresaw both attempts at de-escalation using a single nuclear "warning shot," and use of nuclear weapons against invading forces. It was in this context that Russia abandoned its Soviet-era "no-first-use" strategy in 1991, coming closer and closer to the nuclear policies that NATO had pursued through the years of the Cold War, when it was vulnerable to much more powerful Soviet conventional forces.[22]

Russian experts inside the nuclear weapons complex advanced an argument that developed in parallel with the strategy of using nuclear weapons to compensate for conventional weakness. They became alarmed in the late 1990s that if nuclear weapons transparency measures were pursued, then the United States would gain greater access to Russian nuclear weapons facilities. The Americans would, in effect, breach the inner sanctum on which Russian national security ultimately depended. If that were the case, these experts reasoned, then Russia could find itself in the position of having no means to defend itself against the world's only superpower and its allies.[23]

The U.S. and Russian opposition to nuclear weapon reductions dominated the negotiating scene after 2000. Its effect was to shelve—high up and in the back of the cupboard—existing proposals to pursue controls on nuclear weapons. Even the loose agreement to explore nuclear weapon transparency measures that emerged from the May 2002 Washington summit came to naught. The bilateral working group that was to examine the issue disappeared quickly, seemingly by mutual agreement.

22. For a thorough discussion of the evolution of Russian military doctrine during this period, see Gunnar Arbman and Charles Thornton, "Russia's Tactical Nuclear Weapons, Part I: Background and Policy Issues," Systems Technology, SE-172 90 Stockholm, FOI-R-1057-SE, November 2003, ISSN 1650–1942, pp. 24–34.

23. For more on the Russian attitude toward transparency in their nuclear weapons facilities, see Alexei Arbatov and Rose Gottemoeller, "New Presidents, New Agreements? Advancing U.S.-Russian Strategic Arms Control Agreements," *Arms Control Today*, July–August 2008; see also Harold Feiveson, et al., eds., *The Nuclear Turning Point*, Brookings Institution Press, pp. 181–188.

*Constraints of the Past*

The Short- and Intermediate-Range Nuclear Forces Treaty (INF), which was signed in 1987, was the most successful attempt to constrain forward-deployed nuclear weapons that has been yet undertaken. It banned an entire class of nuclear missiles between 500 and 5500 kilometers in range—and when the missiles left Europe, they took their nuclear warheads with them. For the United States and its European allies, the ban meant that they were no longer facing a highly capable set of new Soviet nuclear missiles—the SS-20—able to strike at targets throughout NATO Europe with little warning and considerable accuracy. For the Soviet Union, it meant that a large number of nuclear weapons and their delivery systems were being removed from NATO Europe, never to be returned.

The INF negotiations were able to finesse that abiding strategic conundrum of the Cold War era: nuclear weapons in Europe were a priority focus of Soviet policy because the Kremlin saw them as a strategic threat, able to attack strategic targets in the heart of Russia at any time. For the United States and its NATO allies, the nuclear weapons in Europe were either tactical assets, to be used on the battlefield, or theater assets. They were different in missions, management, and command and control from strategic nuclear systems deployed in the continental United States.

The USSR persistently tried to draw theater weapon systems into the strategic category in negotiations, for example by insisting that French and British nuclear systems be included in the negotiations, or certain classes of naval cruise missiles. In INF, however, Soviet negotiators eventually accepted an even trade: NATO Pershing-II and ground-launched cruise missiles for Soviet SS-4s, SS-5s, SS-20s and ground-launched cruise missiles. In doing so, they achieved a great victory for Soviet diplomacy, moving a long way toward a denuclearized NATO—the very goal that they had been seeking, canceling out a strategic threat to targets inside Soviet territory.

Today, ironically, Russia seems enthusiastic to restore that threat. INF has been coming in for criticism, with Russian military leaders calling for Russia to withdraw from the treaty in order to free up the possibility of deploying intermediate-range missiles against certain of its neighbors, such as China.[24] They also argue that this step would be a good response to U.S. deployments of missile defenses in Europe. Thus, despite its reputation as a major stepping stone on the road to ending the Cold War, the INF Treaty is under threat. If abandoned, especially in favor of new Russian deployments of nuclear capabilities against Europe, then the United States and its allies will be forced to consider a like response. Although they would be very unlikely to develop new nuclear weapon systems to deploy in Europe—Pershing-II redux—they nevertheless could re-energize existing policies for deploying nuclear weapons in Europe. Certainly the removal of remaining NATO and U.S. nuclear weapons deployed in Europe would be off the table.

A second successful initiative to constrain short-range nuclear weapons in Europe were the Presidential Nuclear Initiatives of 1991–92. President George H. W. Bush and first President Gorbachev, then President Yeltsin, agreed in parallel to control and eliminate certain classes of short-range nuclear weapons. Gorbachev announced, for example, that the USSR would eliminate its entire global inventory of ground-launched short-range nuclear weapons, including artillery shells, ballistic missiles, and land mines. He also pledged that the Soviet Union would remove all nuclear warheads for surface-to-air missiles from combat units, to store them in central storage facilities; likewise, all naval nuclear weapons would be removed from surface

---

24. This issue surfaced first in 2005, when Minister of Defense Sergei Ivanov asked U.S. Defense Secretary Donald Rumsfeld how the U.S. would respond if Russia withdrew from the INF Treaty. According to an account in the *Financial Times*, "Mr. Rumsfeld told Mr. Ivanov that he did not care—but the Pentagon denied this." See Hubert Wetsel, Demetri Sevastopulo, and Guy Dinmore, "Russia confronted Rumsfeld with threat to quit key nuclear treaty," *Financial Times*, March 9, 2005.

ships, multi-purpose submarines, and land-based aircraft to be placed in central storage. Many of these warheads would also be subject to elimination.[25]

These unilateral initiatives were the first attempt at "speed dial" arms control: they moved very quickly in policy terms, ensuing from some rapid consultations between the Soviet or Russian and U.S. Presidents, and also between the Russian President and the leaders of the other newly independent states in 1992. The initiatives were seen as an excellent model to pursue when the threat had dispersed so fundamentally with the break-up of the Soviet Union. They were also seen as an urgent necessity, given concerns that the break-up itself would be the source of new and unpredictable threats from terrorists getting their hands on uncontrolled Soviet nuclear assets. Washington and Moscow seemed to agree that it was vital to get the weapons out of dispersed locations and into central storage facilities, where they could be better protected.

Unfortunately, the early comity that led to rapid agreement on the PNIs did not persist during their implementation—an outcome that was partially the result of the very nature of these reductions. Both the United States and Russia, for example, agreed that they would withdraw the nuclear weapons to central storage facilities. But because they did not agree to a definition for such facilities, as would have occurred during a negotiation, they have continued to argue over what constitutes central storage under the PNIs.

This problem was illustrated in 2001, when a story broke in the Washington press that Russia was moving nuclear weapons into Kaliningrad—a Russian enclave in Europe that is surrounded by Poland and Lithuania.[26] Although the details of this controversy remain murky, it is likely that it is actually a good illustration of differences over the definition of central storage: when the United States moved

25. For an extensive discussion of the PNIs, see Arbman and Thornton, Part I, pp. 12–14.

26. Arbman and Thornton, Part I, pp. 35–38.

short-range weapons into central storage, it moved them back to the continental United States, and it expected Russia to do the same with regard to storage facilities deep in Russia. Russia, however, seems to have defined "central" storage facilities, at least in some cases, as storage facilities still on military bases—only not adjacent to weapon-loading and -handling facilities. Russia may therefore have simply been bringing weapons back to "central storage" in Kaliningrad after routine maintenance, rather than beginning a new deployment in contravention of its PNI promises. The weapons would not have been withdrawn from Kaliningrad in the first place, but would have been placed in central storage at the base there.

Whatever the facts of this situation—no doubt classified in nature—it emphasizes the point that without a serious negotiation resulting in carefully agreed definitions, limitations, procedures, etc., questions are going to arise about how each side is implementing its unilateral initiatives. Therefore, the question for policymakers moving forward is, can the early promise of the PNIs—speedy movement to achieve reductions and even elimination of nuclear weapons—be bolstered by some means to improve confidence in their implementation? This key question will be considered in further detail when we turn to reviewing some arms control approaches.

### The Momentum of New Strategy and Deployments

While the arms control agenda has experienced stasis or even slid backward in the past 15 years, both the United States and its NATO partners, and the Russian Federation, have made many changes in strategy and the deployment of their short-range nuclear forces in that very period. The PNIs are one expression of those changes, but more important is the fact that the USSR and later Russia drove an enormous consolidation of nuclear weapons in Eurasia. In 1988, NATO estimated that the Warsaw Pact countries deployed up to 1,365 short-range nuclear missiles alone. When the Warsaw Pact and the Soviet Union began to crumble in the late 1980s, the Russian Ministry of

Defense undertook a massive withdrawal of non-strategic nuclear weapons from Eastern and Central Europe, and also from the territory of the non-Russian republics. By 1993, all of these weapons had been consolidated in Russia, and many were in a queue for elimination.[27]

This process involving the non-strategic nuclear weapons was followed by an intensive effort to withdraw over 3000 strategic nuclear weapons from Ukraine, Kazakhstan and Belarus; most of these warheads were slated for elimination, although less than 100 single-warhead missiles withdrawn from Belarus were redeployed with their mobile launchers in Russia.

The decision by the USSR and Russia to pursue an all-out consolidation of nuclear weapons on Russian territory was one of the greatest single factors contributing to continued stability in Eurasia following the breakup of the Soviet Union. The countries in the region have experienced much tension in the years since, some of it self-inflicted, some inspired by their neighbors—and here Russia has certainly played a negative role. However, if nuclear weapons had remained widely scattered around the former Soviet space and Warsaw Pact territory, the result could have been serious continuing crisis and perhaps nuclear disaster.

The consolidation also produced some interesting lessons for the arms control process. First and foremost, it clearly showed that the countries in the region are capable of working together to achieve nuclear policy goals, even when tensions are high. Ukraine, for example, never acquiesced easily to Russian proposals on the consolidation front, nor did it work easily with the United States when Washington became involved in the strategic nuclear "trilateral" discussions in 1993. There was always a persistent fear, at least among U.S. negotiators, that Ukraine meant to hold onto some of the nuclear weapons on its territory—a fear that was heightened when Ukraine froze shipments of nuclear warheads several times during the years when they were going on.

27. Gunnar and Thornton, Part I, pp. 14–19.

Ukraine was demanding that it have some assurances that the weapons flowing back to Russia were going to be eliminated, and not simply re-deployed. It eventually won those assurances, and a verification regime to back it up. This regime was comprised of experienced Ukrainian officers, many of whom had previously served in the Strategic Rocket Forces, and other nuclear experts who received access to Russian elimination facilities to ensure that the warheads being received there from Ukraine were actually destroyed. Thus, it became clear that under some circumstances, Russia was willing to accept inspectors into its warhead elimination facilities.

With this positive point, it is worth reiterating that Russia has persistently presented nuclear weapons as the only way in which it will be able to compensate for the weakness of its conventional forces. Therefore, Russia's policy embodied an important contradiction: Its responsible attitude toward ensuring that new nuclear states did not emerge in the wake of the Soviet breakup never translated into an enthusiasm for reducing reliance on nuclear weapons in its own military doctrine and strategy.

As for the United States and NATO, they have had their own share of contradictions. As mentioned above, in the 1990s European politicians did everything they could to keep nuclear weapons deployed in NATO countries out of the limelight. In recent years, however, this view has been changing, driven as much by budget pressures as by political conviction. Today, five countries in Europe—Belgium, Germany, Italy, the Netherlands, and Turkey—deploy an estimated 150–241 B-61 gravity bombs to be delivered by dual-capable aircraft.[28]

In 2005, Belgian and German parliamentarians began actively to debate NATO's policy with regard to these weapons, arguing in advance of the May 2005 Nonproliferation Treaty Review Conference

28. Hans M. Kristensen, "U.S. Nuclear Weapons Withdrawn from the United Kingdom," The Federation of American Scientists, www.fas.org/blog/ssp/2008/06/us-nuclear-weapons-withdrawn-from-the-united-kingdom.php

that NATO should consider withdrawing these weapons from Europe and sending them back to the United States. For the first time, parties in a ruling coalition, the Social Democrats and Greens in Germany, actively called for such changes. Joschka Fischer, then serving a as Germany's Foreign Minister and a member of the Green Party, called such proposals a "reasonable initiative."[29]

On top of these political developments came budgetary reality. With aircraft such as Germany's Tornado PA-200 and the F-16s deployed by Turkey and the Netherlands reaching the end of their service life, NATO countries will have to decide soon whether they will acquire dual-capable aircraft to replace them. Currently, the preference seems to be not to bear the budget burden of acquiring the extra capability to deliver nuclear weapons.[30] As Hans Kristensen has said, "The trend seems clear: Nuclear burden-sharing in NATO . . . is on a slow but steady decline toward ending altogether. The only question seems to be when and whether . . . constrained defense budgets and force structure reorganization or a political decision . . . will end it."[31]

The United States, although actively insisting on the status quo, nevertheless has itself taken serious steps to move away from reliance on nuclear weapons deployed in Europe. In 2008, for example, the United States withdrew nuclear weapons from the Royal Air Force base at Lakenheath, England. This action followed on withdrawls from Ramstein air base in Germany in 2005 and Greece in 2001.[32] Moreover, since the early 1990s, the United States has been working to consolidate nuclear missions in the new Strategic Command based in

29. Oliver Meier, "Belgium, Germany Question U.S. Tactical Nuclear Weapons in Europe," *Arms Control Today*, June 2005, p. 30.

30. Oliver Meier, "An End to U.S. Tactical Nuclear Weapons in Europe?" *Arms Control Today*, July-August 2006, p. 37.

31. Hans M. Kristensen, "U.S. Nuclear Weapons in Europe: A Review of Post-Cold War Policy, Force Levels, and War Planning," Natural Resources Defense Council, February 2005, p. 59.

32. Kristensen,     www.fas.org/blog/ssp/2008/06/us-nuclear-weapons-withdrawn-from-the-united-kingdom.php

Omaha, Nebraska. Once the Bush administration came to office, this process came to embrace the strategy of "Global Strike," and placed greater and greater emphasis on global missions emphasizing conventional rather than nuclear weapons.[33]

This lack of priority focus has manifested itself in Europe in a number of ways, perhaps most seriously in the lack of trained personnel for handling and maintaining the weapons. As early as 1993, evaluation teams were finding that there was a dearth of officers in Europe trained in nuclear operations, and that units handling nuclear weapons suffered from inadequate training across the board.[34] This problem has no doubt been exacerbated by the extra demands placed on military personnel by the war in Iraq.

In light of these trends, it appears that the United States and the NATO allies deploying nuclear weapons have arrived willy-nilly at a new place in their long and stormy marriage, without explicit action but decisive effect: They have decided to sell the nuclear beach house and buy a conventional house in the mountains. Now they just have to figure out how to tell the children.

This metaphor is facetious, but it has a sharp edge to it, honed from the attitudes of the new members of NATO. Although the countries that have been deploying nuclear weapons for decades might be ready to give them up, their new neighbors and NATO partners are likely to be less willing, if only because the neighbor on the other side, Russia, is so nasty and unpredictable—and indeed has been voicing explicit threats lately to deploy more nuclear missiles targeted at Europe, in response to missile defense deployments in NATO countries.

33. For an official statement highlighting this policy development, see Statement by James E. Cartwright, Commander United States Strategic Command Before the Strategic Force Subcommittee of the Senate Armed Services Committee on Global Strike Plans and Programs, 29 March 2006, found at armed-services.senate.gov/statemnt/2006/March/Cartwright%20SF%2003-29-06.pdf, accessed August 2, 2007.

34. Kristensen, pp. 35–36.

This threat can be countered through negotiations, and likely will be. Nevertheless, NATO's newest members will not want to move fast to denuclearize the alliance. Moreover, they will be able to cite NATO documents in support of the status quo. In 1997, NATO assured Russia that it had "no intention, no plan, and no reason" to deploy nuclear weapons on the territory of new members, but it also stated that it does not plan "to change any aspect of NATO's nuclear policy—and do not foresee any future need to do so."[35]

Thus, the Russian Federation on one side and the United States and NATO on the other are both bathed in contradictions. The contradictions will make it difficult to move forward on eliminating short-range nuclear weapons deployed in Europe. In both cases, however, the contradictions contain a seed of possibility: interesting new ideas that might be worth pursuing in the arms control realm. They will either help to set a new environment for arms control deliberations, or in some cases, a new locus for cooperation on confidence-building and arms reductions.

35. See the Alliance's Strategic Concept, approved at the Washington NATO Summit April 23–24, 1999, quoted in Woolf, p. 13.

# Appendix B: U.S. Short-Range Nuclear Weapons† in Europe, 2005

| Country | Base | Custodian[a] | Delivery Aircraft | Vaults | WS3 Capacity | | Weapons | | |
| | | | | | Capacity | Completed | U.S. | Host | Total |
|---|---|---|---|---|---|---|---|---|---|
| Belgium | Kleine Brogel AB | 701 MUNSS | Belgian F-16 | 11 | 44 | Apr 1992 | 20 | 20 | 20 |
| Germany[b] | Büchel AB | 702 MUNSS | German PA-200 Tornados | 11 | 44 | Aug 1990 | 0 | 20 | 20 |
| | Nörvenich AB* | | German PA-200 Tornados | 11 | 44 | Jun 1991 | 0 | 0 | 0 |
| | Ramstein AB | 52 FW | USF-16C/D | 55[c] | 220[e] | Jan 1992 | 90[d] | 40[e] | 130 |
| Greece | Araxos AB* | | | 6 | 24 | Sep 1997 | 0 | 0 | 0 |
| Italy | Aviano AB | 31 FW | USF-16C/D | 18 | 72 | Jan 1996 | 50 | 0 | 50 |
| | Ghedi Torre AB | 704 MUNSS | Italian PA-200 Tornados | 11 | 44 | Jan 1997 | 0 | 40 | 40 |
| Netherlands | Volkel AB | 703 MUNSS | Dutch F-16 | 11 | 44 | Sep 1991 | 0 | 20 | 20 |
| Turkey | Akinci AB* | | Turkish F-16 | 6 | 24 | Oct 1997 | 0 | 0 | 0 |
| | Balikesir AB* | | Turkish F-16 | 6 | 24 | Sep 1997 | 0 | 0 | 0 |
| | Incirlik AB | 39 FW | USF-16C/D | 25 | 100 | Apr 1998 | 50 | 40 | 90 |
| United Kingdom | RAF Lakenheath | 48 FW | USF-15E | 33 | 132 | Nov 1994 | 110 | 0 | 110 |
| TOTAL | | | | 204 | 816 | | 300 | 180 | 480 |

NOTES: †The term "tactical nuclear weapons" is used in Gunnar Arbman and Charles Thornton, "Russia's Tactical Nuclear Weapons; Part 1: Background and Policy Issues," Systems Technology, SE-172 90 Stockholm, FOI-R-1057-SE, November 2003, ISSN 1650-1942. The term "nonstrategic nuclear weapons" is also in common usage (see, for example, Amy F. Woolf, "Nonstrategic Nuclear Weapons," CRS Report for Congress, Order Code RL 32572, updated January 9, 2007, pp. 4–6). For purposes of this analysis, "tactical nuclear weapons," "nonstrategic nuclear weapons," and "short-range nuclear weapons" are treated as synonymous.

*Site is in caretaker status.

[a] Each Munitions Support Squadron (MUNSS) includes approximately 125–150 assigned personnel.

[b] Operational and support responsibilities of USAF and the Bundeswehr for munitions support bases in Germany are described in the 1960 Tool Chest Agreement.

[c] One vault is a training vault.

[d] Assumes 20 weapons removed from Araxos Air Base in 2001 were transferred to Ramstein Air Base rather than to Aviano Air Base to avoid filling the Italian vaults to capacity. Alternatively, the weapons could have been returned to the United States.

[e] Half of these weapons may have been returned to the U.S. after Memmingen Air Base closed in 2003.

SOURCE: This data appeared as Appendix A in Hans M. Kristensen, "U.S. Nuclear Weapons in Europe: A Review of Post-Cold War Policy, Force Levels, and War Planning," Natural Resources Defense Council, February 2005.

# Appendix C: Russian Short-Range Nuclear Weapons†

| Weapons | Total in service in 1991 | Outside central storage in 2000, 2001, and 2002 | Warhead inventory in 2000, 2001, and 2002 | Outside central storage in 2004 | Warhead inventory in 2004 |
|---|---|---|---|---|---|
| Ground forces | | | | | |
| Rocket forces | 4,400 | 0 | >0 | 0 | 0 |
| Artillery | 2,000 | 0 | >0 | 0 | 0 |
| Corps of Engineers | 700 | 0 | >0 | 0 | 0 |
| Air Defense | 3,000 | unknown | 1,500 | unknown | 1,500 |
| Air forces | | | | | |
| Frontal aviation | 7,000 | unknown | 3,500 | unknown | 3,500 |
| General purpose Navy | | | | | |
| Ships and submarines | 3,000 | 0 | 2,000 | 0 | 2,000 |
| Naval aviation | 2,000 | 0 | 1,400 | 0 | 1,000 |
| TOTAL | 21,700 | | 8,400 | | 8,000 |

This table uses as a baseline Alexei Arbatov's figures, supplemented by Russian official statements. The resulting estimate appeared in Gunnar Arbman and Charles Thornton, "Russia's Tactical Nuclear Weapons; Part I: Background and Policy Issues," Systems Technology, SE-172 90 Stockholm, FOI-R-1057-SE, November 2003, ISSN 1650-1942, p. 17. The original Arbatov estimates appeared in Alexei Arbatov, "Deep Cuts and De-alerting: A Russian Perspective," in Harold Feiveson, editor, *The Nuclear Turning Point: A Blueprint for Deep Cuts and De-Alerting of Nuclear Weapons*, The Brookings Institutions, Washington, D.C., 1999, p. 319.

It must be emphasized that estimates of Russian short-range nuclear weapons vary widely, as Arbman and Thornton catalogue in their study. I am grateful to Bruce Blair, Hans Kristensen, and Victoria Samson for pointing out that the Russians might have fewer than 3000 operational tactical nuclear weapons in 2007, of which 700 would be for defensive operations (100 for ABM purposes, 600 for air defense), and 1629 would be for offensive operations (974 for bombers and 655 for naval delivery). As Kristensen points out, however, "These are best estimates. There's no solid information." E-mail exchange with Bruce Blair and Victoria Sampson, September 5, 2007.

†Gunnar and Arbman use the term "tactical nuclear weapons"; the term "nonstrategic nuclear weapons" is also in common usage (see, for example, Amy F. Woolf, "Nonstrategic Nuclear Weapons," CRS Report for Congress, Order Code RL 32572, updated January 9, 2007, pp. 4–6). For purposes of this analysis, "tactical nuclear weapons," "nonstrategic nuclear weapons," and "short-range nuclear weapons" are treated as synonymous.

# 4. Challenges of Verification and Compliance within a State of Universal Latency
## Raymond J. Juzaitis
## John E. McLaughlin

**Executive Summary**

Achieving the vision of a world free of nuclear weapons will require a monitoring and verification effort more challenging, comprehensive, and systematic than anything attempted in arms control heretofore. Whereas most previous arms control arrangements have been geographically and functionally limited, this effort will have to grow to global scope and involve all aspects of the nuclear fuel cycle and weapons cycle while also encompassing actors ranging from established nuclear states to non-state entities.

There are at least four major areas in which monitoring and verification would play a crucial role on the way to the desired end state.

*First*, the established *nuclear weapons states* (NWS) must revive momentum toward further deep reductions in nuclear weapons and ensure the renewal of essential monitoring and verification provisions that otherwise will become moot when the START I agreement expires in 2009. They must also enter into negotiations on non-deployed warheads now in storage, about which little has been revealed in previous bargaining.

- For the first of these tasks—continuing reductions of deployed weapons—intelligence agencies have both a template and a body

of precedent and should be well prepared to monitor and to contribute toward verification of compliance.

- Regarding non-deployed weapons, however, intelligence would
  face a tougher task, for which success would require extensive
  new data declarations to cue intelligence sources.

- Requirements for technology development to support the monitoring and verification mission would need to be tailored to
  achieve the balance between transparency (confidence of the verifying party) and legitimate needs to protect nuclear weapon design information, proprietary information related to process design
  and technology, as well as operations security (opsec) -related
  logistical information critical for protection of materials and weapons.

*Second*, diplomacy will have to focus on slowing and ultimately
stopping the momentum toward nuclear armament in the *non-nuclear
weapons states*—a task that should benefit from any demonstrable
progress toward stockpile reductions in the current nuclear weapons
states. The Non-Proliferation Treaty will need to be enhanced by aug-
menting and expanding the Safeguards regime to develop better confidence in the completeness of member states' declarations.

- Monitoring and verification in this arena will be more difficult by
  an order of magnitude because there is virtually no tradition of
  arms control, with its associated provisions for declarations and
  inspections outside of the NPT regime—nor has much systematic
  thought been given by these countries to deterrence.

- Successful monitoring and verification can occur, but intelligence
  will have to move in lockstep with diplomacy to embed the arms
  control practices developed among the NWS in the past.

- Based on prior experience, it is doubtful that monitoring confidence will come quickly, but it can be achieved if, as in the past,
  we break what will seem to be overwhelmingly difficult problems
  into individual tasks that are achievable.

*Third*, to account for and globally secure *nuclear explosive material*, a number of initiatives would have to converge to produce what might be called a global Fissile Material Control Initiative (FMCI). Current programs and initiatives, such as the Fissile Material Cutoff Treaty (FMCT), if successfully negotiated and brought into force, along with natural follow-on programs to the Cooperative Threat Reduction Program and the Materials, Protection, Control, and Accountability Program could form a foundation for a more rigorous system of accounting and security.

- Confident monitoring and verification of this effort would require an unprecedented aggregation of monitoring techniques.
- Thorough and detailed data declarations would be the crucial starting point to enable essential synergy among National Technical Means, human source reporting, on-site inspections, and other techniques.
- Broadly based, "bottom-up" awareness related to integrated security management of nuclear materials would need to follow a path similar to a World Association of Nuclear Operators in the field of nuclear reactor safety.

*Fourth*, international consensus must be built regarding ways to deter—or in the extreme respond to—secret attempts by countries to "breakout" of any agreements that are achieved. The challenges here are many: developing diagnostic tools to detect and disable any nuclear devices smuggled into the country, building international consensus on the conditions that would justify a "last resort" use of force to deter a potential violator, and initiating cooperative multinational work on a Ballistic Missile Defense capability to counter unexpected threats by treaty violators.

- Intelligence challenges would be substantial but manageable in this environment; by the time the global system had achieved a state of "universal nuclear latency," there would be such an extensive body of data and practice that intelligence would have an excellent basis for detection programs.

- As the National Academy of Sciences noted in its recent study (*Monitoring Nuclear Weapons and Nuclear Explosive Materials: Methods and Capabilities*, 2005), it is very doubtful that a clandestine nuclear weapons program would escape early detection by the intelligence community. The harder questions would center on what to do about it.

Finally it must be noted that efforts to reach a nuclear weapons-free world cannot ignore the growing threat posed by *non-state actors* such as al-Qaeda. Presumably, their access to nuclear material and expertise would diminish as progress is made on all the foregoing objectives. But their clear intent to actually use nuclear capability for attack or blackmail gives them an especially menacing character—made all the more worrisome by uncertainties about how to deter them from such use. Detecting and countering their activities in the future will, as now, require all intelligence capabilities, with HUMINT playing an especially prominent role. Broad information-sharing would enhance the effectiveness of international and domestic law enforcement.

As we progress with force reductions and implementation of the steps toward realizing the vision, as discussed in the *Wall Street Journal* op-ed and in the other papers prepared for this conference, we should expect growing trust between the nations, starting with the U.S. and Russia. This, in turn, can be expected to lead to increasing transparency in all these nuclear matters, thereby improving prospects for being able to monitor compliance and verify that our security interests are not being compromised.

The central argument of this paper is that a coherent and comprehensive technical/policy paradigm should be sought in order to enable attainment of the vision being analyzed at this conference. Such a paradigm would provide the proper vehicle(s) for managing the inevitable security risk, as well as supporting the political confidence and international trust that would be required to reduce nuclear arms to very low levels over time and to provide the pervasive vigilance demanded of a universally latent nuclear world, i.e., a world in which most nuclear weapons have been eliminated but in which many countries would retain the technological know-how and requisite materials to resume nuclear weapons work. Such vigilance would continually address the risk of nuclear material diversion in a world enjoying expansive utilization of nuclear energy, as well as provide early warning of technical activities indicative of weaponization.

## Introduction

Much has been written with regard to the relationship between verification and trust between adversaries when addressing arms control negotiations. The issue is central to our discussion at this conference: will going to the Zero Option result in verification requirements that would simply be unsustainable in any practical sense?

In 1961, President Kennedy's Chief Science Advisor, Jerome Wiesner, proposed a notional model for gauging the amount of inspection required to effectively verify the degree of disarmament achieved [1]. A corresponding graphic is reproduced as Figure 1.

- At high levels of armament, and at a particular specified trust level between parties, fairly high uncertainties in the assessed level of arms could be tolerated from a less than perfect verification regime because the consequences of incorrect assessments were dwarfed by the sheer size of the stockpiles.

- However, as disarmament proceeded and the number of arms held by each side tended to much lower numbers (even approaching "zero"), the marginal utility of each extra warhead becomes more significant, driving the required work of inspection to very high order in order to achieve very exacting conditions on uncertainty.

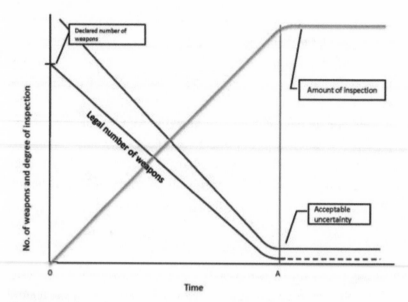

Figure 1.   The Wiesner Curve, showing relationship between extent of disarmament and demand for inspection. (Reproduced from Krass, 1985)

- Simply put, if there are few weapons left, your opponent having
  a few of them hidden means more.

If this, indeed, were the case, our vision of a world of zero nuclear
weapons would be doomed due to the unacceptably high cost of verification. But technology that can more accurately portray what your
counterpart has could reduce distrust. If you have more confidence in
the means of detection, it cancels out the worst concerns in Wiesner's
model. Therefore, we need an explicit and nationally supported program of technology development to prepare for the eventuality of
getting close to zero and therefore needing greater transparency than
current techniques are likely to provide.

In a world completely transformed by paradigm-shifting advances
in microelectronics and sensors, nanotechnologies, and information
technology, it is hard to imagine that the power of technology could
not be engaged to sense, communicate, characterize, and identify the

observables of illicit activity in a timely enough manner to permit effective policy responses.

- The key challenge would be to create coherent government-sponsored programs that would be effective at motivating the development process toward ambitious technology performance goals.

Some means must also be found to quantify relevant concepts and metrics and provide an objective basis for coherently driving the technology requirements. Periodic assessments that would engage the entire technical and policy community and could be broadly reported would aid in creating such requirements. At the least, such assessments would guarantee long-term vigilance.

In this regard, some methodological and practical means for quantifying and periodically assessing "latency" must be developed. We notionally associate "latency" with time delay needed to attain an imminent nuclear threat: thus, higher latency is "good," lower latency is "bad." "Proliferation resistance" is another quality or characteristic that is referenced in multiple forums, but never methodically quantified. It is a quality that is a key component of latency. The challenge remains to quantify these concepts and to transform them to technology requirements.

## The Four Interlocking Verification Strategies of a Comprehensive Framework

*The new paradigm differs from "traditional" notions of arms control*

In constructing a framework and appropriate terms of reference for programs that would implement a path forward for the Zero Option, it is important to reiterate a point made earlier: The confluence of terrorism and proliferation create the basis of a newly emerged threat environment that the United States has not heretofore faced in a coherent manner. Post-9/11 considerations addressing the potential attack on this nation with stolen, smuggled, or improvised nuclear explosives generally characterize such an event as an "asymmetric" attack on the sole remaining superpower. Therefore, more traditional approaches to nuclear disarmament (e.g., those pursued in the SALT and START epochs) must be augmented by more broadly based initiatives that address the ultimate "source" of nuclear threat—the special materials that can be used in relatively small quantities to render a very effective and destructive asymmetric attack.

Such a threat creates renewed urgency to address the Zero Option for this option alone promises to make tractable the challenge of controlling nuclear materials indefinitely on such a global scale. Correspondingly, the focus must shift to the security of, and accountability for, nuclear materials worldwide. The United States government has only partially addressed this concern with the chartering of a Domestic Nuclear Detection Office (DNDO). However, detection by itself is not enough to adequately address the overall risk of the threat, driven as it is by unacceptable consequences. Access to relatively small amounts of the special nuclear materials is all that stands between security and disaster. Such a threat environment does not involve stockpile-size quantities of material, but may indeed be hidden in the uncertainties surrounding such large quantities. Given the huge global landscape on which sources of nuclear material are to be found, ensuring comprehensive security of these materials becomes an imperative. The United States must engage with the other nations of the world to address this problem.

The concept of "virtual stockpiles" has been addressed before. Molander and Wilson [2] identified the "Virtual Abolition of Nuclear Arsenals" as one of several alternative future scenarios ("asymptotes") for post-Cold War (but pre-9/11) deliberations on nuclear strategy. Even then, the unprecedented requirement for the attending intrusive and relentless international inspection regime was well understood. In light of today's threat environment, however, we are compelled to focus on what it would take to reach such as state of "universal latency," and to galvanize our collective resources to go beyond conceptualizing to actually managing our global nuclear security environment to such an end state.

The intelligence community (IC) will play an unarguably pivotal role in this envisioned paradigm. Although we will address several strategies comprising an overarching framework for achieving universal latency, a common denominator across all of them will be successful end-to-end exploitation of information by the IC. The IC has the experience and skills to successfully monitor the various end states we seek in this proposal and to contribute to verification decisions. That said, the intelligence requirements for this will be more challenging and labor intensive than anything else in arms control history and will have to compete with escalating demands for intelligence coverage of complex post-Cold War problems.

- In contrast to earlier arms control intelligence tasks, this one will gradually expand to be global in scope, as compared to the geographically and functionally limited requirements of the Cold War.
- The effort will have to go well beyond the kinds of elements arms control intelligence was previously most comfortable with and skilled in monitoring—silos, deployed nuclear weapons, large conventional formations.
- On the other hand, the goal of a world free of nuclear weapons and with nuclear material effectively secured meshes well with the intelligence community's current highest priority: the potential nexus between terrorism and weapons of mass destruction.

There are basically five tools essential to successful intelligence monitoring:

- *National Technical Means (NTM)* is popularly understood to mean collection of information by satellites capable of taking photographs and intercepting communications. Although this is the most common interpretation of the term, precise definitions of NTM were resisted during Cold War negotiations, largely because neither side wanted to bargain directly over the role of human intelligence (HUMINT), fearing that to do so would implicitly authorize the other side to recruit spies as part of the monitoring process. This imprecision allowed the sides to understand that NTM could actually include all of a country's intelligence capabilities.

- That said, *HUMINT* is unquestionably a vital tool that will become more important in any effort that aims to monitor "universal latency." As we note elsewhere, the closer we get to that end state, the more important will be intent and motivation—facets that technical intelligence can seldom discern and that often only HUMINT, i.e., classic espionage, can confidently gauge.

- *On-Site Inspections* (*OSI*)—everything from periodic visits to in-place observation (portal monitoring)—will also be vital at various stages. Experience has shown that this technique is most effective when it is fairly routine as opposed to aggressive or challenging, particularly when one of the goals is building mutual confidence. To be sure, there is a role for aperiodic, unscheduled visits but these are most effective when integrated into a series of predictable and routine visits.

- *Declarations* of existing capability are essential to give intelligence a baseline from which to make judgments. Without such declarations, all sides start with a deficit of confidence, intelligence has to define its own arena of operations, and it is almost impossible to move beyond a cat-and-mouse mentality.

- *Specialized sensors*, with capabilities ranging from detection of radiation to interpretation of hyper-spectral data, also have an important part to play. Many are useful primarily in close-in rather than remote roles. Their design and operating characteristics must reflect the specific nature of the monitoring task and its physical environment, and new technologies must adapt in a timely way to opportunities that present themselves for exploitation.

*None of these techniques is likely to suffice alone for any particular monitoring task.* While a critical insight may occasionally come from a single intelligence source, the key to monitoring success is *synergy among all of these methods.* For example, declarations can provide the guide for targeting on-site inspections, while NTM can allow you to watch the "back door" to see if anything is being removed from a site slated for examination. Or when NTM detects an anomaly that cannot be squared with declarations or the results of inspections, a good HUMINT source may be able to "get under the roof" or "behind the doors" that NTM cannot penetrate.

The intelligence community will need to focus on how to maximize this synergy as the effort goes forward. A way must be found to develop an effective and timely manner for linking data collection, information analysis and integrative technical assessment, and development/deployment of new collection technologies, in an "end-to-end" manner that creates an endless stream of actionable information to the policy community. The IC must work closely with policymakers to ensure that diplomats negotiate provisions that take advantage of particular capabilities. For example, this means ensuring that if the community has a portable or covert device capable of detecting radiation, that provision is made to install it along a road likely to be used by cheaters to "clean" a facility. *This kind of synergy will be key to the success of monitoring efforts and will increase in importance as we get closer to "universal latency."*

To get to the desired end state, intelligence will have to monitor activities in diverse arenas, ranging from traditional nuclear weapons states to new nuclear weapons states and non-state actors. The difficulty, prominence, and importance of particular techniques—and the requirement for innovation—will increase as the ladder is climbed to higher and higher states of latency. In fact, latency must be quantified in some manner, regularly assessed, and eventually managed across numerous negotiations over time, and at both ends of the nuclear capability spectrum. The respective roles of different states in this regard must be played simultaneously to realize the hoped-for holistic effect.

First, the nuclear weapons states (NWS) must proceed to *increase* the "latency" of their deployed weapon stockpiles, by pursuing measures that would give increased warning time and would systemically shift emphasis onto conventional responses to undergird their strategic posture. In effect, reduction of the nuclear stockpiles would proceed along with steady progress in de-legitimizing the use of nuclear weapons in matters of national defense.

In parallel, the Non-Nuclear Weapon States (NNWS) would be challenged to *maintain* their nuclear capability latency at very high levels, i.e., long time delays before launch, restricting nuclear technology to civilian applications, most notably in meeting the energy needs of developing and developed nations and supporting sustainable development in the global community. The promise of "Atoms for Peace" would be revisited, but this time in a much more controlled manner that pays more than lip service to the imperatives of proliferation resistance.

Assessing and verifying the actual capability latency of nations that participate in fuel cycle activities will require the transparency achievable with an independent, internationally managed inspectorate supported by modern technology. This would allow timely and precise assessments with regard to declared activities and material stocks, but with an intrusiveness level restrained to some degree, reflecting the trust placed in the inspectorate by the inspected nation. Therefore, as noted above, the NTM of member states will still play a very major role in a comprehensive program. The proper "firewalls" will need to be maintained between these two sets of capabilities to ensure the continued effectiveness of each.

The greatest perceived danger to a proposed paradigm of universal latency would be the possibility of breakout. For this reason, a deterrence posture must be redesigned away from historical practice driven by threats and counterthreats of arsenal exchange. Deterrence might now be achieved through implementation of tailored, but credible and timely non-nuclear response capabilities to preclude success of any imminent nuclear threat. Another mechanism might involve institutionalizing some reconstitution capability under appropriate mechanisms of legitimized authority.

It is impossible to imagine how anything like the foregoing proposal for managing nuclear latency could have any chance for success without a return to bilateral and multilateral negotiations. Only such processes can bring forth the attendant verification protocols designed to engage transformational technology, as well as broadly based confidence-building measures, in providing the salutary feedback effects in the reduction process. The latter would build trust and hopefully preclude the types of unbearable cost burdens associated traditionally with effectively verifying very small stockpiles (Wiesner "prediction").

**Strategy 1. Verifying phased stockpile reductions**

The role played by the NWS in a comprehensive global latency management framework involves a demonstrable, effective effort at negotiating a phased reduction in the levels of stockpiled nuclear weapons, consistent with global and national security requirements of the P5, as well as with obligations embodied in Article VI of the Non-Proliferation Treaty. These latter obligations were renewed in 1995 as part of the agreement reached at the 25th Anniversary Review Conference of the NPT, which extended the treaty indefinitely. Pursuing a notional road map consistent with these obligations begins by first identifying the verification challenges along the path of stockpile reductions.

The arguments for and against specific stockpile reduction mileposts are beyond the scope of this paper. Nevertheless, any potential set of these will step through a natural progression of stages that will require special consideration in blending verification technology with trust-enabled procedures to attain the desired transparency objectives. The three general stages will include (a) return to negotiated verification protocols; (b) monitoring of nuclear warhead inventories at various stages or "states" of latency, throughout a prolonged period of stockpile reductions; (c) monitoring nuclear materials and "virtual stockpiles" at the end-state of the Zero Option. We will consider these in greater detail.

*Return to verification protocols*

The first step in following a long path to the Zero Option will obviously begin with a return to the negotiation of verification protocols, presumably to accompany the already agreed-upon strategic arsenal levels of the Moscow Treaty of 2002 (SORT). The clock is running out on the START I accords, which are scheduled to expire in 2009. This treaty imposed reductions in deployed strategic arsenals to the level of 1600 delivery vehicles with an attending number of 6000 warheads. Special counting rules had been agreed upon for imputing numbers of warheads to the verified number of strategic delivery vehicles, which were the actual "countable" entities referenced in the accompanying verification measures.

Meanwhile, the Moscow Treaty was signed between Presidents Bush and Putin in 2002, merely documenting the unilateral declarations by the U.S. and Russian Federation to reduce strategic deployed warheads to 1700–2200 on each side. In the declared interest of ensuring maximum "flexibility," no further accompanying disaggregation of the total numbers was identified and no verification protocols were negotiated. The numerical limits were to take effect (and then immediately expire) on December 31, 2012. Presumably, both sides have been reducing their numbers since 2003.

Given the verification provisions associated with START I are still in effect until 2009, it would seem a most logically straightforward step to immediately begin the required planning to apply the means of verification established under the START process to the numerical limits set by SORT, and extending them to enable adequate verification of further reductions for both deployed and responsive forces.

The technology development challenges for this first step would be, in fact, only incremental. Means and protocols for verification had been worked out in START I and START II with a focus on counting delivery vehicles (missiles and launchers). The arms control experience of the Cold War gives us a proven template for monitoring deployed nuclear weapons in established nuclear weapons states. The traditional combination of declarations, OSI, and NTM provides a solid basis for progress among states such as the U.S., the Russian Federation, the U.K., and France.

Eventually the challenge will shift to bringing other established nuclear weapons states, principally China and Israel, into some kind of negotiation/monitoring regime. This will also be required for newly minted de facto NWS such as India and Pakistan. Most of the "heavy lifting" for this will be in the diplomatic realm. Intelligence has a proven track record and ample precedent to work with.

However, the challenges for intelligence and technology development will increase in moving to the next level; i.e., that associated with providing the necessary transparency and monitoring capability that would be required for building confidence in the process of controlling actual numbers of warheads, both those in responsive as well as deployed status.

*Verification of Warhead Inventories*

As we proceed to the next phase of stockpile reductions, a key principle of latency management would make it imperative to include provisions for ensuring the irreversibility of deeper stockpile reductions. This would involve appropriate monitoring capabilities to enable transparency and resulting confidence in the negotiated joint elimination of nuclear warheads. However, the case of verifying numbers of deployed (and for that matter: stored, disassembled, and destroyed) warheads is much more formidable than counting numbers of the more easily observable missiles and strategic bombers. The former are smaller, more numerous, and can be more easily moved and stored clandestinely than the larger delivery vehicles.

Dealing with non-deployed nuclear warheads will be a tougher challenge for intelligence, with no proven template and very few precedents. Absolutely key to success here will be declarations, followed by on-site inspections. *The importance of HUMINT will begin to increase*, because we will be entering a realm where intent is untested, practice is scant, and suspicions will be more prominent. So will the importance of increasing trust between nations as the goals for reductions to lower force levels proceed.

Thinking about all of these challenges, it is important to recall one of the major lessons of the past: *The key to successful monitoring of arms control and nonproliferation agreements is to break overwhelmingly hard problems into individual tasks that are achievable.* This has historically and successfully been done by implementing a series of unilateral intelligence and multilateral negotiated measures that work synergistically together.

- Negotiated information exchanges provide a framework for understanding normalcy.
- The exchanges declare where material of relevance to an agreement is normally based, outline the ranges of usual behavior in storing and moving such material, and provide checkable facts for on-site inspections, technical verification measures, and intelligence targeting.

In some respects, data declarations are like income tax returns. They provide a basis for a monitoring organization to sample behavior to see if there are discrepancies that require further review. For international agreements, the sampling is done through some combination of negotiated inspection measures, overt technical monitoring, and covert intelligence-collection methods.

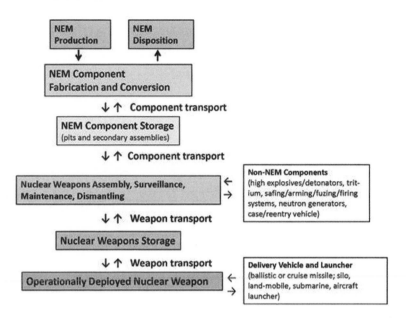

Figure 2.   Life-cycle stages of nuclear warhead showing "latency" gradation. (Reproduced from *Monitoring Nuclear Weapons and Nuclear Explosive Materials: Methods and Capabilities*, Committee on International Security and Arms Control [National Research Council], National Academies Press, 2005)

Actual implementation of such general approaches begs the identification of an appropriate model that would serve as a vehicle for framing discussions that center on the life cycle of nuclear weapons. A model would also provide a framework for guiding the deployment of technologies that would be implemented in somewhat more intrusive verification measures. Such a model is presented in the National Academies report, "Monitoring Nuclear Weapons and Nuclear-Explosive Materials: An Assessment of Methods and Capabilities" [3]. An illustrative schematic is reproduced as Figure 2. ("NEM" refers to "Nuclear Explosive Materials.")

As illustrated by this schema, one could "reverse-track" the stockpile gestation of a nuclear weapon from bulk nuclear material, through component fabrication and storage, weapon assembly, weapon storage, and ultimately operational deployment in the stockpile. By drawing an analogy to NPT Safeguards, a material/unit balance can be identified in such a representation, and provisions implemented for monitoring the in-flows, out-flows, and inferring the accumulated (or depleted) stocks within each material balance unit.

The approach would be straightforward in principle, but would demand special attention to ensure chain of custody could be established while observing materials moving "in" and "out" of "black boxes" that figuratively represent processes that, for security purposes, would be obscured from direct inspection and observation. This would include any activities that could reveal the details of point designs of nuclear weapons, or reveal information that could render them vulnerable.

The overall verification "tasks" could thus be identified in the following graded scheme:

- Number of aggregate deployed and non-deployed missiles and launchers;
- Number of deployed warheads at some alert level;
- Number of non-deployed warheads;
- Number of non-deployed warheads removed/de-mated from carrier systems;
- Locations of facilities at which non-deployed warheads are stored;
- Number of warheads dismantled into components: pits, secondary assemblies, and non-nuclear supporting sub-systems;
- Locations of facilities at which nuclear weapon components are stored;
- Mass of bulk nuclear material declared "in excess" of stockpile requirements;
- Location of facilities at which military stocks of nuclear material are stored.

The overall approach for each step in this graded scheme would proceed along the following general pattern:

- Nation formally *declares* numbers or masses of weapons/components/materials within a general category;
- Verifying nation, through on-site inspections, deploys observers and equipment to *monitor* the transport of declared items into and out of the material balance envelope, as well as sample some number of items of the inventory within the envelope to ensure against clandestine diversion;
- Radiation-detection equipment, often supplemented by deployable simulation capability, is employed to establish the *validity* of the observed items and to infer the status of the declared material balance.

## *Data Exchange and Encryption*

Clearly, baseline information for declared quantities, along with associated uncertainties of this information, would be key to subsequently tracking with confidence any further negotiated reductions in numbers. Declarations may be exchanged at agreed-upon intervals following establishment of the baselines, with frequencies most likely in inverse proportion to numbers being counted. Ultimately, one could envision continuous monitoring with real-time reporting of the relevant quantities. This would obviously presume a significantly high trust level between adversaries, but one that could conceivably be attained through successful implementation and experience in verification activities associated with earlier agreements.

The cost/benefit of such a process is driven by the presumed "value" of confidence one party places in the numbers declared by its adversary and confirmed through verification. The countervailing "costs" include the resources required to implement the verification procedures, and more importantly the enhanced vulnerability associated with the monitored party's nuclear assets or national security posture given the detail of declarations made and confirmed.

- The latter factor takes on much more significance in light of the proliferation and operational security risk that is entailed when technical details related to "point designs" and capabilities, as well as locations of weapons and materials in facilities, are made public.

In this regard, technologies that can protect the identity of the source or encrypt the associated declaration information would be absolutely critical for enabling implementation of verification measures. Technologies like this have already been developed in the commercial sector and would need to be adapted to verification needs. Some of these are described in *Monitoring Nuclear Weapons and Nuclear Explosive Materials* (National Research Council, 2005) [3].

Information to be declared can be broken down into data records. The plain text information in these records will contain certain descriptive details about agreed-upon controlled items and materials, as well as their location. The objective is to allow intelligible access to these details ONLY to the verifying party, and to hide it from everyone else.

- One would ideally like to put each record of data into an opaque envelope and give it to the intended receiver, who would be the only one who can open the envelope to access the data.
- This can be done electronically in a process called "encryption." (Similar techniques are now being broadly applied to protect personal identity information on modern laptop computers in light of highly publicized losses of huge quantities of such data when the computers have been lost or stolen.)
- Data records involved in declarations could be carefully encrypted by the declaring party prior to transmittal. Thereafter, the verifying party would sample the records and would request specific encryption "keys" (algorithms used to descramble the cipher lines).
- These then would be applied and the plain-text descriptions would be reassembled. The verifying party would randomly sample from

among the huge number of encrypted records (sampling rate based on the degree of confidence desired) and would use the information to confirm the declarations with actual inspections.

*On-Site Inspection*

At the core of any verification protocol, the declarations made by a particular state must be *confirmed* to some determined level of confidence by the inspecting party. The declarations discussed in the previous paragraph can be confirmed by several means, but the most straightforward involve some type of on-site inspection (OSI), either routinely scheduled at predetermined intervals, or arising out of specific challenges. Agreed-upon detection technologies and monitoring instruments are used by inspectors to confirm the identity, numbers, and location of declared warheads, all of which give off radiation signatures that are like "nuclear fingerprints." The use of such inspections has been successfully demonstrated in verifying the numbers of missiles and launchers that were the subject of START I and INF (Intermediate Nuclear Force Reductions) treaties.

Monitoring of declared items would be greatly facilitated by extensive data exchanges, which would give inspectors a clear expectation of what they should find on any particular missile or bomber, or at various storage facilities. Deviations from the database, due to lags in notifications or other factors, could be clarified by the host side in their briefings to inspectors at the start of the inspection. Interestingly, whereas NTM can provide valuable information regarding warheads from telemetry data obtained in observing flight tests, usefulness in determining the actual number deployed is significantly less. On the other hand, NTM can be extremely helpful in periodic or persistent surveillance of activities surrounding declared sites and facilities.

In principle, presumed nuclear warheads could be removed and scanned with a portable neutron detector. They may be presented to the inspector, however, inside a simple-shaped container to prevent visual observation of the details of the weapon design. Neutron-detection technology is employed to identify the presence of actual nuclear material. However, the detection equipment must be designed to be "spoof-proof" in order to ascertain that shielding materials have not been inserted to reduce the intrinsic radiation emitted by the warhead, thus forcing the inspector to infer smaller quantities of material.

There are ways to actually detect such spoofing shields. In conjunction with the neutron-measurement procedure, a low-intensity gamma or neutron source may be placed opposite the appropriate detector and an independent measurement taken of the resulting radiation field to characterize multiplication and shielding properties of the cannister assembly. Some computational model of what the "correct" device would look like would be used to enable the proper inferences. Under the INF Treaty, agreed procedures had been developed for neutron-counting to determine that a missile was a permitted SS-25 with one warhead, and not a prohibited SS-20 with three warheads. This was necessary because the Soviets deployed SS-25 ICBMs at former SS-20 IRBM bases.

Depending on the sophistication of detection technology agreed upon in negotiations, it is generally desirable to field detection systems that can identify specific radioactive isotopes, and especially can identify the presence of fissile materials. Such technology, previously only available for laboratory settings, has now been developed for portable applications. For example, a "Fission Meter" has recently been commercialized by ORTEC (developed originally by Lawrence Livermore National Laboratory) that can identify uranium and plutonium by specifically counting neutrons that are emitted simultaneously from a nucleus by the process of spontaneous fission. Such correlated neutrons help in distinguishing source material from cosmic ray background, as well as indicating neutron multiplication by fissioning nuclei. The 57-pound package contains the He-3 neutron detectors as well as the HV supplies and discriminator circuits used to identify the "simultaneous" events. Such technology was previously unavailable to support the earlier verification mission.

## Chain of Custody

However, the requirement for ensuring "chain of custody" from deployment to storage through destruction implies that some process will be required to authenticate the object (observable through detection equipment) inside a black box. Ultimately, how can one be assured that the fissile material presented as "excess" actually came from a nuclear weapon that was dismantled? The importance of establishing "chain of custody" for designated devices and materials would need to be balanced with due regard for protecting secret nuclear weapon design information. The initial authentication process would then be followed by a rigorous accounting process based on tracking tags and seals. This is where technology could play a major role.

The use of "templates," "attributes," and "information barriers" become key enablers in this regard ([3], pp. 97–108). A nuclear weapon, or one of its key special nuclear material-bearing components, has specific physical observables and signatures that may be measured or observed in the process of identification. These are labeled "attributes."

For example, a prototype attribute system was demonstrated to Russian scientists at Los Alamos National Laboratory as part of the Fissile Material Transparency Technology Demonstration in 2000. It had been developed to confirm the authenticity of plutonium pits to be stored in the Russian Mayak facility. Attributes included the presence of plutonium; isotopic composition of plutonium; plutonium age; plutonium mass; symmetry of the plutonium mass distribution; and absence of plutonium oxide. Specific identification of emitted gamma-ray spectra and signals from neutron multiplicity counters were employed to identify "true" pits by inferring the attributes from these measurements.

A "template"-based system would also key on attributes such as emitted gamma-ray spectra from a particular weapon configuration, but could conceivably include other physical observables such as mechanical, thermal, or acoustical properties. The specific signature, effectively a "fingerprint" of the device, would be compared to an established reference object that was known to be an authentic weapon of a particular type, thus establishing the validity of the "test" object. Template approaches bear the security cost of having to store sensitive data associated with the reference device or component.

Clearly, in many cases such measurements could directly reveal secret design features of nuclear weapon assemblies. The protection of this information in the application of template and attribute identification systems is the principle behind "information barriers." Such systems are generally designed to automate the data acquisition and analysis process, with a resulting unclassified "summary" display (such as "green" or "red" light) as the only observable available to an inspector. The information barrier system would be designed in a way that prevents access to any compromising intermediate data or analysis product, with strict system design requirements to prevent unwarranted transmission of signals across the "barrier."

Once a weapon or component is authenticated via procedures described previously, it could be placed inside a specially designed and constructed container, then tagged with a unique identifier (e.g., serial number, barcode, or other intrinsic characteristic that is difficult to alter) and enclosed with a tamper-resistant or tamper-revealing seal. Tags and seals would then be used together, tracked and monitored in the "chain" of events that accompany the life history of the enclosed device. Any observed tampering would provide the unambiguous evidence that a violation has occurred along the chain of custody.

*Perimeter-Portal Continuous Monitoring*

The conceptual model of device/material balance within a physical or imagined "boundary" around declared facilities becomes the basis for the design and implementation of monitoring systems to confirm declarations made by the inspected party, and to track changes from the baseline over time. A minimal monitoring system could involve declarations and perhaps a one-time visit to storage facilities to establish a baseline. Much more intrusive arrangements can also be envisioned.

It would be possible to establish a Perimeter-Portal Continuous Monitoring system (PPCM) at what would presumably be a small number of declared storage sites. The two sides have extensive experience with such systems under the INF and START treaties. Under START, the sides were allowed up to 30 monitors at a PPCM site. They do not enter the site, but have complete access to the perimeter at any time and can examine items leaving the site that have dimensions such that they could be a controlled item. The small size of warheads could make this a burdensome task, but traffic into, or out of, a facility that only stores warheads should be light. The warhead containers could be tagged and/or could contain a unique identifier. Nuclear detectors could be used to verify that the container did contain nuclear material consistent with a warhead.

One possibility that would avoid extreme intrusiveness would be to establish radiation portal monitors at the entry/exit points of the storage facility. These could resemble the portals now being deployed extensively at foreign and U.S. border crossing points, as provided for by the DOE/NNSA Second Line of Defense and DHS/DNDO port inspection programs. Because these could be relatively large, they could be more sophisticated than handheld devices. They could be designed to detect both neutrons and gamma-rays.

Technology development objectives for radiation detection in DOE, DHS, and DoD programs are currently emphasizing the simultaneous portability and resolution capabilities needed to identify isotopes (including uranium enrichments). Precise spectroscopic measurements of gamma-ray emissions have traditionally involved high-purity germanium-based sensors that required bulky support equipment to provide cooling to cryogenic conditions, greatly complicating the logistics associated with verification activities. Recent developments have included battery-operated, ultra-reliable mechanical cryocoolers (e.g., Stirling cycle) or room-temperature semiconductor materials (e.g., cadmium-zinc-telluride or CZT) to allow for handheld spectroscopic identification capability.

The verification technology program for the Zero Option could very easily leverage the investments now being made in Nonproliferation, Homeland Security, and DoD Force Protection programs. Moreover, the high false alarm rates experienced by similar devices at U.S. border crossings, due to agricultural products, ceramics, people with radioactive isotopes in their bodies following medical procedures, etc., should not be a major concern at a warhead storage facility. Each type of warhead could be measured to establish a baseline radiation signature or template. The host side should declare each incoming or outgoing warhead and the portal monitor should be able to confirm this declaration. Accurate logs of all movements of warheads into and out of the facility would be essential. In general, however, while Pu should generally be detectable, HEU may not be, due to its much lower intrinsic radioactivity. Neutron-based "active" detection systems are being developed to induce fissions in uranium and then measure the emitted gamma spectra.

Given the precautions noted above, non-deployed warheads could be tracked into and out of declared storage facilities through designated portals in the engineered facility perimeter, or even between cells or blocks of assembly/disassembly facilities. It would clearly be desirable to have inspection personnel manning the monitors around the clock. If this is considered too intrusive or expensive, it might be possible to establish automated systems, which would transmit data back to an operations center. Such a scheme could draw heavily upon the remote monitoring systems used successfully in Iraq by UNSCOM and UNMOVIC. A system of cameras would be highly desirable to assure that warheads were not entering or leaving the complex at locations other than the designated entry/exit points. A still less intrusive system could dispense with real-time remote monitoring, relying more upon periodic visits to check logs and unmanned monitors. This could resemble the system used by the IAEA to monitor Safeguards Agreements.

Under either the manned or unmanned scenario, periodic inspections could be conducted to provide confidence in the data being accumulated. Attempting to look at all warheads would not be realistic, nor should it be necessary. However, the inspection team could ask to see a number of specific warheads, identified by the unique identifiers on their containers. If this were done successfully at regular intervals, it would provide some confidence that the system was working as intended, without revealing sensitive design information.

*Proceeding to virtual stockpiles*

The overarching objective in designing such a comprehensive framework for verifying stockpile reduction in the NWS would be to "raise" the level of latency in each NW state by managing the number of weapons/mass of special materials along a gradient of increasing "latency" over a period of time.

So how does one quantify the level of latency? In fact, for the NWS with established stockpiles, "latency" most generally reflects the time interval measured between the moment a decision is made to launch a nuclear attack against an adversary, to the time the weapon's explosive yield is released at the intended target site.

- On this time line, weapon materials, components, or weapon systems could conceptually be assigned a "latency factor" that reflects the time interval between its current state and yield released on target.
- A "latency state" would correspond to the different groupings of weapons, components, or material along the life cycle time line (boxes in Figure 2).
- The overall "stockpile latency" would be some appropriate number-weighted or mass-weighted average of latency factors, inte-

grated across the "latency states" along the life-cycle, and nor-malized to the sum total of weapons/components of nuclear explosive devices or mass of material attributed to the nation.

- Verification protocols would be designed to deduce the number of weapons (or mass of material) in each latency state to an accept-able level of confidence.

Using the methods, procedures, and models identified in the pre-vious sections as "building blocks," or implementation elements, a general roadmap composed of critical stockpile reduction mileposts may be postulated. It is clear that progress along the overarching pro-cess we envision will rely most critically on the state of trust existing between nuclear adversaries, or even more generally among all the nuclear weapon states, in order to ensure methodical progress toward the global condition of effectively *virtual stockpiles*.

Progress will be dominated by policy considerations and collective visions of nuclear and global security; however, the disciplined inclu-sion of negotiated verification protocols will provide joint experience, relationship-building, periodic reaffirmation of global end-state vision, and ultimately the necessary feedback mechanism to enhance trust while continuing down the disarmament path. Verification experience, including joint resolution of conflicts and implementation issues, is needed to build up sufficient trust to eventually "beat the Wiesner curve."

Stocks of nuclear explosive material accumulating in the category designated "in excess of military requirements" will carry the highest latency factor of all materiel within the legitimate authority of a na-tion's nuclear weapons complex. Managing the overall transition of material in this framework, beginning with deployed weapons on alert, then "up" the latency gradient toward materials declared as "excess" (and thus scheduled for downblending, final disposition in actinide-burning reactors or in immobilized form for geological disposal), con-stitutes the engine for achieving the Reykjavik II vision.

A successful regime would provide for declarations of the numbers of warheads in each of the "states" or categories illustrated graphically in Figure 2 and discussed previously. Notionally, as negotiations proceed along the lines of this overarching strategy, it should be possible to deduce a quantitative indication of overall stockpile latency represented by the residual nuclear weapons stockpile with supporting storage and processing infrastructure (weapons complex).

- In the end, as it was in the beginning, we are back to the ultimate issue of controlling global stocks of nuclear explosive material.
- It is here that the *de jure* nuclear weapon states "meet" the de facto nuclear weapon states, and together join with today's truly non-nuclear weapon states, all facing the common legacy problem of accounting for and securing special nuclear material on a global scale.

Besides the challenge of returning to verification regimes involving the P-5 states, meeting the end-state objectives of the "Zero Option" will include the challenge of extending the umbrella to include emerging nuclear weapon states. The intelligence challenge likely to be faced in monitoring the situation in the new nuclear weapons states, principally India and Pakistan, and aspiring or near-nuclear weapons states, such as North Korea and Iran, will rely even more on HUMINT. Here, there is virtually no tradition of arms control and its associated provisions for declarations and inspections. Nor is there a well-developed concept of deterrence. The *full suite of intelligence capabilities* would have to move in harmony with diplomacy to help introduce these concepts and to transfer the experience of successful arms control as practiced in the past among established nuclear states.

### Strategy 2. Non-Nuclear Weapon States maintain high latency by eschewing weapons capability

The non-nuclear weapon states (NNWS) similarly play an important role in a global framework of latency management by continuing to resist any temptation to develop nuclear weapons capability. Presumably, with the NWS on the path to stockpile reductions, the political motivations for the NNWS to develop such capability could arguably be reduced, supported also by positive perceptions of their own regional security. The NNWS challenge under NPT will be to remain responsible stewards of civilian nuclear technology. This would be reflected by a collective commitment to strengthen the NPT regime, eventually building and pursuing a more comprehensive global strategy for controlling nuclear explosive materials in partnership with the "former" NWS. As the NWS pursuit of the Zero Option is founded on a regime built on existing treaties and agreements (START, INF, TTBT, CTBT), the NNWS fidelity to maintaining latency also rests fundamentally on the NPT regime administered by the International Atomic Energy Agency (IAEA) since 1970.

However, the contemporary reality is that the NPT regime is at a major crossroads, some would even say at a "tipping point." Without the benefit of a stabilizing world order, some nations (e.g., Iran, North Korea) are strongly tempted to continue to nurture their nuclear weapons ambitions. In the aftermath of the first Gulf War, the limitations of the NPT regime in identifying clandestine nuclear weapons development in Iraq were made quite apparent. Likewise, the example of South Africa (although ending in a much more favorable outcome) indicated how far a determined nation could go in developing nuclear weapons capability in the background of normal military and commercial activities. In general, latency has both a political, as well as the more familiar capability dimension. Political latency would measure a nation state's willingness to live comfortably within the norms of the international power structure; alternatively, a state of "low latency" would indicate intent to challenge or undermine the power structure (e.g., a willingness to develop an asymmetric WMD capability to challenge superpower conventional dominance). The need for early warning to unmask the weaponization intent of a proliferating regime makes it imperative to address both dimensions of the latency problem.

The world faces expansive growth in energy demand over the next 50 years to support the development goals of huge, growing population centers. Nuclear power provides a very credible means for supplying safe, baseloaded, carbon-free energy that does not bring with it the risk of climate change. In the face of such expansion of nuclear energy, the NPT regime must not just be strengthened, it must be transformed to meet the great challenges before it. The three prevailing strategies for doing this include:

- Seeking greater efficiencies and effectiveness in the traditional mission of verifying member states' negotiated comprehensive safeguards declarations in the face of severe resource constraints (INFCIRC/153);

- Seeking transformational capability to also assess the *completeness* of the state's declarations by assuring the international community that no materials or activities required to be declared under safeguards are, in fact, *undeclared*. This involves an aggressive and effective implementation of the Additional Protocol in all of the States that have concluded comprehensive safeguards agreements with the IAEA (Information Circular (INFCIRC)/540);

- Enhancing the scope of nuclear security vigilance to put more attention on rogue, clandestine proliferation networks (à la A. Q. Khan) that procure enabling nuclear materials production technologies hidden in the "background" of globalized trade related to expansive growth in nuclear power or other relevant industries.

In the face of the expected growth in nuclear energy, the $100 million IAEA Safeguards budget, even as augmented by the contributions of Member State Support Programs (e.g., supplying R&D), seems inadequate for executing the traditional nuclear material accountancy mission. Technology development and enhanced inspection training programs are essential to transforming this activity. In the

United States, National Nuclear Security Agency (NNSA) has proposed a visionary technical program to address "Next Generation Safeguards" needs. However, the allocated resources are disturbingly low given the importance of the mission. In the face of a stagnating safeguards technology base, key thrusts have been proposed in the following areas (among others):

- Measurement technologies to improve the "reach" and precision of nuclear measurements, to include non-destructive assay techniques for spent fuel and measurement of plutonium concentrations and isotopics in non-traditional material forms characteristic of new nuclear processes;
- Unattended systems for process monitoring in real time with high reliability;
- Portable inspection equipment allowing high-resolution isotopics identification, e.g., for monitoring enrichment levels of uranium streams.

The most transformational effect could come from investment in advanced information processing and analysis capability. With the strategic and extensive deployment of sensor systems throughout a safeguarded facility to monitor processes in a manner that maximizes the probability of detecting material diversion, real-time integration of the data to facilitate timely analysis becomes a major technology challenge. The application of modern information analysis techniques could address the truly grand challenge problem: create an "activity monitoring engine" that ingests huge amounts of multiple forms of data in real time (text streams, surveillance imagery streams, in-situ sensor streams) and applies automated adaptive learning algorithms to facilitate detection of very small changes on a very "noisy" background of normal plant activity. Knowledge discovery tools could also be adapted to integrate information from state declarations, environmental sample results, commercial imagery, and various open source publications in order to guide and inform the inspection process, as well as facilitate the preparation of accurate, credible State Evaluation Reports.

Such technology could revolutionize the power of an inspectorate that is chronically resource-challenged. The national laboratories are pursuing major research programs in the integration of distributed sensor networks and advanced knowledge discovery and Bayesian inference algorithms, including implementation of computing hardware architectures originally developed for the gaming industry to process huge volumes of information in real time, to create such transformational capability. The Predictive Knowledge Systems initiative at Lawrence Livermore, as well as the Integrated Knowledge Engine being developed at Los Alamos will benefit both the international safeguards regime, as well as the intelligence community.

The Additional Protocol (AP) provides the IAEA with a very powerful means for enhancing the safeguards regime. Under this protocol, a state is required to provide the IAEA with broader information covering all aspects of its nuclear fuel cycle-related activities, including related R&D. In addition to providing inspectors with challenge access to all buildings on a nuclear site, "complementary access" allows access to a much wider range of locations to help verify the absence of undeclared nuclear material and related activities. This includes the collection of environmental samples beyond declared locations. In fact, if enabled by the appropriate technologies, including state-of-the art information analysis/technology as described above, the AP provisions could allow inspectors to detect "telltale" signs of weaponization activities based on multiple signatures that accompany the chain of activities starting with a political decision to manufacture a weapon, through material acquisition and processing, component fabrication, and testing/evaluation. The properly time-correlated indications from multiple data sources and a variety of locations could provide incontrovertible evidence of the "intent" to weaponize.

However, in order to leverage the opportunities accorded the inspectorate by the AP, appropriate technology transfer from the member states must be forthcoming to empower the international regime. Technologies such as airborne air sampling, hyperspectral imaging, commercial satellite imagery, nano-scale secondary-ion mass spectrometry (NanoSIMS), as well as access to export/import data and automated intelligent searches of the International Nuclear Information System, could form the backbone of a very powerful "Information-Driven Safeguards" program.

- For example, processing of materials in a nuclear program will inevitably involve effluent emissions from chemical processing.
- Mobile, precisely tuneable lasers can be used near suspected nuclear locations to stimulate specific airborne molecules that are released from nuclear materials processing.
- Co-located light-sensitive telescopes can scan the atmosphere to detect the presence of signature molecules. This is the general principle behind LIDAR (Light Detection and Ranging) systems.

With another technique, particles as small as 500 atoms in size can be probed by an ion beam to identify the elemental and isotopic composition of the particles that might indicate the chemical and physical processes that produced them. The impact of the beam on the particle sputters the matter, and the liberated atomic clusters are ionized and collected by a mass spectrometer for registration. Forensic analysis enabled by NanoSIMS technology could provide "nuclear CSI" capability to the IAEA ("CSI" refers to the popularized "Crime Scene Investigation").

- A complete suite of instruments like this could allow inspectors to literally build a credible model of a nuclear weapon development program from the indicators and signatures associated with the nuclear fuel cycle.

## Strategy 3. Beyond Safeguards: a comprehensive global Fissile Material Control Initiative (FMCI)

Despite the significant challenges facing the international community in supporting the enhanced Safeguards program of the IAEA, the ultimate enabling capability for a truly Zero Option end state must go to the very heart of universal latency: complete global accountability for all nuclear explosive material. If the NWS are truly successful in driving stockpiles to zero (therefore disposing of huge quantities of excess nuclear material), and IAEA effectively monitors the world's nuclear power programs and supporting infrastructures for diversion of nuclear materials, there is still a nagging problem posed by uncertainties in the quantities of nuclear material accumulated as the end state is approached. Thus, a veritable safety net is required to continuously reduce, secure, and monitor all nuclear explosive materials on the planet.

This state of affairs becomes the necessary complement to the Zero Option; in fact, it becomes the veritable insurance policy for the Zero Option. Halting the production of fissile material for weapons globally becomes the first order of business along the nuclear materials path to the Zero Option. Phasing out the use of highly enriched uranium in civil commerce and removing weapons-useable uranium from research facilities around the world becomes another milestone. Somewhat more difficult, but strongly highlighted by the recent Global Nuclear Energy Partnership (GNEP), is the goal of removing separated plutonium from civil commerce and materials processing infrastructures. This latter mission imperative will remain as long as there is an active nuclear power program throughout the world (whether or not the GNEP survives in its current programmatic manifestation).

Just like the two previously identified strategy elements of our program (phased negotiated stockpile reductions and transformed Safeguards), this one is founded on current programs and initiatives. Most notably, multilateral discussions addressing a *Fissile Material*

*Cutoff Treaty* have been going on for decades. Until recently, and going back to the 1946 Baruch Plan, control over the production of weapons materials had been a consistent U.S. policy objective. Successful negotiation and entry into force of this treaty, along with a negotiated verification protocol, would arguably be the single most straightforward action in support of this strategy. In 1993, the UN General Assembly adopted a consensus resolution that recommended "the negotiation in the most appropriate international forum of a non-discriminatory multilateral and internationally and effectively verifiable treaty banning the production of fissile material for nuclear weapons or other nuclear explosive devices." The U.S. strongly supported the Treaty during the discussions that took place surrounding the indefinite extension of the NPT in 1995. The reader is referred to Chapter 8 by Robert Einhorn for a more complete exposition.

Technology development can also enable verification of a worldwide ban on plutonium production. A recent R&D accomplishment, borrowing science from modern astrophysics and cosmology research, provides a very useful example in this regard. Lawrence Livermore, in partnership with Sandia National Laboratory, has developed and fielded an anti-neutrino detector to provide continuous, nonintrusive, and unattended monitoring of fissile material inventory in an operating nuclear reactor. The cubic-meter-sized (liquid scintillator) detector was located 24 meters from the reactor core in an area of the plant rarely accessed by plant personnel. The anti-neutrino detection rate is sensitive to plutonium inventory in the reactor core (2 percent decrease in count rate correlates to 60 kg increase in Pu). A prototype of the detector was demonstrated over a period of 1.5 years at the San Onofre Nuclear Generating Station in California. With such an instrument, the declared power history and Pu inventory of a reactor can be verified, and the frequency of inspections can be reduced significantly.

Beyond the FMCT, other initiatives address the more distributed nature of nuclear materials outside of material production. Cooperative

Threat Reduction (CTR) complemented by the DOE's successful programs of *Materials Protection, Control, and Accountability (MPC&A)* and the *Global Threat Reduction Initiative*, have addressed the legacy issues associated with nuclear weapons and materials "orphaned" at the end of the Cold War. Some of these programs are actually coming to programmatic conclusion, as targeted by the Bush administration's Global Initiative to Combat Nuclear Terrorism. Admittedly, these are laudable accomplishments. However, there is currently no vision in the U.S. government to comprehensively move this to the next level. In the previous discussion of phased reductions to NWS stockpiles, the verification of weapon dismantlement and destruction inevitably leads to related consideration of a verification regime to assure transparency, monitoring, and destruction of fissile material very similar to that for nuclear weapons.

Just like the methodical consideration given to stockpile reductions, a material control regime would involve historical accounting in each nation of fissile material production (accompanied by requisite "declarations"), exchanges of data regarding existing stocks of materials, and verification of existing fissile material stockpiles. This would cover all processes through storage or other disposition. Conversion of nuclear material for civilian purposes would accordingly be monitored as well.

Ultimately, consideration must be given to the level of security accorded all stocks of nuclear material throughout the world. Although a long-term professional objective of the Institute for Nuclear Materials Management (INMM), physical security of nuclear materials has become an imperative in the post-9/11 terror threat environment. The International Convention on Physical Protection of Nuclear Materials has adopted an amendment that extends protection of nuclear materials from an initial historical focus on international transport, now to all activities within the boundaries of member states. Principles have been established for safeguarding the materials, and the IAEA's Office of Nuclear Security has oversight responsibilities related to compliance with these principles. A four-year Nuclear Security Plan (NSP) has been developed and is owned by the IAEA Department of Safeguards, in support of the strategic goal to establish a "comprehensive and effective international framework for promoting nuclear safety and security."

However, more detailed physical protection standards are needed. To meet this need, the Nuclear Threat Initiative (NTI), partnering with the INMM, has proposed a World Institute of Nuclear Security (WINS), patterned after the nuclear safety-focused World Association of Nuclear Operators (WANO). Its charter presumably would include a professionally managed forum for exchange of information between operators, industry, governments, and government entities; promulgation of "best practices" in physical protection and nuclear material control and accounting; support of IAEA peer review objectives; and assistance with self-assessments related to physical security and material control/accounting. This initiative is another element that integrates into a comprehensive approach for attaining a truly global *Fissile Material Control Initiative*. [See the discussion by Robert Einhorn in Chapter 8.]

Monitoring the state and security of nuclear explosive material would further increase the intelligence challenge. *Declarations* will be critical to establish a baseline. *NTM* will be helpful but not definitive. *On-site inspections* will play a more critical role. *HUMINT* will have to focus on issues such as "insider theft." And it will be particularly important to have a coalition of states equipped with *technical equipment to monitor borders* across which such material might be smuggled.

The challenge is multiplied when plans and capabilities of non-state actors, such as al-Qaeda, are brought into consideration. In most of the foregoing cases examined by this paper, detecting capabilities will be easier than discerning intent. With non-state actors, the challenge is reversed: *intent* is fairly clear—they seem prepared to use nuclear weapons for attack or blackmail—but *capabilities* are hard to define with confidence. Deterrence may be possible, but any calculus would at minimum be more complex than with state-based nuclear weapons. All intelligence capabilities would be in play, but *HUMINT would have an especially prominent role.* Information sharing will be important in order to operationalize any actionable information by empowering international and domestic law enforcement elements.

## Strategy 4. Credible Response Capabilities Ensure Desired System Dynamics

The foregoing sections of this paper have introduced three major elements of a global framework for enabling and monitoring a global state of universal latency: (1) a negotiated and verified reduction of State-controlled nuclear weapon stockpiles to the Zero Option (presumably an end state of essentially virtual stockpiles); (2) a revitalized Safeguards program monitored by international authority that has kept NNWS from subverting nuclear power/fuel cycle programs to develop nuclear weapons capability; and (3) the institution of a global Fissile Material Control Initiative to provide a safety net to protect against the smuggling of even small numbers or amounts of nuclear weapons/materials for malicious purposes.

In earlier parts of this paper we identified means by which NWS and NNWS might be driven to higher degrees of latency, but strong emphasis was placed on carefully designed procedures and technology-enabled monitoring to detect violations of declarations in a timely manner and with high levels of certainty. Such credible information would then trigger predetermined sanctions ("restoring forces" in the overall system dynamics). It is the role of detection and information technology to ensure that evidence collected in this process is *compelling* enough to trigger the response.

In light of political circumstances or perceived threat to security, states may from time to time attempt to deviate from their expected degree of latency in this scheme. For the system to reach its designed end state, restoring forces must act promptly, presumably through a set of graded sanctions, to induce the state to return to an "acceptable" condition. (Although this type of behavior works pretty reliably in a home thermostat, there is no illusion about the level of difficulty this may pose in the international arena among sovereign states with complex security requirements. A case in point is the drama being played out now in North Korea and Iran.) This action-and-response principle must play out long enough in time for the entire global system to move to the ultimate goal.

Nevertheless, even having attained this state of universal latency, there is an existential need to protect the system from the insult of "breakout," for which it must be eternally vigilant. Credible response capabilities, then, must be built into the final solution. These would not be so much for sanctioning moderate transgressions, but rather for creating an ultimate deterrent effect in this new paradigm. We propose three major response modes: tailored emergency disablement; counterproliferation; and ballistic missile defense.

If an improvised nuclear explosive were to be smuggled into the country and detected, there must exist a technologically superior emergency response capability that would not just be capable of detecting the nuclear material in time, but could infer the nature of the design itself via appropriate diagnostics, and then stabilize or effectively disable the device to prevent it from reaching its design objective. This requires a sophisticated nuclear weapon design and diagnostic capability that would rival the capabilities now engaged in Stockpile Stewardship of the enduring stockpile.

Ideally, the collective capabilities of multiple nations could work more collaboratively against the common threat of a rogue adversary armed with a non-state-designed weapon. (The nuclear weapon laboratories do have such capabilities today, but arguably they are not nurtured and developed in a manner robust enough to address the very palpable nature of the contemporary nuclear threat.) Given interdiction of the threat, nuclear forensic capabilities (such as those identified earlier for the detailed characterization of material processing signatures) could be applied to infer the ultimate source and production history of the material in the unexploded device. This would enable a judgment of attribution to be made, establishing ultimate responsibility for the foiled attack (specifically related to the source of the material).

It is quite possible that a nuclear weapons capability breakout could occur somewhere in the world, even from conditions that would accompany the Zero Option end state. This would constitute a very quick transition from latency to imminent threat. Depending on the certainty of the corroborating evidence, as well as the nature of the offense, a politically "transformed" international community that had built high levels of trust might develop agreed procedures for a preemptive attack on the emerging threat by an internationally authorized military force. In short, conventional counterproliferation capability would be a constant companion on the path to universal latency. But in keeping with traditional Just War doctrine, such a capability would be exercised only as a last resort and with careful consideration of collateral effect.

In a similar vein, the issue of Ballistic Missile Defense must also be raised. The subject of the proliferation of missile technology has not been discussed in this paper, nor has there been any presumption made with regard to the future of the Missile Technology Control Regime (MTCR). One could imagine a world of universal nuclear latency, but one that still retained significant numbers of conventionally armed ballistic missiles. The possibility of a clandestine attempt to deliver an improvised nuclear explosive payload cannot be discounted, any more than one can discount smuggling of a nuclear device across the borders of a country. However, the time frame within which to react to the former threat could be orders of magnitude shorter. In this case, Ballistic Missile Defense capability could be regarded as a justified defensive measure in light of an imminent, unexpected threat. Under these conditions, President Bush's characterization would be quite accurate: "America's development of a missile defense (would be truly) a search for security, not a search for advantage."

The problem here is that, although it is fairly easy to justify the implementation of BMD in a presumably de-nuclearized world as an insurance measure against an unexpected WMD attack, it is much more difficult to imagine where on the path to de-nuclearization its introduction would be the most prudent and the least provocative. This topic will not be considered in this paper. It is only interesting to observe that we have come fully back around to Reykjavik in 1986, when the vision of a nuclear weapon-free world and the promise of anti-ballistic missile technology were presented as part of a comprehensive vision. Due to the realities of the time, that particular discussion was not long-lived. It took the end of the Cold War and the advent of global terrorism to lead us to a point where such a relationship could again be revisited.

## Space and ASAT

It is clear that in a world of universal latency, NTM capabilities will be so important that special precautions will be required to protect such assets from attack. There are many reasons to maintain space as a benign environment for satellites circling the globe in orbits above the atmosphere, at lower altitudes above 150 kilometers every 90 minutes, and up to geosynchronous orbits at 36,000 kilometers. They are vital components of the global communications and navigation network, of the global economy, and of the scientific exploration of our universe to the outer extremes of space. Central to our present discussion, they also play a major role in our military capabilities and national security (Graham and Hansen, 2005) [4].

Reconnaissance satellites in space have exploited a broad range of the electromagnetic spectrum for half a century, monitoring the development, testing, and deployment of nuclear weapons. This has enabled nations to enter into verifiable arms control treaties that have been, and remain, of great value to many nations, and particularly to the United States as a leader in space technology. It is anticipated that the importance of unhindered operations of NTM will increase, rather than diminish, as we negotiate deeper reductions in nuclear weapons and negotiate protocols to further restrict nuclear activities en route to a nuclear-free world.

The Chinese ASAT test of January 11, 2007 was a direct ascent interceptor that impacted and destroyed one of their dormant weather satellites at an altitude of 850 kilometers, creating more than 900 pieces of debris large enough to be tracked from Earth. Most are circulating in long-lasting orbits, remaining potentially dangerous to many orbiting satellites at a densely populated altitude. That incident reminds us that destructive collisions of our satellites with such space debris, which in turn would further increase the total debris, are potential threats to the benign space environment. It won't take many such debris-creating intercepts to deny the use of space by satellites whose eyes and ears are now serving important missions for communications, navigation, science, and reconnaissance.

The spread of ballistic missile technology is making it possible for increasing numbers of nations to attack and destroy orbiting satellites. This makes it imperative to address the problem of maintaining space as a benign environment, sooner rather than later.

What we can or should do to meet this challenge is not so simple to decide because satellites have more valuable missions than the ones indicated above for peacetime. They also provide instantaneous command control links for directing military battlefield operations. An approach to the problem of limiting the development of potentially threatening ASAT capabilities has been recently described by Geoffrey Forden [5], who proposes two steps for starters that are practical. The first is to make clear that nations will share basic information available from their civilian satellites with any other nation that has lost a satellite due to hostile action, and that is cooperating in a protocol that forbids such actions. The second is to negotiate an agreement that defines a keep-out region around national space assets. The keep-out range might take the form, as suggested by Forden, of forbidding the testing of an interceptor that approaches within 100 kilometers of another country's satellites with a closing speed greater than 100 meters per second. (Orbital speeds are typically several kilometers per second.)

These are two plausible initiatives to begin to regulate activities in space and develop a confidence among nations that space will not become another dimension in which weapons are deployed in a potentially hostile competition as we seek to reduce nuclear weapons and move toward a world free of them.

*References*

(1) Krass, Allan S., *Verification: How Much is Enough?*, SIPRI, Lexington Books, Lexington, Mass, 1985.

(2) Molander, Roger and Wilson, Peter A., *On Dealing With the Prospect of Nuclear Chaos*, *The Washington Quarterly*, Summer 1994 v17 n3.

(3) *Monitoring Nuclear Weapons and Nuclear Explosive Materials: Methods and Capabilities*, Committee on International Security and Arms Control (National Research Council), National Academies Press, 2005. Download at www.nap.edu.catalog/11265.html.

(4) Graham, Thomas and Hansen, Keith, *Spy Satellites and Other Intelligence Technologies that Changed History*, University of Washington Press, 2007.

(5) Forden, Geoffrey A., *After China's Test: Time for Limited Ban on Anti-Satellite Weapons*, in *Arms Control Today*, Arms Control Association, April 2007 (www.armscontrol.org/act/2007_04/Forden.asp)

# 5. Transparent and Irreversible Dismantlement of Nuclear Weapons
## Matthew Bunn

### Key Judgments

- Prohibition of nuclear weapons will require the dismantlement of some 25,000 nuclear weapons that currently exist in nine states. While this dismantlement will pose major operational challenges, facilities and procedures are in place that can accomplish it.

- The nuclear weapons to be eliminated must be: (a) secured and accounted for; (b) committed to dismantlement; (c) placed under bilateral or international monitoring; and (d) verifiably dismantled. The fissile materials from these warheads must then be: (a) placed in secure storage subject to bilateral or international monitoring; (b) committed never to be returned to weapons; and (c) used or disposed of in a way that would make it impossible or very costly to ever return them to weapons use.

- Technologies and procedures are available which, with some refinement and negotiation, can make it possible to build confidence that these warheads have been placed in secure storage and then dismantled as agreed, without compromising sensitive nuclear weapon design information. Technologies and procedures are also available to confirm secure storage and disposition of the fissile materials from these weapons.

- Many nuclear weapons can also be rapidly, verifiably, and permanently disabled pending dismantlement. This would contribute to both arms reduction and theft prevention.

- Building confidence in nuclear arms reductions as they proceed to very low levels will require making these reductions transparent and difficult to reverse. A comprehensive "transparency and irreversibility" approach would include verifiable dismantlement of delivery systems (and modification of remaining systems to ensure that they could not carry many more than the agreed number of nuclear weapons); verifiable dismantlement of nuclear weapons themselves; disposition of all fissile material beyond the amounts required to support the remaining warheads, along with any agreed remaining purposes (such as naval fuel); and dismantlement or conversion of facilities for producing more delivery vehicles, nuclear weapons, and weapons-useable material.

- If managed appropriately, large-scale nuclear weapon dismantlements and disposition of excess fissile material could reduce the threat of nuclear theft and terrorism. If stringent security measures are not maintained throughout these processes, however, they could *increase* the risk of nuclear terrorism by removing weapons and materials from secure vaults, shipping them from place to place, and processing them.

- Some approaches could make it possible to place thousands of especially dangerous nuclear weapons under internationally monitored lock and key, commit them to eventual verifiable dismantlement, and begin permanently disabling them within months of a decision to do so.

## Background

*"For nuclear disarmament to be real, one has to have procedures for monitoring the dismantling of nuclear munitions and fissionable materials contained in these munitions."*
—Then-Russian First Deputy Minister of Atomic Energy Lev Ryabev, ITAR-TASS, 11 March 1998.

*"Real disarmament is possible only if the accumulated huge stocks of weapons-grade uranium and plutonium are destroyed."*
—Then-Russian Minister of Atomic Energy Victor Mikhailov, address to the International Atomic Energy Agency (IAEA), quoted by TASS, 22 September 1992.

Implementing deep reductions in nuclear weapons stockpiles, and ultimately the prohibition of nuclear weapons, will require the dismantlement of tens of thousands of nuclear weapons and effective control over the stocks of nuclear material that could be used to rebuild these arsenals. To be successful, this process of nuclear weapons reduction will have to be implemented with enough transparency to give other countries confidence that reductions are taking place as agreed, and in a way that would be difficult, costly, and observable to reverse.

As discussed in the paper on verification, a comprehensive approach will be needed, including declarations of all nuclear weapon and nuclear material stockpiles; measures to confirm and build confidence in the accuracy of those declarations; dismantlement of nuclear weapons, with measures to confirm the dismantlement is taking place; and monitored storage and disposition of excess fissile materials, bringing the stocks of such materials down to the minimum necessary to support whatever stockpiles of nuclear weapons exist at each stage. [See Chapter 4.] There will also have to be comprehensive measures to ensure that all nuclear weapons and materials are secure throughout this process. The greatest challenge will not be in confirming that particular declared warheads are dismantled—the subject of this paper—but in building confidence that there are no hidden stockpiles that have not been declared. Absolute verification of that is impossible—but by exchanging data at a large number of points throughout the nuclear warhead and fissile material life cycles, and comparing the information exchanged with data available from national technical means and other sources, it is potentially possible to build good confidence over time that the declarations are accurate and complete.

Moving forward with such an effort will require fundamental changes in both nuclear weapons policies and nuclear secrecy policies in the nuclear weapon states.[1] It is a remarkable fact that today, sixteen years after the collapse of the Soviet Union, the United States and Russia have never told each other (let alone anyone else) how many nuclear warheads they have, and neither country has verified the dismantlement of a single one of the other country's nuclear warheads.

## Numbers of Nuclear Weapons

Today, there are still more than 25,000 assembled nuclear weapons in the world, possessed by nine states. This includes an estimated 15,000 remaining in Russia's stockpile; nearly 10,000 remaining in the U.S. nuclear stockpiles; and over 1,000 warheads in the combined total of other countries' stockpiles.[2] This level of nuclear armament was in-

1. There is a large literature on measures to confirm warhead dismantlement, and other transparency measures for nuclear warheads and materials (of which only a part is classified). For particularly useful recent discussions, see U.S. National Academy of Sciences, Committee on International Security and Arms Control, *Monitoring Nuclear Weapons and Nuclear-Explosive Materials* (Washington, D.C.: National Academy Press, 2005; available at books.nap.edu/catalog/11265.html); Nicholas Zarimpas, ed., *Transparency in Nuclear Warheads and Materials: The Political and Technical Dimensions* (Oxford: Oxford University Press for the Stockholm Peace Research Institute, 2003). The Natural Resources Defense Council and the Federation of American Scientists were early leaders in recognizing the importance of such measures and beginning discussions with Russian experts about what might be done. See, for example, *Third International Workshop on Verified Storage and Destruction of Nuclear Warheads*, Moscow and Kiev, December 1991.

2. See Robert S. Norris and Hans M. Kristensen, "NRDC Nuclear Notebook: Russian Nuclear Forces, 2007," *Bulletin of the Atomic Scientists* (March/April 2007);

*Table 1: World Nuclear Weapon Stockpiles*

| Country | # Weapons | % of World |
|---|---|---|
| Russia | 15,000 | 58% |
| United States | 10,000 | 39% |
| France | 350 | 1% |
| China | 200 | 0.75% |
| United Kingdom | 200 | 0.75% |
| Israel | 60–80 | 0.5% |
| India | 50–60 | 0.3% |
| Pakistan | 40–50 | 0.2% |
| North Korea | 10 | 0.04% |
| TOTAL | 26,000 | 100.00% |

*Sources:* Robert S. Norris and Hans M. Kristensen, "NRDC Nuclear Notebook: Global Nuclear Stockpiles 1945–2006," *Bulletin of the Atomic Scientists*, July/August 2006, updated with the following editions of the "NRDC Nuclear Notebook": for Russia: March/April 2007; for the United States: January/February 2007.

sane in Cold War times; more than a decade later, nuclear arsenals of this size clearly pose far more risk than benefit.

The five states with the largest number of nuclear weapons are the five nuclear weapon state parties to the nuclear Nonproliferation Treaty (NPT): Russia, the United States, China, France, and the United Kingdom. The four other states with nuclear weapons are the only states outside the NPT (North Korea being the only country to have joined the treaty and then withdrawn). See Table 1. In addition to these nine countries that possess nuclear weapons of their own, U.S. nuclear weapons are reportedly located in six other countries—one other nuclear weapons state (the United Kingdom) and five non-nuclear weapons states (Germany, the Netherlands, Belgium, Italy, and Turkey).[3] The larger the number of individual locations where such weapons exist, the higher the risks of accident or theft.

---

Robert S. Norris and Hans M. Kristensen, "NRDC Nuclear Notebook: U.S. Nuclear Forces, 2007," *Bulletin of the Atomic Scientists* (September/October 2007); Robert S. Norris and Hans M. Kristensen, "NRDC Nuclear Notebook: Global Nuclear Stockpiles, 1945–2006," *Bulletin of the Atomic Scientists* (July/August 2006).

3. As a result of the 1991 Presidential Nuclear Initiatives, U.S. nuclear weapons have been removed from South Korea and from surface ships, which previously reg-

## Dismantlement Capacity

The specific steps involved in dismantlement of a nuclear weapon vary somewhat depending on the type of weapon. In general, dismantlement involves removing the weapon itself, or the "physics package" from the outer shell and other components, separating the high explosives from the fissile materials in the weapon, and destroying, storing, or re-using the various weapon components.

In both the United States and Russia, and presumably in other nuclear weapon states as well, nuclear weapons are typically dismantled in the same facilities where they were assembled, as those facilities have the experience and the tooling needed to handle that particular warhead type. The only operational nuclear weapon assembly/disassembly facility in the United States is at Pantex, in Amarillo, Texas. (The Device Assembly Facility [DAF] at the Nevada Test Site was designed to assemble small numbers of nuclear weapons for nuclear tests, but has never been used for that purpose.) Russia has two remaining nuclear weapon assembly/disassembly facilities, at the closed nuclear cities of Lesnoy (formerly Sverdlovsk-45) and Trekhgornyy (formerly Zlatoust-36).

The United States maintained an average dismantlement rate of some 1,300 weapons per year during 1990–1998; in some of those years, the United States dismantled as many as 1,800 weapons. For recent years, dismantlement rates have declined dramatically, though specific numbers are classified. Reportedly, the dismantlement rate in 2003 and the years immediately following was in the range of 130 weapons per year. The Department of Energy (DOE) informed Congress that the rate in 2007 would be 50 percent higher, but that would

---

ularly carried them to countries around the world. The deployments in Europe, and on submarines, are believed to be the only remaining U.S. nuclear weapons deployments beyond U.S. shores. For a detailed discussion of the remaining U.S. nuclear weapons in Europe, see Hans M. Kristensen, *U.S. Nuclear Weapons in Europe: A Review of Post-Cold War Policy, Force Levels, and War Planning* (Washington, D.C.: Natural Resources Defense Council, 2005).

still bring the total to only about 200 warheads per year. Independent experts have estimated that the Bush administration's announced plans to reduce the U.S. nuclear weapons stockpile would, if implemented as planned, eliminate roughly 5,000 of the nuclear weapons in the U.S. stockpile. DOE reports that it plans to complete those dismantlements by 2023, which would suggest a planned dismantlement rate in the range of 300 weapons per year.[4]

This slow pace is primarily the result of warhead dismantlement not being treated as a high priority. Instead, a substantial part of the capacity at Pantex is being devoted to refurbishing existing warheads to extend their lives decades into the future. If dismantlement were made a top priority, it is likely that Pantex could again dismantle more than 1,000 nuclear weapons per year.

The situation appears to be similar in Russia, though Russia is believed to have a larger backlog of weapons that are not in use and are slated for eventual dismantlement. In the 1990s, by some estimates, Russia was dismantling as many as 2,000 nuclear weapons per year. In recent years, Russia has closed two of its four warhead assembly/disassembly facilities (though the two closed facilities, at Sarov and Zarechnyy, had much smaller capacities than the two remaining facilities). One independent estimate suggests that Russia is now dismantling some 400–500 warheads a year, but remanufacturing perhaps 200 of them, for a net dismantlement rate in the range of 200–300 per year.[5] Like the United States, it is likely that if Russia made dismantlement a priority, it would have the capability to dismantle more than 1,000 nuclear weapons per year.

Less is known about nuclear weapons assembly and disassembly

4. For discussions of these points, see Chapter 5 in International Panel on Fissile Materials, *Global Fissile Materials Report 2007* (Princeton, NJ: IPFM, October 2007) and Robert S. Norris and Hans Kristensen, "NRDC Nuclear Notebook: The U.S. Nuclear Stockpile, Today and Tomorrow," *Bulletin of the Atomic Scientists* (September/October 2007).

5. Anatoli Diakov, cited in *Global Fissile Materials Report 2007*, p. 62.

capacities in other countries. Other countries, however, have nuclear stockpiles measured in hundreds of warheads or less; it is likely that these stockpiles could be dismantled relatively quickly if a decision were taken to do so. In short, it appears that it would be technically possible to dismantle all the world's nuclear weapons over a period of 10–20 years.

## Past Discussions of Verified
## Dismantlement and Related Measures

Nuclear weapons themselves are smaller and easier to hide than the missiles and bombers that deliver them. To date, nuclear arms control and reduction agreements have focused on reducing delivery vehicles, not on dismantlement of the nuclear weapons themselves. It has long been understood, however, that as reductions proceed to lower levels, restraints on nuclear weapons themselves, and on the fissile materials needed to make them, will become increasingly important.[6] Official studies of approaches to verifying warhead dismantlement have been underway in one form or another for over forty years.

During the 1990s, the United States and Russia pursued a series of discussions focused on "Safeguards, Transparency, and Irreversibility" (STI) of nuclear arms reductions. By 1995, the U.S. and Russian presidents had agreed to exchange data on how many nuclear weapons and how much fissile material each side had, and a number of transparency and irreversibility commitments were included in a 1995 joint summit statement. The United States made a proposal that called for a detailed data exchange, and for reciprocal visits to fissile material sites to help build confidence in the accuracy of the data. (At that time, verified warhead dismantlement was not included in the proposal.) While Soviet and Russian negotiators had, in the past, agreed to a series of intrusive on-site inspection measures as part of

6. See discussions in U.S. National Academy of Sciences, *Monitoring Weapons and Nuclear-Explosive Materials*; and Zarimpas, ed., *Transparency in Nuclear Warheads and Materials*.

negotiating arms reduction agreements that they believed served their country's interest, in this case the transparency measures were proposed independently of any associated arms reductions—and would have affected not just missiles, bombers, and submarines, but nuclear weapons and materials themselves. Secrecy and suspicion were still pervasive among the nuclear security and counterintelligence establishments in both Russia and the United States. Russia appears to have concluded that the U.S. proposals for data exchange were so broad that they constituted, in effect, an intelligence fishing expedition. Ultimately, these proposals went nowhere, and no data exchanges occurred.[7]

At the Helsinki summit in 1997, however, President Bill Clinton and Russian President Boris Yeltsin agreed that a START III agreement should include "measures relating to the transparency of strategic nuclear warhead inventories and the destruction of strategic nuclear warheads . . . to promote the irreversibility of deep reductions including prevention of a rapid increase in the number of warheads." The two presidents also instructed their experts to "explore, as separate issues" (that is, presumably not as part of a START III agreement itself) "possible measures relating to nuclear long-range sea-launched cruise missiles and tactical nuclear systems, to include appropriate confidence-building and transparency measures," and agreed to "consider the issues related to transparency in nuclear materials." In the discussions that followed, the United States proposed a protocol on nuclear warhead transparency and monitoring in early 2000, but Russian negotiators did not appear interested in pursuing this idea. Ultimately, formal START III negotiations never began. The Bush administration has not chosen to pursue any discussions focused on monitored reductions in nuclear weapon stockpiles.

7. The best published account of these discussions is from James Goodby, the lead U.S. negotiator. See James Goodby, "Transparency and Irreversibility in Nuclear Warhead Dismantlement," in *The Nuclear Turning Point: A Blueprint for Deep Cuts and De-Alerting of Nuclear Weapons*, Harold A. Feiveson, ed. (Washington, D.C.: Brookings, 1999).

Since the 1990s, however, experts from U.S. and Russian nuclear laboratories have cooperated extensively to develop options for confirming warhead dismantlement without revealing sensitive nuclear weapons design information, along with other transparency approaches related to nuclear warheads and fissile materials.[8] (As these efforts included a number of approaches to detection of nuclear material and high explosives, they have been refocused on counter-terrorism missions in the aftermath of the 9/11 attacks, but the cooperation is continuing.) These efforts provide a substantial technical base on which to draw for future agreements on verified warhead dismantlement.

In addition, cooperation on threat reduction has formed habits of cooperation and opened many categories of information. Cooperation to destroy, and confirm the destruction of, ballistic missiles, bombers, and submarines is now routine. In the course of cooperation to improve security for nuclear stockpiles, U.S. experts have visited the vast majority of the buildings in Russia's nuclear weapons complex and numerous nuclear warhead storage sites, with only actual warhead assembly/disassembly facilities and a few buildings at other sites remaining off-limits; Russian experts have visited most of the facilities of the U.S. nuclear weapons complex, including Pantex, the nuclear weapons assembly/disassembly plant.

Moreover, while Russia and the United States have not negotiated any broad transparency regime for nuclear warheads and fissile materials, or any measures specifically related to verifying warhead dismantlement, a few "islands of transparency" have been implemented for particular purposes, and others are still being pursued. The most successful example is the transparency for the U.S.-Russian Highly Enriched Uranium (HEU) Purchase Agreement, under which U.S. monitors visit facilities and check activities related to chopping HEU

8. For a useful overview, see Oleg Bukharin, "Russian and U.S. Technology Development in Support of Nuclear Warhead and Material Transparency Initiatives," in Zarimpas, ed., *Transparency in Nuclear Warheads and Materials*.

warhead components into metal shavings, oxidizing them, purifying them, converting them to uranium hexafluoride, and blending them to low-enriched uranium. Russian monitors check at U.S. facilities to make sure the material delivered is used only for peaceful purposes. Unmanned equipment continuously monitors the actual blending of the HEU to low-enriched uranium.[9] Despite years of effort, a transparency accord for the Mayak Fissile Material Storage Facility had not been reached by early 2008; negotiations continue over monitoring plutonium produced in the plutonium production reactors, and monitoring disposition of excess plutonium.

## Issues

### What needs to be done pending dismantlement?

Verified dismantlement of nuclear weapons would be only one element in a broader political and technical regime for secure, transparent, and irreversible nuclear arms reductions. In particular, if $X$ thousand weapons are to be dismantled, it would be extremely important to know how many there were to start with, and how many will remain after a particular agreed stage of dismantlement is completed.

Hence, a key first step is a comprehensive declaration of how many nuclear weapons each side has. An accompanying declaration concerning the quantities of separated plutonium and HEU would also be important. There is a wide range of possibilities for the kinds of information to be included, how the information would be exchanged, and the measures to be used to build confidence in the accuracy of the declarations.[10]

9. See Matthew Bunn, with James Platte, "Highly Enriched Uranium Transparency," in *Nuclear Threat Initiative Research Library: Securing the Bomb* (Cambridge, Mass., and Washington, D.C.: Project on Managing the Atom, Harvard University and Nuclear Threat Initiative, 2006; available at www.nti.org/e_research/cnwm/monitoring/uranium.asp as of March 2, 2007).

10. For example, if it were considered too sensitive to exchange complete data at present, the two sides could exchange message digests in the form of a secure hash;

In addition, the nuclear weapons to be eliminated must be placed in highly secure storage, and committed to dismantlement—at least as a political commitment initially, or perhaps in a legal agreement. They should then be placed under either bilateral or international monitoring, to confirm that they remain in storage and have not been removed, and remain highly secure.

Since there are nine states with nuclear weapons, and many more with a strong interest in nuclear disarmament, nuclear disarmament will inevitably be a multilateral enterprise. At some stage, monitoring by some international group is likely to be required, to convince all states, not just the United States and Russia, that weapons are being eliminated as agreed. Monitoring by the IAEA, in particular, has a credibility with the vast majority of the world's states (which are already subject to IAEA monitoring) that bilateral monitoring by the United States and Russia will never achieve. But in the near term, there is probably a great deal the United States and Russia would be willing to open to verification bilaterally that they would not be willing to allow international inspectors—who might come from states suspected of pursuing nuclear weapons themselves—to monitor. The best balance between bilateral and international inspection, and the process for transitioning from the one to the other, requires further study.

If desired, nuclear warheads can also be disabled pending their eventual dismantlement, so that they could no longer be detonated; this could reduce the risk these weapons would pose if they were stolen, and, if done in a way that was difficult to reverse, could make it possible to eliminate the capability of these weapons more rapidly than they can actually be dismantled. One approach that could be applied to many warhead types, which could also contribute to veri-

---

these digests themselves would contain no useful information, but would allow information provided later from the data the digests came from to be confirmed as authentic. See discussion in U.S. National Academy of Sciences, *Monitoring Nuclear Weapons and Nuclear-Explosive Materials*, pp. 92–94.

fication of disablement and dismantlement, is referred to as "pit-stuffing." Modern boosted thermonuclear weapons typically have a hollow-shell primary, or "pit," surrounded with high explosives. A tube leads from the outside of the pit to the inside, allowing tritium to be injected into the pit for boosting. If the hollow pit is filled with other material—such as wire inserted through the pit tube—the explosives can no longer crush the pit to a critical configuration and the weapon cannot go off. Steps can be taken to make it effectively impossible to pull the wire back out without disassembling the weapon and cutting open the pit (such as equipping the wire with small toggle bolts similar to those used to mount shelves on hollow walls, for example). Monitors could observe as the inspected party inserted such wires before the weapons were disassembled (with appropriate shrouds used to avoid revealing sensitive information); a gamma-ray image of a small section of the warhead could confirm that it contained a hollow plutonium shell with a tangle of metal inside it.[11] Pit-stuffing, however, could not be applied to all nuclear weapon types. Moreover, it has received only a modest level of study, and further detailed examinations of implementation issues would be needed before this approach could be adopted on a large scale.

As discussed further below, these steps could in principle be taken relatively quickly—in many cases within months or a year after a decision to do so. Once the warheads are secure, under monitoring, and committed to dismantlement, the dismantlement itself can proceed at the careful pace required.

### What is the best approach to confirming dismantlement?

A variety of approaches to building confidence that dismantlement is taking place as agreed have been proposed; these offer varying levels of confidence and varying obstacles to implementation.

11. See Matthew Bunn, "'Pit-Stuffing': How to Rapidly Disable Thousands of Warheads and Easily Verify Their Dismantlement," *F.A.S. Public Interest Report*, March/April 1998, with commentary by Richard L. Garwin.

If there were high confidence that there were no secret stockpiles of unassembled nuclear weapons components, the simplest approach would be simply to monitor disassembled nuclear weapon components building up in storage. Each additional nuclear weapon primary, or "pit," being added to storage would be assumed to mean one additional weapon dismantled. This approach is simple, low-cost, and avoids the sensitivities of monitoring at dismantlement sites, but is relatively low confidence, since the pits building up in storage might possibly be coming from some secret stockpile or from new manufacturing, if those possibilities were not effectively monitored. If the focus is on very deep reductions, and potentially complete nuclear disarmament, this approach alone is probably insufficient, though it can contribute in concert with other approaches.

Another approach, known as "chain of custody," would track nuclear weapons up to the door of the building or area where the weapon was to be dismantled, and then track their components when they left the building. Unless other monitoring measures were included, however, it would be possible to bring warheads in and bring them back out again without dismantling them, and bring components in and bring them back out as though they were from dismantled weapons.

Hence, many analyses have focused on "perimeter-portal" monitoring. In this approach, inspectors would count the number of warheads entering the perimeter of a dismantlement facility, through one or more agreed portals; and the number of fissile material components leaving the facility.[12] There would be occasional inspections of the interior of the facility (during periods when no nuclear weapons were being dismantled) to confirm that there was no buildup of nuclear weapons or materials within the facility.

12. If the same facility were also remanufacturing weapons for maintenance purposes, the monitors could count the number of weapons going in and the number coming out, to determine the *net* number going in. Alternatively, remanufacturing could be segregated at a different facility or area of the facility; some monitoring would still be needed to ensure that what was taking place was not the production of significant numbers of new warheads.

A key issue in such approaches is how to confirm that an object entering the dismantlement facility that is declared to be a warhead is in fact a warhead. Two main approaches have been examined, one based on "attributes"—characteristics that all nuclear warheads and few other objects would generally have—and the other based on "templates"—detailed signatures specific to particular warhead types.[13] In an attribute approach, for example, the parties might agree that an object that was declared to be a nuclear weapon, was of an appropriate size to be a nuclear weapon, was confirmed by detectors to contain at least $x$ kilograms of weapons-grade plutonium in metal form, and which was also confirmed to contain high explosives in close proximity to the plutonium, would be considered a nuclear weapon.[14] Key disadvantages include the need to have very broad standards in order to encompass all the varying characteristics of different types of nuclear weapons, and the possibility the system could be spoofed with dummy objects that contained explosives and weapons-grade plutonium but were not weapons. (Whether there would be any incentive for a party to go to the considerable expense of manufacturing hundreds or thousands of objects that contained weapons-grade plutonium metal and high explosives but were not weapons is an open question.)

In the "template" approach, measurements—typically radiation measurements, but others could be used as well—would be taken on particular warhead types, and the signatures from these measurements would be compared to the signatures from objects declared to be weapons of that type entering a dismantlement facility. In U.S. tests, such systems have shown an excellent ability to distinguish real weapons from other objects. A key issue for the "template" approach is how to confirm that the objects measured to get the templates are actually nuclear weapons: in the case of weapon types still deployed

13. See, for example, U.S. National Academy of Sciences, *Monitoring Nuclear Weapons and Nuclear-Explosive Materials*, pp. 97–106.

14. Except in nuclear weapons, high explosives are generally kept separately from radioactive materials for safety reasons.

on strategic ballistic missiles, this may not be a great difficulty, as particular missiles could be selected at random and measurements taken on one of their warheads. But in the case of air-delivered bombs and other weapons that are all in storage, the task of confirming that the templates are themselves authentic is a non-trivial one.

The "pit-stuffing" approach just described could also be used to confirm nuclear weapon dismantlement. As already noted, a gamma-ray image of a small section of the weapon (from outside a container) could confirm that it contained a hollow plutonium shell with a tangle of metal inside it; after dismantlement, a similar gamma-ray image could confirm that a container which was declared to be the pit from that weapon could confirm that it also contained a hollow plutonium shell with a tangle of metal.[15] As noted earlier, the approach could not be used for all warhead types, and would require additional study before implementation.

All of these approaches have advantages and disadvantages. In the end, it is likely that some combination of these approaches will be required.

All of these approaches pose the problem that the measurements of radiation from nuclear warheads and components that they require are likely to contain sensitive information. To deal with that problem, a variety of approaches to "information barriers" have been developed—systems which would take the measurements in a way that could be authenticated, but would tell the monitors only "yes" or "no"—the object had the expected attributes or template, or it did not. To ensure that these systems could not be programmed to report, for example, that an object was a nuclear weapon when it was not, the systems can be built with simple hardware and software, where every line of the code can be inspected; arrangements can also be made in which the systems are built by the inspecting side, which would build extra copies of the systems so that the inspected side could choose

15. Bunn, "Pit-Stuffing."

which one would be used and take another apart to confirm that it was not designed to collect information beyond that agreed to. The "template" approach poses particularly difficult challenges for the protection and control of sensitive information, since the radiation templates themselves would be highly sensitive and would have to be stored and moved from place to place.[16]

In short, technologies and procedures are available which can make it possible to confirm the dismantlement of declared nuclear weapons with reasonable confidence, without revealing sensitive nuclear weapon design information.

## What should be done with fissile materials from dismantled weapons?

If dismantlement is to be permanent, the huge stockpiles of plutonium and HEU that now exist must also be addressed. Once weapons are dismantled, the first steps would be to place the resulting fissile materials in highly secure storage facilities; commit them never again to be used in nuclear weapons; and open them to bilateral or international monitoring.

Over time, stockpiles of fissile materials should then be reduced to the minimum required to support the remaining nuclear weapon stockpiles at each stage (and to support whatever other purposes for these materials are still permitted, such as the use of HEU for naval fuel).[17]

A comprehensive program to make it difficult, costly, and observable to reverse nuclear arms reductions would include verifiable dismantlement of delivery systems (and modification of remaining systems to ensure that they could not carry many more than the agreed

16. See U.S. National Academy of Sciences, *Monitoring Nuclear Weapons and Nuclear-Explosive Materials*, pp. 107–8.

17. U.S. National Academy of Sciences, Committee on International Security and Arms Control, *Management and Disposition of Excess Weapons Plutonium* (Washington, D.C.: National Academy Press, 1994).

number of nuclear weapons); verified dismantlement of nuclear weapons themselves (as just discussed); disposition of all fissile material beyond the amounts required to support the remaining warheads, along with any agreed remaining purposes; and dismantlement or conversion of facilities for producing more delivery vehicles, nuclear weapons, and weapons-useable material. Disposition of excess HEU and plutonium would be one very important element of this program, but only one.

Technically, reducing HEU stockpiles is straightforward, as HEU can be blended with other uranium to produce low-enriched uranium (LEU) that cannot be used in a nuclear bomb but is the standard fuel for commercial nuclear power plants. This approach is already being implemented on a large scale: the U.S.-Russian HEU Purchase Agreement has already destroyed enough HEU for more than 10,000 nuclear weapons. Remarkably, roughly one in ten light bulbs in the United States is fueled with material from dismantled Russian nuclear weapons. Additional blending of HEU to LEU, if managed appropriately so as not to damage uranium and enrichment markets, can help address current shortages of uranium and enrichment services, filling the gap until additional uranium mines and enrichment capabilities are brought on-line to support a growing nuclear energy enterprise.

Disposition of excess plutonium is more difficult. As nearly all mixes of plutonium isotopes can be used in a nuclear bomb, simple blending with other plutonium does not eliminate the security hazard posed by plutonium as it does in uranium's case. Plutonium can be mixed with uranium to produce a mixed oxide (MOX) that can be used as reactor fuel—but doing so is more expensive than using LEU fuel (except when uranium prices are unusually high), even if the plutonium itself is considered "free." Alternatively, plutonium can be immobilized and disposed of as a waste, possibly mixed with highly radioactive fission products to provide a radiation barrier to any effort to recover the plutonium for use in nuclear weapons. Either of these means could make the plutonium from excess nuclear weapons as difficult to use in weapons as the much larger amount of plutonium in the spent fuel from commercial power reactors around the world—the "spent fuel standard."

It is essential to ensure that the highest practicable standards of security and accounting are maintained throughout these processes. Otherwise, removing these materials from secure vaults, processing them in bulk, and shipping them from place to place could *increase,* rather than decrease, the risk of nuclear theft. Measures that are already being implemented for the HEU Purchase Agreement and for civilian use of HEU and plutonium can verify the disposition of these materials.[18]

**What distinctions should be made between strategic and tactical warheads?**

Arms control negotiations to date have focused primarily on strategic nuclear weapons. Only the voluntary and unverified 1991–1992 Presidential Nuclear Initiatives, and other unilateral decisions, have led to large-scale reductions in tactical nuclear weapons.

The United States has sought at least transparency measures for tactical nuclear warhead stockpiles. Russia, which has a large tactical stockpile it regards as an important backup for its comparatively weak conventional forces, has been reluctant to pursue formal controls on tactical nuclear weapons.

Initially, it is very likely that reductions in strategic weapons and in tactical nuclear weapons will be pursued separately. As reductions proceed to low levels, however, it would be desirable to focus more simply on the total number of nuclear weapons. Attempting to distin-

18. For a seminal discussion of these issues, see Committee on International Security and Arms Control, *Management and Disposition of Excess Weapons Plutonium.* For recent updates, see Matthew Bunn and Anatoli Diakov, "Disposition of Excess Highly Enriched Uranium," and "Disposition of Excess Plutonium," in International Panel on Fissile Materials, *Global Fissile Materials Report 2007* (Princeton, N.J.: IPFM, October 2007).

guish strategic nuclear weapons from tactical nuclear weapons in approaches to monitoring warhead dismantlement introduces substantial complications—particularly as some weapon types are used for both tactical and strategic purposes. Thus, the ultimate objective should be a transparency and reductions regime that applies to all nuclear weapons and the stocks of fissile material needed to make them.[19]

**What is the best balance between transparency and secrecy?**

Activities related to nuclear weapons remain shrouded in secrecy. While there has been some increased transparency in some weapons states (particularly the United Kingdom and the United States), the secrecy remains pervasive. So far, secrecy concerns have blocked transparency measures of the kind described in this paper. Although the United States and Russia came close to completing negotiation of a legal framework for exchanging classified nuclear information in the 1990s, many people in the nuclear and security establishments of the United States, Russia, and other weapons states remain extraordinarily reluctant to change traditional secrecy policies.[20]

Ultimately, however, a program of deep, transparent, and irreversible nuclear arms reductions, pointing in the direction of nuclear prohibition, will require major changes in secrecy policies. Increased

19. See, for example, U.S. National Academy of Sciences, *Monitoring Nuclear Weapons and Nuclear-Explosive Materials*.

20. An anecdote illustrates the degree of the problem, even in the United States, which has allowed more transparency than most nuclear weapon states. In the 1990s, after President Clinton announced that excess U.S. plutonium and HEU would be submitted to International Atomic Energy Agency (IAEA) monitoring, the National Security Council staff directed the State Department to chair an interagency discussion of what monitoring measures IAEA inspectors could be allowed to conduct on containers that held components from dismantled weapons without revealing sensitive information. At the meeting, the representatives from the Defense Department and the Defense Programs part of the Department of Energy said that they objected to even holding such an interagency meeting, and that they would not even describe the reasons for their objections. For an argument of the near-completion of the agreement for exchange of classified information, see Goodby, "Transparency and Irreversibility in Nuclear Arms Reductions."

transparency will be required to build international confidence in the ongoing reductions process, and to help each party be confident in the size and management of the others' remaining nuclear stockpiles.

In general, the rule should be that all information related to nuclear weapon design and information that could substantially contribute to planning a nuclear theft should remain secret. All other information could be exchanged, either publicly or on a confidential basis, to the extent to which it contributes to the joint objective of transparent reductions. For each piece of information to be exchanged or opened to monitors, there should be a consideration of the benefits and the risks of providing that information, and it should be provided wherever the benefits outweigh the risks.

### What warhead and fissile material reduction initiatives could have significant security benefits quickly?

It is not possible to dismantle thousands of nuclear weapons quickly. There are, however, a number of initiatives that could have significant security benefits and could be implemented quickly:

- The United States and Russia could launch another round of reciprocal reduction initiatives, while adding limited monitoring arrangements. Thousands of nuclear weapons could be placed in secure storage, committed to eventual verified dismantlement, and opened to monitoring by the other side—in effect placing them under jointly monitored lock and key—within months of a decision to do so. Ideally, such initiatives should include particularly warheads that pose particular security risks—such as readily portable tactical weapons not equipped with modern, difficult-to-bypass electronic locks.

- Commitments can be made quickly. A U.S.-Russian commitment to pursue deep reductions in their nuclear stockpiles, to implement verified dismantlement of weapons, to reduce their plutonium and HEU stockpiles to the minimum required to support reduced nuclear weapon stockpiles, and to open all excess plutonium and HEU to international monitoring could radically transform international perceptions of their commitment to fulfilling their nuclear disarmament obligations. This could be particularly important in the lead-up to the 2010 NPT review conference.

- The United States and Russia already have large stockpiles of plutonium and HEU which have already been declared to be in excess of their military needs. In their Trilateral Initiative with the IAEA, they have already developed legal and technological approaches to placing these materials irrevocably under international monitoring, without revealing sensitive information. A U.S. and Russian announcement that they would open thousands of bombs' worth of material to international monitoring could, in itself, have significant benefits for building support for the nonproliferation regime.

- Declarations of total numbers of nuclear weapons and total stockpiles of fissile materials can be exchanged essentially as soon as decisions can be taken to do so. The sooner such declarations are exchanged, the sooner the governments involved can begin building confidence in their accuracy and completeness.

**Recommendations**

- The United States and Russia, eventually joined by all other states, should work to build a comprehensive transparency regime for nuclear warheads and fissile materials, including measures to confirm the dismantlement of nuclear weapons. This regime should be designed to provide confidence in the size and security of nuclear stockpiles, and confidence in the process of reducing them.

- The United States and Russia should move quickly to commit themselves to deep reductions in their stockpiles of nuclear weapons and materials. Ideally, this commitment should be made prior to the opening of the 2010 NPT review conference. All states should eventually join in these reductions.

- The United States and Russia should move quickly to put thousands of unneeded nuclear weapons in secure, jointly monitored storage, and commit them to be dismantled verifiably as soon as appropriate arrangements can be agreed. They should also take steps to disable these weapons pending dismantlement. Such measures should be considered as part of a post-START reductions and verification regime.

- The United States and Russia should move rapidly to place all of their excess plutonium and HEU under IAEA monitoring—ideally prior to the opening of the 2010 NPT review conference.

- The United States and Russia should work with other nuclear weapons states and non-nuclear weapons states to agree on approaches to confirming warhead dismantlement that all concerned can have confidence in.

- All states participating in dismantlement of nuclear weapons and disposition of excess nuclear material should ensure that the highest practicable standards of security and accounting are maintained throughout these processes.

# 6. Monitoring Nuclear Warheads

## Edward Ifft

**Summary**

The effective verification of deep reductions in, and eventual elimination of, nuclear weapons will be an essential and challenging task, posing verification issues never before encountered in an arms control agreement. The emphasis will be on monitoring warheads, which are considered the most important component of weapons systems. They are also the smallest and contain the most sensitive technology. It is possible to distinguish among four monitoring tasks—deployed warheads, non-deployed warheads, virtual warheads, and disassembled/dismantled warheads.

Fortunately, the successful implementation of the SALT, INF, and START Treaties has provided us with a number of powerful and proven tools. These include National Technical Means, data exchanges, on-site inspection, Perimeter and Portal Continuous Monitoring, nuclear detection devices, and remote monitoring techniques. The experience of UNSCOM and UNMOVIC in Iraq can also be useful.

Counting warheads which are *deployed*, or considered to be deployed, is straightforward and can be carried out with high confidence

The views expressed in this paper are the views of the author and do not necessarily reflect the policies of the United States government.

using techniques which have previously been agreed between the U.S. and the Russian Federation. Monitoring the numbers of *non-deployed* warheads has never been attempted in an arms control agreement. Since this was on the agenda of the 1997 Helsinki Framework (START III), some work was done in the U.S. on how one might approach the task. The appropriate level of intrusiveness also became an issue in the Cooperative Threat Reduction Program. Keeping track of warheads removed from deployed status under agreed procedures should be possible, but an agreed baseline should also be established. Depending upon the degree of confidence required, rather intrusive inspections might be necessary.

Keeping track of "*virtual*" warheads would be similar to the problems posed by non-deployed warheads. If virtual is understood to be simply warheads removed from deployed status under agreed procedures, the problem should be manageable. However, there are systems which have never been deployed, but which are "real" and need to be accounted for, especially at very low levels of deployed systems. In addition, a realistic accounting of a virtual force should also consider the capability of missiles and bombers to carry additional warheads. One reason for this is that it will probably be difficult to account for all non-deployed warheads with high confidence. Another is that a portion of reductions will almost certainly result from "downloading" existing systems. Thus, although the focus will properly be on warheads, one cannot ignore the other components—missiles, missile launchers, and bombers, especially as the numbers get very low.

Monitoring the *disassembly/dismantlement* of warheads and accounting for their special nuclear material will be the final task. Some useful work related to this task was done in anticipation of the Helsinki Framework, most specifically the Trilateral Initiative among the U.S., Russia, and the IAEA. This work should be revived.

Existing, proven verification techniques are adequate for levels significantly lower than presently exist. At very low levels, however, new and quite intrusive measures will be needed, along with higher levels of transparency and trust than exist today. As reductions proceed, things may fall into place faster than we can now anticipate. On the other hand, verification and compliance problems may arise that will make further reductions politically difficult. Thus, it might be wise to plan for strategic pauses or plateaus to assess how well we have designed our verification regime and to make adjustments as necessary.

**Introduction**

Determining numbers of nuclear warheads could well be the most important single task in monitoring a future arms control regime.* Of the three major components of strategic offensive arms—delivery vehicles (missile launchers and heavy bomber airframes), missiles, and warheads—warheads are the most important. They are also by far the smallest and most numerous. They can be moved and stored clandestinely with relative ease, compared to the other components. Thus, a well-designed and rather intrusive verification regime is essential. Even that may not be sufficient to verify effectively certain possible constraints. Fortunately, we do have a number of relevant verification tools that are well-understood and accepted by the U.S. and Russian Federation:

- National Technical Means (NTM)
- Data exchange/Notifications
- On-Site Inspection (OSI), both routine and challenge
- Perimeter and Portal Continuous Monitoring (PPCM)
- Nuclear detection devices, both handheld and fixed
- Remote monitoring techniques developed by UNSCOM and UN-MOVIC in Iraq

One could distinguish among four general monitoring tasks. These

---

*"Warheads" in this paper are understood to mean reentry vehicles for strategic ballistic missiles, as well as bomber armament (ALCMs, SRAMS, gravity bombs).

involve deployed warheads, non-deployed warheads, virtual warheads, and dismantled/disassembled warheads.

## Monitoring Deployed Nuclear Warheads

Warheads deployed on, or attributed to, missiles and bombers are the most likely subjects of monitoring and the case with which we have the most experience. NTM can provide valuable information regarding warheads obtained in observing flight tests. However, NTM is of little use in determining the actual number deployed. Under the START Treaty, the U.S. and the Russian Federation each may conduct up to 10 RV OSIs per year. In the first 10 years of START, the U.S. conducted 99 such inspections, failing to use its full quota only once. The Russians conducted 87. Inasmuch as the procedures are very well established and accepted by both sides, there would seem to be no obvious reason to change them. The number of inspections allowed, of course, could be altered or could be combined with other types of inspections. Factors such as the rights and privileges of inspectors (largely drawn from the Vienna Convention on Diplomatic Relations), timelines, entry/exit points, escorting procedures, financial factors, etc., are all well understood and could be adapted to a new agreement with little change.

Under START, each type of ballistic missile is attributed with a fixed number of RVs. This greatly simplifies the verification task. A missile can be deployed or flight tested with fewer than this number (or with none at all), but not with more. The inspection team declares a specific ICBM or SLBM for inspection, is quickly taken to the site and keeps the missile front section under constant visual observation until the process is completed. The inspection may be carried out at the launcher or in a separate building. The shroud is removed and a hard or soft cover is placed over the RVs. This process is not carried out within the direct sight of the inspectors, but is done in a way that guarantees that no RVs could have been removed. This cover must be of a size and shape that enables the inspection team to determine that no more than the allowed number of RVs could be present under the cover. All members of the team (ten inspectors) are permitted to observe the cover from all angles at fairly close range, but not to touch or photograph it. Thus the procedures are designed to enable inspectors to determine the maximum number of RVs that could be present on the missile, but not their precise shapes or details of their structures or mountings.

It is clear that the procedure above does not distinguish between nuclear and conventional RVs. This is not important in START because the Treaty counts nuclear and conventional warheads equally. If it is desired to count only *nuclear* RVs in a future agreement, the task is clearly more difficult. However, the START Treaty does provide at least the beginnings of how this could be done. The Joint Compliance and Inspection Commission has developed agreed procedures for determining whether an object on the front end of a missile, which could resemble an RV, is nuclear or not. The object can be removed and scanned with a portable neutron detector ($He^3$ tube, moderated with polyethylene). The detector is calibrated using an Americium$^{241}$/Lithium neutron source and the background measured. Under the INF Treaty, agreed procedures were also developed for neutron-counting to determine that a missile was a permitted SS-25 with one warhead, and not a prohibited SS-20 with three warheads. This was necessary because the Soviets deployed SS-25 ICBMs at former SS-20 IRBM bases.

Under START, it is also necessary to monitor the numbers of warheads on heavy bombers. Again, a specific number of warheads is attributed to each type of heavy bomber. Under a special "discounting rule," this number may or may not correspond to the number for which a heavy bomber is actually equipped, but there is no ambiguity regarding the maximum allowed for any specific bomber. The inspection team is allowed to inspect the bomb bay and any rotary or fixed ALCM launcher, if present, as well as attachment points on the wings. From the dimensions measured, along with information provided about both bombers and launchers during technical exhibitions, it is possible to determine that the allowed number of warheads has not been exceeded.

There is also a nuclear dimension to the verification of heavy bomber armament. Because nuclear-armed and conventionally-armed heavy bombers are counted differently and geographically separated, no nuclear armaments are permitted at bases for conventional bombers. Therefore, inspectors may take measurements, using the neutron detectors described above, in the weapon storage areas at conventional bomber bases to determine that no nuclear armaments are present. Because weapons such as ALCMs may be in containers in such storage areas, there are procedures for measuring the nuclear-shielding properties of any such containers.

Under the Moscow Treaty (SORT), life is more complicated. Although this Treaty has no verification regime at all (thus far), it is instructive to consider how it might be verified, since some of its features might be present in a future agreement. There are no "type rules" in SORT. Any particular missile or heavy bomber can have any number of warheads at any particular time, so long as the agreed overall aggregate is not exceeded. These numbers could change from day to day, so that it is not easy to say how much confidence would be gained from spot checks of actual numbers. Monitoring of START is greatly facilitated, not only by agreed counting rules, but also by quite extensive data exchanges, which give inspectors a clear expectation of what they should find on any particular missile or bomber. Deviations from the database, due to lags in notifications or other factors, are clarified by the host side in their briefings to inspectors at the start of the inspection.

The START Treaty is set to expire in December 2009. It could be renewed, but this is not the preferred position of the sides. Negotiations are underway for an agreement to replace START. It is not clear what verification measures will be agreed or what the relationship of a new agreement will be to SORT. In any case, it seems clear that the replacement agreement will have neither the reductions, nor the verification measures contemplated in this study.

Presumably, one would like to have a future agreement that is less complicated than START, but more amenable to verification than SORT. It is not appropriate to go into great detail here, but some guiding principles would be useful. Among these would be that there must be some OSIs, though one would not expect these to be sufficiently numerous as to be statistically significant. There should be a sufficient data exchange that the inspectors have some reasonable expectation of what they will find. It should also be such that the sides can make sense of what they learn from NTM. If only nuclear warheads are to be counted, there should be some geographical separation between nuclear and conventional warheads. For example, ICBMs with nuclear warheads should be based separately from those with conventional warheads. In the case of SSBNs with mixed loads, it should be known which tubes have which type of armament.

It is clear that monitoring a regime that allows no deployed warheads at all is a special case of the above. The concept of eliminating all deployed warheads was put forward in the article in the *Wall Street Journal* by Shultz, Perry, Kissinger, and Nunn on January 4, 2007. This was given a further boost in an important speech by former U.K. Foreign Secretary Margaret Beckett on June 25, 2007, in which she called for a renewed dedication to the goal of complete nuclear disarmament, together with serious new work on how to verify such a regime. The OSI procedures noted above would clearly be applicable to a regime which allowed deployed missiles and bombers, but without nuclear warheads. In principle, determining that there were no warheads would be easier than deducing the maximum number under a cover. Access to the front section of a missile and the bomb bay of a bomber would be sufficient. Of course, this would not guarantee that warheads could not be rapidly installed and, in fact, the sides might insist on such a capability as a hedge. Presumably, there would be some minimum distance between the deployed systems without warheads and the storage sites where the warheads were located. There are similar geographical constraints in START and these can be verified by a combination of NTM and OSI.

## Monitoring Non-Deployed Nuclear Warheads

Monitoring *non-deployed* warheads has never been attempted in an arms control agreement. As reductions in deployed systems proceed, the numbers of non-deployed warheads are increasing and dealing with them is becoming more important. The numbers and locations of such warheads are classified, but there are clearly thousands on each side. The U.S. has announced that it will cut its stockpile in half by 2012, but without revealing what the number is now or what it will be when these reductions are completed. As long as deployed systems exist, there will be a need for some non-deployed systems. There should be declarations of the numbers of non-deployed warheads by systems. If the precise number is considered too sensitive, or is changing rapidly, the declarations could specify a range. The locations should also be declared. Counting these objects would be possible in theory, but difficult and intrusive in practice. As a minimum, there should be a right to challenge inspections to assure the sides that there are no illegal undeclared storage sites. Presumably, the evidence that such might be the case would come from NTM.

A *minimal* monitoring system could involve declarations and perhaps a one-time visit to storage facilities to establish a baseline. Much more intrusive arrangements can also be envisioned. It would be possible to establish a PPCM system at what would presumably be a small number of storage sites. The sides have excellent experience with such systems under the INF and START Treaties. Under START, the sides are allowed up to 30 monitors at a PPCM site. They do not enter the site, but have complete access to the perimeter at any time and can examine items leaving the site that have dimensions such that they could be a controlled item. The small size of warheads could make this a burdensome task, but traffic into, or out of, a facility that only stores warheads should be light. The warhead containers could be tagged and/or could contain a unique identifier. Nuclear detectors could be used to verify that the container did contain nuclear material consistent with a warhead. Experience with designing the Russian Mayak facility would be quite helpful. However, the problems with monitoring and access which arose in connection with this project also illustrate that it may not be possible to establish a highly intrusive system.

One possibility that would avoid extreme intrusiveness would be to establish radiation portal monitors at the entry/exit points of the storage facility. These could resemble the portals now being used at U.S. border crossing points. Because these could be relatively large, they could be more sophisticated than handheld devices. They could be designed to detect both neutrons and gamma-rays. The detectors themselves could be NaI, activated with 1% thallium, and He$^3$ gas tubes. These would not require cooling. The high false alarm rates experienced by similar devices at U.S. border crossings, due to agri-cultural products, ceramics, people with radioactive isotopes in their bodies following medical procedures, etc., should not be a major con-cern at a warhead storage facility. Each type of warhead could be measured to establish a baseline radiation signature or template. The host side should declare each incoming or outgoing warhead and the portal monitor should be able to confirm this declaration. Accurate logs of all movements of warheads into and out of the facility would be essential. In general, however, while Pu should generally be de-tectable, HEU may not be, due to its much lower activity.

It would clearly be desirable to have inspection personnel man-ning the monitors around the clock. If this is considered too intrusive or expensive, it might be possible to establish automated systems, which would transmit data back to an operations center. Such a scheme could draw heavily upon the remote monitoring systems used successfully in Iraq by UNSCOM and UNMOVIC. A system of cam-eras would be highly desirable to assure that warheads were not entering or leaving the complex at locations other than the designated entry/exit points. A still less intrusive system could dispense with real-time remote monitoring, relying more upon periodic visits to check logs and unmanned monitors. This could resemble the system used by the IAEA to monitor Safeguards Agreements.

Under either the manned or unmanned scenario, periodic inspections could be held to provide confidence in the data being accumulated. Attempting to look at all warheads would not be realistic, nor should it be necessary. However, the inspection team could ask to see a number of specific warheads, identified by the unique identifiers on their containers. If this were done successfully at regular intervals, it would provide some confidence that the system was working as intended, without revealing sensitive design information.

It is clear that monitoring non-deployed *tactical* nuclear warheads would be quite similar. However, this task would be complicated by the smaller size and portability of such warheads, as well as the fact that we would be starting with a less reliable intelligence baseline. In any case, the prospects for a negotiation on tactical nuclear weapons in the near future do not appear bright.

**Monitoring Virtual Nuclear Warheads**

Monitoring "virtual" or "latent" nuclear warheads will become increasingly important as countries gradually shift away from operational, deployed forces. Such forces would be similar, but not identical to, those considered "non-deployed" as discussed above. In START, there are systems which have legitimate purposes which are separate from the operational deployed forces, but which have the potential to circumvent the central limits on these deployed forces. Examples are systems used for spares, testing, training, space launch, static displays, etc. These are not counted in the central limits, but are subject to a variety of specific numerical and geographical constraints to limit the possibility that they could be used for hostile purposes. Some of these systems—for example, those used for space launch at designated space launch facilities—should not carry warheads at all. Others—for example, missiles used for testing at designated test ranges—must be allowed to carry dummy warheads.

In order for the concept of virtual forces to be effective, serious consideration must be given to how to define such forces and to verify, at least to some degree, the numbers, locations, and status of these forces. One could then focus on the actual number of warheads in existence, along with the credible capability of the *deployed* delivery force to deliver them. As noted above, while it seems necessary to require declarations of at least the approximate numbers of virtual nuclear *warheads*, verifying these numbers would be very challenging. It might not even be desirable to try (beyond the use of NTM), since any use of OSI would require revealing the locations of these warheads, which in turn would compromise their survivability. Thus, it becomes important to control the *delivery vehicles* on which these warheads could be deployed. These would be fixed and mobile ICBM launchers, SLBM launchers, and bombers. The missiles themselves should also be included. Under the START Treaty, we have extensive successful experience in monitoring non-deployed missile launchers, missiles, and bombers.

Assuming that the primary virtual limit is on *warheads*, there might be no limits *per se* on missiles, launchers, and bombers, but the numbers of such systems must be consistent with the limit on virtual warheads. As an example, if a side declared that it had 1000 virtual ICBM warheads, the capacity of its ICBMs and ICBM launchers should not be wildly in excess of what would be required to deliver these 1,000 warheads, since the 1,000 warhead number itself will probably not be effectively verifiable. A further complication is that one must take into account more than just missiles, launchers, and bombers in storage, mothballed, or otherwise non-deployed. If, as seems highly likely, some portion of the reductions is achieved through "downloading," the capacity of the still-deployed forces should also be taken into account. Thus, if a type of missile which previously was tested and deployed with 10 warheads has been down-loaded to, say, 5 warheads, it would be logical to require that the additional 5 warheads that could be reinstalled on it should be counted in the virtual force. One might decide to count in this way even if the 5 downloaded warheads had been dismantled, since the capability would remain and it could not be ruled out that 5 additional warheads were available or could be readily produced.

Another way of posing the issue is to ask whether virtual warheads are simply all existing warheads which are not deployed, or, alternatively, virtual warheads represent the capability of the existing launchers, missiles, and bombers to deliver warheads beyond those warheads actually deployed. The former would be easy to define, but hard to verify. The latter might be difficult to agree upon, but relatively straightforward to verify once the counting rules were established.

There will clearly be definitional issues to be solved. For example, should missiles and launchers at test ranges and space launch facilities be considered part of the virtual force? What about systems scheduled for dismantlement? Following the example of START, one would probably decide that such systems with legitimate roles would not be considered part of the virtual force. However, this judgment could change as reductions drive the numbers of deployed forces to very low levels. Dealing with bombers could be particularly complicated because of their inherent dual capability. In START, "discounting" rules count the warheads attributed to certain bombers far below their actual capacity. Heavy bombers equipped for non-nuclear arms, train-ing heavy bombers, and former heavy bombers are not counted in the central limits at all, but are subject to an aggregate limit of 75 units. In SORT, the U.S. has taken the position that any heavy bombers it unilaterally declares to be conventionally armed will not count, which will exclude about 100 B-1 and B-2 heavy bombers. In a world with limits on virtual warheads, it seems unlikely that this would be ac-cepted at face value by other countries, without some convincing proof that these bombers could not carry nuclear weapons. Another consideration is that, as levels come down, the fact that bombers of lesser ranges can also deliver nuclear weapons will likely come into play.

In all of these cases, the amount of time and modification required to return virtual forces to operational status will be relevant in deciding what should be included in the virtual force. None of these issues should be insuperable, but it is clear that serious thought, negotiation, and compromise will be required.

## Monitoring the Disassembly/Dismantlement of Nuclear Warheads

This is clearly the most intrusive and most difficult task related to warheads. Some work was done in connection with the 1997 Helsinki Framework, which did envision such monitoring. A prime consideration is the legal barriers which exist on both sides, some of which also apply to the previous section. For the U.S., the 1954 Atomic Energy Act, as amended, requires a special agreement for sharing stockpile information with other nations in support of a program for the control and accounting of nuclear weapons and fissile material, as well as other weapons material. In addition, certain guarantees would be required regarding the protection of such information. There appear to be similar legal requirements on the Russian side.

A successful regime should provide for declarations of the numbers of warheads in retired status and those designated for retirement, along with their locations. A dismantlement schedule should be created, along with notification of warheads actually dismantled, by number and type. For completeness, one would presumably also need information on weapons-grade fissile material not in nuclear weapons—for example, in naval reactors, research reactors, and space systems. It is clear that there is some overlap with a Fissile Material Cutoff Treaty, which has its own set of problems.

A further difficult problem concerns how one can be assured that the fissile material presented actually came from a nuclear weapon. In theory, a system of seals, tags, and intrusive OSI could verify the origin and chain-of-custody of the material. Whether this is achievable in practice, and whether it is really necessary, are open to question. On the technical side, the Trilateral Initiative among the U.S., Russia, and the IAEA led to the concept of an "information barrier." The objective would be to determine that objects in containers have certain attributes of nuclear weapon pits. The device would use gamma spectrometry to detect the presence of Pu, high-resolution gamma spectrometry to determine that the object contains at least a threshold ratio of $Pu^{239}$ to total Pu and neutron multiplicity counting to determine the presence of at least a threshold mass of Pu. The answer would be indicated by a red or green light, showing whether or not the object met the criteria, but without revealing sensitive design information, such as shape or specific isotopic composition. Although all three parties seemed pleased with the technical progress made, the Trilateral Initiative has stalled. The reasons for this are not entirely clear, though the legal issues noted above may be part of the problem. In any case, the effort should be revived, since success seems crucial to any attempt to monitor and control the dismantlement of nuclear warheads.

Efforts should also be resumed to consider how inspectors could be granted access to sensitive disassembly/dismantlement facilities— e.g., Pantex on the U.S. side. Monitoring the final disposition of fissile material, whether as reactor fuel, vitrification or by some other method is beyond the scope of this paper.

As reductions proceed, things may fall into place faster than we can now anticipate. On the other hand, verification and compliance problems may arise that will make further reductions politically difficult. Thus, it might be wise to plan for strategic pauses or plateaus to assess how well we have designed the verification regime and to make adjustments as necessary.

# 7. Securing Nuclear Stockpiles Worldwide
**Matthew Bunn**

## Key Judgments

- Nuclear terrorism is a real and urgent threat. Both al Qaeda and Aum Shinrikyo (and possibly some Chechen factions) have sought nuclear weapons and the materials to make them. If a sophisticated and well-financed group got separated plutonium or highly enriched uranium (HEU), it is plausible they could make a crude nuclear explosive.

- The most effective tool for reducing this risk is to strengthen security for all nuclear weapons and weapons-usable nuclear materials worldwide. Preventing theft of nuclear weapons and materials would also block a major shortcut for states seeking nuclear weapons. After nuclear material has been stolen, all later lines of defense are variations on looking for needles in haystacks.

- Accurate and transparent accounting of nuclear weapons and materials stockpiles—a key part of a comprehensive nuclear security approach—will also be an essential part of a verifiable path to deep reductions in, or prohibition of, nuclear weapons.

- Although current efforts to improve security for nuclear weapons and materials have made substantial progress, particularly in Russia, unacceptable risks remain. Hundreds of buildings with plutonium or HEU in many countries around the world are demonstrably not secured against the kinds of outsider and insider threats that terrorists and criminals have shown they can pose.

- Efforts to improve nuclear security around the world must meet three goals: to improve security *fast enough* so that the security upgrades get there before the thieves do; to improve security to a *high enough level* to protect stockpiles of nuclear weapons and materials against plausible terrorist and criminal threats; and to *sustain* effective security over time. There are inevitable tensions between these three goals, but all must be met to reduce the risk of nuclear terrorism substantially for the long haul.

- The main obstacles to achieving these goals are: (a) complacency about the threat; (b) resistance from nuclear managers and officials who would have to pay the costs and bear the inconveniences of improved security; (c) secrecy; (d) concerns over national sovereignty; (e) bureaucratic inertia; and (f) the sheer difficulty of changing the attitudes and daily behavior (the "security culture") of thousands of people around the world who handle or guard nuclear weapons and materials.

*Recommendations*

- *Sustained leadership.* The most important ingredient for overcoming the obstacles to securing nuclear stockpiles is sustained leadership from the highest levels of government, in Washington, Moscow, and capitals around the world. The U.S. president should appoint a senior full-time official in the White House to ensure that preventing nuclear terrorism gets the sustained high-level attention it requires, and encourage Russia and other states to do likewise.

- *Explaining the urgency of the threat.* Making the needed action happen will require convincing political leaders and nuclear managers around the world that nuclear terrorism is a real and urgent global threat worthy of their time and resources. A variety of approaches should be pursued to make this case, including joint briefings on the threat (by U.S. experts and experts from the particular country concerned); nuclear terrorism war games and simulations; fast-paced reviews of whether the nuclear security measures in place are sufficient to defeat specified outsider or insider threats (by experts from each country, or foreign experts if the country so wishes); and realistic tests of the performance of nuclear security systems in defeating plausible outsider and insider threats.

- *A global nuclear security campaign.* The United States and Russia should seek to lead a fast-paced global campaign to achieve effective and sustainable security for all nuclear weapons and weapons-usable nuclear materials worldwide as quickly as practicable, using all policy tools available. The recent Global Initiative to Combat Nuclear Terrorism is one, but only one, of the policy tools that must be brought to bear. This campaign should pursue partnership-based approaches which respect national sovereignty and draw on ideas and resources from all participants—and which can be implemented while protecting nuclear secrets.

- *An expanded and accelerated global cleanout of vulnerable nuclear stockpiles.* A key element of such a campaign must be an expanded and accelerated global effort to remove the weapons-usable nuclear material entirely from vulnerable sites around the world. This must include stronger efforts to convert research reactors from HEU to low-enriched fuels and to shut down unneeded HEU-fueled reactors; expanded efforts to ship the HEU from such sites to secure locations; and targeted incentives to convince states and reactor operators to convert or shut down and give up their HEU.

- *Forging effective global nuclear security standards.* The United States and other leading nuclear weapon and nuclear energy countries should seek to put in place global nuclear security standards that will ensure that all nuclear weapons and every significant cache of plutonium or HEU has adequate protection from theft.

UNSC Resolution 1540 already legally requires all states to pro-vide "appropriate effective" security and accounting for nuclear stockpiles; the United States and its partners should seek a com-mon understanding on the essential elements of such "appropriate effective" systems and seek to help (and pressure) states to put them in place.

- *Building sustainability and security culture.* Another key element of the global campaign will be helping states put in place the resources, organizations, and incentives needed to sustain effective security for the long haul, and strong security cultures. Effective and effectively enforced nuclear security rules are particularly im-portant, as without them, most nuclear managers will not invest in expensive security measures.
- *Beyond nuclear security.* The United States and other leading states should also take new steps to detect and disrupt potential nuclear terrorist groups; interdict nuclear smuggling; deter and prevent nuclear transfers from states to terrorist groups; strengthen the norm against mass slaughter of civilians in the Muslim world and elsewhere; and address the root causes of terrorist violence.

## Background

Effectively securing the world's stockpiles of nuclear weapons and the materials needed to make them is the single most effective step that can be taken to reduce the deadly risk of nuclear terrorism—and to block a major potential shortcut for states seeking nuclear weapons as well.[1] Moreover, accurate and transparent accounting of these stocks—an important element of a comprehensive nuclear security

---

1. This paper addresses only terrorist use of actual nuclear explosives—either stolen nuclear weapons, or crude nuclear explosives terrorists might be able to make from nuclear material they managed to acquire. It does not address more likely but much less catastrophic radiological "dirty bomb" attacks; nor does it address sabotage of major nuclear facilities. It draws heavily on Matthew Bunn, *Securing the Bomb* (Cambridge, Mass.: Project on Managing the Atom, Harvard University and Nuclear Threat Initiative, 2007).

system—is also a key element of a verifiable path to deep reductions in, or prohibition of, nuclear weapons. Unfortunately, the obstacles to rapidly and sustainably achieving stringent standards of security for all nuclear stockpiles worldwide are substantial.

Nuclear terrorism remains a real and urgent danger. The facts that frame the danger are stark.

*Terrorists are seeking nuclear weapons.* By word and deed, al Qaeda and the global movement it has spawned have made it clear that they want nuclear weapons.[2] Osama bin Laden has called acquiring nuclear weapons a "religious duty." Despite the post-9/11 disruptions it has faced, the evidence suggests that al Qaeda continues to seek nuclear weapons and the materials and expertise to make them. In his memoir, former Director of Central Intelligence George Tenet provides frightening new information on al Qaeda's nuclear efforts— including a report from a senior al Qaeda operative that the group's nuclear weapons program had advanced to the point of conventional explosive testing. Tenet says that he is "convinced" that Osama bin Laden still "desperately" wants a nuclear bomb.[3] The removal of al Qaeda's sanctuary in Taliban-led Afghanistan and the disruption of al Qaeda's central command reduced the risk, but it appears that al Qaeda is rebuilding in the Pakistan-Afghanistan border areas. U.S. intelligence assesses that the al Qaeda leadership "continues to plan high-impact plots" with "the goal of producing mass casualties," and continues to seek nuclear, chemical, biological, and radiological weapons.[4] Nor is this only an American fear: In late 2005, for example,

2. See discussion in Matthew Bunn and Anthony Wier with Joshua Friedman, "The Demand for Black Market Fissile Material," in *Nuclear Threat Initiative Research Library: Securing the Bomb* (Cambridge, Mass.: Project on Managing the Atom, Harvard University and Nuclear Threat Initiative, 2005; available at www.nti.org/e_research/cnwm/threat/demand.asp as of January 2, 2007).

3. George Tenet, *At the Center of the Storm: My Years at the CIA* (New York: Harper Collins, 2007), pp. 275, 279.

4. U.S. National Intelligence Council, *National Intelligence Estimate: The Terrorist Threat to the U.S. Homeland* (Washington, D.C.: Office of the Director of

Russian Interior Minister Rashid Nurgaliev, in charge of the MVD troops guarding nuclear facilities, confirmed that in recent years "international terrorists have planned attacks against nuclear and power industry installations" intended to "seize nuclear materials and use them to build weapons of mass destruction for their own political ends."[5]

*Huge stockpiles of nuclear weapons and potential nuclear bomb material exist worldwide.* Today, world stockpiles include some 25,000 nuclear weapons and an estimated 2,300 tons of highly enriched uranium (HEU) or separated plutonium. Nine countries possess nuclear weapons, and U.S. nuclear weapons are physically located in several additional countries. Weapons-usable nuclear materials exist in more than 40 countries, in hundreds of individual buildings. Hundreds of transports of nuclear weapons or potential nuclear bomb material—the part of their life cycles where they are most vulnerable to overt, violent theft—occur every year. Many thousands of people around the world have access to either nuclear weapons or the materials needed to make them.

*Some nuclear stockpiles are dangerously insecure.* Security at some of these buildings is excellent; at others, it amounts to little more than a night watchman and a chain-link fence.[6] Many sites have security and control measures that are demonstrably insufficient to defeat the kinds of sophisticated insider conspiracies or large-scale outsider attacks that terrorists and criminals have successfully carried out in a variety of countries around the world. No binding global standards currently exist specifying how secure nuclear weapons and the materials needed to make them must be.

Remarkably, it appears that neither the U.S. government nor the

---

National Intelligence, 2007; available at www.dni.gov/press_releases/20070717_release.pdf as of August 3, 2007).

5. "Internal Troops to Make Russian State Facilities Less Vulnerable to Terrorists," *RIA-Novosti*, October 5, 2005.

6. For discussion, see, for example, Bunn, *Securing the Bomb*, 2007.

International Atomic Energy Agency (IAEA) yet has a prioritized list assessing which facilities around the world pose the most serious risks of nuclear theft, integrating assessments of the quantity and quality of material at each site, the security at that site, and the level of capability adversaries could bring to bear for an attempted theft at that site. Such a prioritized assessment should be prepared urgently, and updated regularly. Based on the limited publicly available data on these factors, it appears that the highest risks of nuclear theft today are in Russia, Pakistan, and at HEU-fueled research reactors.

Nuclear security in Russia has improved dramatically since the mid-1990s, as a result of U.S. and international assistance, Russia's own efforts, and Russia's newfound economic strength. The most egregious security weaknesses have been fixed, and it is unlikely that one person with no particular plan could steal HEU or plutonium at any nuclear facility in the Russian Federation today, as occurred in several cases in the 1990s. But real risks remain, from persistent under-funding of nuclear security systems, weak nuclear security regulations, widespread corruption, and conscript guard forces rife with hazing and suicide, coupled with threats ranging from surprise attack by scores of heavily armed terrorists to sophisticated insider theft conspiracies. The 2006 firing of Major General Sergey Shlyapuzhnikov, deputy chairman of the section of the Ministry of Interior (MVD) responsible for law and order in the closed territories (including the closed nuclear cities), for helping to organize smuggling in and out of those closed territories, is an indicator of the systemic corruption that creates dangerous possibilities for sophisticated insider conspiracies.[7] Russia has the world's largest stockpile of nuclear weapons and materials, and remains the only state in the world where authorities have confirmed that terrorists have been carrying out reconnaissance at nuclear warhead storage sites.

7. "The President Issued a Decree to Dismiss Deputy Chairman of the MVD Department in Charge of Law and Order in Closed Territories and Sensitive Sites, Major General Sergey Shlyapuzhnikov," *Rossiyskaya Gazeta*, June 2, 2006.

Similarly, in Pakistan, nuclear insiders have met with bin Laden to discuss nuclear weapons, and have marketed sensitive nuclear technologies around the world; the outsider threat includes both a reconstituted al Qaeda and a wide range of other jihadi groups. Serving Pakistani military officers cooperating with al Qaeda operatives have twice come close to assassinating the Pakistani president; who can be confident that officers guarding nuclear weapons will never cooperate with al Qaeda?

HEU-fueled research reactors pose another high-priority theft risk. More than 140 research reactors in dozens of countries around the world are still fueled by HEU (though usually in forms that would require modest chemical processing before the material could be used in a bomb), and many of these facilities have modest security in place—again, no more than a night watchman and a chain-link fence in some cases. Beyond these three highest priorities, other nuclear theft risks exist around the world, from large-scale transports of civilian plutonium to nuclear stockpiles in developing states such as China and India.

*Nuclear theft is an ongoing reality.* The seizure of stolen 89% enriched HEU in Georgia in early 2006 is a stark reminder that nuclear theft and smuggling is not a hypothetical worry but an ongoing fact of international life. The IAEA has documented some 17 cases of seizure of stolen HEU or separated plutonium confirmed by the states concerned; there are additional cases that certainly occurred (the relevant individuals have confessed and been convicted) but that the relevant states have not yet officially confirmed to the IAEA. U.S. intelligence assesses that additional undetected thefts have occurred.[8]

8. Probably the best available summary of what we know and what we cannot know from the known cases of nuclear and radiological smuggling is "Illicit Trafficking in Radioactive Materials," in *Nuclear Black Markets: Pakistan, A. Q. Khan and the Rise of Proliferation Networks: A Net Assessment* (London: International Institute for Strategic Studies, 2007). There are 18 cases currently on the IAEA's list, but one is a case of discovery of substantial HEU contamination which may not have involved stolen material. For the U.S. intelligence assessment, see U.S. National In-

The critical question which cannot be answered is, How many cases, of what magnitude, have gone undetected?

*State transfers to terrorists are a real, but lower, risk.* Because of the immense danger of being found out, under all but a few circumstances, states are extremely unlikely to consciously decide to transfer a nuclear weapon or weapons-usable nuclear materials in their possession to a terrorist group. Such a decision would mean transferring the most awesome military power the state had ever acquired to a group over which it had little control—a particularly unlikely step for dictators or oligarchs obsessed with controlling their states and maintaining power. Such transfers might be more plausible, however, if (a) the state became desperate enough that the money or other items that might be gained in return for nuclear material were seen as critical to the survival of the regime (or of its key leaders), or (b) the regime was convinced that it was about to collapse or be overthrown in any case, and such a transfer was seen as a last act of revenge. In addition, the line between theft-and-transfer and conscious state transfer may not always be a bright one: While the North Korean regime presumably exercises tight control over its small nuclear stockpile, for example (given its importance to the regime), in the pervasive corruption of the North Korean state, one could imagine a scenario in which a leading general (or a small clique of officers) concluded that there was enough plutonium available that a bomb's worth could be sold to terrorists for cash without the rest of the government becoming aware of the transfer. Hence, steps to convince states such as North Korea and Iran to verifiably abandon their nuclear weapons efforts and eliminate any weapons or weapons-usable nuclear material in their possession are clearly also an important part of a nuclear-terrorism-prevention agenda. Efforts to make such transfers more difficult—such as the current program to put radiation detectors at key border cross-

---

telligence Council, *Annual Report to Congress on the Safety and Security of Russian Nuclear Facilities and Military Forces* (Washington, D.C.: Central Intelligence Agency, 2006; available at www.fas.org/irp/nic/russia0406.html as of May 16, 2007).

ings from North Korea into China—should also be pursued, but given the immense difficulties of stopping such transfers, no one should rely on such measures to reduce the risk by more than a few percent.

*Nuclear smuggling is extraordinarily hard to stop.* Whether terrorists got a nuclear bomb or nuclear material from a state or after it had been stolen, it would be extraordinarily difficult to find and recover it, or to stop it from being smuggled within or between countries. Attempting to protect the United States or any other large country from nuclear terrorism by detecting and stopping nuclear contraband at the country's borders is like a football team defending at its own goal line—but with that goal line stretched to thousands of kilometers, much of it unguarded wilderness, with millions of people and vehicles legitimately crossing it every year. After all, thousands of tons of illegal drugs and hundreds of thousands of illegal immigrants cross U.S. borders every year despite massive efforts to stop them.

The nuclear materials needed to make a nuclear bomb would fit in a suitcase. Moreover, the radioactivity from these materials is weak and difficult to detect from any substantial distance. The radiation detectors now being installed at borders around the world would have little chance of detecting the radiation from a shielded package of HEU. Technologies such as active nuclear detectors (which probe the items they are searching with beams of radiation) and combining nuclear detection with X-rays to detect shielding may help, but pose their own problems and difficulties.

In any case, the obvious question is why a nuclear smuggler would bring his HEU or plutonium through an official border crossing with readily observable inspectors and radiation detectors in the first place. There are countless other opportunities for going uninspected across the wild borderlands of the world—including U.S. borders. In the United States, it remains perfectly legal to sail up the Hudson or the Potomac with an uninspected oceangoing yacht, to give just one example.

Despite the difficulties, there is a wide range of steps that can and should be taken to make smuggling more difficult, including measures to strengthen international police and intelligence cooperation, to pursue additional demand stings (posing as buyers of nuclear material or expertise) and supply stings (posing as sellers), and to encourage the semi-feudal chieftains who control some of the world's most dangerous borders to let us know about transports of nuclear material.[9] It is also worth investing in improved border detection systems to make the nuclear smuggler's job more difficult and uncertain. But this line of defense will inevitably be highly porous, and the world should not place undue reliance on it.

*A terrorist nuclear attack would be a devastating catastrophe, with global effects.* Finally, detonation of even a crude terrorist bomb in a major city would be a catastrophe of historic proportions. A bomb with the explosive power of 10,000 tons of TNT (that is, 10 "kilotons," somewhat smaller than the bomb that obliterated Hiroshima), if set off in midtown Manhattan on a typical workday, could kill half a million people and cause more than $1 trillion in direct economic damage.[10] Neither the United States nor any other country in the world is remotely prepared to cope with the aftermath of such an attack—the need to care for tens of thousands of burned, wounded, and irradiated victims (far more than the entire country's supply of burn or radiation treatment beds), the need to evacuate hundreds of thousands of people in the path of the fallout, the enormous challenge of restoring essential services to a partly burned and irradiated city, and more.[11] Devastating economic aftershocks would reverberate through-

9. See, for example, Rensselaer Lee, "Nuclear Smuggling: Patterns and Responses," *Parameters: U.S. Army War College Quarterly* (Spring 2003; available at carlisle-www.army.mil/usawc/Parameters/03spring/lee.pdf as of July 9, 2007).

10. See Matthew Bunn, Anthony Wier, and John Holdren, *Controlling Nuclear Warheads and Materials: A Report Card and Action Plan* (Cambridge, Mass. and Washington, D.C.: Project on Managing the Atom, Harvard University and Nuclear Threat Initiative, 2003; available at www.nti.org/e_research/cnwm/cnwm.pdf as of January 2, 2007), pp. 15–19.

11. Ashton B. Carter, Michael M. May, and William J. Perry, *The Day After:*

out the country and the world. America and the world would be transformed forever—and not for the better.

Nor is nuclear terrorism a threat only to the United States. Al
Qaeda or al Qaeda-inspired attacks intended to inflict mass casualties
have occurred throughout the world. The Japanese terror cult Aum
Shinrikyo, which launched a nerve gas attack in the Tokyo subways
and attempted to build a nuclear bomb, was a wholly homegrown
Japanese phenomenon—and such a group might sprout the next time
in virtually any country. Moreover, even if the target was the United
States, the effects would be global. While UN Secretary-General, Kofi
Annan estimated that the reverberating global economic effects of a
nuclear terrorist attack would be sufficiently severe to push "tens of
millions of people into dire poverty," creating "a second death toll
throughout the developing world."[12] In short, insecure weapons-usable
nuclear material anywhere is a threat to everyone, everywhere.

*Existing programs are making real but insufficient progress in
reducing the threat.* Since the 1990s, the original seed sown through
the vision of Senator Sam Nunn and Senator Richard Lugar in 1991
has grown into a broad suite of programs to reduce nuclear, chemical,
and biological threats, sponsored by many countries. Such cooperative
programs have drastically reduced the risks posed by some of the
world's highest-risk nuclear stockpiles, providing a benefit for U.S.
and world security far beyond their cost—and demonstrating what can
be done to address these threats. As already noted, the progress in the
former Soviet Union has been particularly substantial; the most egre-

---

*Action in the 24 Hours Following a Nuclear Blast in an American City*, a report based
on a workshop hosted by the Preventive Defense Project (Cambridge, Mass. and
Stanford, Calif., Harvard and Stanford Universities, Preventive Defense Project, May
2007; available at belfercenter.ksg.harvard.edu/files/dayafterworkshopreport_
May2007.pdf).

12. Kofi Annan, "A Global Strategy for Fighting Terrorism: Keynote Address to
the Closing Plenary," in *The International Summit on Democracy, Terrorism and
Security* (Madrid: Club de Madrid, 2005; available at english.safe-democracy.org/
keynotes/a-global-strategy-for-fighting-terrorism.html as of July 9, 2007).

gious security weaknesses there (gaping holes in fences, sites with no security camera in the nuclear material area and no detector to set off an alarm if HEU or plutonium is removed) have been fixed. By the end of fiscal year (FY) 2006, more comprehensive U.S.-sponsored security upgrades had been completed for over half of the buildings with weapons-usable nuclear materials and over half of the nuclear warhead sites.[13] The United States and Russia have set a joint goal of completing cooperative upgrades by the end of 2008; while that goal will be very challenging to meet, upgrades at the sites where the two countries have agreed to cooperate are likely to be completed either by the agreed deadline or within a year or two thereafter. The United States and Russia, however, have never agreed to cooperate on a significant number of nuclear material buildings believed to contain large quantities of nuclear material, or on some of Russia's nuclear warhead sites (especially temporary sites).

With the agreed upgrades nearing completion, the most important policy questions now focus on more intangible, difficult-to-measure factors: Are sufficient security measures being put in place, given the scope of the outsider and insider threats in Russia? Will effective security be sustained over time, after U.S. assistance phases out? Will security cultures at all of these sites be strong enough to ensure that the equipment will actually be used in a way that provides effective security, and guards will not be turning off intrusion detectors or staff propping open security doors? DOE and Rosatom reached an accord in April 2007 on specific steps toward sustainability to take at each Rosatom site, which is a major step forward. There is significant progress on security culture as well—but both sustainability and security culture remain major challenges, not only at Rosatom sites but at non-Rosatom nuclear material sites and nuclear warhead sites as well.

Outside of the former Soviet Union, many nuclear security improvement efforts are still in their early stages, and significant gaps

13. For a detailed discussion, see Bunn, *Securing the Bomb*, 2007.

remain. The United States and other countries have provided assistance to upgrade security for more than three-quarters of the world's HEU-fueled research reactors whose physical protection did not match IAEA recommendations, but only a small fraction of these has been upgraded to levels designed to defeat demonstrated terrorist and criminal threats. U.S. nuclear security cooperation with Pakistan is underway, but what precisely has been accomplished remains a secret. In China, one civilian site with HEU has had extensive security and accounting upgrades, and a broad dialogue is underway regarding a range of security and accounting measures, but it remains unclear how much effect this dialogue has had on improving security for other Chinese facilities, and cooperation on military stockpiles remains stymied. Nuclear security cooperation was not included in the summit pact on nuclear cooperation with India, and India has so far refused any cooperation in this area. Both sustainability and security culture are likely to be serious issues for nuclear security improvements worldwide (as they are in the United States).

Efforts to remove nuclear material from potentially vulnerable sites and to convert research reactors to use non-weapons-usable low-enriched uranium (LEU) as their fuel have accelerated since the establishment of the Global Threat Reduction Initiative (GTRI) in 2004. Moreover, in the last year, GTRI expanded the list of reactors it hopes to convert. But only a small fraction of the HEU-fueled research reactor sites around the world have yet had all their HEU removed. Even with its expanded scope, however, the conversion effort will leave roughly 40 percent of the world's currently operating HEU-fueled reactors uncovered. Large amounts of weapons-usable nuclear material are also not yet being addressed. For example, only 5.2 tons of the 17 tons of U.S.-origin HEU abroad is covered by the current U.S. offer to take it back, and GTRI currently plans to take back less than a third of the eligible material (though GTRI does plan to address almost a ton of additional U.S.-origin HEU in its "gap" material program). Some of the material not covered is being reprocessed or oth-

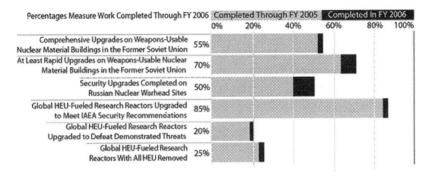

**Figure 1.  Progress of U.S.-Funded Programs to Secure Nuclear Stockpiles**

erwise addressed abroad, and some of it is at sites with highly effective security—but some of it is not. See Figure 1 for a summary of several key measures of the progress of U.S.-funded programs to improve nuclear security.[14] Clearly, while these programs have been excellent investments in U.S. and world security, there is much more yet to be done.

The Global Initiative to Combat Nuclear Terrorism, launched in July 2006, may become an important tool for convincing governments around the world that nuclear terrorism is a real and urgent threat, and focusing them on specific actions they can take to reduce the risk. Unfortunately, the principles the participants have accepted are extremely general, and there appears to have been little effort to use this format to gain agreement on effective standards for nuclear security that all participants would agree to maintain. As yet, there is little evidence that the initiative has led to any substantial improvements in nuclear security, and the jury is still out on how important it will prove to be.

## Issues

Urgent action is needed to prevent a nuclear 9/11. While much has been accomplished—demonstrating the potential for international co-

14. For the data and discussion behind this figure, see Bunn, *Securing the Bomb*, 2007.

operation to reduce the risk—much more remains to be done. Efforts to improve nuclear security around the world must meet three goals: to improve security *fast enough* so that the security upgrades get there before the thieves do; to improve security to a *high enough level* to protect stockpiles of nuclear weapons and materials against plausible terrorist and criminal threats; and to *sustain* effective security over time. There are inevitable tensions between these three goals, as slapped-together systems can be put in place quickly, but may not provide high enough levels of security or be sustainable for the long haul; but all must be met to reduce the risk of nuclear terrorism substantially for the long haul. Success will require addressing several key issues.

*How much nuclear security is enough?* No nuclear security system can defend against every conceivable threat.[15] Designing nuclear security systems to defend against more capable insider and outsider threats reduces the risk that adversaries might be able to overcome those security systems—but costs more, and creates new inconveniences. Where does the best balance of risk and cost lie?

There is no one clear answer to this question. But given the terrorist threats the world now faces, it seems clear that at a minimum, every nuclear weapon and every significant cache of HEU or separated plutonium worldwide should at least be protected against a modest group of well-trained and well-armed outside attackers (capable of operating in more than one team, and with access to inside information about the security system), one or two well-placed insiders, or both working together. In some countries, where terrorists and thieves are particularly active and capable, it will be necessary to defend against

---

15. Indeed, while nuclear security improvements can greatly reduce the risk of nuclear terrorism, policymakers should understand that they are not a panacea. If Pakistan becomes a failed state, for example, or a faction allied with the Taliban takes power, better fences and intrusion detectors at its nuclear sites will not solve the problem. Similarly, if a general commanding a nuclear site decides to sell off nuclear material, or 200 well-trained and well-armed attackers assault a facility, most currently contemplated nuclear security measures would be of little help.

even more capable threats to reduce the remaining nuclear terrorism risk to a low level.

*How much will it cost, and how long will it take?* Here, too, there is no single, well-understood answer. As far as is publicly known, no government or international organization has a listing of all the facilities and transport organizations handling nuclear weapons and weapons-usable materials worldwide and what level of security upgrades they would each require to meet a particular chosen level of security. There is good reason to believe, however, that a further investment in the range of $5 billion would be enough to remove the nuclear stockpiles entirely from the world's most vulnerable sites and provide sufficient security to reduce the risk of nuclear theft at the remaining sites to a low level, and that this could be accomplished within approximately four years. (In current threat-reduction programs, cooperative security upgrades at a site are typically completed within 18 months of the start of work, except at the largest, most complex sites.) There would then be a continuing requirement for hundreds of millions of dollars a year in spending by countries around the world to sustain effective security.

*How can we overcome the obstacles that have constrained progress?* Rapidly achieving such security standards for all the many caches of nuclear weapons and materials worldwide will not be easy. Key obstacles that will have to be overcome include (a) complacency about the threat; (b) resistance from nuclear managers and officials who would have to pay the costs and bear the inconveniences of improved security; (c) secrecy; (d) concerns over national sovereignty; (e) bureaucratic inertia; and (f) the sheer difficulty of changing the attitudes and daily behavior (the "security culture") of thousands of people around the world who handle or guard nuclear weapons and materials.

Overcoming these obstacles will require a sea-change in the level of sustained leadership from the highest levels of government in Washington, Moscow, and other capitals around the world. Day-in, day-out engagement will be required, not just occasional encouraging statements. To overcome the current widespread complacency, new steps to convince policymakers and facility managers around the world that nuclear terrorism is a real and urgent threat will be needed; several such steps are recommended below. These steps to increase the sense of urgency should also make policymakers more likely to be willing to override resistance to new nuclear security measures in their nuclear bureaucracies (as occurred in the U.S. Department of Energy (DOE) complex after the 9/11 attacks); bypassing such resistance is also likely to require seeking initial broad commitments at high political levels, where officials are more likely to be able to balance the threat to their nation from the risk of nuclear terrorism against the cost of increased security measures. A range of approaches can make it possible to confirm that a donor state's money is being used appropriately while protecting legitimate nuclear and security secrets—and ongoing cooperation with countries such as Russia and Pakistan makes clear that these approaches can go a long way toward addressing secrecy concerns.

To address concerns over national sovereignty—and to build the kind of "buy in" among the people who will be using and maintaining nuclear security systems—it will be essential to pursue partnership-based approaches to nuclear security cooperation which allow states to choose different approaches to similar nuclear security objectives and which draw on ideas and resources from all participants in ways that serve each of their national interests, not just the donor state's interests.[16] For countries like India and Pakistan, for example, the opportunity to join with the major nuclear states in jointly addressing a

16. For a useful account of what genuinely partnership-based approaches would look like in the U.S.-Russian context, see U.S. Committee on Strengthening U.S. and Russian Cooperative Nuclear Nonproliferation, National Research Council, and Russian Committee on Strengthening U.S. and Russian Cooperative Nuclear Nonproliferation, Russian Academy of Sciences, *Strengthening U.S.-Russian Cooperation on Nuclear Nonproliferation* (Washington, D.C.: National Academy Press, 2005; available at fermat.nap.edu/catalog/11302.html as of July 9, 2007).

global problem is more politically appealing than portraying the work as U.S. assistance necessitated because they are unable to adequately control their nuclear stockpiles on their own. In the past, concerns over national sovereignty and other obstacles have blocked efforts to negotiate stringent global nuclear security standards in formal treaties, and this is likely to be the case in the near-term future as well; other approaches to forging global standards are recommended below.

Overcoming bureaucratic inertia is likely to require new approaches to institutionalizing high-level attention to the problem in Washington, Moscow, and other leading capitals. Finally, building sustainability and changing security cultures is likely to begin with convincing the staff of nuclear organizations around the world of the reality of the threat; even once that has been accomplished, success is likely to require high-level management commitment and creative approaches.

## Recommendations

### *A Global Campaign to Prevent Nuclear Terrorism*

The danger of nuclear theft and terrorism is a global problem, requiring a global response. President Bush, working with other world leaders, should launch a global campaign to lock down every nuclear weapon and every significant cache of potential nuclear bomb material worldwide, as rapidly as that can possibly be done—and to take other key steps to reduce the risk of nuclear terrorism. This effort must be at the center of U.S. national security policy and diplomacy—an issue to be raised with every country with stockpiles to secure or resources to help, at every level, at every opportunity, until the job is done.

This campaign should creatively and flexibly integrate a broad range of policy tools to achieve the objective—from technical experts cooperating to install improved security systems at particular sites to presidents and prime ministers meeting to overcome obstacles to cooperation. In some cases, the recently launched Global Initiative to

Combat Nuclear Terrorism may provide the right forum to pursue these goals; in others, high-level bilateral initiatives such as the nuclear security agreement reached between President Bush and Russian President Putin in 2005 may offer the most effective approach; in still others, cooperation led by international organizations such as the IAEA may be the forum that other countries most readily accept. Such a campaign should also include expanding the mission, personnel, and funding of the IAEA's Office of Nuclear Security, as there are many steps the widely-respected international organization can take more effectively than the United States can unilaterally.

*Adapting Nunn-Lugar.* The cooperative threat-reduction approaches developed in the former Soviet Union will be a critical tool in achieving the objectives of such a global campaign, which should focus on working with countries around the world to ensure that all stockpiles of nuclear weapons and weapons-usable materials are sustainably secured against the outsider and insider threats terrorists and criminals have shown they can pose. These cooperative approaches will have to be adapted to the circumstances of each country, including its nuclear infrastructure, national culture, secrecy concerns, and more. Pakistan, for example, has now acknowledged that nuclear security cooperation with the United States is taking place, but has made clear that U.S. personnel will not be allowed to visit Pakistani nuclear weapon sites or other sensitive nuclear sites.[17] Tools that have been developed to address such sensitivities in Russia include U.S. provision of equipment that the host state installs at its own expense, without the involvement of U.S. personnel; U.S. reliance on photographs or videotapes to confirm that nuclear security equipment has been installed as agreed, if the United States is paying for the installation; and certification of work done by a "trusted agent," such as an individual with a security clearance from the host country, who is em-

17. Nirupama Subramanian, "Pakistan Accepted U.S. Help on N-Plants," *The Hindu,* 22 June 2006 (available at www.thehindu.com/2006/06/22/stories/2006062205201400.htm as of July 9, 2007).

ployed by a U.S. contractor. Offering reciprocal visits to comparable U.S. sites (such as the Russian visits that have occurred to U.S. nuclear weapon storage sites, nuclear weapons laboratories, and even the U.S. nuclear weapons assembly/disassembly facility) can also be important in addressing such sensitivities, building a sense of partnership, and demonstrating good security practices that might be implemented elsewhere. Similarly, exchanges in key areas such as drafting and enforcing effective nuclear security rules; approaches to assessing vulnerabilities at nuclear sites and designing improvements; methods for testing the real-world performance of nuclear security systems; building strong security cultures; building up appropriate budgetary, training, manufacturing, and maintenance infrastructures for nuclear security; and coping with insider threats can and should be pursued without compromising nuclear secrets, improving countries' ability to ensure effective and sustainable nuclear security on their own through the exchange of best practices and approaches. Similar adaptations of Nunn-Lugar approaches are likely to be necessary in states such as India (where nuclear security cooperation has not yet begun) and China (where such cooperation is in its early stages) as well.

*Building the sense of urgency.* The fundamental key to the success of such a campaign is convincing political leaders and nuclear managers around the world that nuclear terrorism is a real and urgent threat to *their* country's security, worthy of a substantial investment of their time and money to reduce the danger. If they are convinced, they will take the actions necessary to achieve effective and lasting security for their nuclear stockpiles; if they are not, they will not take the political risks of opening sensitive sites to nuclear security cooperation, give their nuclear regulators the mission and power to enforce effective nuclear security rules, or provide the resources necessary to sustain high levels of security. The United States and other countries should take several steps to build the needed sense of urgency:

- *Joint threat briefings.* Upcoming summits with political leaders of key countries should include detailed briefings for both leaders on the nuclear terrorism threat, given jointly by U.S. experts and experts from the country concerned. These would outline both the very real possibility that terrorists could get nuclear material and make a nuclear bomb, and the global economic and political effects of a terrorist nuclear attack.

- *Nuclear terrorism exercises and war games.* The United States and other leading countries should organize a series of exercises and war games with senior policymakers from key states, with scenarios tailored to the circumstances of each country or region where the exercises take place. Participating in such a war game can reach officials emotionally in a way that briefings and policy memos cannot.
- *Fast-paced nuclear security reviews.* The United States and other leading countries should encourage leaders of key states to pick teams of security experts they trust to conduct fast-paced reviews of nuclear security in their countries, assessing whether facilities are adequately protected against a set of clearly-defined threats. (In the United States, such fast-paced reviews after major incidents such as 9/11 have often revealed a wide range of vulnerabilities that needed to be fixed.)
- *Realistic testing of nuclear security performance.* The United States and other leading countries should work with key states around the world to implement programs to conduct realistic tests of nuclear security systems' ability to defeat either insiders or outsiders. (Failures in such tests can be powerful evidence to senior policymakers that nuclear security needs improvement.)
- *Shared databases of threats and incidents.* The United States and other key countries should collaborate to create shared databases of unclassified information on actual security incidents (both at nuclear sites and at non-nuclear guarded facilities) that offer lessons for policymakers and facility managers to consider in deciding on nuclear security levels and the steps required in light of those incidents.

## Effective Global Nuclear Security Standards

As part of this global campaign, President Bush and other leaders of major nuclear weapon and nuclear energy states should immediately seek agreement on a broad political commitment to meet at least a common minimum standard of nuclear security. A plausible standard might be the one described above—all nuclear weapons and significant caches of weapons-usable nuclear materials be protected at least against two small groups of well-armed and well-trained outsiders, one to two well-placed insiders, or both outsiders and insiders working together. Where countries believe bigger threats are possible, they should provide greater protection. This would be specific enough to make it possible to hold states accountable for fulfilling their commitment, but general enough to allow each state to take its own approach to nuclear security.

United Nations Security Council Resolution 1540, which legally requires all states to provide "appropriate effective" security and accounting for any nuclear stockpiles they may have, provides an excellent opportunity, as yet unused, to back up such a high-level political commitment. If the words "appropriate effective" mean anything, they should mean that nuclear security systems could effectively defeat threats that terrorists and criminals have demonstrated.

Hence, the United States should seek the broadest possible agreement that UNSCR 1540 already legally binds states to meet a minimum level of nuclear security comparable to the one just described. The United States should immediately begin working with the other Global Initiative participants and the IAEA to detail the essential elements of an "appropriate effective" system for nuclear security, to assess what improvements countries around the world need to make to put these essential elements in place, and to assist countries in taking the needed actions. The United States should also begin discussions with key nuclear states to develop the means to build international confidence that states have fulfilled their commitments to take

effective nuclear security measures, without unduly compromising nuclear secrets.

International discussions of a new revision to the IAEA's physical
protection recommendations are just beginning. The United States
should seek agreement that the revised text recommend that all states
require facilities with the most sensitive materials to be effectively
protected against a minimum threat such as that described above.

A "security Chernobyl" resulting from a successful sabotage of a
nuclear plant or a nuclear theft leading to nuclear terrorism would be
both a human catastrophe and a disaster for the global nuclear industry, ending any plausible chance for a large-scale nuclear renaissance.
Hence, complementing government efforts, the nuclear industry
should launch its own initiative focused on bringing the worst security
performers up to the level of the best performers, through defining
and exchanging best practices, industry peer reviews, and similar measures—a World Institute for Nuclear Security (WINS) on the model
of the World Association of Nuclear Operators (WANO) established
to improve global nuclear safety after the Chernobyl accident. The
Nuclear Threat Initiative (NTI) has launched an effort to build such
an organization, working with the Institute for Nuclear Materials Management (INMM) and other stakeholders.

### Building Sustainability and Strong Security Cultures

If the nuclear security and accounting equipment is broken or unused
five years after its installation by the U.S. or other countries, or if
guards are turning off intrusion detectors and staff are propping open
security doors for convenience, efforts to drastically reduce the danger
of nuclear theft and terrorism will fail. Hence, ensuring that high levels of security will be sustained for the long haul, and forging strong
security cultures where all relevant staff put high priority on security,
is absolutely critical to success.

Here again, convincing foreign leaders and nuclear managers of
the reality and urgency of the threat is the most important ingredient

of success; without that, they are unlikely to take the actions needed to sustain high levels of security, or to build strong security cultures.

Building on the recent DOE-Rosatom agreement on sustainability, the United States and other leading states should be working with countries around the world to put in place the *resources, organizations*, and *incentives* that are required to sustain effective nuclear security for the long haul. In particular:

- The United States should seek a presidential-level commitment from Russia to provide enough money and capable people to sustain effective nuclear security and accounting at all facilities (and transport operations) with nuclear weapons or weapons-usable nuclear materials. Ultimately other countries where upgrades are taking place should make similar commitments as well.

- The United States and other leading states should seek to ensure that every facility and transport operation with nuclear weapons or weapons-usable material worldwide has all the capacities needed to sustain effective nuclear security, including the necessary procedures, training, and maintenance arrangements.

- The United States and other leading states should work to ensure that every facility and transport operation with nuclear weapons or weapons-usable nuclear material worldwide has an organization focused on nuclear security and accounting, and that these organizations have the needed resources, expertise, and authority. The ministries, agencies, or companies that control these facilities and transport operations should also have appropriate organizations in place to focus on sustaining effective nuclear security.

- The United States and other leading states should seek to ensure that every country with nuclear weapons or weapons-usable nuclear materials has effective nuclear security and accounting rules, effectively enforced. Most nuclear managers will only invest in the expensive nuclear security measures the government re-

quires—so nuclear security regulation is central to effective and
lasting nuclear security.

- The United States and other leading states should take additional
  steps to ensure that states and facilities have strong incentives to
  provide effective nuclear security, including establishing prefer-
  ences in all contracts for facilities that have demonstrated superior
  nuclear security performance.

At the same time, the United States and other leading states should
do everything possible to build strong security cultures for all organizations involved with managing nuclear weapons and weapons-usable
nuclear materials. Organizational cultures start from the top, so it is
essential to convince nuclear managers to build cultures focused on
high security. This requires, at a minimum: intensive training on the
threat; coordinators in each organization whose job is developing security culture awareness; and incentives for strong security performance. Here, too, realistic performance testing and other kinds of
simulations and exercises can help convince guards and staff of the
reality of the threat and what needs to be done to defend against it,
and shared databases of confirmed security incidents can educate security personnel about the threats that exist. Both the nuclear industry
and other industries have broad experience in building strong safety
cultures in high-risk organizations; all countries with nuclear weapons
or weapons-usable nuclear material should take steps to strengthen
security cultures that build on that experience.

## An Accelerated and Expanded Global Cleanout

The only foolproof way to ensure that nuclear material will not be
stolen from a particular site is to remove it. As a central part of the
global campaign to prevent nuclear terrorism, the United States should
immediately begin working with other countries to take steps to accelerate and expand the removal of weapons-usable nuclear material
from vulnerable sites around the world. Where material cannot im-

mediately be removed, the United States must speed steps to ensure that high levels of security are implemented and maintained. The goal should be to remove all nuclear material from the world's most vulnerable sites within four years—substantially upgrading security wherever that cannot be accomplished—and to eliminate all HEU from civil sites worldwide within roughly a decade. That is a challenging goal, but potentially achievable with sustained high-level leadership. The United States should make every effort to build international consensus that the civilian use of HEU is no longer acceptable, that all HEU should be removed from all civilian sites, and that all civilian commerce in HEU should be ended as quickly as possible.

Achieving these goals will require a strengthened, broadened effort, including:

- *Incentives.* The United States and other leading countries should provide substantial packages of incentives, targeted to the needs of each facility and host country, to convince research reactors to convert from HEU to low-enriched uranium or to shut down and to convince these and related sites to ship their HEU elsewhere for secure storage and disposition.

- *Shut-down as an additional policy tool.* To date, U.S. efforts to reduce the use of HEU at potentially vulnerable research reactors have focused only on conversion to LEU. Many research reactors, however, are difficult to convert, and many more are underutilized and no longer offer benefits that justify their costs and risks. For these, the cheaper and quicker answer is likely to be to provide incentives to help convince reactors to shut down—including arrangements to support their scientists doing research as user groups at other facilities. To maintain the trust needed to convince reactor operators to convert to LEU, however, any shut-down effort should be institutionally separate from the conversion effort—perhaps under the rubric of a "Sound Nuclear Science Initiative" focused on ensuring that the world gets the highest-quality research, training, and isotope production out of the smallest number of safe and secure reactors at the lowest cost.

- *An expanded set of reactors.* While the Global Threat Reduction Initiative has expanded it scope to include 129 research reactors they would like to convert (48 of which were already converted or shut down by the end of 2006), some 40 percent of the research reactors operating with HEU around the world today are still not covered by the conversion effort. But with an expanded set of tools—including shut-down in addition to conversion—many of these difficult-to-convert reactors can and should be addressed. To remove threats inside U.S. borders and enable American leadership in convincing others to do the same, the United States should also convert or shut down its own HEU-fueled research reactors, and implement effective nuclear security measures to protect them while HEU is still present.

- *An expanded set of material.* The United States and other leading states should greatly expand and accelerate their programs to take back or otherwise arrange for the disposition of potentially vulnerable HEU and separated plutonium around the world. The focus should be on whether the particular stock poses a security risk, not whether it fits within the stovepipe of a particular program. The goal should be to remove all potential bomb material from sites that cannot easily be effectively secured as rapidly as possible, and to reduce the total number of sites where such material exists to the lowest practicable number. The United States should expand its own take-back offer to cover *all* stockpiles of U.S.-supplied HEU, except for cases in which a rigorous security analysis demonstrates that little if any risk of nuclear theft exists; on a case-by-case basis, the United States should also accept other weapons-usable nuclear material that poses a proliferation threat. The United States should seek agreement from Russia, Britain, France, and other countries to receive and manage high-risk materials when the occasion demands, to share the burden. The

United States should also seek to eliminate vulnerable stocks of separated civilian plutonium where practicable, should renew the effort to negotiate a 20-year U.S.-Russian moratorium on separating weapons-usable plutonium, and should work to ensure that its reconsideration of modified approaches to reprocessing in the Global Nuclear Energy Partnership does not encourage the spread of plutonium separation facilities.

## Beyond Nuclear Security

While upgrading nuclear security and removing nuclear weapons and weapons-usable nuclear materials from vulnerable sites are the most important measures that can be taken to reduce the risk of nuclear terrorism, the United States and other leading states should pursue a layered defense that includes a range of other approaches as well.

- *Disrupt.* Counterterrorist measures focused on detecting and disrupting those groups with the skills and ambitions to attempt nuclear terrorism should be greatly strengthened, and new steps have been taken to make recruiting nuclear experts more difficult (including addressing some of sources of radical Islamic violence and hatred, and challenging the moral legitimacy of mass-casualty terror within the Islamic community). This will require greatly strengthened international police and intelligence cooperation, particularly focused on observable indicators of terrorist nuclear activities, such as attempts to recruit nuclear physicists or metallurgists.
- *Interdict.* A broad system of measures to detect and disrupt nuclear smuggling and terrorist nuclear bomb efforts should be put in place, including not only radiation detectors but also increased emphasis on intelligence operations such as supply and demand "stings" (that is, intelligence agents posing as buyers or sellers of nuclear material or nuclear expertise), and targeted efforts to encourage participants in such conspiracies to blow the whistle.

- *Prevent.* The international community must convince North Korea and Iran to verifiably end their nuclear weapons efforts (and, in North Korea's case, to give up the weapons and materials already produced). At the same time, the global effort to stem the spread of nuclear weapons should be significantly strengthened, reducing the chances that a state might provide nuclear materials to terrorists (though conscious decisions by states to give nuclear weapons or weapons-usable material to terrorists are already a less likely path for terrorists to get the bomb than nuclear theft).

- *Deter.* The United States should put in place the best practicable means for identifying the source of any nuclear attack and announce that the United States will treat any terrorist nuclear attack using material provided by a state as an attack by that state, and will respond accordingly. A significantly expanded investment in nuclear forensics, and new efforts to convince countries around the world to cooperate in collecting data on the characteristics of nuclear material from different places and processes, should be a key component of this effort. But nuclear forensics must be combined with traditional intelligence approaches, which may often offer more information on where nuclear material may have come from. After all, there were no isotopes to study after the 9/11 attacks, but it did not take long to identify what group, and what individuals, had perpetrated them. Whatever the technical limits of nuclear forensics, the United States and other leading countries should make clear that states that might consider providing nuclear materials to terrorists stand a high risk of being caught and facing overwhelming consequences.

## Getting the Job Done

None of these initiatives will be easy. A maze of political and bureaucratic obstacles must be overcome—quickly—if the world's most vulnerable nuclear stockpiles are to be secured before terrorists and thieves get to them. A sea-change in the level of sustained leadership from the highest levels of government in Washington, Moscow, and elsewhere will be essential. The substantial results when top political leaders have taken action—such as the acceleration of work following the Bush-Putin nuclear security summit accord at Bratislava in 2005—hint at what could be accomplished with a sustained push from the Oval Office.

To ensure that this work gets the priority it deserves, President Bush should appoint a senior full-time White House official, with the access needed to walk in and ask for presidential action when needed, to lead these efforts and keep them on the front burner at the White House every day. At the same time, President Bush should encourage other key national leaders to do the same. In the United States, this official would be responsible for finding and fixing the obstacles to progress in the scores of existing U.S. programs scattered across several cabinet departments of the U.S. government that are focused on pieces of the job of keeping nuclear weapons out of terrorist hands—and for setting priorities, eliminating overlaps, and seizing opportunities for synergy.

That full-time leader should be charged with preparing an integrated and prioritized plan for the many steps needed to reduce the risk of nuclear terrorism. Of course, that plan will have to be adapted and modified as obstacles and opportunities change. The president and Congress should ensure that sufficient resources are provided so that none of the key efforts focused on reducing this risk are slowed down by a lack of funds. And President Bush should direct the intelligence community to give top priority, working with the policy and implementation agencies, to collecting the information needed to focus this effort, ranging from assessments of the level of security in place at nuclear facilities around the world, to morale and corruption among guards and staff.

In short, with so many efforts under way tackling different pieces of the nuclear terrorism problem, it is time—in the United States, in Russia, and in other leading countries around the world—to put in place a single leader for the effort, an integrated plan, and the re-sources and information needed to carry out the plan.

## *Appendix:* **Nuclear Material Accounting and the Limits of Verification**

An accurate and timely nuclear material accounting system is an important part of a comprehensive approach to nuclear security. By confirming whether or not the protected items and materials are still present, a good accounting system can confirm that the other elements of the protection system have worked—or sound the alarm when they have not. Timely and accurate accounting can detect a protracted insider theft while it is still in progress, potentially allowing the theft to be stopped. And a good accounting system can deter potential insider thieves frightened that a theft would be revealed.

On the path to deep reductions and ultimately prohibition of nu-clear weapons, it is likely to be increasingly important to monitor not only nuclear weapons stockpiles, but also stockpiles of the plutonium and HEU from which weapons could be made.[18] An accurate and transparent accounting of these stocks will be an important element of a comprehensive verification approach.

Nuclear weapons themselves can simply be counted, and in gen-eral states with nuclear weapons are likely to have accurate records concerning their nuclear weapon stockpiles. But when nuclear mate-rials are processed in bulk, inevitable processing losses and measure-ment uncertainties arise. In a bakery making tons of bread every year, it is impossible to account for every kilogram of flour; much the same is true of a plant processing tons of plutonium every year. Thus, at the end of each year, such a plant will have an "inventory difference," sometimes known as "material unaccounted for"—the difference be-

18. U.S. National Academy of Sciences, Committee on International Security and Arms Control, *Monitoring Nuclear Weapons and Nuclear-Explosive Materials* (Wash-ington, D.C.: National Academy Press, 2005; available at books.nap.edu/catalog/11265.html as of July 9, 2007).

tween what the records say should be on hand and what current measurements say is in fact on hand. No other nation will ever be able to verify a country's nuclear stockpile more accurately than that country can account for it itself, so these uncertainties are important for considering how precise the purely technical results of verification of nuclear material stockpiles can ever be.

Non-nuclear weapon states party to the Nonproliferation Treaty (NPT) are already required to maintain national nuclear material accounting systems that meet acceptable standards of accuracy. Nuclear weapon states and non-parties to the NPT have no such multilateral discipline. During the Cold War, in both the United States and the Soviet Union, the emphasis was on maximizing weapons production, not on accounting for every kilogram. In the 1990s, the United States went through an elaborate process of accounting for its stockpiles, checking its records of production and use of plutonium and HEU against the stockpiles that still existed. These reports indicated that 2.8 tons of plutonium and some 3.2 tons of HEU is officially "inventory differences," with another 3.4 tons of plutonium and 4.9 tons of HEU considered to have been lost to waste—enough material in total for many hundreds of nuclear weapons. It will never be possible to verify that these amounts are precisely correct.

Russia has not yet undertaken a similar exercise of matching production and usage records to current stocks (though for a period the United States and Russia discussed cooperating on such an effort). But it seems clear that its Cold War accounting was less accurate than the U.S. system; its accounting systems were designed to ensure that sites met production quotas, not to detect theft, and at many sites the difference between output and input was simply *defined* as losses to waste, defining away the very possibility that material had been stolen. While improved material accounting equipment has been put in place at many sites, most sites with large inventories of material built up over decades have still not performed an actual measured physical inventory to confirm whether all their hundreds or thousands of canisters of nuclear material still contain the material the paper records say they do. China, France, Britain, India, and Pakistan, with their much smaller military nuclear programs, will presumably have smaller uncertainties in their accounting—but it seems likely that in all these cases the irreducible uncertainties will amount to several bombs' worth of nuclear material.

The United States found, in preparing its inventory analyses, that the original production records and the knowledge of the people who produced them were crucial to an accurate understanding of what happened. Around the world, records from decades ago are being thrown out, and the people involved are retiring or dying. Similarly, if "nuclear archaeology" techniques are going to be used to help confirm that levels of production that might be declared in an arms reduction agreement are consistent with the physical condition of the production facilities, it will be crucial to get that work done before these facilities are decommissioned and destroyed.[19]

In short, it would be highly desirable to undertake cooperative efforts to improve nuclear material accounting worldwide, to contribute both to nonproliferation and arms reduction—and there is some urgency in doing so, driven not only by the need to strengthen security against nuclear theft but also by the ongoing and impending loss of crucial information to improve the accuracy of the accounting.[20] Given the sensitivities that still exist, it may be important to begin with helping countries improve their own accounting, rather than insisting

19. Steve Fetter, "Nuclear Archaeology: Verifying Declarations of Fissile Material Production," *Science & Global Security* 3 (1993; available at www.princeton.edu/~globsec/publications/pdf/3_3-4Fetter.pdf as of August 7, 2007).

20. Thomas B. Cochran and Christopher Paine of the Natural Resources Defense Council were early advocates of rapid U.S.-Russian, and ultimately global, cooperative efforts to measure, tag, and seal nuclear materials, as an approach that would contribute to both nonproliferation and disarmament. See, for example, Thomas B. Cochran and Christopher Paine, "Nuclear Warhead Destruction" (Washington, D.C.: Natural Resources Defense Council, 1993; available at docs.nrdc.org/nuclear/nuc_11169301a_118.pdf as of August 7, 2007).

that they provide detailed information on their stockpiles to others. In particular, the United States should work to convince and assist Russia in preparing a detailed accounting of Russia's stockpiles as they compare to what was originally produced (and to preserve production records and knowledge to the extent possible)—without insisting, for the present, that Russia provide the resulting data to the United States.

# 8. Controlling Fissile Materials Worldwide

*A Fissile Material Cutoff Treaty and Beyond*

## Robert J. Einhorn

Over the last decade of futile efforts to get negotiations underway on a Fissile Material Cutoff Treaty (FMCT), the United States has viewed an FMCT as a modest arms control measure of limited scope that could codify the existing de facto moratorium on fissile material production for nuclear weapons by the five NPT nuclear weapon states and cap the fissile material weapons stocks of the three nuclear powers that never joined the NPT. Those goals remain valid, especially now that India and Pakistan appear poised to ramp up their bomb-making capabilities.

But current circumstances—including the fear that terrorists could get their hands on the wherewithal to build nuclear bombs and the growing quantities of excess fissile materials now being created as a by-product of reductions in U.S. and Russian nuclear arsenals—provide grounds for taking a more ambitious approach toward controlling fissile materials. Instead of only banning the production of fissile materials for use in nuclear weapons, an FMCT should also prohibit the production of highly enriched uranium (HEU) for civil purposes and either phase out or adopt a long-term moratorium on the production of HEU for naval propulsion.

Moreover, while the scope of an FMCT itself should focus only on the production of fissile material *after entry into force*, the treaty should be accompanied by parallel steps initially of a voluntary character—under a multilateral framework that might be called a Fissile Material Control Initiative (FMCI)—that would also address the challenges posed by *pre-existing* fissile materials and, over time, help monitor, manage, and reduce existing stocks of fissile materials around the world.

Taken together, the FMCT and FMCI would not only address critical problems posed by vast and growing stocks of fissile materials; they would also establish an essential foundation for moving toward a world with few or no nuclear weapons. But building the necessary international support will not be easy. Some key states may not be prepared to forgo future production of fissile materials for nuclear weapons as required by an FMCT, and some may resist the transparency, verification, and disposition measures called for under an FMCI. Strong leadership by the U.S. will be needed to get the growing problem of fissile material stocks under control.

## A frustrating record

The record of international efforts to achieve an FMCT is a long and frustrating one. Fifty years ago, a 1957 United Nations General Assembly (UNGA) resolution calling for an FMCT first put the issue on the international agenda. But Cold War nuclear buildups and mistrust among the major powers made an FMCT impractical for over 30 years. In the post-Cold War era—with the collapse of the USSR and the focus on reducing the Cold War's nuclear legacy—the idea of an FMCT was resurrected. A 1993 UNGA resolution, co-sponsored by the United States, India, and others, supported the conclusion of "a non-discriminatory, multilateral, and internationally and effectively verifiable treaty banning the production of fissile material for nuclear weapons and other nuclear explosive devices." Thereafter, resolutions calling for an FMCT became hearty perennials in annual UNGA disarmament debates.

The FMCT, or "cutoff," has also figured prominently in the Nonproliferation Treaty (NPT) context. At the 1995 NPT Review and Extension Conference, agreement to pursue an FMCT was an integral part of the consensus that enabled the NPT to be extended indefinitely. At the 2000 Review Conference, as one of 13 "practical steps for the systematic and progressive effort" toward nuclear disarmament, NPT parties agreed to call on the Conference on Disarmament (CD) to commence immediately negotiations on a cutoff treaty with a view to concluding the treaty within five years.

So far, the CD—the Geneva-based, 65-nation body charged with negotiating an FMCT—has hardly been up to the task. In March 1995, after more than a year of consultations, Canadian Ambassador Gerald Shannon announced agreement on a mandate for an Ad Hoc Committee of the CD to negotiate an FMCT. However, notwithstanding the adoption of the "Shannon mandate," the CD, which operates on the basis of consensus, soon bogged down over disagreements on the priority to be assigned to the various items on its agenda. With the exception of a few weeks in the summer of 1998—when alarm over the May 1998 nuclear tests by India and Pakistan temporarily motivated CD members to set aside their differences—the CD has been unable to proceed with negotiations on an FMCT. Non-aligned countries have resisted giving FMCT priority over their preferred agenda items—nuclear disarmament and legally-binding negative security assurances—while Russia and China have linked negotiations on an FMCT to their desire to pursue an agreement that would prevent an arms race in outer space. With no consensus on a program of work, the CD has been paralyzed.

In July 2004, the Bush administration abandoned the longstanding U.S. requirement that an FMCT be effectively verified. Contrary to the Shannon mandate's call for an "internationally and effectively verifiable treaty," the U.S. stated that, after a lengthy internal review, it had concluded that an effectively verified FMCT could not be achieved. Several CD members, including close allies of the U.S., took issue with this assessment, and basic differences on the question of verifiability became another impediment to moving ahead on FMCT.

In May 2006, the United States tabled a draft cutoff treaty in the CD. One of the motivations for the U.S. initiative was to undercut opposition to the July 2005 U.S.-India deal on civil nuclear cooperation, which reversed the decades-old American policy of engaging in nuclear commerce only with NPT parties. A major criticism of the deal was that, by allowing India to import uranium for its civil nuclear program, it would free up India's limited indigenous uranium supplies for use in its nuclear weapons program and would therefore facilitate a significant increase in India's production of fissile material for nuclear weapons. In anticipation of such criticism, the U.S. and India had pledged in their July 2005 joint statement that they would work together for the conclusion of a multilateral FMCT. The tabling of the U.S. draft treaty in 2006 was an effort to show Congressional critics that the administration was serious about that pledge and that concerns about an Indian fissile material buildup were unwarranted in light of the prospect of a cutoff treaty. Consistent with its 2004 decision on verification, the Bush administration omitted provisions for international verification from its very short treaty text and called instead for reliance on the parties' own national means of verification and on consultations among parties to resolve questions of compliance.

Despite the tabling of the U.S. draft treaty, negotiations did not get underway. In an effort to break the impasse in the CD, a compromise work program was floated in March 2007 which called for "negotiations" on an FMCT and "substantive discussions" on the three agenda items that some delegations had long sought to link to the cutoff: nuclear disarmament, prevention of an arms race in outer space, and negative security assurances. U.S. Ambassador Christina Rocca supported the draft work program, noting ominously that, "if the CD cannot agree to this compromise, we do not believe it will ever be able to break out of its stalemate, and member states will have to reconsider their commitment to this body." But so far, a consensus has still not been reached—with China, Iran, and Pakistan the main holdouts—and prospects are uncertain.

Although the stalemate in Geneva is often described in procedural terms, it actually reflects significant substantive differences—both on priorities in the area of arms control and nonproliferation and on the desirability of stopping the production of fissile materials for nuclear weapons. Some states whose positions on a cutoff treaty are crucial may be determined to continue fissile material production in the near term (India, Pakistan), may wish to keep open their option to resume production in an uncertain strategic environment (China), or may see the FMCT as a challenge to their overall strategic posture (Israel, Iran). And other states whose strong support for an FMCT would be essential to its success (e.g., U.S., Russia) have not yet assigned it the necessary high priority.

**Scope of an FMCT**

In terms of the nuclear activities and materials that would be covered by an FMCT, the United States and the other nuclear weapon states party to the NPT have traditionally favored a relatively modest approach. They have taken the view that the scope of an FMCT should be confined to prohibiting the production of additional fissile material—mainly highly enriched uranium[1] and separated plutonium—for use in nuclear weapons. The idea that the treaty would "cut off" new production—production after entry into force—is what put the "C" in FMCT. Under this approach, the following would *not* be covered:

- highly enriched uranium (HEU) or separated plutonium already produced before entry into force, including for nuclear weapons or any other purpose;
- any production of low-enriched uranium (LEU);
- new production of HEU or separated plutonium for civil purposes

---

1. Uranium enriched to more than 20% U-235 or U-233.

(e.g., plutonium for use as fuel in nuclear power reactors, HEU for use in reactors to produce medical isotopes);

- new production of HEU for military, non-explosive purposes (mainly for use in reactors for naval propulsion).

An FMCT with this scope would not have much practical effect on non-nuclear weapon states (NNWS) party to the NPT that decided to join. Under the NPT, those states are *already* prohibited from producing fissile materials for nuclear weapons and are obliged to accept comprehensive IAEA safeguards to verify that they are abiding by that prohibition. The FMCT, therefore, would not add to their existing obligations (other than to require them to adhere to the Additional Protocol to their existing comprehensive safeguards agreements).

The impact of an FMCT with this scope would fall mainly on the states with nuclear weapons that decided to join—both states that are not party to the NPT (India, Israel, and Pakistan and North Korea if it does not re-join the Treaty) and the five NPT nuclear weapon states (China, France, Russia, U.K., and U.S.). None of these states now has any legal restriction on its ability to enrich uranium or reprocess plutonium for nuclear weapons.

An FMCT would codify the de facto moratorium on the production of fissile materials for nuclear weapons that is now in place for the five NPT nuclear weapon states. France, Russia, the U.K., and the U.S. have declared that, as a matter of policy, they have stopped such production and have no plans to resume. (The United States has not produced HEU for use in nuclear weapons since 1964 and not produced plutonium for use in weapons since 1988.[2]) China is believed not to be producing fissile material for nuclear weapons at present but has been reluctant to join a declared moratorium and apparently wishes to retain the option to resume production if warranted by future

2. Statement by Christopher A. Ford, U.S. Special Representative for Nuclear Nonproliferation, to the Conference on "Preparing for 2010: Getting the Process Right," Annecy, France, March 17, 2007.

strategic circumstances (e.g., a perceived need to expand Chinese strategic capabilities to penetrate U.S. missile defenses). Adherence by all five to an FMCT would give legal force to the current de facto moratorium and lock in Chinese restraint.

The impact would be more significant for the nuclear powers *not* party to the NPT that elected to join the FMCT because all of them are continuing to produce fissile materials for nuclear weapons (with the exception of North Korea if it maintains the current shutdown of its Yongbyon facilities and if it is not now covertly producing HEU). Indeed, a major benefit of an FMCT is that it could head off a potential nuclear arms race in South Asia. In its civil nuclear cooperation deal with the U.S., India insisted on keeping outside of IAEA safeguards—and therefore eligible for producing fissile material for nuclear weapons—its existing reprocessing and enrichment facilities, eight current or planned nuclear reactors, and any future reactors that it chooses to keep outside safeguards, including fast breeder reactors capable of producing large quantities of weapons-grade plutonium. Together with its newly-acquired ability to import uranium for civil uses and dedicate indigenous uranium to its weapons program, this will enable India to vastly expand its stocks of fissile material for nuclear weapons.

Meanwhile, Pakistan is not sitting on its hands. It is now constructing two plutonium production reactors which, added to its first production reactor at Khushab and its existing enrichment and reprocessing facilities, will give Islamabad the ability to accelerate its own accumulation of fissile material for nuclear weapons. A stepped-up competition in fissile material production between India and Pakistan could eventually persuade China that it needs to resume its own production.

**Fissile material issues not covered**

An FMCT with the scope described above—limited to banning new production of fissile materials for use in nuclear weapons—would not address a range of issues associated with the accumulation of fissile material stockpiles around the world.

- *Civil plutonium.* The amount of plutonium that is currently being created by reprocessing spent fuel from civil reactors far exceeds the amount of plutonium that is being recycled as reactor fuel. As a result, global stocks of civil plutonium are growing at a rate of roughly 10 tons per year.[3] At present, France, India, Japan, Russia, and the U.K. are all engaged in large-scale reprocessing of civilian spent fuel. The U.K. and Russia—owning 75 and 40 tons of separated civilian plutonium, respectively—have no plutonium recycle program currently in place and therefore will continue to build up their stocks (until the U.K. stops reprocessing in 2012).[4] With the 2006 startup of Japan's Rokkasho reprocessing facility and no plutonium reprocessed there scheduled to be recycled before 2012, Japan's plutonium stocks are expected to grow from today's 40 tons to more than 70 tons by 2020.[5] Before long, the world's stocks of civil plutonium are likely to exceed global stocks of plutonium produced for nuclear weapons.[6] While "reactor-grade" plutonium is not as advantageous as "weapons-grade" plutonium in nuclear bomb-making, it can still be used to fabricate workable, effective nuclear weapons.
- *Excess weapons material.* As the United States and Russia have reduced their nuclear arsenals, various amounts of HEU and plutonium have been declared by both countries as excess to their nuclear weapons needs, and a portion of that surplus has been converted into material unusable in nuclear weapons. In 1993,

---

3. *Global Fissile Material Report, 2007*, International Panel on Fissile Materials, p. 7.

4. *Strategy Options for the UK's Separated Plutonium*, The Royal Society, September 2007, p. 9.

5. *Japan's Spent Fuel and Plutonium Management Problems*, Tadahiro Katsuta and Tatsujiro Suzuki, International Panel on Fissile Materials, 2006.

6. *Global Fissile Material Report 2007*, op.cit.

Russia declared 500 metric tons of HEU from dismantled nuclear weapons as excess and agreed, in the U.S.-Russia HEU Purchase Agreement, to blend the material down to LEU and sell it to the U.S. as reactor fuel. Well over half that material has already been down-blended. In 1994, the U.S. declared 174 tons of HEU as excess, roughly 87 tons of which has been down-blended. In 2005, the U.S. declared an additional 200 tons of HEU as excess and said it planned to down-blend 52 tons, reserve 128 tons for naval-reactor fuel, and allocate 20 tons for space and research reactors.[7] In 2000, the U.S. and Russia each agreed to dispose of 34 tons of excess, former weapons plutonium, but their plans to burn the excess plutonium in reactors ran into legal, financial, and other obstacles. With the U.S.-Russian "mutual understanding" of November 19, 2007, on funding and on disposition paths for Russian plutonium (burning in the BN-600 and BN-800 fast-neutron reactors), that agreement seems to be back on track, but the disposal of the material is still decades away.[8] At the 2007 IAEA General Conference, Secretary of Energy Samuel Bodman announced that an additional nine tons of plutonium from nuclear weapon "pits" had been declared excess to weapons needs and eventually would be converted to reactor fuel. However, despite these initial steps by Russia and the United States, both countries still have large quantities of weapons materials that they have been reluctant to declare as excess. Moreover, the conversion of excess HEU and plutonium to materials no longer usable in nuclear weapons has proceeded much too slowly, especially in the case of plutonium for both countries and HEU for the U.S. This problem of large stocks of surplus material—no longer needed for weapons but still readily usable for weapons—will be magnified as the two sides

7. Ibid, p. 20.
8. Joint Statement on Mutual Understanding Concerning Cooperation on the Program for the Disposition of Excess Weapon-Grade Plutonium, November 19, 2007.

implement the nuclear weapons reductions called for in the 2002 Moscow Treaty and pursue even deeper reductions.

- *Naval reactor fuel.* A significant military, non-explosive use of HEU is to fuel nuclear reactors on naval vessels, both submarines and surface ships. With HEU, it is easier than with LEU to design reactor cores that are highly compact (a critical requirement for submarines) and yet do not need re-fueling for long periods of time. Indeed, all U.S. submarines have HEU cores designed to last for the entire design life of the submarine. In addition to submarines, all U.S. aircraft carriers are HEU-powered. Most Russian submarines and nine civilian icebreakers operate with HEU, as do British submarines whose nuclear propulsion systems rely heavily on the United States. France has both HEU- and LEU-powered submarines but is planning to fuel future naval reactors with LEU. China is believed to rely on LEU or near-LEU fuel for naval propulsion, and India is also pursuing nuclear-powered submarines, probably HEU-fueled. The U.S. hasn't produced HEU for naval reactors since 1991. To meet its naval propulsion needs, the U.S. has set aside a reserve of 128 tons of HEU from excess weapons stocks. In announcing the allocation of HEU to naval propulsion, Secretary of Energy Samuel Bodman said that it would have the effect "of postponing the need for construction of a new uranium high-enriched facility for at least 50 years."[9] On the basis of estimates that the U.S nuclear fleet consumes roughly two tons of HEU annually, independent experts calculate that the naval propulsion reserve would be sufficient to power U.S. ships for 40–60 years.[10] In addition to those 128 tons and an undisclosed amount of HEU held by the Navy before the 2005 allocation, the

9. Statement by Secretary of Energy Samuel Bodman at the Carnegie Endowment for International Peace, November 7, 2005. Bodman's November 2005 announcement called for allocating 160 metric tons to the nuclear Navy but that was later changed to 128 tons.

10. *Global Fissile Materials Report*, 2007, p. 11.

naval propulsion program will presumably be able to draw upon HEU released from future nuclear weapons reductions. Despite the abundance of HEU the Navy has at its disposal, the U.S. draft FMCT would still permit new production of HEU for military, non-explosive uses.

- *Civil HEU.* Civil HEU—highly enriched uranium used to fuel civilian research reactors and produce isotopes for a range of peaceful applications—constitutes a small percentage of global HEU stocks. But civil HEU is widely dispersed at over 100 research centers in over 28 countries around the world, and many of those sites and their nuclear materials are inadequately protected against theft or seizure. Given the relative ease of making first-generation nuclear bombs out of HEU (as compared to plutonium), the security of HEU stocks worldwide has become a priority in U.S. efforts to prevent nuclear terrorism. In part due to its concerns about terrorists getting access to HEU, the U.S. has long sought to end the use of HEU in civil nuclear programs worldwide. Since 2004, it has actively pursued the Global Threat Reduction Initiative (GTRI), which is aimed at removing HEU fuel from potentially vulnerable research reactor sites around the world, sending HEU fuel back to its countries of origin (mostly the U.S. and Russia), and converting research reactors to operate on non-weapons-usable LEU fuel. After a slow start, GTRI is now making progress. But much remains to be done and the pace of the "global cleanout" of civil HEU needs to be accelerated. Moreover, at least so far, the initiative does not cover a substantial number of facilities that contain large quantities of HEU, including over 50 HEU-fueled research reactors and 15 icebreaker reactors in Russia. Under the U.S.-Russia Material Consolidation and Conversion Program, however, 17 tons of excess civil HEU from Russian research institutes will be blended down to LEU by the end of 2015.[11]

11. Ibid, p. 28.

## A broader scope?

While the U.S. and the other NPT nuclear powers have favored an FMCT prohibiting only new production of fissile materials for use in nuclear weapons—and not addressing the four categories of fissile materials discussed above—some governments and non-governmental experts have suggested a more ambitious approach, broadening the scope of an FMCT in a number of possible ways.

For example, instead of prohibiting new production of fissile material only for use in nuclear weapons, an FMCT might also ban new production for other uses. An FMCT, at least theoretically, could prohibit further reprocessing of plutonium for use in civil reactors, further production of highly enriched uranium for civil uses, and/or further production of HEU for military, non-explosive uses. Each of these possible expansions of the scope of the prohibition would have strong opponents.

Another way to broaden the scope of an FMCT would be to address not just the production of fissile material after entry into force (the traditional "cutoff") but also material produced *before* entry into force. An approach addressing existing fissile material stocks:

- could cover one or more categories of such stocks (e.g., civil HEU, HEU for naval propulsion, civil plutonium);
- could call for one or more kinds of measures to be applied to such categories of materials (e.g., declarations, safeguards, conversion to non-weapons-usable forms);
- could be voluntary or legally binding; and
- could be an integral part of an FMCT or adopted separately and in parallel with it.

The question of whether an FMCT should deal with existing stocks of fissile material has been a contentious one. While the five NPT nuclear powers and India have opposed addressing existing stocks, Pakistan, Egypt, other non-aligned countries, and even some

Western countries have pressed for covering them in some fashion. Their motives and proposed methods for dealing with existing stocks have varied widely.

Pakistan said it sees the FMCT as an opportunity to "seek a solution to the problem of unequal stockpiles"[12]—presumably between Pakistan and India—but has not been clear on how an FMCT would deal with such asymmetries. Similarly, Egypt has suggested that an FMCT could provide a way to get at Israel's existing nuclear capability. South Africa proposed that material declared excess to military needs be placed under a special verification arrangement until it can be converted to a less sensitive form. Canada suggested a "separate but parallel process" to deal with existing stocks. Still others expressed the view that an FMCT that simply capped existing weapons stocks at very high levels and didn't require reductions would not meet the requirements of NPT Article VI. Given the differences of approach, the 1995 Shannon mandate left the issue open, specifying that agreement to begin negotiations on a treaty banning the production of fissile materials for nuclear weapons "does not preclude raising for consideration past production or management of such material."[13]

## Pursuing an FMCT in today's strategic environment

During the 1990s, when the CD first began struggling with a mandate for FMCT negotiations, the United States viewed a cutoff treaty as a modest arms control measure that could codify the de facto moratorium on the production of fissile material for nuclear weapons by the five NPT nuclear powers, cap fissile material production for weapons by the nuclear powers outside the NPT, and demonstrate progress in fulfilling NPT Article VI. In today's circumstances, there are several reasons for considering a more ambitious approach that would regard

12. Statement by Ambassador Munir Akram to the Conference on Disarmament, July 30, 1998.

13. The Shannon Report and Mandate, March 1995, http://www.acronym.org.uk/fissban/Shannon.htm

the FMCT not just as a modest arms control measure but also as an opportunity to give greater impetus to international efforts to control, monitor, manage, and dispose of fissile materials worldwide.

- Since 9/11 and the realization that al-Qaeda and other terrorist groups are seeking to acquire nuclear weapons, preventing non-state actors from getting their hands on nuclear weapons and fissile materials has become a top national security priority. Denying them access means adopting strong physical protection measures for nuclear installations and fissile material stocks. But because larger stocks will be more difficult and costly to protect, it also means minimizing the growth of fissile material stocks worldwide and accelerating their conversion to non-weapons-usable forms.

- During the Cold War, most fissile materials were contained in nuclear weapons which, for the most part, are subject to rigorous accountability and protection measures. In the post-Cold War period, with the reduction and dismantling of nuclear weapons, there are much greater quantities of fissile material outside of weapons and those materials may wait many years before being disposed of in a manner that renders them non-weapons-usable.

- If reliance on nuclear power grows in coming decades as many expect, we may see an increase of sensitive fuel-cycle facilities in various parts of the world which, in turn, may mean a growth in the production of fissile materials, both for peaceful and military uses.

- Finally, if the international community is serious about moving toward a world without nuclear weapons, it will have to get a handle not just on the number of nuclear weapons and the fissile material contained in weapons but also on the vast stocks of fissile material outside of weapons that could be used to re-generate a nuclear weapons capability. Of course, the risks of re-generation are most acute when the numbers of nuclear weapons reach very low levels. But trying to get a handle on fissile material stocks only when those low levels are reached would be too late. If the international community is eventually to have confidence that substantial fissile material breakout capabilities do not exist, it will have to start soon to try to gain a better understanding of worldwide fissile material stocks and how they might be brought under greater control.

For these reasons, the U.S. should take another look at the scope and objectives of a fissile material cutoff treaty, and particularly at whether the treaty itself—or separate measures adopted in parallel with it—should seek to address some of the problems associated with fissile material stocks outside of weapons.

The remainder of this paper will address the challenge of controlling fissile materials worldwide. It will first look at some of the questions that arise in negotiating an FMCT and then will discuss how issues associated with existing fissile material stocks might be approached.

## Key issues in pursuing an FMCT

*Scope of the prohibition.* Summarizing informal discussions on FMCT issues by CD members in February and March 2007, Italian CD Ambassador Carlo Trezza noted that it was "generally accepted" that only fissile materials for use in nuclear weapons—and not materials for naval and space propulsion or civil research reactors— should fall within the scope of the Treaty.[14] Notwithstanding this broad support for covering only materials for use in nuclear weapons, however, the possibility of expanding the scope to cover the production of fissile materials for *non*-weapons purposes should be considered.

Banning the production of plutonium for civil purposes would be a bridge too far. Countries currently reprocessing civil reactor spent

14. Report on informal meetings in the Conference on Disarmament on item 2 of the CD agenda, contained in CD/1827, 16 August 2007.

fuel and planning to recycle plutonium as fuel—including France, Japan, Russia, and India—would strongly oppose a prohibition on production of civil plutonium. And because these are countries whose support for an FMCT would be critical, it makes little sense to seek such a ban. Instead, concerns about the worldwide buildup of civilian separated plutonium stocks should be addressed outside an FMCT (see below).

A broader ban on producing HEU—that is, broader than the ban on producing HEU for use in nuclear weapons—may be more feasible. As a result of the widely-supported U.S. policy to eliminate the worldwide use of HEU for civil purposes—including by converting HEU-fueled research reactors to operate on LEU—we can expect demand for civil HEU to fall over time. For those few civilian and research applications that cannot readily make the transition to LEU, existing HEU stocks (including excess from weapons programs) can keep them supplied for a substantial period pending conversion. Indeed, the U.S. has already set aside more than 20 tons of excess weapons HEU for this purpose. Consideration should therefore be given to banning new production of HEU for civil purposes.

As noted above, the U.S. naval propulsion program already has a dedicated stockpile of HEU that can last at least 50 years and probably more. Moreover, additional weapons-grade uranium made excess to U.S. weapons needs by nuclear force reductions could be allocated to the naval program if necessary. Therefore, there will be no need, at least for a considerable period of time, for the U.S. to produce more HEU for military, non-explosive uses. The Russians, drawing on their own excess weapons HEU, and the British, relying on their own resources as well as ours, should also have no near-term requirement for producing additional HEU for naval reactors. The French, whose future naval propulsion programs are likely to use LEU, may see no need for HEU production. The future direction of Chinese and Indian propulsion programs are less well known. One approach would be for the FMCT to allow HEU production for naval propulsion for a grace period of 20–25 years, after which production would be banned. The 20–25-year period would provide an opportunity for current users of HEU for naval propulsion to make the transition to LEU if they so desired. An alternative would be to ban production for naval fuel for 20–25 years, after which the ban would automatically end unless all FMCT parties that have naval reactors agree to extend the ban.

So, depending on which HEU option is chosen, it might be possible to have an FMCT that permitted civil plutonium production but prohibited HEU production for civilian use and phased it out for naval propulsion. This would somewhat simplify the verification task and end production of the material most useful to terrorists in fabricating a nuclear bomb.

*Should the FMCT contain international verification provisions?* As noted above, the Bush administration has reversed longstanding U.S. policy and proposed an FMCT without international verification. A U.S. White Paper states that "the United States has concluded that, even with extensive verification mechanisms and provisions—so extensive that they could compromise the core national security interests of key signatories, and so costly that many countries would be hesitant to implement them—we still would not have high confidence in our ability to monitor compliance with an FMCT."[15] Instead of relying on international measures, the U.S. approach calls on all parties to use their own national means to reach judgments about compliance, with the U.N. Security Council serving as the ultimate arbiter on compliance questions.

Among the insurmountable verification challenges claimed by the administration is the small likelihood of discovering covert centrifuge enrichment facilities, the difficulty of determining whether detected fissile material was produced legally (before entry into force) or illegally (after entry into force and for a proscribed purpose), and the

---

15. United States of America: White Paper on a Fissile Material Cutoff Treaty, http://geneva.usmission.gov/Press2006/0518WhitePaper.html

complications involved in verifying the non-diversion to weapons of HEU produced for naval propulsion (because naval propulsion facilities and processes are too sensitive to monitor). In addition, the administration argues that developing a consensus on verification arrangements in the 65-nation CD would take several years—during which countries would continue to build up their fissile material stocks—whereas the "normative treaty" proposed by the U.S. could be finished quickly.

Although the U.S. is not completely isolated in its opposition to international verification, it is in a small minority. Proponents of verification measures note that the IAEA has plenty of experience confirming the shutdown of facilities and verifying that only legal production is taking place at declared reprocessing and enrichment facilities. They point out that familiar "managed access" procedures can be used to deny inspectors sensitive information at nuclear weapon states' facilities. Moreover, while they recognize the difficulty of finding clandestine production facilities, they believe that "special inspection" and "complementary access" procedures, available to the IAEA under NPT safeguards agreements and the Additional Protocol, can take advantage of such techniques as environmental sampling and wide-area environmental monitoring of Krypton-85 (for detection of reprocessing) to significantly reduce the likelihood of undetected cheating. (While the Bush administration cites the difficulty of detecting clandestine enrichment facilities as a key reason why an FMCT is unverifiable, the same verification challenge exists for monitoring NNWS' compliance with the NPT—and the administration has not claimed that it is not worthwhile for the IAEA to attempt to verify the NPT.)

While no verification system is perfect, it should be possible to construct an FMCT verification system that is capable of protecting U.S. security interests better than having no international verification arrangement. The U.S. official responsible for FMCT in the late 1990s came to that conclusion: "We think that a strong regime of routine monitoring of all [fissile] production facilities and all newly produced material and a regime for non-routine or so-called challenge inspections would give us enough building blocks to build an effective verification regime."[16]

If an FMCT is seen not as an isolated arms control measure but as a step toward a world without nuclear weapons, then the debate on whether to include international verification measures in an FMCT is won decisively by the proponents of verification. Moving to a world of few or no nuclear weapons will require that we have high confidence in a verification system. But such confidence will have to be built in stages and over an extended period of time. Clearly, the security stakes of non-compliance with an FMCT (which might involve an existing nuclear power producing additional fissile material rather than capping its capability) would be far lower than the stakes of cheating in the endgame of total nuclear disarmament (where the covert production or retention of a few nuclear weapons would have major security consequences). And so the FMCT provides an opportunity, at relatively low risk, to test the effectiveness of international verification and to gain experience that can be used to evaluate whether, and with what kind of verification, to proceed further down the path toward a nuclear-free world.

*Should verification measures be an integral part of the FMCT or negotiated separately and subsequently?* One of the arguments the Bush administration makes for excluding international verification provisions from an FMCT is that it would avoid years of negotiation on a verification regime and allow the prohibition to take effect before much more fissile material is produced. A better way to avoid such a lengthy delay in halting production would be to negotiate and bring into force quickly something like the Bush administration's short "normative" treaty (i.e., without verification) but to include a provision

16. Michael Guhin, Statement at the Carnegie International Nonproliferation Conference, Washington D.C., January 11-12, 1999.

obligating the parties and the IAEA, within a realistic period of time (e.g., two years), to work out a verification regime. Unlike the approach adopted in the Chemical Weapons Convention, which contained detailed verification measures in the Convention itself, this approach would follow the precedent of the NPT, which called for verification in Article III but left the verification system to be elaborated separately (which later took the form of bilateral "safeguards" agreements between each party and the IAEA based on a model agreement contained in IAEA document INFCIRC/153). A two-step FMCT approach along these lines was suggested by Australia.[17]

Separating the political obligations and verification measures in this way involves some drawbacks. In particular, it would require parties to begin implementing a cutoff without knowing what verification measures will eventually be agreed—indeed, without knowing whether agreement on a verification system will be reached at all. Some states may be reluctant to halt their own production without knowing whether the verification regime to be worked out will be adequate to detect possible noncompliance by other states. Such a two-step approach, however, would also have benefits—not just the advantage of not having to defer a production halt until detailed verification measures can be negotiated but also greater flexibility to strengthen the verification system in the future without having to amend the treaty itself.

Assuming the negotiating parties decide, contrary to the current U.S. position, that international measures should be adopted to verify an FMCT, the choice between integral and separate verification provisions will be an important issue for the negotiations. If it appears that agreement can be reached relatively soon on detailed verification measures, then the best approach would probably be to make them an integral party of the treaty text. But if it becomes clear that negotiating

---

17. Australian Working Paper, "Suggestions for Progressing the Fissile Material Cutoff Treaty," CD/1775, 17 May 2006.

verification provisions would significantly delay a production halt, then one of the following two alternatives should be pursued. The first would be the approach discussed above—bring the treaty into force soon and negotiate the verification system later. The second would be for key countries—perhaps the five NPT-nuclear-weapon states or the seven countries that have declared themselves nuclear powers and tested nuclear weapons (the five plus India and Pakistan)[18]—to adopt a moratorium on producing fissile materials for nuclear weapons pending completion and entry into force of an FMCT containing integral verification provisions. Because the moratorium would not be legally binding and therefore be more easily reversible, it might have greater appeal to countries reluctant to accept a legal obligation to stop production without knowing what the FMCT's verification measures will be.

*Comprehensive vs. focused verification.* Assuming that an FMCT will contain international verification measures, compliance by non-nuclear weapon states would be monitored by their existing NPT safeguards agreements and Additional Protocols (which should be mandatory for FMCT parties). To monitor compliance by the nuclear weapon states that join the FMCT, whether or not they are party to the NPT, a choice would have to be made between two differing approaches:

- A *focused* approach would monitor all enrichment and reprocessing facilities to confirm either that the facility had been shut down or that any continued production of HEU or separated plutonium was for non-proscribed purposes (e.g., plutonium fuel for civil reactors). Any plutonium or HEU produced for non-proscribed purposes would continue to be monitored at "downstream" facil-

18. North Korea and Israel would not be included in this group. North Korea has tested a nuclear weapon and occasionally declared itself a nuclear weapon state, but is now claiming that it is willing to give up its nuclear capability. Israel is universally believed to have nuclear weapons, but it has not declared itself a nuclear weapon state and there is no proof that it ever carried out a nuclear test.

ities (e.g., fuel fabrication plants) until they are no longer weapons-usable—until, for example, the plutonium in MOX fuel is loaded in a reactor or HEU is down-blended to LEU. In addition to monitoring at these declared locations, there would be agreed inspection and monitoring procedures (e.g., environmental sampling) to enable the IAEA to search for undeclared fissile material production.

- A *comprehensive* approach would include everything in the focused approach but would also include the entire civilian fuel cycles of the nuclear weapon states, including all civilian nuclear reactors, fuel fabrication, and storage facilities and exempting only military facilities and existing fissile material stocks.

Since separated plutonium and HEU can only be produced in reprocessing or enrichment facilities, it is sufficient, for the purpose of verifying new production of fissile material, to monitor reprocessing and enrichment facilities (and to try to detect any undeclared enrichment and reprocessing plants). Monitoring a wide range of other civil nuclear facilities in nuclear weapon states could add marginally to confidence in compliance, but that increment of confidence is more than offset by the additional cost of applying safeguards to a much larger number of facilities and the possibility that the more extensive verification arrangements would drive some countries away from the treaty.

The principal argument for the comprehensive option is a political one—that it would reduce the discriminatory nature of the nonproliferation regime by narrowing the gap between safeguards coverage in the nuclear and non-nuclear states and therefore make the safeguards burden more equitable. Minimizing discrimination is a worthy goal, but it would be better to ask the nuclear powers to shoulder a greater burden in areas that produce real payoffs (e.g., converting fissile materials to materials not usable in nuclear weapons, see below) than to ask them to make what are little more than symbolic gestures. For these reasons, the focused approach to FMCT verification is preferable.

*Entry into force requirement.* The legal-sounding issue of entry into force has huge consequences for the value of an FMCT. To get the maximum benefit from an FMCT, we would want all nuclear weapon states, whether NPT parties or not, to join the treaty. But given the current reservations of some of those states toward an FMCT, requiring them all to get on board from the start, could delay entry into force indefinitely.

One option would be to require, as a condition for entry into force, the adherence of all states that have tested nuclear weapons and declared themselves to be nuclear weapon states—the NPT five plus India and Pakistan.[19] But there are several problems with this approach, not the least of which is that both India and Pakistan may be determined to continue building up their fissile material stocks, in which case they will refuse to adhere and entry into force will be blocked. Moreover, Indians (and perhaps Pakistanis too) would regard this option as an attempt to pressure them on a vital national security matter and could produce a nationalistic backlash against the FMCT (as happened in the case of the CTBT, whose entry into force provision included India among the states required for entry into force). In addition, many states, especially from the Arab world, would question why Israel was not on the list.

Another option would be to require adherence by all states with unsafeguarded nuclear facilities—which would add Israel to the seven in the first option. While this has the virtue of including all states whose participation would make the FMCT a success, it has most of

19. As indicated in the preceding footnote, the DPRK has tested a nuclear weapon and declared itself a nuclear weapon state, but is now claiming that it is willing to give up its nuclear capability. Moreover, to put North Korea in the category of states whose adherence is necessary for entry into force would tend to give it recognition as a nuclear weapon state at a time when the Six Party Talks are attempting to achieve its de-nuclearization.

the problems of the first option plus some of its own, the most critical of which is that Israel has made clear that, at least under current conditions in the Middle East, it wants nothing to do with an FMCT. Its opposition to an FMCT probably has little to do with a desire to produce more fissile material (it probably has enough plutonium for any reasonable deterrence requirements) and more to do with concerns about intrusive inspections at Dimona and possible transparency provisions that could compromise its longstanding policy of strategic ambiguity.

The preferred option—and the one included in the U.S. draft treaty—is to condition entry into force on adherence by the five NPT nuclear weapon states. Given their responsibilities as NPT parties, especially under Article VI, this is fitting. Moreover, since none of the five is currently producing fissile material for nuclear weapons, there is a reasonable possibility that the five will be prepared to adhere at an early date. (The one question mark is China.) By not requiring the non-NPT nuclear powers to join from the beginning, this option would avoid putting undue pressure on them and risking a backlash. Indeed, the initiative and leadership of the five would provide strong encouragement for the others to follow suit and, before long, if not from the outset, it would, one hopes, be possible to bring some or all of them on board. This option also avoids the perception—which might accompany the first two—that the non-NPT nuclear powers were being given *de jure* status as nuclear weapon states.

## Addressing existing stocks of fissile materials

As suggested above, there are several reasons why existing fissile material stocks should not be ignored while pursuing an FMCT, including the risks of terrorist access to bomb-making materials, the possibility that existing non-weapons stocks could be diverted to weapons uses in circumvention of the FMCT, and the need to begin laying the foundation for going to very low levels of nuclear forces.

A number of countries want the issue of existing fissile materials to be handled in the CD as part of an FMCT. However, there are strong reasons for not doing so:

- Several unilateral, bilateral, and multilateral efforts are already underway to address problems associated with fissile materials outside weapons (e.g., HEU Purchase Agreement, GTRI) and nothing done in the context of FMCT negotiations should be allowed to interfere with those efforts.
- Dealing with existing stocks could import bilateral disputes into the FMCT negotiations (e.g., India-Pakistan, Egypt-Israel) which could politicize deliberations and lead to paralysis.
- Not all nuclear weapon state stakeholders on the fissile material issue are ready or willing to accept new responsibilities with respect to their existing stocks, which could lead to gridlock in the negotiations.
- Some NNWS would be tempted to try to deal with the issue of existing stocks as a nuclear disarmament measure (i.e., seek reductions in fissile materials contained in weapons) and this would soon bog down the process.

In view of these factors, it would be better to handle the FMCT and the issue of existing stocks separately. However, given the number of states that insist on dealing with existing stocks in the FMCT, this may not be easy to do without stirring up major controversy. Consideration should therefore be given to how the two processes might be linked. Perhaps the most promising approach would be to include in the FMCT text a general provision or provisions that would obligate those parties possessing fissile materials to develop arrangements separately that would serve particular goals—for example, increasing quantities of fissile material declared excess to weapons needs, placing additional excess material under IAEA safeguards, and converting former weapons material as soon as possible to forms not usable in weapons. Such a legally binding commitment regarding existing stocks—albeit of a non-specific character and designed to be further

developed separately—might be sufficient to satisfy the desire to address existing stocks in some fashion while avoiding the gridlock certain to result from trying to negotiate detailed provisions on existing
stocks in the Treaty itself.

*Fissile Material Control Initiative (FMCI).* Assuming there is
support for loosely linking an FMCT with existing stocks but for
addressing the latter in detail only on a separate basis, what should
be done separately on existing stocks? In principle, it might be desirable to have a formal regime covering existing stocks with clear legal
obligations binding all states possessing fissile materials. But in practice, it would not be possible at the present time to get such a diverse
group of states—with very different fissile material holdings and security perspectives—to agree on a common set of obligations.

Instead of seeking such a formal regime, it would be more promising to create a voluntary multilateral arrangement that would establish common goals and guidelines with respect to fissile material
stocks, but would allow each participant to proceed at its own pace.
The arrangement—perhaps called the Fissile Material Control Initiative—would be open to any country that possessed fissile material
(whether safeguarded or not) and was willing to sign on to a set of
agreed principles. It could include NPT nuclear weapons states, nuclear powers not party to the NPT, and NPT NNWS such as Japan
and Germany that have safeguarded civil plutonium or HEU. The
IAEA would be invited to participate as an observer. FMCI would
serve as an umbrella under which individual states or groups of states
could act unilaterally or work out agreements, legally binding or not,
with other states. It would not affect existing arrangements such as
the U.S.-Russia Plutonium Management and Disposition Agreement
or GTRI. Participants would meet periodically to share information
and discuss new steps that members might wish to take.

The overall goals of FMCI would be to reduce the risks associated
with existing stocks of fissile materials (e.g., seizure by terrorists), to
move fissile materials verifiably and irreversibly out of nuclear weap-

ons and into forms unusable for nuclear weapons, and in general to help prepare for a world with far fewer or no nuclear weapons. A set of guidelines would be established that partners would be encouraged to follow—if not immediately, then as soon as they can. Not all guidelines would be relevant to all of the partners. For example, a guideline on declaring material excess to nuclear weapons requirements would obviously not be relevant to NNWS partners, and a guideline on managing civil plutonium would not be relevant to partners without civil plutonium programs. The guidelines would cover a wide range of measures:

- *Declarations.* Partners would be requested to make regular declarations on fissile material stocks. They would be asked to provide total HEU and separated plutonium inventories, together with production histories, as well as data broken down by categories— for example, material in weapons and weapon components; material declared excess to weapons requirements but still in classified forms; material declared excess already in unclassified forms; material in naval and other non-explosive military programs (broken down into reserve stocks in unclassified forms, material in fuel assemblies and reactors, and material in spent fuel storage); civil HEU and separated plutonium (with their planned uses and locations), and so on. Some of this information is already publicly available. For example, the U.S. and U.K. have already provided extensive data on their HEU and plutonium holdings, both aggregated and disaggregated. And participants in the "Guidelines for the Management of Plutonium" initiative[20] (Belgium, China, France, Germany, Japan, Russia, Switzerland, the U.K., and U.S.) provide annual data on civil plutonium and, to a lesser extent, civil HEU. But so far, information on military stocks other than for the U.S. and U.K. has rarely been available. Partners may wish

---

20. *Guidelines for the Management of Plutonium*, International Atomic Energy Agency, INFCIRC/549, 16 March 1998.

to proceed incrementally with their declarations, starting with aggregate holdings and proceeding to more detailed reporting over
time. Declarations would be a key part of FMCI. They not only
demonstrate transparency internationally, but can assist domestic
authorities in planning their own material-management programs.
And accurate declarations provide an indispensable baseline for
moving to nuclear disarmament.

- Physical protection. FMCI partners would be asked to apply the
  highest standards of physical protection and accountancy to all
  their fissile materials, whether military or civilian. They would be
  encouraged, if they have not already done so, to adhere to the
  Convention on the Physical Protection of Nuclear Material, as
  recently amended. Although they are unlikely to interact on questions specifically related to their military fissile materials or nuclear weapons, they should be encouraged to engage one another
  on "best practices" in the generic area of nuclear security, and
  perhaps establish peer review procedures or use IAEA assessment
  teams to confirm that physical protection measures at their civilian
  facilities are up to the highest standards.

- *Excess material and safeguards.* As reductions in nuclear weapons proceed, large additional quantities of fissile material will
  become excess to nuclear weapons needs. Under the FMCI, the
  nuclear powers should be requested to declare regularly as much
  excess material as possible and, as soon as practicable, to make
  such material available for international safeguards under their so-
  called "voluntary offer" safeguards arrangements with the IAEA.
  Making excess material available for safeguards would provide
  assurance that it will not be returned to weapons use. A commitment to this effect was made at the 1996 G-8 summit in Moscow.
  The Moscow Nuclear Safety and Security Summit Declaration
  stated: "We pledge our support for efforts to ensure that all sensitive nuclear material (separated plutonium and highly enriched
  uranium) designated as not intended for use for meeting defense

requirements is safely stored, protected and placed under IAEA safeguards (in the Nuclear Weapon States, under the relevant voluntary offer IAEA safeguards agreements) as soon as it is practicable to do so."[21] So far, only the U.S., Russia, and the U.K. have declared any former weapons material as excess, but substantially more of their material could be. Moreover, of the material already declared excess, only a small portion has been made available for IAEA safeguards. An impediment to putting excess materials quickly under safeguards is that much of the declared material is often in sensitive, classified forms (e.g., weapons components). In the late 1990s, the U.S., Russia, and the IAEA participated in a Trilateral Initiative aimed at developing techniques that could ensure inspectors that materials made available for safeguards came from weapons without revealing sensitive weapons characteristics. Although the Trilateral Initiative was abandoned before it could be put into effect, it should now be resurrected (perhaps with additional participants) and, if proven to be effective, should be used to place classified excess material under international safeguards. If the effort to develop "information barriers" capable of concealing sensitive characteristics proves unsuccessful, states should be encouraged to convert the sensitive materials as quickly as possible to unclassified forms so they could be made available for regular IAEA safeguards.

- With respect to *civil* plutonium and HEU, that material is already under safeguards in NNWS, and is already under Euratom/IAEA safeguards in the U.K. and France. FMCI should request that civilian materials in the other nuclear weapon states, including non-NPT states, also be placed under IAEA safeguards. With respect to HEU for *naval* reactors, national security sensitivities preclude the normal application of safeguards. Under FMCI, however,

21. Text of the Moscow Nuclear Safety and Security Summit Declaration, IAEA Information Circular, 4 June 1996. http://www.iaea.org/Publications/Documents/Infcircs/1996/inf509.shtml

approaches should be developed that provide assurance about aggregate quantities of material assigned to naval programs and confidence that material assigned to the program is not being diverted to nuclear weapons. For example, monitoring naval reserve stocks of HEU and the amounts of material periodically withdrawn from those reserves and sent to naval fuel fabrication facilities might, without divulging sensitive information, provide confidence that the material withdrawn was roughly consistent with requirements for naval reactor operations.

- *Disposition.* Converting fissile materials to forms that cannot be used for nuclear weapons is the best way to provide confidence in the irreversibility of the disarmament process. Various conversion programs are already underway, including the HEU Purchase Agreement, the Plutonium Management and Disposition Agreement, the Material Consolidation and Conversion Program, and the Global Threat Reduction Initiative. FMCI should encourage the acceleration of these programs, especially the program for weapons plutonium disposition, which has not yet disposed of a single gram of plutonium. Moreover, even once these programs discharge their current mandates, there will remain huge stocks of HEU and separated plutonium—a substantial share of which has already been declared excess to weapons needs—that have yet to be moved to the queue for disposition. For example, the 34 tons of plutonium Russia is now committed to dispose of is estimated to be only one-quarter of Russia's total stock of weapons plutonium, while for the U.S. the 34 tons is only one-third of its plutonium inventory.[22] For civil plutonium, the main path for dis-

22. Matthew Bunn of Harvard's Managing the Atom Project writes that Russia is thought to have about 145 tons of separated weapons-grade plutonium (with an uncertainty of 25 tons) and about 40 tons of civilian separated plutonium, while the U.S. has about 92 metric tons of plutonium separated from spent fuel. "Troubled Disposition: Next Steps in Dealing with Excess Plutonium," in *Arms Control Today*, April 2007.

position is burning the material in reactors, but much more plutonium is being produced today than consumed. The Guidelines for the Management of Plutonium that were developed a decade ago noted "the importance of balancing supply and demand," so as to keep on hand only "reasonable working stocks" of plutonium rather than the glut we are now accumulating.[23] FMCI should take a new look at those guidelines with a view to reducing existing stocks of civil plutonium.

While ideally we would want all states with fissile materials to join FMCI from the outset and subscribe to all of its guidelines, in practice it would be a voluntary, evolutionary process in which participants, at least initially, choose "a la carte" which elements they are prepared to implement. As FMCI partners become more receptive to addressing their fissile material stocks internationally, FMCI's agenda would become more ambitious—and could include establishing benchmarks and a road map that would provide target dates for when benchmarks should be met. The goal, over time, would be to make FMCI an increasingly rigorous, comprehensive (in terms of materials covered), inclusive (in terms of participants), and perhaps even legally-binding regime for the accounting, management, and disposition of fissile material stocks worldwide.

## Outlook for negotiations

As noted earlier, the longstanding impasse on getting FMCT negotiations underway has less to do with procedural difficulties than with substantive reservations about the treaty itself. Some countries, like India and Pakistan, seem reluctant to stop producing fissile materials for nuclear weapons. Others, like China, may wish to keep their future options open. Still others, like Egypt and some other non-aligned countries, may have unrealistic expectations that an FMCT can be

---

23. *Guidelines for the Management of Plutonium*, International Atomic Energy Agency, INFCIRC/549, 16 March 1998.

used to promote nuclear disarmament (including by Israel). And the Bush administration's approach toward verification has become another divisive and impeding factor.

The United States will have to play a leading role in ending the stalemate. A good first step would be to return to its traditional support for a treaty with verification provisions. It should also use its recently improved relationship with India to encourage a more forthcoming posture by New Delhi. During the last two years of negotiations with the U.S. on the U.S.-India nuclear deal, India has felt compelled, in the face of domestic criticism, to oppose all constraints on its strategic programs. One hopes that in due course the Indian government will show greater willingness to end its production of fissile materials for nuclear weapons. If India becomes more receptive to FMCT negotiations, Pakistan will come under strong international pressure to follow.

Even if the key countries are prepared to begin the process, the CD may prove to be unwieldy as a negotiating forum. If we see that various countries are inclined to abuse the consensus rule to push their own hobby horses, we should consider assembling an ad hoc group of countries with a strong stake in fissile material issues (the NPT nuclear powers, the non-NPT states, and NNWS with fissile material production capabilities) and seek to begin the process there. If agreement on the central elements of an overall FMCT-FMCI package could be worked out in that ad hoc group, the group could decide whether to bring the FMCT portion of the package to the CD for completion of the negotiations, send it to a different body (perhaps a committee convened by the IAEA Board of Governors), or simply complete it in the ad hoc group and send it to the UNGA for endorsement.

## Toward a world without nuclear weapons

Among the practical steps to be taken on the way to a world with few or no nuclear weapons, controlling fissile materials may deserve a somewhat lower priority than reducing operationally deployed nuclear weapons, non-deployed nuclear weapons, or even nuclear-capable delivery vehicles. But stopping the production of more fissile material for nuclear weapons is a necessary step toward capping and reducing worldwide nuclear capabilities, which is why an FMCT has long been considered an indispensable part of the nuclear disarmament process.

Stopping additional production of fissile material for nuclear weapons, however, is not enough—not for preventing nuclear terrorism and not even for preventing a further buildup of nuclear weapons capabilities, because of the risk that large stocks of fissile materials produced for civilian or non-explosive military purposes could be diverted to use in nuclear weapons. Indeed, as nuclear weapons are reduced to lower and lower levels, the potential risks associated with materials in civilian programs or materials no longer needed for nuclear weapons become more acute. And that is why the agenda for controlling fissile materials should go beyond the FMCT to a broad international effort to account for, secure, manage, and reduce stocks of fissile materials on a worldwide basis.

# 9. Preventing the Spread of Enrichment and Reprocessing
## James Timbie

### Key Judgments

- As many countries consider nuclear energy, the potential spread of sensitive fuel cycle technologies (enrichment of uranium and reprocessing of spent fuel to separate plutonium) poses a serious challenge to nuclear nonproliferation.
- The latent potential to produce fissile material for weapons inherent in enrichment and reprocessing capabilities could be a substantial obstacle to further reductions of nuclear weapons.
- The most reliable and economical approach to nuclear energy is to rely on the international market for nuclear fuel services. But some will advocate indigenous enrichment and reprocessing capabilities to promote energy security, to avoid falling behind regional peers technologically, and to gain security benefits, despite the economic and political costs and risks.
- Advanced nuclear countries can offer a package of incentives to countries aspiring to nuclear energy as an alternative to sensitive fuel cycle activities, including:
  - Assurances of reliable supply of nuclear fuel, including a back-up safety net mechanism.
  - Reserves of enriched uranium.
  - Infrastructure assistance.

- Facilitation of financing.
- Spent fuel management.

- A practical and successful package of incentives would balance a number of competing interests in order to:
  - Provide tangible benefits to countries considering nuclear energy.
  - Respect the widespread desire not to foreclose rights.
  - Respect the national laws and regulations of supplier countries governing transfer of nuclear materials and technology.

**Background**

The Non-Proliferation Treaty (NPT) acknowledges the right to develop and use nuclear energy for peaceful purposes, provided this is done in conformity with the basic obligation of the Treaty not to acquire nuclear weapons.

Nuclear fuel cycle technologies, particularly uranium enrichment and spent fuel reprocessing, can be used to produce weapons-usable highly enriched uranium and plutonium, one of the most difficult steps in attaining a nuclear weapons capability. The spread of these sensitive elements of the nuclear fuel cycle is widely recognized as a major weakness of the nuclear nonproliferation regime. IAEA Director General ElBaradei has called it the Achilles Heel.

This weakness has been well understood since the 1960s. Over 30 years ago the International Nuclear Fuel Cycle Evaluation project looked into ways to curb proliferation of sensitive fuel cycle technologies, and developed ideas—a fuel supply safety net, an international fuel bank, and international spent fuel management—that are still being considered today. A recent multinational study, the February 2005 report of the IAEA Director General's Expert Group on Multilateral Approaches to the Nuclear Fuel Cycle, addressed similar ideas.

Four decades of talk and study have produced a range of good ideas, but today a country starting out in nuclear energy and considering whether or not to invest in fuel cycle facilities will find nothing in place to provide confidence that if it encounters problems in fuel supply or spent fuel management, it can turn to the international community for help.

The goal is not in question. If additional countries enrich uranium or separate plutonium, that would bring them close to a nuclear weapons capability. We don't want to change the NPT, as that would open a counterproductive debate. So we want to create incentives to encourage countries considering nuclear energy to choose not to pursue indigenous enrichment and reprocessing.

The Iranian programs to enrich uranium and produce plutonium add urgency to the effort to encourage other states to choose a different path. Many of the incentives addressed here have already been offered to Iran by the EU (such as assured supply of fuel and return of spent fuel), as well as measures that go well beyond those addressed here. The impressive incentives the EU has offered have not led to a change in the course Iran is on, an indicator that the goal of the Iranian program is not just energy production.

The following is a brief discussion of a range of incentives that can be offered to countries considering nuclear energy as alternatives to indigenous enrichment and reprocessing. These incentives are not mutually exclusive, and in fact are mutually reinforcing. A diversity of approaches can help in the development of combinations that meet the needs of individual countries.

*Fuel supply assurances*

Fuel supply assurances have been discussed for decades as an incentive to pursue nuclear energy without indigenous sensitive fuel cycle facilities. In an effort to transition from discussion to actually putting a fuel supply mechanism in place, the United States led a group of six states that supply enriched uranium to the world market (the United States, France, Russia, and the URENCO partners Germany, the United Kingdom, and the Netherlands) that put forward to the

IAEA Director General in May 2006 a Concept for a Multilateral Mechanism for Reliable Access to Nuclear Fuel.

The six-country concept envisions several tiers:

- The existing commercial market, which is functioning well as a reliable and economical source of enriched uranium fuel.
- Establishment of a fuel supply assurance mechanism at the IAEA. If commercial supply arrangements were interrupted for reasons other than questions about nonproliferation obligations, and cannot be restored through normal commercial processes, a country could approach the IAEA and seek help through the mechanism. Following an assessment of, inter alia, the country's safeguards obligations and whether it had chosen to obtain fuel on the international market and not to pursue sensitive fuel cycle activities, the IAEA would seek to facilitate new supply arrangements.
- Mutual backup arrangements by commercial companies.
- Establishment of reserves of enriched uranium. The United States is converting to low-enriched uranium 17 tons of highly enriched uranium excess to our national security needs, to create a reserve to support fuel supply assurances. This will create a reserve of about 290 tons of LEU, enough to provide about 10 annual reloads for a typical nuclear power reactor. Russia intends to establish a reserve at Angarsk, and others are encouraged to establish similar reserves. The Nuclear Threat Initiative has pledged $50 million toward the creation of a reserve administered by the IAEA.

The six-country concept would focus initially on enriched uranium, and could be developed over time in a step-by-step manner to include natural uranium, fabricated fuel, and eventually the more complex question of spent fuel management.

Some on the IAEA Board (including South Africa, Brazil, and Argentina) have opposed the six-country concept on grounds that rights to nuclear technology should not be restricted.

*Global Nuclear Energy Partnership*

The United States launched the Global Nuclear Energy Partnership (GNEP) in February 2006 to promote international cooperation to enable expansion of nuclear energy worldwide, including cooperation on fuel cycle approaches that enhance energy security and nonproliferation. Partner nations aim to develop comprehensive fuel services, including assured supply and spent fuel management, to allow countries to enjoy the benefits of nuclear energy without indigenous enrichment and reprocessing.

The initial partners (the United States, France, Russia, Japan, and China) cooperate bilaterally and multilaterally under GNEP on the development of more proliferation-resistant fuel cycle approaches and reactor technologies, including advanced technologies for recycling spent fuel, advanced fast reactors, and power reactors appropriate for developing countries.

Ministers and other senior officials of these initial GNEP partners met in Washington in May 2007 to address international cooperation to support expansion of nuclear energy, including to nations currently without nuclear power. They agreed to convene a follow-on high-level conference with broader participation, which was held in September 2007 on the margins of the IAEA General Conference. Seventeen nations representing a broad range of nuclear energy experience have adopted a GNEP statement of principles, which addresses expansion of nuclear energy, enhanced safeguards, international fuel service frameworks, and advanced technologies. Multinational working groups were established to address comprehensive fuel services and nuclear infrastructure development.

*International Uranium Enrichment Center at Angarsk*

Russia has proposed the establishment of international centers providing nuclear fuel cycle services, beginning with enrichment. The first such center has been established at an existing enrichment plant at

Angarsk. Participants would conclude intergovernmental agreements with Russia, and could invest in the center and share in any profits. Russia intends to set aside a quantity of enriched uranium at the center as a reserve. Participants would have no access to enrichment technology. Kazakhstan, a major uranium producer, has become the first partner.

Participation in such a center could enhance confidence in enriched uranium supply in a number of ways:

- The existence of government-to-government agreements in addition to commercial contracts.
- The leverage as an equity investor.
- The establishment of a reserve at the center.

In addition, a country which believes enrichment is a potentially profitable endeavor would have the opportunity to invest in the center and share its financial returns as an alternative to investing in indigenous facilities.

## Nuclear Threat Initiative (NTI) proposed reserve

The NTI has pledged $50 million toward the creation of an enriched uranium reserve to be owned and managed by the IAEA, provided this grant is matched by at least another $100 million from others. $150 million would purchase sufficient LEU for 2–3 annual reloads for a typical power reactor. The reserve is intended to support assurances of international supply of nuclear fuel to states that are meeting their nonproliferation obligations. The IAEA could draw on the reserve as a last resort in event of a supply disruption.

Conditions for access to the reserve would be determined by the IAEA Board, along with conditions required by the suppliers of the enriched uranium. A diversity of reserves would increase confidence in assurance of reliable access to nuclear fuel by increasing the likelihood that a country facing a supply disruption could have access to a reserve.

## World Nuclear Association (WNA) proposal

The WNA, an international nuclear industry organization, proposed in May 2006 that enrichment supplier firms commit to back up each other in event of certain types of disruption. These mutual backup commitments would be included in commercial contracts between enrichers and customers.

These commitments by enrichers would be supported by commitments by their governments to allow exports of enriched uranium when called on to do so by the IAEA, and by commitments of all IAEA member governments not to retaliate against enrichment suppliers engaged in implementing these arrangements.

The WNA approach is a form of insurance against supply disruption. Enrichment suppliers would be compensated for the costs associated with providing this insurance (the cost of reserves, standby capacity, etc.). This commercial mutual backup supply arrangement would establish a safety net under the existing enrichment market, and would in turn be backed up by reserves established by governments.

The six-country concept and the possible framework suggested in the report of the IAEA Director General both drew on the ideas developed by the WNA.

## Report of the IAEA Director General

Following up on the Chairman's report of the September 2006 IAEA Special Event on Assurances of Supply and Assurances of Non-Proliferation, the Director General issued a comprehensive report in June 2007, "Possible New Framework for the Utilization of Nuclear Energy: Options for Assurance of Supply of Nuclear Fuel." The report summarizes the full range of proposals for fuel supply assurances, and identifies common themes for a possible framework.

The suggested framework would have three levels:

- The existing global market arrangements for nuclear fuel.
- Backup commitments provided by suppliers of enrichment and

fuel fabrication services, and commitments of their respective governments.

• A physical reserve of enriched uranium and arrangements for fuel fabrication services.

The framework outlined in the Director General's report provides a useful basis for further development of a mechanism for reliable access to nuclear fuel. The suggested structure is compatible with the six-country concept and the WNA ideas, and the framework could readily accommodate any of the proposals that have been put forward (including the Russian fuel center, various enriched uranium reserves, a U.K. proposal for a bond backed by URENCO's production capability, a Japanese proposal for enhanced transparency in the nuclear fuel market, a German proposal for a multinational enrichment plant controlled by the IAEA, and others).

The way forward is to proceed with a step-by-step approach to put in place elements of a fuel assurance mechanism at the IAEA along the lines sketched out in the Director General's report, adding elements as they mature and as policy, technical, and legal issues are worked out.

*U.S.-Russia Declaration on Nuclear Energy and Nonproliferation*

In July 2007 the U.S. and Russian presidents declared their intention to work together and with others to develop a viable alternative to the acquisition of sensitive fuel cycle technologies. This effort draws upon and complements a range of existing activities, including the work at the IAEA on fuel supply assurances, the U.S. GNEP initiative, the Russian fuel center initiative, IAEA Technical Cooperation, and many others.

The intent is to develop an attractive offer for countries considering nuclear energy to encourage them to pursue nuclear energy without indigenous sensitive fuel cycle facilities. Such an offer would include a range of reactors and arrangements for fuel supply and spent fuel management, assistance in infrastructure development (regulatory framework, safety and security culture) through IAEA Technical Co-operation, facilitation of national and multinational financing, and grid development.

Discussions have begun among interested supplier countries to develop the commercial and intergovernmental elements of such an attractive offer, with the intention of getting into a position in the near term to begin to engage with states considering nuclear energy.

**Issues**

*Expansion of nuclear energy*

A long list of countries is seriously considering nuclear power (Algeria, Australia, Azerbaijan, Belarus, Chile, Egypt, Georgia, Ghana, the Gulf Cooperation Council, Indonesia, Jordan, Kazakhstan, Libya, Lithuania (in partnership with Poland), Malaysia, Mexico, Morocco, Namibia, Nigeria, Norway, Syria, Turkey, Venezuela, Vietnam, and Yemen).

In part this interest in nuclear energy is a logical response to increasing energy demand for economic development, rising fossil fuel prices, and the pollution and greenhouse gas issues associated with fossil fuels. In many cases there may be other motivations as well, including a desire to participate in an advanced technology sector and avoid being left behind by the developed world, an interest in acquiring the "deterrent" inherent in a nuclear fuel cycle, and a perceived need to keep pace with regional rivals (e.g., Iran) in this field.

It follows that the decisions on nuclear energy that these countries will be making, in some cases soon, will include the question of whether to pursue nuclear fuel cycle activities, including enrichment and reprocessing. They will weigh the energy security, deterrence, and technology development considerations favoring investment in fuel cycle facilities against the economic and political costs and waste burden that favor relying on the international market.

There is therefore an opportunity to influence these decisions by taking steps to deal with concerns about the reliability of nuclear fuel services, assist in the development of necessary infrastructure, and offer ways to participate in nuclear technology. Such development of an attractive alternative to indigenous fuel cycle activities could make a positive difference in the outcomes of such deliberations worldwide.

### Conditions/Rights/Beneficiary commitments

Many proposals explicitly condition access to the benefits of fuel supply assurances to countries that refrain from sensitive fuel cycle activities. For example, the mechanism envisaged in the six-country concept would be for states that have "chosen to obtain supplies on the international market and not to pursue sensitive fuel cycle activities." The Russian International Uranium Enrichment Center at Angarsk and the NTI enriched uranium reserve are also intended for states that do not have indigenous enrichment capabilities.

Many countries have expressed substantial opposition to such a condition for eligibility, including South Africa, Brazil, and Argentina, on grounds that rights to nuclear technology should not be restricted. Citing Article IV of the NPT ("the inalienable right of all the Parties to the Treaty to develop research, production and use of nuclear energy for peaceful purposes without discrimination and in conformity with Articles I and II"), they argue that any assurance mechanism should be open to all IAEA member states in good standing, including those engaged in enrichment and reprocessing. There is strong and widespread resistance to the creation of another division between haves and have-nots based on fuel cycle technology.

For this reason, the possible framework developed by the IAEA in the June 2007 report of the Director General would be open to participation by all IAEA member states meeting safeguards, safety, and security standards. Many believe that any fuel supply framework established and administered at the IAEA would need to be open to all member states in good standing, and could not be restricted to states without enrichment and reprocessing. Even without such conditions established by the IAEA, such restrictions might be attached by supplier states to their nuclear material, or be part of a contract or agreement between supplier and beneficiary states.

This raises a fundamental issue in the construction of incentives to encourage countries to make decisions not to pursue sensitive fuel cycle activities: should access to the benefits be restricted to states that do not have (or, in a stronger form, commit not to have) sensitive fuel cycle activities, or should the benefits be available to all to encourage, but not require, states not to pursue sensitive fuel cycle activities.

This is a difficult issue. Restricting eligibility to states without enrichment and reprocessing would create a stronger incentive, but would face widespread opposition in the IAEA, including many prospective target countries. A structure alleviating concerns about the supply of fuel services that is open to all could provide a weaker, but still positive, incentive to forgo indigenous activities.

There could be mixed approaches. An IAEA mechanism open to all could be supplemented by:

- Additional incentives as part of an agreement between supplier and beneficiary states that specifies the absence of indigenous sensitive activities.
- A commercial contract for the supply of a reactor and fuel that includes a provision not to pursue enrichment capabilities.
- Conditions a supplier state could apply to material provided by that state.

This is not a question of rights, but the development of incentives to encourage sovereign decisions not to pursue sensitive activities.

*Supplier state commitments*

Commitments of supplier states are an important element of assurances of reliable access to nuclear fuel services. This issue is complex because supplier firms must navigate national laws and regulations, international standards and guidelines, and, in some cases, the terms of international agreements, all of which serve to control the transfer of nuclear materials. Given these legal requirements and standards, it is not possible for most supplier states to make unqualified commitments concerning what they will or will not do during the useful life of a reactor, a period of several decades.

Supplier states can commit, in principle, to endeavor to allow and expedite the export of nuclear materials in implementation of the mechanism, and to avoid opposing exports of others. The six-country concept calls for supplier states to make such qualified commitments.

At the other extreme are proposals for pre-negotiated agreements committing all participating supplier governments to guarantee all necessary export and transit licenses, and not to retaliate against substitute enrichment suppliers. While such an approach would increase confidence of potential beneficiaries, setting the standard this high risks extended (perhaps endless) discussion and failure.

Intermediate approaches include granting of long-term licenses for export of nuclear material (e.g., for multiple reloads, or for a duration that extends to the anticipated life of a reactor). While such long-term licenses would not guarantee that all future deliveries could be made, putting in place long-term licenses could expedite supply and increase confidence that supplier states would support implementation of a fuel supply mechanism.

## Multinational Facilities

Establishment of multinational facilities to provide enrichment and other fuel cycle services has been studied extensively as an alternative to national facilities, and features prominently in the February 2005 report of the IAEA Expert Group on Multilateral Approaches to the Nuclear Fuel Cycle. In principle, multinational facilities under IAEA control might mitigate concerns about reliance on a few developed countries for nuclear fuel, and represent an alternative to the costs and risks of indigenous efforts.

Potential problems with multinational facilities include:

- *Technology security.* A multinational enrichment facility staffed by nationals of many countries could facilitate the spread of enrichment technology. (The enrichment programs of Pakistan and Iran, for example, are based on technology stolen from URENCO, a multinational organization, by a Pakistani national employee.)
- *Incompatibility with the existing, partially privatized, enrichment industry.* Today's efficient and competitive technology is the proprietary intellectual property of enrichment enterprises in Europe, the United States, and Russia. The existing industry functions well as a reliable and economical supplier, and would not welcome multilateralization of existing facilities.
- *Cost.* Start-up costs for a new enrichment plant would be substantial (more than a billion dollars), and operation in competition with existing efficient enrichment suppliers would be costly as well.

A potential approach could be to establish a facility with multilateral ownership under IAEA control as a "black box," with equipment and operations supplied by an existing enrichment enterprise and no transfer of technology. An enrichment plant is being constructed in New Mexico by a European enrichment enterprise as a "black box."

*Back end of the fuel cycle*

Assistance in spent fuel management would represent a substantial benefit for countries considering nuclear energy, helping with (or perhaps relieving) the burden of disposition of spent fuel and waste. If advanced nuclear states were in a position to lease fresh fuel and take back spent fuel, this would be a strong incentive to forgo the costs and burdens of indigenous fuel cycle activities.

Unfortunately, the advanced nuclear states have not resolved questions concerning disposition of their own spent fuel, as the worldwide accumulation of spent fuel and reprocessed plutonium attests, and are not now in a position to take back the spent fuel of others. Russia takes back Russian-supplied fuel for storage and reprocessing in limited circumstances (Iran and a few long-term European customers). France is prepared to reprocess spent fuel, but returns the resulting plutonium, uranium, and fission products.

GNEP is developing advanced technology for recycling spent fuel, including consumption of transuranic elements in fast reactors. This would greatly reduce waste burdens and open a path for countries with advanced nuclear economies to lease fresh fuel and take back spent fuel for recycling.

In the interim, there is a need to develop a near-term approach to assistance with spent fuel management. This could involve:

- Arrangements for safe and secure storage of spent fuel for a period of time at the reactor site.
- Exploring the feasibility of arrangements for subsequent storage at regional or international facilities, pending recycling or final disposition.
- Exploring the feasibility of taking back spent fuel, opening up an option for suppliers to lease fresh fuel and take it back after it has been used.

States with advanced nuclear technology could offer countries considering nuclear energy technical advice and assistance on interim storage of spent fuel at the reactor site. Assistance could include help with site selection, establishment of wet or dry storage facilities, development of a regulatory framework, meeting international physical protection standards, and training of personnel. A more substantial commitment would be for the provider of fresh fuel to offer to assume responsibility for the safe and secure storage of the spent fuel at the reactor site.

A more difficult but more attractive approach would be to offer to move spent fuel (after cooling for a few years) to an international repository for long-term storage. Finding an appropriate site would be a major challenge. A suitable site would need to be secure, geologically stable, accessible by ships and aircraft, and politically acceptable to the host nation and its neighbors. International storage on U.S. territories in the Pacific has been considered in the past, but abandoned following opposition from Pacific states and in Congress. A determined effort could be undertaken by supplier states and the IAEA to resume a search for an acceptable site for an international facility for temporary storage of spent fuel. If successful, this could allow an offer to states considering nuclear energy to remove spent fuel and place it in international storage.

The most attractive step that suppliers could take to help countries aspiring to nuclear energy would be to accept the return of spent fuel for storage, recycling, or disposition. With the partial exception of Russia, supplier states are not today in a position to make such an offer. The United States could examine the possibility of taking back spent fuel from states that are considering nuclear energy and do not pursue sensitive technologies, for near-term storage and eventual recycling once advanced technologies are available. This would be controversial pending the development of a disposition path for spent fuel generated in the United States.

Assistance in management and disposition of spent fuel for countries aspiring to nuclear energy could make an important contribution to encouraging them to forgo indigenous sensitive fuel cycle facilities, but will require substantial creative work to develop storage and disposition possibilities that do not now exist.

### Elements of a solution

The elements listed here are not mutually exclusive, but are intended to be mutually supportive. They can be developed, combined, and drawn upon to produce packages appropriate for the specific situations of individual target countries as incentives not to pursue sensitive fuel cycle activities.

- *Appropriate reactors.* Develop, in cooperation with potential customers, a range of reactors appropriate for the energy needs and grid capacities of a range of countries. For many developing countries, appropriate reactors may be smaller or modular in design to fit with national grids, and should be relatively easy to use safely and securely and relatively difficult to misuse. Small reactors (on the order of 300 Megawatts, about one-third the size of typical power reactors) would be appropriate for the grids of many developing countries. Such reactors could be available in 10–15 years. Some designs for such reactors could be loaded at the outset with a lifetime supply of fuel.
- *Assurances of a reliable supply of fuel.* Establish at the IAEA a mechanism for reliable access to nuclear fuel, following up on the framework suggested in the Director General's June 2007 report and incorporating a range of concepts outlined in that report. The mechanism would have several levels:

1. The existing commercial market.

2. A backup mechanism at the IAEA which could be invoked if commercial supply arrangements are interrupted (for reasons other than questions about compliance with nonproliferation obligations). The IAEA could then seek to facilitate alternative supply arrangements, and arrangements could be made for suppliers to back up each other. Initial elements of such a mechanism could be put in place in the coming months.

3. As a last resort, reserves of enriched uranium could be drawn upon. There would be national reserves (as the U.S. and Russia are creating) and reserves administered by the IAEA (as the NTI has proposed). Such reserves can be established now and filled with LEU over the next few years.

The fuel supply mechanism would initially cover enriched uranium (and perhaps fuel fabrication). Supplier states would support levels 2 and 3 by granting long-term licenses and making (qualified) commitments to endeavor to allow and expedite the export of nuclear materials in implementation of the mechanism, and to avoid opposing exports of others. The mechanism would be open to all IAEA member states in good standing; supplier states could impose additional conditions on the use of their materials. Other compatible ideas (e.g., the enrichment bond) could be included.

This global mechanism could be supplemented with fuel supply assurances that suppliers and supplier states can provide directly on a case-by-case basis to individual states aspiring to nuclear energy.

- Reserves of enriched uranium. Establish a number of enriched uranium reserves to support fuel supply assurances, including:
  - The reserve being created by the United States by converting 17 tons of HEU excess to military needs. This reserve will be located in and administered by the United States, and exports from it will be subject to the requirements of U.S. law.
  - The reserve to be administered by the IAEA proposed by the Nuclear Threat Initiative. States can contribute to the IAEA reserve in cash and in kind, to meet the $100 million in matching contributions required by the NTI grant. Subject to whatever restrictions are imposed by donors on material purchased through their contributions or provided in kind, the material in the IAEA reserve could be available for transfer at the discretion of the IAEA.
  - A reserve associated with the fuel center at Angarsk.

Diversity of reserves, with differing restrictions on access to their nuclear material, would increase confidence that enriched uranium in a reserve would be available and accessible to resolve a supply disruption.

- *Infrastructure assistance.* Offer assistance through IAEA Technical Cooperation to develop infrastructure necessary for responsible management of a nuclear power program. Some countries considering nuclear power have extensive experience in nuclear technology, some have none, and some are in between. In many cases a great deal of work must be done to put in place a nuclear regulatory framework, develop safety and security systems and cultures, and train specialized personnel. The IAEA is developing a document on infrastructure milestones which can be used to identify assistance needs. Financing such infrastructure development would be a substantial benefit to developing countries and an incentive for responsible nonproliferation decisions.

- *Financing.* International financial institutions routinely finance energy projects in developing countries, but have traditionally not supported nuclear projects. Such organizations can be encouraged where appropriate to reconsider this policy for states that have responsible nonproliferation policies. More generally, states can seek to facilitate financing of nuclear energy projects through national and international financial institutions for states pursuing nuclear power without sensitive fuel cycle facilities.

- *Spent fuel management.* Assistance in spent fuel management is a difficult but potentially important area for developing incentives to forgo sensitive fuel cycle activities. It would address and potentially ameliorate a serious problem for states considering nuclear energy. A multilateral effort can be undertaken to develop an approach including assistance in safe and secure storage at the reactor site for a period of time, followed by safe and secure storage at an international facility or return to the supplier country, pending disposition or recycling using advanced technologies as they become available.

The joint initiative launched by the July 3 Declaration on Nuclear Energy and Nonproliferation is designed to bring together this range of activities in a comprehensive way to offer economical and reliable access to nuclear energy and create an attractive alternative to the acquisition of sensitive fuel cycle facilities.

# 10. Internationalizing the Nuclear Fuel Cycle
## James E. Goodby

## Summary: Where We Are Right Now

The Bush administration has tried to persuade the Nuclear Suppliers Group (NSG) not to sell technology and equipment for enrichment and reprocessing to any state that does not already possess full-scale, functioning plants of this type. The proposal was rejected, even by close friends of the United States. The United States is now trying to accommodate its policy to a "criteria-based" approach proposed by France and other NSG members. Efforts to block the spread of enrichment and reprocessing capabilities have fallen short for four main reasons: (1) access to the base technologies required for entry into the field is relatively easy; (2) several states were determined to acquire their own enrichment and/or reprocessing capabilities for various reasons, e.g., to reduce energy dependence, conserve energy resources, or to manage nuclear wastes; (3) no combination of incentives and threats short of military action have sufficed to dissuade nations intent on acquiring a nuclear weapons capability from exploiting these technologies; and (4) many nations that have no current intention of building nuclear weapons and no special animosity toward the United

I acknowledge, with thanks, the invaluable help that many people gave me in writing this paper. They include Chaim Braun, Sidney Drell, Amitai Etzioni, Mark Fitzpatrick, Geoffrey Forden, Charles Forsberg, Subrata Ghoshroy, Daryl Kimball, Pierre Goldschmidt, Laura Holgate, Fred McGoldrick, Marvin Miller, Pavel Podvig, Burton Richter, Geoffrey Rothwell, Harry Rowen, Larry Scheinman, Andy Semmel, George Shultz, Jim Timbie, and Frank von Hippel. The way in which this paper has turned out is my responsibility.

States reject the idea of a two-tier system as regards possession of enrichment and reprocessing facilities, believing they have every right to develop all aspects of a civil nuclear power program. Stopping the further proliferation of nuclear weapons will depend on developing policies that deal effectively with these four factors.

## Key Issues

1. Would it be useful to take credible steps to eliminate the "two-tier" system, both in civil nuclear power and in nuclear weapons?

2. Can equal rights to fuel cycle services be satisfied through assurances of reliable access at reasonable cost to fuel for civilian reactors?

3. Could a stronger effort to internationalize the fuel cycle help to limit the spread of technology and facilities?

4. Would it be feasible to create an international norm requiring that sensitive nuclear fuel cycle facilities be placed under some form of multinational control?

5. Are there criteria beyond (1) multinational ownership and management and (2) IAEA safeguards, which could gain international acceptance as a means to limit the number of uranium enrichment facilities in the world and prevent the spread of enrichment technologies?

6. How could agreements to internationalize nuclear fuel cycle services be enforced?

## Conclusions and Recommendations

1. It should be U.S. policy to work, step-by-step, toward the goal of a world free of nuclear weapons. In this framework, the credibility of actions to remove the "two-tier" stigma from the arena of fuel cycle service would be enhanced and efforts to block the spread of technology and equipment that can be used to build atomic bombs are likely to be more successful.

2. Current programs and proposals advanced by several nations to assure reliable supplies of nuclear fuel at reasonable costs to states

with responsible nonproliferation records should be supported, while recognizing that these programs are not a complete answer to demands for an end to the "two-tier" system. One of these programs, the Bush administration's Global Nuclear Energy Partnership (GNEP), should include a wider array of technical options than it currently does, especially ones that do not require more emphasis on reprocessing with existing technology to produce mixed oxide (MOX) fuel. The partnership also should make infrastructure development, including internationalization of the nuclear fuel cycle, one of its priority goals.

3. Priority attention should be given to establishing uranium enrichment facilities under multinational control. The United States should take the lead in proposing that: (1) as of a given date, all plans for new commercial uranium enrichment facilities should be based on the presumption that the facilities will be multinationally owned and their operations safeguarded under conditions approved by the Nuclear Suppliers Group (NSG). After that date, the NSG should give preference to such facilities when considering selling enrichment equipment and technology; (2) existing commercial facilities or those under construction that are not already multinationally owned should be encouraged to convert to multinational ownership, with their operations similarly safeguarded.

4. Models of multinational enrichment facilities include:
- Urenco, a multinational board of directors with plants in Germany, The Netherlands, and the United Kingdom. Major policy committees, plant management, and operating staff includes nationals of the three founding countries. Technology is shared among these countries but not with others. Urenco shares are not for sale.
- Eurodif, owned by Areva, has a plant located in France, managed and run by French personnel. Although Areva is a multinational corporation, Eurodif is wholly owned by France. Technology is not shared. Angarsk, a Russian enrichment fa-

cility partly owned by Kazakhstan, apparently will follow the Eurodif model. GE Hitachi may adopt this pattern as well.
- A generic model in which the board, senior management, and operating staff is multinational. Access to sensitive technology would be limited to participants who already possess such technology.

5. U.S. policy should continue to seek to limit the number of uranium enrichment facilities in the world and to limit the spread of sensitive enrichment technology. In addition to conditions imposed by U.S. laws and policies, NSG conditions for transfers of enrichment technology and equipment should include the following:

- A recipient of enrichment equipment or technology must be a member in good standing of the NPT and have an IAEA "Additional Protocol," in effect or in the process of being put into effect;
- Proposals for new enrichment facilities should be based on sufficient domestic demand or in cases where the export market is a consideration, exports of enriched uranium must be in compliance with NSG guidelines;
- Protecting sensitive technology must be a priority objective, including "black box" arrangements for uranium enrichment facilities;
- All exporters of enriched uranium fuel assemblies, including the nuclear weapon states, must support an increase in the IAEA safeguards budget sufficient to provide for the actual application of IAEA safeguards using Limited Frequency Unannounced Access (LFUA) at their uranium enrichment facilities;

6. The most difficult question is whether multinational enrichment facilities should be encouraged in potentially unstable areas in return for rolling back incipient nuclear weapons programs. The test case is Iran. The Iranian government stated on May 8, 2008, that it is ready to consider "establishing enrichment and nuclear fuel production con-

sortiums in different parts of the world—including in Iran." This should be explored in appropriate channels. A requirement for international staffing should be a part of the agreement in cases like Iran where regional security considerations are a factor.

7. Enforcement mechanisms should be devised in case of violations of NPT/IAEA agreements, enabling the UN Security Council to establish a "response mechanism," including a series of pre-agreed incremental sanctions.

8. Ideally, the presidents of the United States and Russia should launch a nonproliferation initiative by declaring, early in 2009, that their mutual intention is to work toward a world without nuclear weapons. Tangible evidence of this would be their agreement to reduce the numbers of warheads in the 2002 Strategic Offensive Reductions Treaty from 1700–2200 to 1000 and to add to that treaty verification provisions drawn from START.

9. In any case, the United States should begin consultations with other countries at an early date (1) to make the elimination of nuclear weapons a truly global enterprise and (2) to ensure that all states in compliance with their nonproliferation obligations have access to the benefits of peaceful nuclear energy, including reliable fuel supplies and, if desired, the possibility of partial ownership of multinational enrichment facilities.

10. The United States should consider opening domestic uranium enrichment facilities to joint ownership and co-management with entities of other nations, under conditions approved by the NSG. The goal would be to make safeguarding multinational uranium enrichment the normal way of doing business and to make substantial progress toward that goal not later than the 2010 Review Meeting of the Nonproliferation Treaty.

## Internationalizing the Nuclear Fuel Cycle

*Nuclear Dilemmas*

The fact that nuclear energy can be exploited both for weapons and for civil purposes has presented a dilemma which has been managed but never resolved in over six decades. Uranium and plutonium can provide abundant, carbon-free energy but also the means for producing the most destructive weapons ever invented. Enriching natural uranium is useful for producing nuclear fuel for reactors, and for bomb-making. Removing pure plutonium from spent fuel produces material from which a bomb can be made. In his "Atoms for Peace" speech of December 8, 1953, Dwight Eisenhower put it this way: "If the fearful trend of atomic military build up can be reversed, this greatest of destructive forces can be developed into a great boon, for the benefit of all mankind." This dilemma has never been satisfactorily resolved. In the context of a serious international commitment to work for the goal of a world without nuclear weapons, perhaps it can be.

Two interconnected concepts that might resolve the dilemma were advanced in the Acheson-Lilienthal Report not long after the bombing of Hiroshima and Nagasaki. The ideas were to eliminate nuclear weapons and to create an international authority to manage the peaceful uses of nuclear energy. Eliminating the very few nuclear weapons that existed in the late 1940s would have been relatively easy to do as a technical matter. Conflicting national objectives at the time made the task impossible. Today, in contrast, eliminating nuclear weapons is a more complex task, as a technical matter. But the national objectives of the major nations may be more in alignment, as they consider the threat posed by nuclear weapons.

As in 1946, establishing some form of international authority over the most dangerous aspects of the nuclear fuel cycle is likely to be the most effective long-term remedy for the proliferation problem. And, as in 1946, the key to success is to carry out the process of internationalizing the nuclear fuel cycle in parallel with the process of eliminating nuclear weapons. Decisions to act cooperatively in this sensitive area were impossible for the major governments in the 1940s and 1950s. Cooperation on nuclear energy will be politically difficult, but perhaps not impossible, in the 2010s. In contrast to 1946, an incentive-driven, "bottom-up" approach may augment public policies and this combination could lead, over time, to an international authority of limited scope.

The goal of a world without nuclear weapons should serve as a compass to guide public policy in the here and now, not in some distant future. Nowhere is such a policy framework more necessary than in decisions concerning the nuclear fuel cycle. The end of the Cold War, the globalization of the economy, and deadly challenges posed to all states by non-state organizations have created an environment that should make the need for international cooperation more apparent. The level of cooperation that would insulate the nuclear fuel cycle from potential misuse is on a lesser scale than the authority envisaged in the Acheson-Lilienthal Report. The technical/material obstacles confronting the task of eliminating nuclear weapons are formidable, but probably can be overcome if the task is addressed carefully and incrementally. Progress in escaping from the nuclear deterrence trap altogether is dependent on significant improvements in the relations among the major nations but progress in one should breed progress in the other.

### The Nuclear Renaissance

One solution to the nuclear dilemma would be to phase out nuclear reactors, which is precisely what some people advocate, but even a world without nuclear weapons is not likely to be a world without civil nuclear power plants.[1] The rising demand for energy, especially in Asia, has made it all but inevitable that a surge in the construction

1. Helen Caldicott, *Nuclear Power is Not the Answer* (New York: The New Press, 2006)

of new reactors will occur over the next two decades. That will pose issues regarding the building of new uranium enrichment facilities and of reprocessing facilities, or the expansion of existing facilities. The question of assured nuclear fuel supply already is on the table, as are the perennial questions of what to do with spent fuel and whether to exploit for power-generation purposes the plutonium that is contained in the spent fuel. Getting the answers right will be a crucial test for public policies, in the United States and elsewhere.

Growing energy demands and the need to curb greenhouse gases have created the much publicized "renaissance" in proposals for new nuclear reactors. Many projects have reached the advanced planning stage or are already being constructed. Centrifuge technology for enriching uranium also has made significant advances and the cost of separative work has been reduced. The cost will drop further as the transition to centrifuge technology from gaseous diffusion technology continues. The base technology is spreading. There may be exaggerated expectations associated with the renaissance and the time frame for its full flowering is likely to be very long, but new reactors are being planned on a scale unseen in recent years. All that remains uncertain is the *rate* of nuclear power growth.

Assumptions suggesting that nuclear power growth will be slow depend primarily upon some level of stability in the Middle East so that oil supplies from there are not interrupted, and on there being no rapid and major change in the earth's climate. If these conditions changed, or if dependence on oil from unstable regions simply becomes too risky for major oil exporters to tolerate, the world could decide to make a transition to a heavy dependence on nuclear power. If the example of France is a guide, it could do so on a global scale in 25 years.[2] On the other hand, if there were another Chernobyl-like

2. Dr. Charles W. Forsberg, Executive Director, MIT Nuclear Fuel Cycle Study, private communication. Dr. Forsberg notes that oil hit $133/barrel on May 21, 2008, and "that is over $3.00 per gallon for gasoline in just the oil costs. It implies that about $2 trillion per year is being transferred primarily to five oil exporters: Saudi

accident or some dramatic diversion of nuclear materials from civil power programs to a nuclear bomb, the predicted expansion of dependence on nuclear power might be slowed down or even stopped.[3] On balance, the best bet is that nuclear power plants will become a larger part of the energy mix, which means that managing the nuclear fuel cycle will present "front burner" issues for governments. In the United States, these issues come in the form of a transition to centrifuge-based enrichment technology and possibly to laser-based enrichment, persisting problems regarding storage of nuclear waste material, and whether to begin encouraging the use of plutonium as a reactor fuel.

*Rejection of a Two-tier World*

In addition to uncertainties about the rate of growth of nuclear power generation, there are very strong political currents in the world that distort the picture provided by objective economic analyses. One of these is the view held by many nations that a "two-tier" world is unacceptable, that it is not right that some nations are allowed to have enrichment and reprocessing facilities for peaceful nuclear energy programs while others are forbidden to have that infrastructure. Very few nations would willingly be caught on the inferior side in a permanent "two-tier" system where some nations are entitled to the infrastructure for a civil nuclear power industry and others are not. Assurances of reliable, uninterrupted supply of nuclear fuel, while removing some incentives, do not respond to the "entitlement" motivation. To address that, a mechanism that gives any nation that wants it at least some form of vested interest in one or more major elements of fuel cycle services is required.

---

Arabia, Iran, Iraq, Kuwait, and Venezuela. It is the largest and fastest transfer of wealth in the history of mankind. If it continues for a decade, much of the U.S. economy will be owned by these countries. That is noteworthy because it's tough to argue with our banker about nonproliferation."

3. Dr. Henry Rowen, Stanford University, private communication.

Another powerful determinant of national policies is the desire to have an option to acquire nuclear weapons. This consideration has played a major role in several national decisions to build uranium enrichment facilities. To address this motivation, expectations about the future have to be changed. Nations have to become convinced that global trends are in the direction of less dependence on nuclear weapons for security, and that there are better alternatives. Otherwise, they will try to keep the nuclear weapons option and will build the infrastructure needed to do so.

The Bush administration has tried valiantly to make a two-tier system work, offering assurances of reliable supplies of nuclear fuel as an incentive. A notable example of this was the president's speech at the National Defense University, in Washington, D.C., on February 11, 2004, perhaps his most comprehensive policy statement on nuclear proliferation. He proposed seven steps to block nuclear proliferation. One of them was:

The world's leading nuclear exporters should ensure that states have reliable access at reasonable cost to fuel for civilian reactors, so long as those states renounce enrichment and reprocessing—the 40 [*now 45*] nations of the Nuclear Suppliers Group should refuse to sell enrichment and reprocessing equipment and technologies to any state that does not already possess full-scale, functioning enrichment and reprocessing plants.

The administration tried to obtain the agreement of the members of the Nuclear Suppliers Group to this new rule but ran into strong opposition from states, including Canada, that insist on maintaining the option to develop their own fuel cycle capabilities. Non-nuclear weapons states parties to the Nonproliferation Treaty (NPT) believe that Article IV of the treaty gives them the right to participate fully in the peaceful uses of nuclear energy.[4] Currently, the administration

4. Earlier in 2008 Canada told the United States that it would no longer support the G-8 moratorium on not transferring technology to any state that does not already possess enrichment or reprocessing capabilities This led the U.S. to shift its position

has modified its policies to fit with a "criteria-based" approach proposed in the Nuclear Suppliers Group by France and accepted by all others. This would permit transfers of enrichment technology and equipment under certain specified conditions.

On a case-by-case basis, the administration also has sought to reinforce a "two-tier" rule with sanctions, but these have been aimed only at countries deemed to be unfriendly, like Saddam Hussein's Iraq, Iran, and North Korea, not friendly nations like Brazil, India, or Pakistan.

Most of the nations that are interested in acquiring energy from nuclear sources are not presently contemplating the building of a nuclear arsenal. Presently, the demand for small, nationally-controlled enrichment facilities is fairly limited but high prices for uranium, as well as uncertainties about supply may be enough to encourage some countries to build enrichment facilities just on economic grounds. Thus, the current economic situation may not act as a sufficient economic disincentive to the building of small-scale enrichment facilities.[5]

Most nations in this category are opposed to the acquisition of nuclear weapons by Iran and North Korea. But still they are not comfortable with a two-tier system. This attitude was captured in a statement made by the IAEA director-general, Mohamed ElBaradei, at the Oslo Conference on "Achieving the Vision of a World Free of Nuclear Weapons," on February 26, 2008:

---

at the Nuclear Suppliers Group (NSG) away from a moratorium and toward the inclusion of criteria in the NSG Guidelines. For background see www.armscontrol.org/act/2008_05/NuclearExport.asp and ap.google.com/article/ALeqM5ipQB9GzyPIIY_UCu2oLvVfTgyA4wD90719AO0

5. This point has been developed by Dr. Geoffrey Rothwell, Department of Economics, Stanford University. See presentation by Dr. Rothwell, "The Economics of International Supplier States and Recipient State Regimes for Worldwide Nuclear Fuel Services," presented at the Howard Baker Jr. Center for Public Policy, October 3, 2007. Rothwell believes that market intervention to stabilize prices near reasonable cost, as mentioned by President Bush on February 11, 2004, may become necessary.

we *must develop a new framework for the utilization of nuclear energy.* As I continue to advocate, a multilateral approach would ensure security of supply of nuclear fuel, while reducing the risk of proliferation. A number of proposals have been made, including a fuel bank under IAEA auspices and multinational enrichment facilities. The ultimate goal in my view should be to bring the entire fuel cycle, including waste disposal, under multinational control, so that no one country has the exclusive capability to produce the material for nuclear weapons. I do not believe that any country will give up its right to engage in fuel cycle activities unless the multinational framework is based on equal rights and obligations for *all* participants.

Thus, added to the economic and technical dimensions of nuclear energy is the imperative identified by Dr. ElBaradei: the need to create a level playing field through a new framework that is based on equal rights and obligations.

## Back to the Future?

A new framework for the peaceful uses of nuclear energy must also prevent the proliferation of facilities useful for manufacturing nuclear weapons. A tall order? Yes, and the magnitude of the challenge can be appreciated by recalling the solution to the same problem offered by the authors of the Acheson-Lilienthal Report, in 1946.[6] The Acheson-Lilienthal Report was written in a world free of nuclear weapons, or very close to it, and its authors tried to imagine how to keep it that way. Faced with this challenge, the authors proposed the creation of an Atomic Development Authority, which would own and operate the basic means of producing materials that could either fuel power plants

6. www.learnworld.com/ZNW/LWText.Acheson-Lilienthal.html    A ground-breaking work in this field was written by Dr. Lawrence Scheinman in 1981. Published originally in *International Organization* as "Multilateral Alternatives and Nuclear Nonproliferation," it was republished under the title "The Nuclear Fuel Cycle: A Challenge for Nonproliferation" in *Disarmament Diplomacy*, No. 76, March/April 2004, The Acronym Institute.

or be used to build an atom bomb. Access to uranium and plutonium was regarded as a key choke point in preventing nuclear weapons development. The Acheson-Lilienthal Report specifically left in national hands the construction and operation of energy-producing nuclear reactors, provided there was some oversight of reactor design, construction, and operation.

That report was amended by the Truman administration in ways that made it less acceptable to other nations, and specifically to the Soviet Union. It was then presented to the United Nations by Bernard Baruch on behalf of the United States government, and became known as the Baruch Plan. After years of futile debate in the depths of the Cold War, the proposal was withdrawn, long after it had ceased being a topic of international negotiation. The vision of a world free of nuclear weapons was not discussed seriously again by American leaders until 1986, when President Ronald Reagan and Soviet General Secretary Mikhail Gorbachev met at Reykjavik. They failed there to reach an accord on total elimination of nuclear weapons, but they did succeed in launching a trend toward many fewer warheads in the U.S. and Soviet/Russian stockpiles.

In 2006, on the 20th anniversary of the Reykjavik meeting, Reagan's Secretary of State, George P. Shultz, and Dr. Sidney Drell convened a meeting at Stanford University's Hoover Institution for the purpose of discussing whether Reagan's hopes could be rekindled. That meeting of knowledgeable people from around the country led to an extremely influential article published in the *Wall Street Journal* on January 4, 2007, signed by Shultz, former Secretary of State Henry A. Kissinger, former Secretary of Defense William Perry, and former Chair of the Senate Armed Services Committee, Sam Nunn. It endorsed "setting the goal of a world free of nuclear weapons and working energetically on the actions required to achieve that goal."

Another conference held a year later, sponsored by the Hoover Institution and the Nuclear Threat Initiative, resulted in a second article by the same four authors. It reaffirmed the vision of moving toward zero nuclear weapons and called for "developing an international system to manage the risks of the nuclear fuel cycle." And so today, in 2008, the dilemma faced by the authors of the Acheson-Lilienthal Report in 1946 has re-surfaced, again in the context of a world free of nuclear weapons. The Acheson-Lilienthal recommendations would have required sweeping political changes that were not possible in the 1940s. Even in 1986 the world was not ready for such a dramatic shift in policies and public attitudes. Today, the attitude is more like: "Why has it taken so long?" And nearly everyone who has thought about the dilemma now believes that if a world free of nuclear weapons is to be achieved, international authorities of *limited* scope, on a more modest scale than the one proposed in the Acheson-Lilienthal Report, will become necessary at some point in the process.

## A Goal and a Compass

If that is the case, then policies in the United States and elsewhere should begin laying the foundation for an international authority, recognizing that steps in that direction will have to be incremental, building on what exists today. Examples of international authorities of limited scope exist today in the nuclear field, and while they are much less ambitious in their reach than the authority envisaged in the Acheson-Lilienthal Report, they are multinational. Some provide for joint ownership and operations of key functions of the power industry, specifically uranium enrichment.

The process of institution-building in the nuclear field may come to resemble the function-oriented process advocated by Jean Monnet as he imagined how a united Europe could be created. Monnet's scheme started with a Coal and Steel Community, although his longer-term vision was to re-create the political structure of Europe. Similarly, the creation of an international authority to manage civilian nuclear power could begin with multinational organizations of fairly limited scope which later might coalesce.[7] Economic incentives, not

7. Many scholars, particularly those adhering to the "constructivist" school of

top-down directives, can provide much of the motivation for progress in this direction. But a clear and convincing U.S. policy framework is needed to chart the course.

The past history of efforts to internationalize the nuclear fuel cycle does not give grounds for optimism about current efforts—but times have changed. The anticipated surge in construction of nuclear power reactors may create a steeply rising demand for nuclear fuel services, including enrichment of uranium. Four new enrichment facilities now are being planned or actually being built in the United States alone.

A second factor is the growing realization among nations that present trends in the nuclear arena court disaster. The two *Wall Street Journal* articles by Shultz, Kissinger, Perry, and Nunn received enormous public attention around the world. Their warning that the world is at a tipping point in terms of nuclear proliferation resonated strongly. As states such as Iran and North Korea have acquired the means of enriching uranium and to separate plutonium and as the clandestine network operated by A. Q. Khan has shown the ease with which technology can be transferred to states such as Iran, Libya, and North Korea, the proliferation of the infrastructure for bomb-making has become a pressing concern. Instability and terrorist activities in

---

international relations, have written about international institutions as they have developed in the era of globalization. These institutions, such as the World Trade Organization, can have supranational characteristics in the specialized field in which they function. Professor Amitai Etzioni has written cogently about emerging global governance through the new institutions for transnational cooperation that have been created incrementally without benefit of a single overarching organization. As an example, Etzioni points to international cooperation in the field of counterterrorism and counterproliferation. He regards the Bush administration's Proliferation Security Initiative as a nascent enforcement mechanism for such an authority. See "Genocide Prevention in the New Global Architecture." *The British Journal of Politics and International Relations*, 2005 Vol. 7, 469–484. He also envisages a branch of the "Global Safety Authority" that would deal with what he calls "deproliferation." For a comprehensive analysis, see his *From Empire to Community: A New Approach to International Relations* (New York: Palgrave Macmillan, 2004). The informal accumulation of responsibilities by an international authority acting on behalf of national governments is a process that could occur in the fuel cycle area.

Pakistan suggest that nuclear programs there also must be considered a potential crisis.

On the positive side, the rise of the global economy has created economic and political conditions that are more receptive to multinational cooperation, including the nuclear fuel cycle.

### First Priority to the Front End of the Fuel Cycle

Construction of new nuclear reactors is a slow process and this affords time for deliberation and for building a consensus regarding appropriate multilateral responses to the anticipated demand for enriched uranium. A successful effort to internationalize the nuclear fuel cycle is likely to be an incremental process and so a basic policy question arises: Should the process take place across the spectrum of fuel cycle operations or on a sector-by-sector basis?

The main sectors are 1) uranium mining, 2) uranium enrichment, 3) fuel fabrication and supply to recipient countries, and 4) reprocessing or storing spent fuel and storing waste material. Three types of fuel cycle facilities entail high capital costs and large economies of scale: uranium enrichment, reprocessing, and storage of waste and spent fuel. These economies of scale can be used to support nonproliferation policies.[8] It appears that uranium enrichment could be the spearhead in the process of internationalizing the fuel cycle. The lower costs of nuclear fuel provided by large, modern centrifuge facilities should help to discourage, on economic grounds, the building of small, high-cost enrichment facilities. It would be far less expensive for nations and companies to take part ownership in a multinationally-owned facility, perhaps using leased centrifuge machines under "black box" conditions, than to build their own. But the case for this choice of priority is based not only on economics but also on the fact that centrifuge technology is becoming more efficient, less expensive to

8. As is stressed by Charles W. Forsberg in a private communication and elsewhere.

operate, and more widely available. The transition from gaseous diffusion to centrifuge and laser technology means that plans have been developed to build new enrichment facilities in the United States, which makes the political and economic dynamics more favorable for multinational ownership than in the past. Furthermore, there is considerable experience in managing multinationally owned enrichment facilities. And interest has been expressed by the Permanent Members of the U.N. Security Council, among others, in a multinational mechanism as a viable alternative to indigenous development of nuclear fuel services.

A few large enrichment facilities, as opposed to many smaller facilities around the world, should help to contain the spread of national capabilities for constructing nuclear weapons.[9] The participation of several nations in ownership management, and, in some cases, in plant operations should help to deter cheating. *It must be recognized that for this plan to work, some jointly owned and managed enrichment facilities must be open to participation by those nations that are the consumers of enriched uranium supplied by multinational facilities. One of the principal purposes of encouraging multinational enrichment facilities is to give consumers a stake and a say in the running of such facilities so that they have fewer legitimate incentives to build their own facilities.*

Multinationally owned and managed uranium enrichment facilities situated in various regions of the world should develop common ground rules for supplying nuclear fuel. They should agree on effec-

9. According to the IAEA, uranium enrichment facilities exist in Argentina, Brazil, China, France, Germany, India, Iran, Japan, The Netherlands, Pakistan, Russia, the United Kingdom, and the United States. Some of these are quite small and some already are multinationally owned and operated. It has been estimated that existing uranium enrichment facilities are capable of supplying all the reactors on-line or expected to come on-line in the next decade or so with the type of enriched uranium useful for reactors. But a transition from high-cost gaseous diffusion technology to less expensive centrifuge technology is underway and the rate of growth of reliance on nuclear power is uncertain. See the IAEA's INFCIRC/640.

tive approaches for safeguarding the plants to prevent diversion of enriched uranium to non-civil purposes and to ensure that enrichment does not proceed beyond a certain level. They should work closely with the IAEA to develop effective safeguards to detect and deter the construction of separate clandestine enrichment facilities. Such multinational facilities, some of which would be quite small to begin with, would have the potential to evolve into the sole lawful suppliers of enriched uranium, fulfilling one element of ElBaradei's vision.

If the United States takes the lead in encouraging multinational facilities, fuel centers might be developed in the following locations:

a. Brazil, based on the Resende uranium enrichment facility. Argentina already is associated with Brazilian nuclear activities.[10]

b. Russia, based on the Angarsk facility.

c. Iran, if that proves to be feasible or, if not, another Middle East-dedicated facility outside the region as proposed by the Saudis. Germany has a similar plan.

d. The United States/Canada.

e. China and/or Japan.

## A Different Solution for the Back End of the Fuel Cycle

The proposition that reprocessing facilities should be established on a multinational basis has been the subject of discussion for many years. The proliferation potential of nationally-owned facilities, which produce plutonium useable for nuclear weapons, is the basis for this interest. A thorough analysis of this idea was conducted as early as 1976 by private-sector experts, most of whom considered that it was feasible and had nonproliferation advantages.[11] This was at a time when

10. Irma Arguello, "Confidence Building in Regional Conflicts Involving Nuclear Dangers," presented at the Oslo Conference, February 26, 2006. A new Brazil-Argentina company that will engage in nuclear enterprises, including enrichment, has been created.

11. Abram Chayes and W. Bennett Lewis, *International Arrangements for Nuclear Fuel Reprocessing* (Cambridge, Mass.: Ballinger Publishing Company, 1977).

it was also thought that reprocessing spent fuel and burning MOX was going to be economically beneficial. This has not been the experience with existing technology.

The very few commercial reprocessing facilities that exist today perform all the services required by nations that want pure plutonium for manufacturing fuel for civil nuclear reactors, either as mixed uranium and plutonium oxides (MOX).

The basic issue is whether to encourage the nuclear power industry to move on a large scale into building reactors that burn plutonium as fuel. The proliferation potential of such a move has made the United States and some other governments hesitant, until recently. Currently proposed technical solutions have not answered the concerns that many still have. It still makes sense, at this time, for the United States to be skeptical about the widespread use of plutonium as a fuel and to discourage the building of reprocessing facilities. Burning already separated plutonium as a means of disposing of it, however, is another matter.

There are three uses for plutonium separation facilities: for weapons, for waste management, and for producing plutonium for use as fuel in reactors, now or in the future. Plutonium is being used as a fuel today, as MOX. In a pure form it can be "burned" in fast neutron reactors, as a form of waste management and power generation. Exploiting plutonium as a reactor fuel may, with improved technology, grow to the point where a multinational approach to reprocessing would be justified, because of economies of scale. France and Japan already are exploiting MOX fuel as a very high-cost energy source as are some other nations. Japan and France already have MOX fuel fabrication facilities and related reprocessing plants. India has plans to follow suit on a large scale.

The rate of growth of energy production from plutonium-based fuel (primarily MOX) over the next two decades is not likely to be on a scale that would justify large multinational facilities. The costs are very high and current reserves of uranium are adequate to provide fuel for reactors for a long time to come. If that picture changes, perhaps due to rising costs of uranium, then expansion of the plutonium-based reactor economy could proceed more rapidly than now anticipated.[12] But for now, it appears that there is no need to move to MOX-based reactor fuel except to perhaps eliminate existing stocks of separated plutonium (in particular in the UK).[13] In the future, nationally-controlled MOX fuel centers in Europe or Asia might be considered as candidates for multilateralization, perhaps as "energy parks."[14]

### Spent-Fuel Storage

A more urgent near-term need is an international used nuclear fuel storage center. Storage of spent fuel is a valid interim or even long-term procedure. The technology exists, the costs are low, it could be done quickly, and the benefits are large. An international used nuclear fuel storage center would encourage supply policies that provide for

12. According to the World Nuclear Association, more than 30 reactors use MOX fuel in Europe (Switzerland, Germany, and France) while about 40 reactors are licensed to do so. In Belgium all the plutonium recovered from the reprocessing of 670 tonnes of spent fuel has been recycled as MOX fuel in two nuclear power plants. Japan also has a plan to use MOX fuel in about 20 of its reactors. Most reactors today accept 50% MOX assemblies. (www.world-nuclear.org/info/inf29.html). India is planning to embark on a very ambitious breeder reactor program.

13. Burton Richter states that while "MOX fuel has become a standard product . . . there is no real necessity for its use now." "Nuclear Power and Proliferation of Nuclear Weapons," Stanford University, February 22, 2008.

14. See Lawrence Scheinman's, "Safeguarding Reprocessing Facilities: The Impact of Multinationalization," *International Arrangements for Nuclear Fuel Reprocessing*, edited by Abram Chayes and W. Bennett Lewis, (Ballinger Publishing Company, 1977). Also see, pg. 4 "The Future of Nuclear Power," MIT interdisciplinary study, July 2003, at web.mit.edu/nuclearpower/. "Energy parks" are proposed. Charles Forsberg notes that energy parks present two challenges. If electricity is the product, there are many transmission lines to the customers. The longer the electric transmission lines, the greater are the electrical loses. Second, all power systems require cooling water. That can be a limitation to the power output of the energy park. If the energy park is producing a fuel such as hydrogen, the energy transport problem disappears, because a relatively small pipeline moves far more energy than many power lines. Private communication.

spent fuel to be returned to the supplier, since the question of where to put waste material would be easier to answer. This option deserves serious attention as a prime candidate for multinational cooperation.

## Implications for U.S. Policy

One of the first concerns of U.S. policy should be to deal equitably with those states that believe they have the right, as a matter of principle, endorsed by the Nonproliferation Treaty (NPT) itself, to own facilities essential to a nuclear power program, including uranium enrichment facilities. Such states may find multinationally-owned enrichment facilities attractive because of (1) the economic advantages over creating and operating their own infrastructure and (2) a strong commitment by the United States and other nuclear-armed states to work seriously for a world without nuclear weapons. In that case, the very small number of states that insist on having their own facilities, for military purposes, can be more easily isolated. Their decisions can possibly be reversed. Iran and North Korea already have been influenced by international pressure, and this should have even more effect in the framework of ending the "two-tier" system.

How to proceed? The United States should propose that: (1) as of a given date, all plans for new commercial uranium enrichment facilities should be based on the presumption that the facilities will be multinationally owned with their operations subject to effective safeguarda. After that date, the Nuclear Suppliers Group should give preference to such facilities when considering selling enrichment equipment and technology; (2) existing commercial facilities or those under construction that are not already multinationally owned should be encouraged to convert to multinational ownership, with their operations similarly safeguarded.

The former proposal is a variation on one already advanced by the Bush administration. The second would require a new decision, taken jointly by government and private industry. It would mean that the U.S. Enrichment Corporation would create a joint venture out of its planned new enrichment facility near Portsmouth, Ohio.

Another U.S.-based enrichment facility under construction in New Mexico already is owned by a multinational entity, Urenco. Such a decision might also mean that the French corporation Areva should be encouraged to enlarge its plans for an enrichment facility in Idaho to include part ownership by American and Canadian entities, and others. GE Hitachi, a multinational corporation, is planning another enrichment facility in North Carolina. The Canadian firm Cameco has taken a 24 percent stake in GLE, the company created by GE Hitachi.

*The possibility of participating in some way in a multinational facility is the key to discouraging totally national enrichment facilities for nations that are the consumers of enriched uranium. Many of these nations may be satisfied with assurances of reliable fuel supplies at reasonable costs. For those that are not, the multinational option should be available.* The case for relying for enrichment services on a few large enrichment facilities (roughly, one for each continent) is persuasive economically if properly designed, and can provide major nonproliferation benefits. That case may not be accepted, however, unless it is seen in the context of a new deal between the current possessors of advanced nuclear technologies, including weapons capabilities, and those nations that are still considering their nuclear options. USEC could benefit from an infusion of capital and its new facility does not have international partners. A move to internationalize that new facility would help to convince other nations that a new deal is in the making. Furthermore, opening the facility to participation by consumer states may be a more practical proposition than in the other three enrichment facilities. USEC's Congressional mandate (Privatization Legislation) stipulates that there is a public interest in domestic enrichment facilities and there are restrictions on board membership but Congress may agree that the public interest would be met by a multinational facility on U.S. soil, open to broader multi-national involvement.[15]

An equally important component of this course of action would be a U.S.-led effort to encourage China, Japan, and Brazil to open their enrichment facilities to multinational ownership and management, not an easy task. But Russia has already embarked on this course in its Angarsk facility and has advocated a network of multinational enrichment facilities. China has worked closely with Russia on enrichment services. During President Medvedev's May 2008 visit to China, Russia signed a new agreement with China whereby Russia will help to build a fourth stage of a Chinese enrichment facility. China might see commercial advantages in replicating Russia's Angarsk initiative, also as part of a network of multinational enrichment facilities. Japanese firms have many joint ventures with U.S. and European companies in the nuclear field, including the GE Hitachi enrichment project. Brazil and Argentina already are engaged in a modest degree of nuclear cooperation; the question is whether to deepen it and open it to other nations, especially in Latin America. It should be noted that the Japanese and Brazilian facilities are quite small, not oriented presently toward export.

A political impulse will have to be provided by high-level governmental leaders if a program of internationalizing the nuclear fuel cycle is to gain any traction. Nations that have nuclear weapons and those that do not should join in making this program a truly joint enterprise.

### Complementary Policies

Commercial markets have generally worked satisfactorily in terms of assurance of nuclear fuel supply. But energy security, naturally, is a matter of prime concern for any nation and the high costs of building

---

15. Laura Holgate, NTI, has suggested the possibility of Canadian participation in the new Areva facility. Private communication.

a nuclear power industry cause governments to be extra wary about the reliabilities of fuel supplies. Several plans already have been advanced by the United States, Britain, Japan, and other nations to provide assurances of reliable fuel supply. These should be encouraged and should be developed further.[16] These may not meet perceived requirements for a level playing field, but they weaken one argument for developing indigenous fuel cycle services. They may well satisfy the economic and political interests of most consumer-nations. Each of the proposals has the advantage that it adds to the diversity of suppliers, which is one of the most effective guarantees of uninterrupted supply of nuclear fuel. This also is true, of course, of multinational enrichment facilities, provided that the geographic distribution and the political complexion of the owners/managers are diversified.[17]

The nuclear fuel bank option, advanced by the Nuclear Threat Initiative (NTI) and endorsed by many others, should be an excellent form of assurance, depending on conditions of supply set by the IAEA and the nation supplying the fuel. The fuel bank is both multilateral, in the sense that the IAEA supervises it, and responsive to demands for equality. Dr. Pierre Goldschmidt, former deputy director general of the IAEA, has suggested that

> an IAEA low enriched fuel reserve should, for practical reasons, be physically located (in the form of UF6) at the sites of all commercial enrichment plants. In addition, the Agency should conclude contracts with all manufacturers of fuel assemblies, whereby it would have

16. See Chaim Braun, "Nuclear Fuel Supply Assurance" (unpublished draft) for a comprehensive review and assessment of these plans. Another excellent review is a Congressional Research Service Report for Congress, "Managing the Nuclear Fuel Cycle: Policy Implications of Expanding Global Access to Nuclear Power," updated January 30, 2008, by Mary Beth Nikitin, Jill Marie Parillo, Sharon Squassoni, Anthony Andrews, and Mark Holt.

17. Charles W. Forsberg puts it well: "there have to be multiple enrichment suppliers that do not have strong political ties to each other, and preferably, dislike each other."

the assurance to have access, in case of necessity, to some fabrication capacity.[18]

## The Global Nuclear Energy Partnership

The Global Nuclear Energy Partnership (GNEP) is one of the Bush administration's efforts to answer concerns about reliability of fuel supply. The Department of Energy's research and development under GNEP currently is predicated on the concept of a U.S.-developed reactor (most likely a sodium-cooled fast reactor) that will use "recycled" fuel, but this is still in the early stages of development. The Department of Energy also is investigating a more proliferation-resistant separation process (UREX+1 and UREX+1a). GNEP's current focus appears to be too narrow at this point in time. A broader array of technology options could be added to its programs.

## Precedents and Possibilities for
## Multinational Enrichment Facilities

A first step toward gaining control of the nuclear fuel cycle through internationalizing it could be private-sector initiatives within a policy framework established by governments and backed by government support. In contrast to the "top down" approach of the Acheson-Lilienthal Report, a mixed approach, relying in part on private-sector initiatives, could become a major motivator.

This approach has to be understood in the context of three uranium enrichment facilities, owned wholly or in part by foreign entities, being planned for construction in the United States. These entities are multibillion-dollar enterprises with multibillion-dollar investments in proprietary technology developed over decades. They operate in a business that has very high barriers to entry and that requires complex risk/reward calculations. One facility located in Lea County, New Mexico, is being built by LES, which is owned by Urenco. It will be

18. Dr. Pierre Goldschmidt, lecture at the 24th Conference of the Nuclear Societies, Israel, February 19–21, 2008.

on-line in 2009 as the first centrifuge plant in the United States. A second, to be built near Idaho Falls, Idaho, will be owned by the French firm Areva. It also will use centrifuge technology. Technology will be protected in these two cases by "black boxes." The third, using laser technology, is planned by the U.S.-Japan joint venture GE Hitachi Nuclear Energy and its subsidiary, Global Laser Enrichment (GLE). The technology was developed by Silex Systems Limited of Australia. The plant will be built at Wilmington, North Carolina and is expected to be in operation on a commercial scale in 2012. Cameco, a Canada-based uranium producing company, recently has brought a 24 percent stake in GLE.

A fourth new plant will be built by the U.S. Enrichment Corporation. USEC is planning to operate its centrifuge plant at Piketon, Ohio, on a commercial scale in late 2009 and will have 11,500 machines deployed in 2012. It will use American technology, the only plant in the United States to do so.

Urenco is a particularly interesting model of a multinational facility but it may also be unique because of its membership. It is a multinationally owned and operated facility in which technology is shared among the founding participants. The United States will have access to the technology only to the extent necessary to grant licenses. Urenco was established by the Treaty of Almelo, signed March 4, 1970, by Great Britain, Germany, and The Netherlands. The treaty entered into force in 1971. Urenco, as of 2007, had 23 percent of the world's market share for enriched uranium.[19] All three founding countries are close allies and share basic values so decision-making, which is based on unanimity, has not been a problem. Urenco was the source of A.Q. Khan's blueprints for an advanced centrifuge which later became the basis for Pakistan's uranium-based nuclear weapons program, which is an obvious blight on its record. The overall experience shows that, among like-minded states with resources available for

19.  www.urenco.com/

large-scale investment, multinational facilities are practical and com-
mercially viable. GE Hitachi is more in the mold of a classic multinational corporation, which means that many nations potentially could
become shareholders, if not real managers of operations. Management
and staff operations are limited to nationals of the nations that dom-
inate these companies.

## Iran

The most difficult question about multinational enrichment facilities
is whether they should be encouraged in unstable areas in return for
rolling back incipient nuclear weapons programs. The test case is Iran,
where a study by John Thomson and Geoffrey Forden, of MIT, suggests that measures can be taken to prevent the expropriation of a
multinational facility by the Iranian government and that the likelihood of discovery of any concealed enrichment facility in Iran would
be enhanced by establishing such a facility.[20]

They have postulated a multinationally owned and operated enrichment facility located in Iran, using Urenco or Russian centrifuges,
which would supplant Iran's nationally-operated enrichment facility.
In their analysis they describe legal, organizational, and technological
barriers to nuclear proliferation, as well as barriers to nationalization.
They point out that increased potential for detection of overt enrichment facilities could result from this arrangement, based on UN-
MOVIC and UNSCOM experience in Iraq. This is an example of the
model where consumer countries would be heavily involved in ownership and management, although the technology would be "black
boxed." It is a model that may answer the level playing field arguments but, as should be expected in violence-prone regions, has proliferation risks of its own. An alternative that should be explored is a
Saudi proposal for a multinational enrichment facility to supply re-

20. mit.edu/stgs/irancrisis.html

actors located in the Middle East, including Iran. The facility would be located outside the region, possibly in Switzerland.

Forden and Thomson report that Iranians with whom they have talked have expressed an interest in involving India and South Africa in such a facility. In a letter dated May 8, 2008, to the UN Secretary-General from the Foreign Minister of Iran, it was stated that the government of Iran is ready to consider "establishing enrichment and nuclear fuel production consortiums in different parts of the world—including in Iran." The letter also spoke of "nuclear disarmament."[21]

Preventing the spread of advanced centrifuge or laser uranium enrichment technology would be a matter of concern in any multinational enterprise, even if the partners were on good terms. The technology is sensitive, and in cases of multinationally owned and managed facilities where the partners may not be equally advanced in enrichment technology, or even on very good terms with each other, that technology will not be shared among all the owners and managers, or with IAEA inspectors. This problem has been resolved in the past by the "black-box" approach to protecting technology and an on-site inspection system developed for the Urenco situation known as "Limited Frequency Unannounced Access." This gives inspectors unannounced access to the cascade hall under specified conditions. This system should be adopted by all states involved in a multinational enrichment enterprise. The question of conditions is common to all fuel supply options but applies with special force in unstable regions.

---

21. The text of the nuclear section of the Iranian proposal is as follows: "With regard to the nuclear issue, Iran is ready—in a comprehensive manner, and as an active and influential member of the NPT and the IAEA—to consider the following issues: [1] Obtaining a further assurance about the non-diversion of the nuclear activities of different countries. [2] Establishing enrichment and nuclear fuel production consortiums in different parts of the world—including Iran. [3] Cooperation to access and utilize peaceful nuclear technology and facilitating its usage by all states. [4] Nuclear disarmament and establishment of a follow-up committee. [5] Improved supervision by the IAEA over the nuclear activities of different states. [6] Joint collaboration over nuclear safety and physical protection. [7] An effort to encourage other states to control the export of nuclear material and equipment."

Treaties or contracts should include provisions for: (1) enforcing Nuclear Suppliers Group conditions for supply of fresh fuel; (2) safeguards against the host nation's seizing unilateral control of the enrichment facility; (3) a method of preventing the transfer of sensitive nuclear technology to participants in a plant who did not previously have access to that technology, in accordance with NPT and Nuclear Suppliers Group rules.

## Asia

Asia presents special complications. India, Pakistan, China, and Japan each have enrichment facilities ranging from pilot plants in the case of India to full-scale production facilities in the other countries. Japan has a commercial uranium enrichment facility (Rokkasho) and China has two, Lanzhou 2 and Shaanxi. China also has a gaseous diffusion plant for production of highly enriched uranium. Pakistan has a centrifuge facility at Kahuta and probably one at Golra Sharif, as well. India has two pilot-scale uranium enrichment facilities.

China's commercial enrichment facilities use Russian technology, apparently under "black box" conditions and are under IAEA safeguards. Russia and China are cooperating actively in uranium enrichment services and nuclear fuel transfers. *With Russia now strongly promoting a network of international uranium centers, it is conceivable that China might agree, if only for its own commercial interests, also to open one or more of its enrichment facilities to international ownership and joint management.* It certainly should be asked, perhaps by Russia.

Japan and the United States signed a Joint Nuclear Energy Action Plan on April 18, 2007. One of its four main areas of cooperation is "establishment of a nuclear fuel supply assurance mechanism."[22] In the meantime, Japan's strategy has been to form joint ventures with companies operating in the nuclear field. This includes GE and Hi-

22. U.S. DOE press release, April 25, 2007.

tachi, Areva and Mitsubishi, and Toshiba's acquisition of Westing-house.[23] The purpose is to capture part of the market for building new reactors. Japan Nuclear Fuel Limited (JNFL), owned largely by Japanese electric companies, controls the nuclear fuel cycle in Japan, including the Rokkasho uranium enrichment plant and a new mixed oxides (MOX) fabrication plant. A reprocessing plant is now under construction. *Consultations with Japan should start soon, aimed at investigating the possibilities for transforming the Rokkasho enrichment facility into a multinationally owned joint venture in parallel with a similar development in the United States, and possibly China.*

Pakistan and India require special consideration as non-members of the Nonproliferation Treaty that have also tested nuclear weapons. There is a great deal of well-documented sensitivity in both countries about rights to fuel cycle technologies. Each nation also has growing needs for energy. Nuclear power plants clearly will figure importantly in the mix of electric power-generating capacity in the subcontinent in the decades ahead. In the near term there is little chance either India or Pakistan will give up its enrichment facilities and each will retain an interest in domestic reprocessing facilities, most of which are involved in their weapons programs. But two developments might change this outlook over the mid-term: First, a growing coalition of the nuclear weapons states and others to move toward a world without nuclear weapons, a movement that would change current expectations about the future salience of nuclear weapons in defense strategies; second, a global movement toward multinationally owned and operated enrichment facilities in which the United States, Canada, Russia, China, Western Europe, Japan, and other nations are involved.[24] *A policy of relying on a few multinationally owned and operated enrichment facilities for the supply of fuel for reactors can become a serious possibility even in India and Pakistan if the goal of a world*

23. "GE, Hitachi to join nuclear-power businesses," Reuters, November 13, 2006.

24. Judgments regarding India and Pakistan are derived in part from Subrata Ghoshroy, MIT, in a private communication.

*without nuclear weapons is generally adopted and if multinational enrichment facilities become the norm.* In fact, if India succeeds in its current plans to develop and build a large number of breeder reactors, India's requirements for enriched uranium may not grow at the same pace as its nuclear power program. A Fissile Material Cutoff Treaty would also help, as could the Iran international enrichment facility advocated by Forden and Thomson.

The major challenge to nonproliferation policies lies in the arc of uncertainty from South Africa, through the Middle East, to South Asia, and on to Australia. South Africa and Australia both appear to be considering their indigenous enrichment options. There are opportunities for cooperation in this area, since several nations are well disposed to the idea of preventing the proliferation of nuclear weapons. But there are also serious obstacles.

## Enforcement

Although this paper focuses as a first priority on internationalizing facilities for enriching uranium, several other actions must be taken to prevent nuclear weapons proliferation. They include:

1. Limiting the spread of reprocessing facilities and technology;
2. Controlling exports of nuclear materials and technology;
3. Removing high-enriched uranium from exposed locations to secure storage facilities.

All of these actions, as well as the effort to ensure that uranium enrichment is used only for peaceful purposes, will be successful only if the international community is willing to take enforcement actions in cases of violations of NPT or IAEA obligations. This requires an international consensus, or something close to it, that violations of nuclear-related norms and agreements present a serious challenge to international peace and security. This consensus has been impossible, thus far, to achieve. Unless that problem can be effectively addressed,

nuclear proliferation will proceed and the vision of a world without
nuclear weapons will not be realized.

*An international review, perhaps sponsored by the UN Security
Council, should be conducted as to whether enforcement mechanisms
could be devised that could be put into practice in case of violations
of agreements.* The issue of enforcement is fundamental and has never
been satisfactorily resolved in nuclear matters. It needs a thorough
airing in international arenas, and discussions by the UN Security
Council. UNSC Resolution 1540 might be a suitable base for exploring what the Council could agree to, in advance, to deal with non-
compliance.

Dr. Mohamed ElBaradei has drawn attention to this problem and
to the need for the UN Security Council to have a "response mechanism."[25] Several levels of sanctions agreed in advance should be identified, for example: removal of nuclear-related equipment supplied to
a nation that withdraws from the NPT; an embargo on all future nuclear-related transfers; mandatory transparency measures; financial
and commercial restrictions; and disabling of key nuclear facilities. If
military action is necessary, it should focus on compliance issues, and
hold the sitting non-compliant regime to account for correcting any
violations.[26]

25. In a discussion at the Council on Foreign Relations in New York on May 14,
2004, Dr. ElBaradei remarked that the French foreign minister had told him that
"maybe you have to have an agreed system of sanction, agreed in advance in the case
of a country's withdrawal, so you would know the cost in advance before you decide
to withdraw."
26. The IAEA's "Report of the Commission of Eminent Persons on the Future of
the Agency," released on May 23, 2008, recommends that "The UN Security Council
should go beyond its Resolution 1540 by: passing a new resolution making clear that
the proliferation of nuclear weapons is a threat to international peace and security;
legally prohibiting any state that withdraws from the Nonproliferation Treaty from
using for military purposes any nuclear facility, materials, or technologies that it
received for peaceful purposes while a party to the NPT; and legally imposing safeguards obligations, going well beyond the Additional Protocol, on any state that substantially violates its safeguards obligations." Dr. Goldschmidt has written extensively
on this subject. He has recommended that the UN Security Council should adopt a

Military actions obviously would be warranted only by an apparent and imminent threat to international peace and security, but a Statement of the UN Security Council president on January 31, 1992, would seem to support that interpretation in most cases of a nation's withdrawal from the NPT. A scenario involving the use of force might include limited naval or air forces in an intercept mission similar to those for which the Proliferation Security Initiative (PSI) was created. Aerial surveillance, such as was carried out in Iraq during the years prior to the invasion in 2003, is another possible scenario. An idea that might represent a "last resort" in an escalating situation was advanced by Dr. Jessica Mathews, president of the Carnegie Endowment for International Peace in 2002.[27] It was a plan for "coercive inspections." Her proposal dealt with the issue of UN inspections in Iraq, but it is an enforcement mechanism which could have relevance in other dire situations. Dr. Mathews suggested that the UN Security

---

generic and legally binding resolution stating that if a state withdraws from the NPT (an undisputed right under its Article X) after being found by the IAEA to be in non-compliance with its safeguards undertakings, then such withdrawal constitutes a threat to international peace and security as defined under Article 39 of the UN Charter. He suggests that it would be logical and legitimate for the Security Council to pre-agree that, in these circumstances, all military cooperation with the non-compliant state would be suspended. Also, "all materials and equipment made available to such a state or resulting from the assistance provided to it under a Comprehensive Safeguards Agreement would have to be forthwith removed from that state under IAEA supervision and remain under Agency's Safeguards."

Dr. Goldschmidt also proposed several ways in which enforcement could be mandated by the UN Security Council. He has suggested, for example, that in cases of a state's noncompliance with safeguards agreements: "the non-compliant state [must] provide the Agency with the necessary additional verification authority . . . prompt access to persons, broader and prompter access to locations, in site access to original documents and copies thereof, broader and faster access to information, and the lifting of other types of restrictions which experience has shown can be employed as obstructive tactics." See his "Mechanisms to Increase Nuclear Fuel Supply Guarantees," Pierre Goldschmidt, Carnegie International Non-Proliferation Conference, Washington, D.C., November 7–8, 2005 and lecture at the 24th Conference of the Nuclear Societies, Israel, February 19–21, 2008.

27. "Iraq: A New Approach," August 2002, Carnegie Endowment for International Peace.

Council might adopt a resolution authorizing multinational enforcement action to enable inspectors to carry out their UNSC mandate. She envisaged that the Security Council would authorize the creation of an "Inspections Implementation Force" to act as an enforcement arm for IAEA. The IAEA inspection team would be *"accompanied by a military arm strong enough to force immediate entry into any site at any time with complete security for the inspections team."* (Italics added.) Dr. Mathews made it clear that the "military arm" would be a very powerful force consisting of air and armored cavalry units with substantial air support. "Use of all necessary means" would be the next step beyond the use of an Inspections Implementation Force.

## A World Without Nuclear Weapons:
## Relating the Vision to the Steps

In any estimate of the current nuclear situation, it is impossible to ignore the core problem. This is the general assumption, shared alike by nuclear-armed nations and by those nations that have forgone nuclear weapons, that the development and acquisition of nuclear weapons will proceed, that a nuclear-armed world is here to stay. That assumption has to be changed, for assurances of fuel supply by any imaginable means will not be sufficient indefinitely to block the gradual spread of nuclear-armed states. Eliminating the two-tier system of nuclear and non-nuclear armed states must go hand in hand with eliminating the two-tier system in civil nuclear power because otherwise, slowly but surely, more states will become capable of making nuclear weapons and those states will have at least the option of starting a weapons program.

A basic proposition of this paper is that a solution to the fuel cycle problem depends on embedding it in a broad commitment to a world free of nuclear weapons and vice versa. The way to move forward is, first, to engage the United States and Russia in a commitment, at the highest levels, to work jointly toward a world free of nuclear weapons. The leaders of the two countries should follow this up with specific programs to reduce their strategic nuclear forces below the levels specified in the May 24, 2002, Treaty of Moscow. While implementing this commitment, and others, the presidents of the United States and Russia should invite other nations to join their two countries in working toward a world free of nuclear weapons. Each nation would be asked to commit to achieving a world without nuclear weapons and also to make a contribution to this goal, according to its special circumstances. A commitment to multinationally owned and managed nuclear fuel centers should be a key part of this program.

Unless impending decisions in several countries regarding the fuel cycle are made in a coherent way, with a view to how they contribute to the achievement of a world without nuclear weapons, these decisions will instead contribute to the spread of nuclear weapons capabilities. Conversely, if the goal of a world free of nuclear weapons is accepted by the international community and actions regarding the fuel cycle are consistent with that goal, it should be easier to expand the use of nuclear power without running the risk of nuclear weapons proliferation. The two have to be linked, not in lockstep, but in a way that permits each track to proceed as rapidly as events permit. Progress in one area should encourage progress in the other but, conversely, sensible progress in one area should not be delayed while waiting for progress in the other. The basic condition for success in escaping from the world's nuclear dilemma lies, as it did at the beginning of the nuclear age, in broad acceptance of the goal of a world without nuclear weapons.

# 11 Comprehensive Nuclear-Test-Ban Treaty and U.S. Security
## Raymond Jeanloz

**Summary**

The Comprehensive Nuclear-Test-Ban Treaty (CTBT) offers a significant opportunity toward implementing President Ronald Reagan's vision of establishing a global verification regime for nuclear weapons. A review of the past decade's developments shows that i) the CTBT is effectively verifiable, ii) it does not undermine the U.S. ability to sustain a nuclear deterrent, and iii) its entry into force would enhance the United States' security by constraining development of the most destructive weapons known. The latter conclusion is not new, but is stronger in the post-9/11 era that identifies radical terrorism as one of the gravest threats to national and international security. Additional steps for the U.S. to pursue in order to increase its security include: 1) Initiating an informed domestic political dialogue leading to CTBT ratification; 2) Reinstating full funding supporting the CTBT Organization; 3) Enhancing international transparency and confidence-building measures associated with sub-critical experiments and other aspects of nuclear weapon stockpile stewardship; 4) Establishing a periodic review of the CTBT, to be based on information from the national laboratories (and other sources) but led by an independent entity commissioned by Congress; and 5) After ratification, taking the lead in bringing about the treaty's entry into force.

**Table 1    Objections to Ratification\***

Too little time for debate
Utility questioned
    For abolishing nuclear explosions
    For advancing nuclear non-proliferation
Concern about ability to maintain U.S. nuclear arsenal
Verification questionable

\*Based on October 7, 1999, Statement of Senator Richard Lugar

## Introduction

The Comprehensive Nuclear-Test-Ban Treaty (CTBT) is intended to constrain the development and deployment of new nuclear weapons worldwide by prohibiting nuclear explosion tests that are used to validate weapon designs and advance weapons science. The Treaty was opened for signature on September 24, 1996, and has been ratified by 140 nations as of September 2007 (e.g., www.ctbto.org; Medalia, 2007a). Through a vote on October 13, 1999, however, the U.S. Senate declined to give its advice and consent to the Treaty's ratification, and the CTBT's entry into force awaits ratification by nine key nations including the United States.

The Senate debate preceding this vote was informed by testimony from a number of military, political, and technical specialists, including the directors of the three nuclear weapons laboratories (Los Alamos, Lawrence Livermore, and Sandia National Laboratories). Key issues at the time included (1) whether the United States can sustain its nuclear deterrent under a CTBT; (2) whether the Treaty is effectively verifiable; and (3) whether it serves U.S. security interests (Table 1). Subsequent to the vote, two of the most detailed studies of the CTBT's implications for U.S. security, by former Chairman of the Joint Chiefs of Staff, General (ret.) John Shalikashvili (2001), and by the National Academy of Sciences (NAS) (2002), specifically considered these issues.

The present paper reviews developments over the past decade, and

**Table 2    Accomplishments of Stockpile Stewardship**

---

Successful annual assessments of stockpile
Successful life-extension programs of weapons
Successful re-establishment of pit production
Retention of core capabilities
    Advances in understanding weapon performance
    Advances in understanding materials
    Developments at experimental facilities
Implications of Future Planning

---

re-examines the Shalikashvili and NAS reports: Have their findings and conclusions stood up over time? Have new considerations come into play, and is there any indication whether potential benefits of a CTBT have increased or decreased in the past ten years?

## Sustaining the U.S. Deterrent

The modern Stockpile Stewardship Program was initiated in 1994 to sustain the U.S. nuclear arsenal without nuclear explosion testing; its long-term success was therefore not well established at the time of the Senate debate on CTBT. Building on almost 40 years' prior experience with surveillance and refurbishment, the past decade's successes have clearly demonstrated the effectiveness of stewardship during a nuclear-test moratorium. This conclusion is documented by at least five developments since the program's inception (Table 2).

### Annual Assessment

The safety, reliability, and effectiveness of the U.S. nuclear weapons stockpile are assessed each year, with the technical need for nuclear explosion testing explicitly considered. Detailed information for this evaluation comes largely from the Department of Energy's nuclear weapons complex: especially from the three national laboratories responsible for design and certification, but also from Pantex and other sites where assembly, disassembly, and surveillance of weapons or their components take place. It is performed under the auspices of U.S. Strategic Command, however, which means that the assessment team is responsive to the military "customer" of the nuclear-weapons complex and can more objectively evaluate the national laboratories' work.

The result is an assessment that is—and is widely viewed as being—both technically sound and devoid of conflicts of interest. Indeed, the surveillance program has uncovered defects in stockpile weapons over the years, and these have been addressed. The fact that the stockpile has been certified to the president to be safe, reliable, and effective every year since establishment of the modern Stewardship Program, with no need for resumption of nuclear-explosion testing, is therefore a significant indication of the U.S. capability to sustain its nuclear arsenal during a test moratorium.

*Life-Extension Programs*

In addition to evaluating the state of the stockpile, stewardship addresses the need to periodically refurbish nuclear weapons as part of their ongoing maintenance. The design and military mission remain unchanged, but materials and components of the weapon may be changed out during these "life-extension" programs (LEPs). Most of the upgrades affect components outside the nuclear-explosive package, such as the arming, fuzing, and firing system, the idea being to sustain or even enhance safety, security, reliability, and ongoing maintainability.

A major challenge for life-extension is that a nuclear weapon is an aggregate of several sub-systems, such that any change to one part of the weapon has to be carefully vetted in order to ensure that no new faults or vulnerabilities have been introduced in the functioning of other parts. This is accomplished through an extensive review of the LEP, and certification of the refurbished weapon system before it is re-introduced into the stockpile.

Considerable research has gone into the first life-extension programs in order to assure their effectiveness and reliability, and the resulting certification of refurbished weapons (e.g., W87 LEP) is one indication of the success of stewardship. That a major new life-extension program is currently underway for the W76, which comprises the largest number of deployed warheads in the U.S. stockpile, testifies to the confidence that both the military and nuclear-weapons laboratories have in the process as well as products of LEPs (see p. 12 of Medalia, 2007b).[1]

*Pit Production and Certification*

Another milestone of the Stewardship Program is the establishment of pit production at Los Alamos. The key component of the primary stage of a thermonuclear weapon, the plutonium pit, releases nuclear energy in response to the chemical energy of high explosives; it is the nuclear trigger for the secondary stage, which then releases the bulk of the weapon's yield.

Pits had been manufactured at the Rocky Flats plant until it was shut down for environmental violations in 1989. Re-establishing a capability to manufacture and certify pits for what is arguably the most sophisticated of U.S. weapons, the W88, was a significant challenge requiring thorough vetting. This validation has been accomplished through a combination of extensive scientific and engineering studies, including sub-critical experiments; the latter are performed at the Nevada Test Site, to allow dynamic studies of fissile materials, but they do not produce a nuclear yield (Jeanloz, 2000).

The fact that new manufacturing processes performed by new people could be successfully established in a new location is a clear indication of the robustness of Stockpile Stewardship.

---

1. "The W76 LEP that is currently underway is an excellent program in terms of technology, schedule, and cost. This LEP is successfully proceeding toward completion as of August 2008. I believe it meets the Navy's needs," said Dr. Barry Hannah, Branch Head, Reentry Systems, Strategic Systems Program, U.S. Navy (quoted in Medalia, 2007b).

*Core Capabilities*

More generally, the success of stewardship has rested on advances in the underlying understanding of weapons performance and materials. Cessation of nuclear-explosion testing has not caused the laboratories to lose technical competence, as had been feared by some when the Stewardship Program started. To the contrary, significant advances have been made as researchers were able to study the physics under-lying weapon performance in great depth, undistracted by what had been the unrelenting demands of the nuclear-weapons program during the time of nuclear-explosion testing. Notable developments in un-derstanding primary- and secondary-stage performance, as well as the link between the two, characterize the Stockpile Stewardship Pro-gram's first decade of accomplishments.

Recently completed studies of plutonium (Pu) aging are another illustration of the scientific capability that has been established under the Stewardship Program. Plutonium ages as do other materials, but it also experiences degradation due to its radioactive decay and con-sequent self-irradiation. Therefore, one must consider how pits within the stockpile may suffer from unanticipated degradation due to plu-tonium aging.

A five-year program of research by the Los Alamos and Lawrence Livermore National Laboratories documented that plutonium ages far more slowly than had been feared, and that the effective lifetime for the metal in U.S. stockpile weapons exceeds 80–100 years (Hemley, et al., 2007). This does not mean that aging of pits can be ignored, but that the timescale for monitoring degradation of Pu is long—decades or more—relative to the time periods required for decisions about the United States' future nuclear stockpile.

Arguably, more was learned during this five-year study period than had previously been known about plutonium. A notable com-ponent of the program has been the international engagement of sci-entists—from Russia (and, to a more limited degree, China) as well as Britain and France—in technical discussions about plutonium with U.S. scientists (e.g., Cooper, 2000; see also www.pu2008.org/). These unclassified discussions have helped to advance the science, and have also enhanced mutual confidence between technical communities in the different countries' defense and nuclear establishments.

Similarly, it would be useful for U.S. national laboratory researchers to publish in the international, peer-reviewed literature the (unclassified) details of how they ensure that sub-critical experiments truly have zero yield; that is, are not capable of sustaining a nuclear chain reaction. Computer simulations are performed ahead of time to determine that an experiment will not produce nuclear yield, even by accident, and measurements during the experiment verify that there has indeed been no yield. Describing these methods in the open scientific literature would do more than build confidence; it would also help establish what the U.S. means by a zero-yield criterion, by documenting how that criterion is met.

Returning to the Stockpile Stewardship Program, numerical simulation and experimental validation have provided the foundation for recent technical advances in understanding weapon materials and performance, and served well in attracting, retaining, and developing scientists and engineers at the national laboratories. Indeed, a case can be made that—supported by major advances in computational capability, and the establishment of such facilities as the Dual-Axis Radiographic Hydrodynamic Test Facility (DARHT) at Los Alamos and the National Ignition Facility (NIF) at Livermore—the U.S. is in a technically *stronger* position for maintaining its nuclear-weapons capability than had it continued with underground nuclear-explosion testing.

Retaining core capability in nuclear weapons is essential not only for responsibly maintaining the stockpile, so long as it is U.S. policy to have a nuclear arsenal, but also for reasons of threat evaluation, counterproliferation and counterterrorism around the world. For example, the national laboratories provide key technical support for the

IAEA and other organizations' inspection, treaty-verification and threat-assessment capabilities. They also have unique capabilities for developing new detectors, analytical methods (e.g., in nuclear forensics), computer algorithms, and other tools required for national and international security.

*Future Planning*

In addition to past accomplishments, a positive assessment of stewardship is strongly indicated by discussions of future activities being considered for the U.S. nuclear weapons programs. For example, the recently proposed Reliable Replacement Warhead program would leverage the capabilities established through stewardship in order to potentially deploy a new warhead without returning to nuclear-explosion proof testing (Medalia, 2007b). To be sure, the design would have to be closely rooted in the results of the U.S.'s 1000-plus nuclear tests. With no new military mission, and no need for nuclear-explosion testing, the new design would be an extension of the LEPs now successfully underway, focusing on enhancements in safety, security (e.g., preventing unauthorized use of the weapon), and maintainability.

It is not yet technically clear that the Reliable Replacement Warhead can be successfully realized, but the ability to consider the option in a responsible manner—with a strong scientific grounding—is in place (American Association for the Advancement of Science, 2007). Put another way, even contemplating such a possibility requires great confidence in the capabilities of the national laboratories and the nuclear-weapons complex, as they approach a generation's experience with stockpile stewardship under a nuclear-test moratorium.

In summary, the evidence from accomplishments of the recent past, as well as future activities being considered, clearly establishes that the U.S. is now able to sustain its nuclear deterrent without the need to resume nuclear-explosion testing.

## Verification

The feasibility of monitoring nuclear-explosion tests, hence of verifying a test-ban treaty, has been of concern for many years, the issues being both political and technical (e.g., Gallagher, 1999). The focus here is on the latter, because high-confidence verification is impossible unless technical feasibility has been documented. From a technical perspective, effective verification means monitoring with high confidence that militarily significant nuclear explosions will be detected in a timely manner.[2]

The CTBT Organization's International Monitoring System (IMS) includes 321 seismic, hydro-acoustic, infrasound, and radionuclide stations, and 16 laboratories (Figures 1–5), and is due to be 90 percent complete at the beginning of 2009 (e.g., www.ctbto.org). The seismic, hydro-acoustic, and infrasound stations monitor sound waves transmitted through Earth's crust, oceans, and atmosphere, respectively, and provide estimates of the time, size, and geographic location of an explosion; they generally cannot distinguish a nuclear from a non-nuclear blast. In contrast, the gases and debris collected at radionuclide stations can prove that an explosion was nuclear, but do not in general resolve the time and location of the explosion to much better than a day and (part of) a continent. The seismo-acoustic and radionuclide methods are thus complementary.

Evidently, the IMS offers the capability to detect explosions down to yields of about 0.1–0.5 kiloton (kt) worldwide, identifying the character of the event as an explosion—rather than an earthquake, or an implosion as is the case for mine collapses (Richards, 2007)—as well as its time and location (see Figures 1–4 in color insert section after page 000). This raises two questions: (1) Is a fraction of a kiloton

2. After Testimony of Kathleen Bailey, former Assistant Director for Nuclear and Weapons Control, Arms Control and Disarmament Agency, in U.S. Congress, Senate Committee on Armed Services. *Comprehensive Test Ban Treaty.* S.Hrg. 106–490, 106th Congress, 1st Session, hearings held October 6 and 7, 1999, USGPO 2000, p. 201; see also Jonas (2007).

good enough for monitoring a CTBT that has a zero-yield threshold, and (2) How reliable are the estimates of monitoring sensitivity?

*Utility of Monitoring with Low-Yield Threshold*

Chapter 3 (and classified supporting material) of the NAS (2002) report addresses the first of these questions explicitly, distinguishing the benefits of testing at various yield levels either i) for nations with limited (or no) experience with nuclear-explosion testing or ii) for nations having significant experience with nuclear-explosion testing. The latter, for example, could use extremely low-yield tests to validate "one-point safety" of their existing designs, but this does not threaten U.S. security. More provocatively, the NAS group considered the possibility that a nation having considerable test experience could potentially get away with proof-testing a low-yield (1–2 kt) weapon if the blast can be effectively muffled ("decoupled"): a difficult task with significant probability of failure, that would in any case result in a design less-well validated than such nations already possess. The NAS (2002) study concluded that, though potentially politically significant, none of these scenarios poses new challenges to U.S. security from a technical perspective.

Similarly, a variety of scenarios could be considered for surreptitious nuclear-explosion testing by states having relatively little experience with nuclear weapons. In addition to their having far greater difficulty in preventing their test(s) from being detected, in comparison with nations having much more experience, such limited-experience countries may have less to gain from low-yield testing in terms of technical validation of their designs (NAS, 2002).

In short, being able to monitor a complete moratorium on nuclear-explosion tests to a fraction of a kiloton (tamped) yield has been found effective from the technical perspective of national and international security, but can one be assured that such sensitivity is actually in hand? The answer is yes, because the IMS provides only part of the world's detection capability, and this global capability has been—and continues to be—used, verified, and improved (e.g., Suda et al., 1998; Webb, 1998; Richards, 2007; Hafemeister, 2007).

*Monitoring Sensitivity and Its Validation*

i) Seismology and hydro-acoustics

The North Korean test of October 9, 2006 offers a case in point. This explosion was well recorded by the IMS, with 22 seismic stations (10 primary and 12 auxiliary) serving to locate the event to within the 1000 km$^2$ required by the CTBT, as reported in a Reviewed Event Bulletin of October 11 (CTBT Organization Preparatory Commission, 2007). It is also significant that many additional stations recorded the test, documenting its yield at about 0.5 ( $\pm 0.3$) kilotons, and validating that it was indeed an explosion, based on the small amount of shear relative to compressional energy released (see Figures 6–7 in color insert section after page 000). Nearby explosions carried out for scientific research on Earth's structure show that a test as small as 4–5 tons would have been detected at station MDJ (Figure 6, bottom), well below the 60-ton sensitivity expected for the primary IMS stations (Figure 2) (Kim and Richards, 2007; Richards, 2007).

Even a decade ago, at the time of the nuclear tests conducted by India and Pakistan, a seismic-detection threshold of less than 10–20 tons could be established from the noise level at non-IMS seismic stations recording those explosions (Barker, et al., 1998): again, much less than the detection limit for the primary IMS stations. As another example, the fact that the August 7, 1998, bombing of the U.S. Embassy in Nairobi, Kenya, was well recorded, with an amplitude corresponding to 4 ( $\pm 2$) tons of TNT, is an indication that even small blasts can be identified in completely unexpected locations (Koper, et al., 2002).

In comparison with these land-based explosions, sensitivity is far greater in the oceans. The explosions causing the Russian submarine *Kursk* to sink in the Barents Sea on August 12, 2000, were recorded at more than 20 seismic stations, located at distances up to 5000 km: a small blast—estimated at less than 20 kilograms yield—was discerned prior to the main explosion(s); the latter had a total yield of 4 tons and sealed the vessel's fate (Koper, et al., 2001; Savage and Helmberger, 2001). This seismological capability complements the high sensitivity indicated in Figure 4 for the hydro-acoustic system.

Such examples illustrate monitoring accomplishments over the past decade; but the actual capability at present and in the future is even better, if for no other reason than that deployment of modern, high-quality (e.g., broadband digital) seismometers continues at a significant pace worldwide. Only a fraction of that deployment is explicitly for CTBT verification, so it is important to recognize the complementary role played by the rest of the seismological community and by those utilizing national technical means in monitoring activity around the entire planet. Not only are more instruments becoming available for observations, but the underlying science is also experiencing dramatic advances.

One unexpected scientific development, for instance, is the recent discovery that horizontal variations in seismic-wave velocities throughout Earth's crust can be imaged from analyses of the ambient background noise recorded on seismometers (see Figure 8 in color insert section). The reason this is interesting is that the velocity heterogeneities act like lenses, refracting (bending) seismic rays and modifying the intensities of waves recorded at each seismic station. Therefore, it is useful to know the seismic-wave velocities throughout the crust in order to quantify seismic recordings of explosions (or earthquakes) at regional distances; that is, at ranges less than 300–700 kilometers, within which one can reliably detect small or decoupled nuclear tests. The noise-based method helps provide this information, with the potential of improving results beyond the current capability illustrated in Figures 6–7.

The background seismic noise is generated by storms, surf, and other ocean-atmospheric processes, to the point that the entire planet is constantly humming at the natural frequencies of Earth's acoustic harmonics (e.g., Webb, 1998; Rhie and Romanowicz, 2004; Gerstoft, et al., 2006; Shapiro, et al., 2006; Gerstoft and Tanimoto, 2007). The method amounts to correlating the background noise recorded at pairs of seismic stations, the correlated signal being sensitive to the wave velocities between each of the two stations. Tomographic analysis of the results, analogous to medical imaging by CT scan, produces the final images of wave-velocity variations (such as Figure 8), which can then be used in subsequent analysis of small events, whether earthquakes or explosions.

To be sure, noise-based tomography is not intrinsically better than the traditional methods of determining seismic-wave velocities between an earthquake (or explosion) and a seismic station. What the ambient-noise method offers, however, is important complementary information that helps to validate the results from traditional approaches, and to fill in the gaps where natural earthquakes or human-caused explosions are insufficient for determining velocity variations in a given region of the world (e.g., due to low levels of seismicity, or inaccessibility of a region of interest). Models of crustal seismic-wave velocities are thereby improved, to the benefit of the monitoring as well as the academic-research communities.

In the meantime, existing capability can also be made more effective. For example, one recommendation is to operate the IMS Auxiliary Network continuously as an enhancement to the Primary Network, thus improving detection capability and allowing supplementary stations to be used more easily to assist with identification of seismic events.

ii) Infrasound

Infrasound refers to low-frequency (0.001–20 Hz) acoustic waves in the atmosphere. This type of monitoring is less-well developed than seismology, but major advances are underway as more infrasound sensors are being deployed for the IMS than were ever available in the past. Many natural sources of infrasound are being documented, and a vibrant research community is establishing itself as experience is being gained from the deployed systems (e.g., Hedlin and Romanowicz, 2006).

For example, infrasound has recently documented the amount of meteorite and comet debris that continuously impacts Earth's atmosphere, showing that our planet experiences the equivalent of a 30-ton explosion twice a week, a 5-kiloton explosion about once per year, and a 10-megaton (Mt) explosion roughly once per millennium (Brown, et al., 2002; Edwards, et al., 2006, 2007). Many of these events are recorded by satellites designed to monitor Earth's surface for nuclear explosions, although the most recent known case of a 10-Mt comet- or meteorite-impact event is the Tunguska explosion that devasted more than 2,000 square kilometers of forest in Siberia on June 30, 1908.

Another notable example is the December 26, 2004, tsunami, which is estimated to have killed more than 200,000 people around the Indian Ocean (see Figure 9 in color insert section after page 000) (e.g., LePichon, et al., 2005; de Groot-Hedlin, 2005; Tolstoy and Bohnenstiehl, 2005; Satake and Atwater, 2007). It is now understood that many casualties might have been avoided if the combination of existing seismic, hyrdo-acoustic, and infrasound sensors had been coordinated into an effective tsunami-warning system: a task for which they were not designed (nor were there adequate means in place, at the time, to communicate such a warning). A tsunami warning system does exist in the Pacific, but such devastation was previously unanticipated for the Indian Ocean; elements of a warning system are now being deployed (e.g., Normile, 2007).

Other natural events being monitored by infrasound include explosive volcanic eruptions that can eject sufficient ash up to stratospheric heights to threaten commercial aviation (Garcés, et al., 2007). Experience being gained with these natural sources is helping researchers to better understand the propagation of sound waves through

Figures 1–10 for Chapter 11,
"Comprehensive Nuclear-Test-Ban Treaty
and U.S. Security" by Raymond Jeanloz

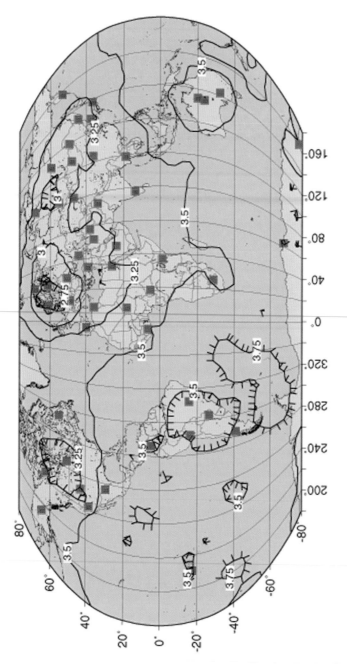

**Fig. 1.** Contours of seismic magnitude for which signals would be expected at 3 or more stations of the IMS primary seismic network (50 stations, shown as purple squares) from 90 percent of the events at or larger than the given magnitude. Contour interval is 0.25 magnitude units, and the detection threshold for Europe, Asia, North America and North Africa is in the magnitude range 3.0–3.5 or lower (from National Academy of Sciences, 2002).

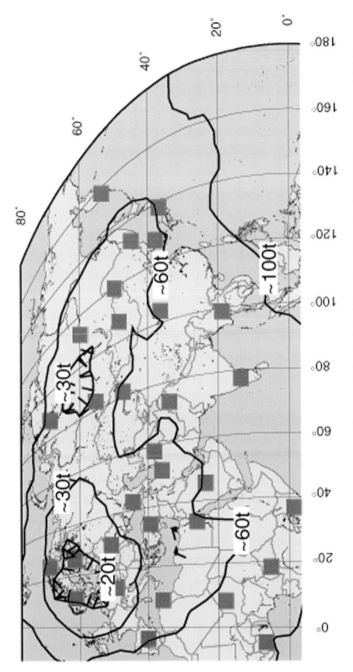

**Fig. 2.** Contours of approximate yield (tons = thousands of kilograms TNT equivalent) of tamped explosions, for which detections can be expected at 3 or more IMS primary stations (purple squares). These contours are the same as in Fig. 1, but with an expanded view of Europe, Asia and North Africa, and with seismic magnitude translated to yield (from NAS, 2002).

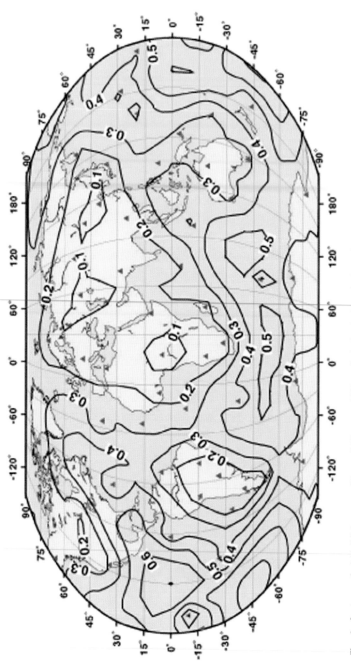

**Fig. 3.** Contours of yield (kilotons = millions of kilograms TNT equivalent) of atmospheric explosions that would be detected with 90 percent probability at more than 1 station for the planned IMS network of 60 infrasound stations (red triangles) (from NAS, 2002).

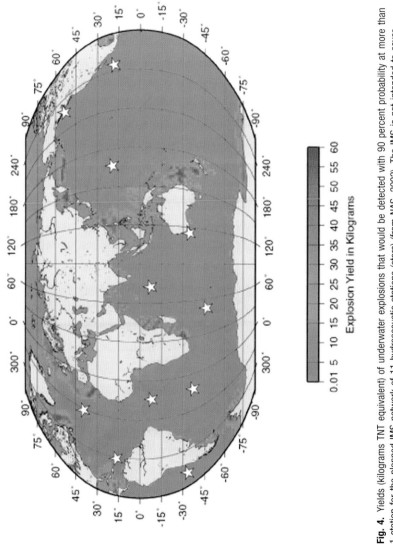

**Fig. 4.** Yields (kilograms TNT equivalent) of underwater explosions that would be detected with 90 percent probability at more than 1 station for the planned IMS network of 11 hydroacoustic stations (stars) (from NAS, 2002). The IMS is not intended to cover inland seas (grey), but the text provides examples of global monitoring capability in these regions.

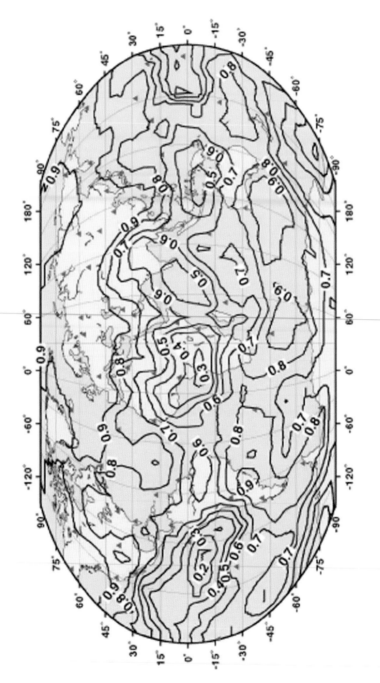

**Fig. 5.** Probability of one-station detection of a 1-kiloton nuclear explosion within 5 days by the planned 80-station IMS radionuclide network (red triangles) (from NAS, 2002).

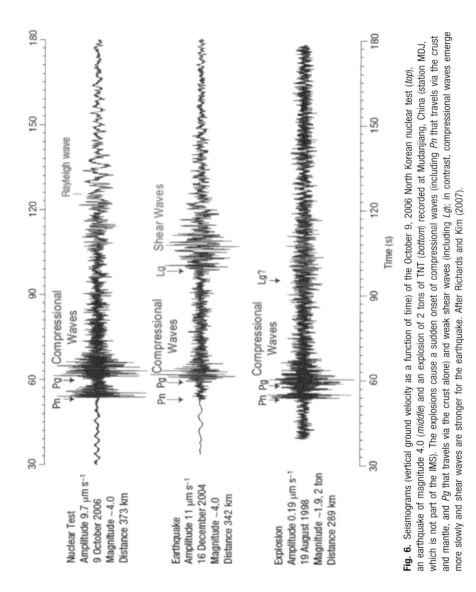

**Fig. 6.** Seismograms (vertical ground velocity as a function of time) of the October 9, 2006 North Korean nuclear test (*top*), an earthquake of magnitude 4.0 (*middle*) and an explosion of 2 tons of TNT (*bottom*) recorded at Mudanjiang, China (station MDJ, which is not part of the IMS). The explosions cause a sudden onset of compressional waves (including *Pn* that travels via the crust and mantle, and *Pg* that travels via the crust alone) and weak shear waves (including *Lg*); in contrast, compressional waves emerge more slowly and shear waves are stronger for the earthquake. After Richards and Kim (2007).

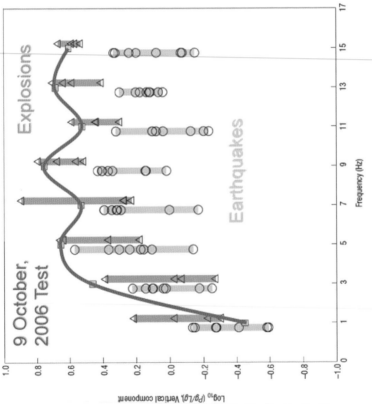

**Fig. 7.** Logarithm of the ratio of amplitudes of compressional (*Pg*) to shear (*Lg*) waves determined as a function of frequency from vertical-velocity recordings (Fig. 6). Explosions (triangles, full range marked in pink) consistently show higher values than earthquakes (circles, full range marked in yellow) at the higher frequencies, and measurements for the October 9, 2006 test (squares linked by red line) clearly fall in the range characteristic of explosions. After Richards and Kim (2007).

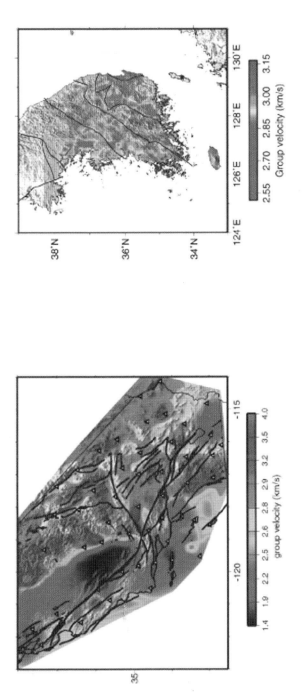

**Fig. 8.** Variations in velocities of seismic surface waves in Southern California (*left*) and South Korea (*right*) imaged using background seismic noise. Red and blue show velocities that are slower and faster, respectively, than average. As these variations effectively cause the observed seismic energy to bend, into fast-velocity and around slow-velocity regions, they affect the focusing of waves reaching each station. Understanding such focusing leads to more accurate locations, magnitudes and source mechanisms for earthquakes or explosions, and to enhancing the sensitivity of seismological methods. From Shapiro, et al. (2005), and Kang and Shin (2006); see also Sabra, et al. (2005).

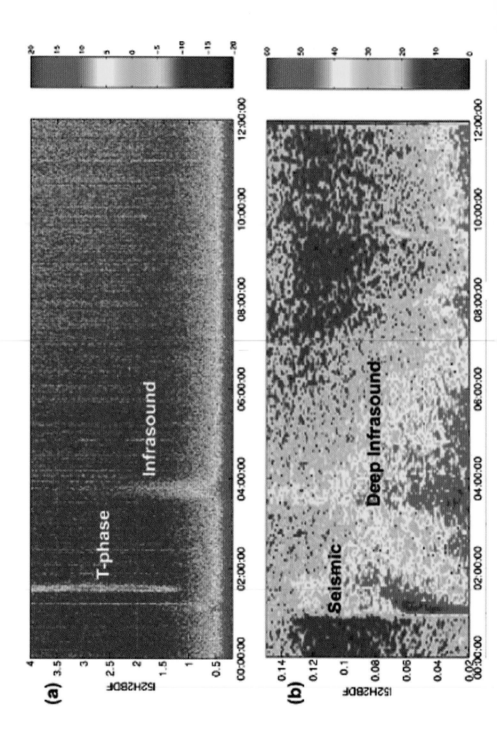

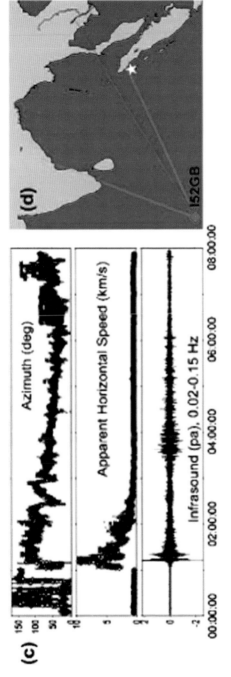

**Fig. 9.** Infrasound signal of the December 26, 2004 Sumatra earthquake and resultant tsunami, recorded 3000 km away at station IS52GB on Diego Garcia. (a) Spectrogram showing the frequencies between 0 and 4 Hz observed as a function of time, with detail between 0.02 and 0.15 Hz given in (b); (c) arrival azimuth (clockwise from north), apparent horizontal propagation speed across the array, and acoustic signature from the 0.01–0.15 Hz band; (d) range of azimuths inferred from array (see c), swinging from ENE to NNE (green lines) during the 4-hour record of infrasound, shown in comparison with locations of the earthquake (white star) and station (red diamond) (from Garcés, et al., 2005).

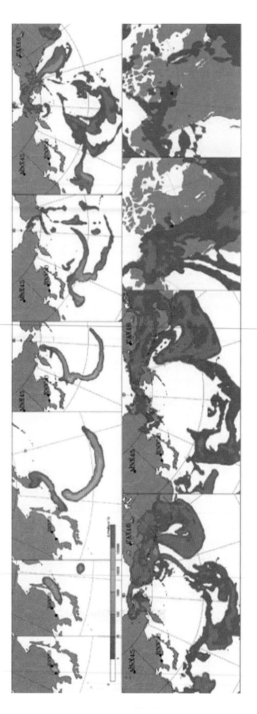

**Fig. 10.** Calculated location of $^{133}$Xe plume generated by the Oct. 9, 2006 North Korean test, shown as a function of time from upper left to lower right as it reaches Canada. From Saey, et al. (2007b).

the atmosphere, thereby improving the ability to determine the location and size of an explosion recorded by infrasound.

In actuality, the situation is developing even more quickly than might have been anticipated, due to the fact that infrasound is now being recognized on recordings from broadband seismometers (e.g., Ishihara, et al., 2004; Langston, 2004; Cochran and Shearer, 2006; Edwards, et al., 2007). As seismometers are far more numerous and widely distributed than infrasound detectors, this means that many more observations of an event can potentially be made than from the IMS infrasound network alone. More experience can be gained, better atmospheric-propagation models developed, and—through engagement of the large seismological research community—scientific advances can be greatly accelerated. A related development is the recording of infrasound by Global Positioning System (GPS) receivers (e.g., Calais, et al., 1998), which again broadens both the technology and community involved with nuclear-explosion monitoring.

## iii) Radionuclides

As with infrasound, radionuclide capability has improved significantly due to deployment of the International Monitoring System (Figure 5) and complementary stations. Remarkably, even the small (sub-kiloton) yield of the North Korean test released a noble-gas signal ($^{133}$Xe) consistent with a nuclear (as distinct from chemical) explosion, as reported from systems deployed in South Korea. In fact, a xenon-isotopic anomaly was predicted using advanced atmospheric transport models, and then detected at the Yellowknife, Canada, IMS station CAX16—more than 7,000 km away—12 to 18 days after the event (Figure 10) (Saey, et al., 2007a, b). It may not offer conclusive attribution by itself, especially as to location and time, but the signal is compatible with the North Korean event having been a nuclear test.

There remains considerable opportunity for enhancing the science and therefore the monitoring of radionuclides. Specifically, deployment of additional atmospheric-gas and aerosol stations for academic research, and further analysis and modeling of the measurements, could significantly expand current capabilities. Indeed, there is much scientific interest in improving this type of global atmospheric monitoring, and an enhanced capability could serve fields ranging from climate modeling to environmental monitoring.

iv) Satellite imagery

Finally, a significant resource that has emerged since the IMS was first being planned is the commercial availability of high-resolution satellite images. Such groups as www.isis-online.org/ and www.globalsecurity.org/ provide an important service in monitoring activities potentially related to nuclear-weapons development worldwide. Using commercial imagery, for example, D. Albright and P. Brannan of the Institute for Science and International Security have proposed an identification of the likely site of the October 9, 2006, North Korean test to within a few square kilometers. There can also be a close synergy between satellite and ground-based monitoring (e.g., Garcés, et al., 2004).

Moreover, evidence from imagery of preparations for nuclear-explosion testing can trigger special attention by IMS and non-IMS sensors, and quantitative analysis of images can place strong constraints on the likelihood that decoupling has been (or will be) attempted at a given site. New software tools such as those available at earth.google.com also facilitate the analysis and display of results.

Commercial imagery and private groups do not replace government analysts using national technical means, but do potentially offer greatly expanded capability in tracking activities around the world. In addition, they engage a large public community, thus decreasing the chances of surreptitious activity going unnoticed. It is also notable that commercial imagery can potentially be used to document conclusions reached on the basis of national technical means, thus making it easier to openly discuss government analysts' findings without revealing sensitive methods or capabilities.

In summary, the combination of national technical means, the International Monitoring System, and the academic and non-governmental organization research communities ensures a level of sensitivity—and cross-validation—that is effective for monitoring a CTBT. The monitoring capability is remarkably self-correcting, as was already demonstrated in response to the Kara Sea earthquake of 1997 (van der Vink, et al., 1998) and is even more the case today. Future research will further enhance this capability, for instance by expanding the fraction of the world that is fully monitored to the lowest yields.

## Role of CTBT

### Objectives and Limitations

The significance of a CTBT can be easily overstated, so it is important to acknowledge the limitations to such a treaty. No test-ban treaty can prevent the development of a fission bomb having a yield in the range of 15 kilotons, for example, as the gun-type weapon dropped on Hiroshima was built with sufficient confidence that nuclear-yield testing was not required.

More than half a century later, the technical knowledge for building such a weapon has to be considered widely accessible. And, with an excess of 60 tons—2,400 weapons' worth—of highly enriched uranium in civilian stockpiles around the world, the materials required to build such weapons have to be considered available, in principle (military stockpiles amount to an additional 1,840 tons or 73,600 weapons' worth of HEU)[3] (National Academy of Sciences, 2005). Indeed, South Africa had a small stockpile of gun-type weapons until it relinquished its nuclear arsenal. The detonation of such a weapon in an urban environment, whether in a military or a terrorist action, would be catastrophic.

---

3. The IAEA's definition of 25 kilograms of highly enriched uranium (HEU) being a "Significant Quantity" is used here to derive the equivalent number of weapons' worth of material.

Nevertheless, an objective of the CTBT is to prevent the development and deployment of far more sophisticated and devastating weapons, such as thermonuclear devices combining fission and fusion processes to release yields tens, hundreds, or even thousands of times larger. More specifically, plutonium-based implosion designs generally require nuclear-explosion testing when new (Garwin and Simonenko, 1997), and even a well-tested design may call for further testing if modifications are made, or the device is in new hands. Miniaturization so as to fit into long-range missiles, and other enhancements in military effectiveness, were among the developments of sophisticated nuclear warheads during the Cold War. These are the weapon designs that require nuclear-explosive testing, and the development and deployment of which a CTBT is intended to contain (see also NAS, 2002).

In comparison with the 10–20 kiloton yield of a gun-type fission device that would not need testing, it is clear that international capability available right now can monitor nuclear-explosion tests having much smaller yields: not only through the International Monitoring System and national technical means, but also through the complementary instrumentation of the academic, governmental (e.g., U.S. Geological Survey), and non-governmental research communities. Systems can fail and errors can be made, so it is impossible to rule out that a nuclear-explosion test might take place without being detected. However, the capability now in place makes this highly implausible, and the possibility of unrecorded (even decoupled) explosions yielding militarily useful information is therefore very limited.

Ironically, after spending hundreds of millions of dollars to deploy instruments and develop scientific capability at the cutting edge of global monitoring, the United States is currently forfeiting its role in the international effort of nuclear-test monitoring through neglect of its full annual dues to the CTBT Organization (Medalia, 2007a). This neglect jeopardizes future access to IMS data, and undermines U.S. leadership in mobilizing states party to the CTBT regime responding to a nuclear explosion should a test be conducted. After leading in so many technical aspects of monitoring capability, the United States' position is self-defeating in this regard.

*Security Benefits*

Still, there is a legitimate question as to whether, on balance, U.S. security does benefit from a CTBT. Several events of the past decade bear on Shalikashvili's (2001) and the NAS's (2002) conclusion that a CTBT is in the interest of U.S. security. The most recent is the North Korean nuclear-explosion test of October 2006, which clearly demonstrated the capability of both IMS and non-IMS stations in characterizing a low-yield test. The yield was so low, and well below the level announced by North Korea, that some have labeled it a failure. It was not a failure, however, in documenting North Korea's ability to detonate a nuclear device—and much is often learned from tests having lower yields than expected.

Thus there is a strong international incentive to avoid further nuclear-explosion testing by North Korea, and current diplomatic efforts appear to be accomplishing this goal. There is little doubt, however, that international pressure would be ineffective—perhaps even impossible to initiate—were any of the major nuclear powers testing at present. The current moratorium on nuclear-explosion testing is thus playing a key role in constraining the actions of North Korea in developing a militarily effective nuclear arsenal.

Similarly, the 1998 Indian testing series produced lower yields than announced, and instigated testing by Pakistan, so there remains a corresponding international incentive to avoid either nation initiating a new program of nuclear-explosion testing. As India and Pakistan have nuclear deterrents, the objective is to limit the development of weapons that are both more powerful and more readily delivered to long distances than already in these nations' stockpiles. Specifically, there is a high probability that resumption of nuclear-explosion testing by either nation would lead to renewed testing by the other, likely resulting in a spiraling arms race both in terms of sophistication and numbers of nuclear weapons deployed by India and Pakistan (and potentially triggering the resumption of testing by China).

These cases illustrate why major nuclear powers must expect to maintain a nuclear-testing moratorium for the indefinite future, if international pressure is to be sustained to dissuade all nations from undertaking nuclear-explosion testing.

Thus, the no-testing norm is effectively accepted by the global community of nations; the need for its ongoing observation means that the current moratorium is as constraining as the CTBT, but without the potential benefits of the Treaty. To be sure, a nuclear-weapon state may be driven by technical reasons to resume nuclear-explosion testing (e.g., due to a newly discovered vulnerability in its deterrent), and language currently in the CTBT allows for this eventuality, but the motivation would have to be strong in order to justify breaking the present international norm against testing.

*International Norms*

One may then question the need for a legally binding treaty, such as the CTBT, rather than a self-imposed moratorium as is currently in place. Indeed, some hold the view that no treaty restraining U.S. actions is in the security benefit of the United States. The NAS (2002) study addresses this issue through a review of the relative technical benefits and threats to U.S. security under distinct circumstances, such as: a) no constraints on nuclear-explosion testing; b) a voluntary moratorium on testing, as is currently in place; and c) entry into force of the CTBT.

A world with unconstrained nuclear-explosion testing advances other nations' capabilities relative to the United States', so does not serve the security interests of the U.S. Detailed analysis of the second option, a voluntary moratorium, shows that it has deficiencies in responding to nations that start testing, whether surreptitiously or openly. Those deficiencies are addressed by a CTBT, both through technical and political means; the former include an operational IMS and system of response to any nation testing, and the latter include confirmation of international norms (see below). As, on balance, the CTBT provides technical and political benefits without significantly challenging U.S. security under presently foreseeable circumstances, the Treaty is evidently in the interest of the United States (NAS, 2002).

However, the 9/11 attacks brought an additional, entirely new perspective to the question of international norms and legally binding treaties. In particular, it led to international terrorism being identified as the United States' highest security priority, and it is the potential combination of modern technology—nuclear weapons being among the most extreme examples—and radical terrorism that is acknowledged as a core threat facing the world today (Bush, 2002, 2006; National Commission on Terrorist Attacks Upon the United States, 2004).

In truth, it is exactly the civilized norms represented by international law that terrorism challenges, and 9/11 is a powerful reminder of why these norms are required. Therefore, only through a global consensus to embrace such norms can radical terrorism be effectively contained: they are necessary, though not necessarily sufficient, and the CTBT is but one example of legal norms that need strengthening. Others have made this point (e.g., Doyle, 2006), and it is more generally the case that nuclear weapons must play a different role in U.S. defense now, in the post-9/11 era, as compared with the Cold War period during which the nuclear arsenals were built up.

The current test-ban moratorium is a weak reflection of such norms, however, as it makes no formal commitment to partner nations intended to stand with the U.S. against those attacking a regime of international law. The existing moratorium—even when violated—has demonstrably played a role in constraining nuclear-explosion testing and therefore the development and deployment of new nuclear-weapon designs (so far), but the continued threats of proliferation call for a stronger system of international constraint. This stronger commitment to international norms is what the CTBT offers, and highlights not only the U.S. interest in ratification but—once ratified—in taking the lead in bringing about the treaty's entry into force.

*Periodic Review and Laboratory Privatization*

Recent developments thus reinforce the conclusion that a CTBT is in the interest of U.S. security, even more than could be appreciated before 9/11. Still, the future is uncertain, and a CTBT might be less effective—or allow new vulnerabilities—under circumstances that may emerge over the coming years or decades. Therefore, as part of a decision to support its entry into force, it would be prudent for the United States to establish an internal process for reviewing the CTBT's role in national and international security. This would be complementary to the international review process specified in Article VIII of the Treaty, and would enhance the utility of the safeguards associated with U.S. implementation of the Treaty.

Indeed, Shalikashvili (2001) recommended that the administration and Senate should jointly review the CTBT regime once per decade after ratification. Doing so would provide a periodic check that the Treaty continues to serve the nation's security interests, with due consideration of the United States' nuclear-weapons policy and posture as these evolve. Technical questions about sustaining U.S. defense capability, as well as the ability to verify the CTBT, would be among the central topics of such a review. More than enough capability exists, in the national laboratories and elsewhere, for periodic review of the CTBT regime.

As with annual assessments of the stockpile, developing a trustworthy process would be central to establishing the credibility of such a review. In this regard, matters have changed somewhat in the past few years. At the time of the 1999 Senate debate, for instance, the national laboratories could be viewed as public institutions providing independent technical information to advise a wider political dialogue.

In particular, Los Alamos and Lawrence Livermore National Laboratories were managed by the University of California (UC), a non-profit public institution with a reputation for fostering openness and free expression. The laboratory directors, testifying in the Senate, no doubt weighed the potential impact of a CTBT on their organizations' future, but they were not constrained from presenting a technically reliable, balanced and complete analysis.

The present situation is different, however, as the nuclear design laboratories are now managed by limited-liability companies (LLCs) in which UC partners with private, for-profit entities. These young LLCs have not yet had the opportunity to establish a record for fostering free expression, so their credibility could be viewed as yet-to-be fully established. Therefore, although the laboratories have the requisite technical expertise to inform a debate about CTBT, they may not—on their own—be in a position to communicate that information as effectively as was previously the case.

This is a recent development, suggesting the need for a new mechanism if the overall security—technical, military, foreign relations—basis of the CTBT regime is to be perceived as objectively reviewed within the U.S. The national laboratories' technical expertise must be an important component of such a review. As successfully demonstrated by the annual assessment of the nuclear-weapons stockpile, however, an independent and broader entity that is competent at the task can be made responsible for leading the review itself.

## Conclusion

Results of the past decade strongly reinforce the conclusions that the CTBT i) does not undermine the United States' ability to sustain an effective nuclear deterrent; ii) can be monitored with a sensitivity more than adequate for effective verification; and iii) does enhance U.S. security by constraining development and deployment of the most devastating weapons currently known. It serves to reinforce international norms that are all the more important at a time when radical terrorism has become the leading security priority of the U.S..

In the past, many of the major treaties bearing on nuclear weapons—INF, SALT, START, and SORT—have been bilateral rather than global in extent; neither SALT, START, nor SORT (or LTBT and TTBT) attempted a zero-level threshold, as does CTBT. In this sense, the Comprehensive Test-Ban Treaty exemplifies the global-verification regime envisaged by President Ronald Reagan for controlling nuclear weapons worldwide.

To be sure, significant nuclear arms control and disarmament efforts date back to the Baruch-Lilienthal Plan (1946) and the Eisenhower administration, and led to the Nuclear Non-Proliferation Treaty (NPT) and IAEA regime presently in force. An end to nuclear-explosion testing is cited in the Preamble of the NPT, and establishing an effective CTBT is one of the key objectives identified at the 1995 Review Conference extending the NPT for an indefinite duration. The CTBT is thus viewed by most of the world, including the nuclear-weapons states, as being intimately connected with nuclear non-proliferation (e.g., Medalia, 2007a; Jonas, 2007).

Based on the findings reviewed here, several actions have been identified for enhancing the CTBT regime and U.S. security, as summarized in Table 3. Though technically feasible on the timescales indicated, it is clear that these recommendations involve significant political issues that must also be addressed (e.g., Gallagher, 1999; Medalia, 2007a). For example, both Congressional and presidential election cycles will plausibly influence the pace as well as the content of a debate toward CTBT ratification. And, although the technical information is readily available, its political consequences may likely take time to work out. Similarly, establishing a nuclear-weapons policy and posture will be an important task for the new administration that takes power in 2009.

These considerations suggest that one to two years may have to be added to the schedule identified for the Intermediate-Term actions

**Table 3    Technically Feasible Actions Enhancing Security**

*Near Term (6–12 months)*
Reinstate full assessed U.S. funding for CTBT Organization*
Publish descriptions of U.S. sub-critical-experiment monitoring in scientific
  literature
Begin background discussions of CTBT in the U.S. Senate, including specific
  steps to build support for ratification and entry into force
*Intermediate Term (1–2 years)*
Establish post-9/11 U.S. nuclear-weapons policy and posture
Enhance coordination between the international verification regime, which
  includes the IMS, and other (academic-research, NGO) monitoring efforts
Debate CTBT, leading to ratification
  (e.g., establish internal periodic review mechanisms, as necessary)
*Long Term (5–10 years)*
Review and enhance CTBT regime
  Utility in controlling proliferation
  Ability to monitor
  Ability to sustain U.S. security needs

*The current implementation of the CTBTO—until the CTBT enters into force—is the CTBT
Organization Preparatory Commission.

in Table 3 to allow for the political activities that will necessarily be required. Still, developments both within the U.S. as well as internationally, including the opportunities and challenges of the upcoming 2010 NPT Review Conference, indicate the need for timely action on the CTBT.

The first concern about U.S. Senate ratification of the CTBT was that there had been inadequate time for the policy debate in 1999 (Table 1). There is no excuse for that continuing to be the case. The United States should start an informed discussion of the Comprehensive Nuclear Test Ban Treaty without delay.

ACKNOWLEDGMENTS

I thank J. F. Ahearne, R. M. Allen, S. Andreasen, J. H. Birely, T. W. Bowyer, L. Branstetter, J. C. Browne, D. S. Dreger, S. D. Drell, S.

Fetter, W. R. Frazer, N. W. Gallagher, M. Garcés, R. L. Garwin, J. E. Goodby, R. J. Hemley, J. I. Katz, K. D. Koper, M. Levi, J. Medalia, W. H. K. Panofsky, R. Peurifoy, P. G. Richards, M. H. Ritzwoller, P. M. Shearer, J. Sterngold, C. B. Tarter, A. Thunborg, and H. F. York for helpful discussions or comments on parts or all of this paper.

ACRONYMS

| | |
|---|---|
| CTBT | Comprehensive Nuclear-Test-Ban Treaty |
| CTBTO | CTBT Organization or, as currently, its Preparatory Commission |
| DARHT | Dual-Axis Radiographic Hydrodynamic Test Facility |
| GPS | Global Positioning System |
| HEU | Highly Enriched Uranium |
| IAEA | International Atomic Energy Agency |
| IMS | International Monitoring System |
| INF | Intermediate Forces Treaty |
| LEP | Life Extension Program |
| LLC | Limited Liability Company |
| LTBT | Limited Test Ban Treaty |
| NAS | National Academy of Sciences |
| NGO | Non-Governmental organization |
| NIF | National Ignition Facility |
| NPT | Nuclear Non-Proliferation Treaty |
| SALT | Strategic Arms Limitation Treaties |
| SORT | Strategic Offensive Reduction Treaty |
| START | Strategic Arms Reduction Treaties |
| TTBT | Threshold Test Ban Treaty |
| UC | University of California |

REFERENCES

American Association for the Advancement of Science (2007) *The United States Nuclear Weapons Program, The role of the Reliable Replacement Warhead*, AAAS, Washington, DC, 34 pp. www.aaas.org/news/releases/2007/media/rrw_report_2007.pdf

B. Barker, M. Clark, P. Davis, M. Fisk, M. Hedlin, H. Israelsson, V. Khalturin, W.-Y. Kim, K. McLaughlin, C. Meade, J. Murphy, R. North, J.

Orcutt, C. Powell, P. G. Richards, R. Stead, J. Stevens, F. Vernon and T. Wallace (1998) Monitoring nuclear tests, *Science* 281, 1967–1968.

P. Brown, R. E. Spalding, D. O. ReVelle, E. Tagliaferri and S. P. Worden (2002) The flux of small near-Earth objects colliding with the Earth, *Nature* 420: 294–296.

G. W. Bush (2002) *National Strategy to Combat Weapons of Mass Destruction* (December 2002), 6 pp. www.fas.org/irp/offdocs/nspd/nspd-wmd.pdf

G. W. Bush (2006) *The National Security Strategy of the United States of America* (March 2006), 49 pp. www.whitehouse.gov/nsc/nss/2006/

E. Calais, J. B. Minster, M. Hofton and M. Hedlin (1998) Ionospheric signature of surface mine blasts from Global Positioning System measurements, *Geophys. J. Int.* 132: 191–202.

E. S. Cochran and P. M. Shearer (2006) Infrasound events detected with the Southern California Seismic Network, *Geophys. Res. Lett.* 33: L19803, doi:10.1029/2006GL026951.

N. G. Cooper, Editor (2000) Challenges in Plutonium Science, *Los Alamos Science* 26, 1–493 (2 vols.). www.fas.org/sgp/othergov/doe/lanl/pubs/number26.htm

CTBT Organization Preparatory Commission (2007) Verification Science, *CTBTO Spectrum* 9: 24, 28. www.ctbt.org

C. D. de Groot-Hedlin (2005) Estimation of the rupture length and velocity of the Great Sumatra earthquake of Dec. 26, 2004 using hydroacoustic signals, *Geophys. Res. Lett.* 32: L11303, doi:10.1029/2005GL022695.

J. Doyle (2006) Strategy for a new nuclear age, *Nonprolif. Rev.* 13: 1746–1766.

W. N. Edwards, P. G. Brown and D. O. ReVelle (2006) Estimates of meteoroid kinetic energies from observations of infrasonic airwaves, *J. Atm. Solar-Terrestr. Phys.*, 68: 1136–1160.

W. N. Edwards, D. W. Eaton, P. J. McCausland, D. O. ReVelle and P. G. Brown (2007) Calibrating infrasonic to seismic coupling using the Stardust sample return capsule shockwave: Implications for seismic observations of meteors, *J. Geophys. Res.* 112: B10306, doi:10.1029/2004JB004621.

N. W. Gallagher (1999) *The Politics of Verification*, Johns Hopkins University Press, Baltimore, MD, 311 pp.

M. Garcés, C. Hetzer, H. Bass, M. Hedlin, K. Lindquist, J. Olson, C. Wilson, D. Drob and M. Picone (2004), Forensic studies of infrasound from massive hypersonic sources, *EOS Trans. Am. Geophys. Union*: 85, 433, 440.

M. Garcés, P. Caron, C. Hetzer, A LePichon, H. Bass, D. Drob and J. Bhttar-charyya (2005) Deep infrasound radiated by the Sumatra earthquake and tsunami, *EOS Trans. Am. Geophys. Union* 86: 317, 320.

M. Garcés, D. McCormack, R. Servranckx, H. Bass, M. Hedlin, and H. Yepes (2007), Acoustic Surveillance for Hazardous Eruptions (ASHE): Preliminary results from a pilot infrasound experiment, *4th International Workshop on Volcanic Ash* (VAWS/4): 26–30 March, Rotorua, New Zealand.

R. L. Garwin and V. A. Simonenko (1997) Nuclear weapon development without nuclear testing? Pugwash Workshop on Problems in Achieving a Nuclear-Weapon-Free World, London, England (25–27, Oct. 1996). www.fas.org/rlg/dev_no_test.htm

P. Gerstoft, M. C. Fehler and K. G. Sabra (2006) When Katrina hit California, *Geophys. Res. Lett.* 33: L17308, doi:10.1029/2006GL027270.

P. Gerstoft and T. Tanimoto (2007) A year of microseisms in southern California, *Geophys. Res. Lett.* 34: L20304, doi:10.1029/2007GL031091.

D. Hafemeister (2007) Progress in CTBT monitoring since its 1999 Senate defeat, *Science & Global Security* 15: 151–183.

M. Hedlin and B. Romanowicz (2006) The sound of silence, *Physics World* 19: 21–25.

R. J. Hemley, D. Meiron and others (2007) *Pit Lifetime*, JSR-06-335, MITRE Corporation, McLean, VA, 20 pp. www.fas.org/irp/agency/dod/jason/pit.pdf

Y. Ishihara, M. Furumoto, S. Sakai and S. Tsukuda (2004) The 2003 Kanto large bolide's trajectory determined from shockwaves recorded by a seismic network and images taken by video camera, *Geophys. Res. Lett.* 31: L14702, doi:10.1029/2004GL020287.

R. Jeanloz (2000) Science-based stockpile stewardship, *Physics Today* 53: 44–50. www.physicstoday.org/pt/vol-53/iss-12/p44.html

D. S. Jonas (2007) The Comprehensive Nuclear Test Ban Treaty: Current legal status in the United States and the implications of a nuclear test explosion, *Int. Law and Politics* 39: 1007–1046.

T.-S. Kang and J. S. Shin (2006) Surface-wave tomography from ambient seismic noise of accelerograph networks in southern Korea, *Geophys. Res. Lett.* 33: L17303, doi:10.1029/2006GL027044.

W.-Y. Kim and P. G. Richards (2007) North Korean nuclear test: Seismic discrimination at low yield, *EOS Trans. Am. Geophys. Union*, 88: 157, 161.

K. D. Koper, T.C. Wallace, S.R. Taylor and H.E. Hartse (2001) Forensic seismology and the sinking of the Kursk, *EOS Trans. Am. Geophys. Union* 82: 37, 45–46.

K. D. Koper, T. C. Wallace, R. E. Reinke and J. A. Leverette (2002) Empirical scaling laws for truck bomb explosions based on seismic and acoustic data, *Bull. Seism. Soc. Am.* 92: 527–542.

C. A. Langston (2004) Seismic ground motions from a bolide shock wave, *J. Geophys. Res.* 109: B12309, doi:10.1029/2004JB003167.

A. LePichon, P. Herry, J. Vergoz, N. Brachet, M. Garcés, D. Drob and L. Ceranna (2005) Infrasound associated with 2004–2005 large Sumatra earthquakes and tsunami, *Geophys. Res. Lett.* 32: L19802, doi:10.1029/2005GL023893.

J. Medalia (2007a) *Nuclear Weapons: Comprehensive Test Ban Treaty*, Congressional Research Service Report for Congress RL33548 (July 12, 2007) 36: www.fas.org/sgp/crs/nuke/RL33548.pdf

J. Medalia (2007b) *The Reliable Replacement Warhead Program: Background and Current Developments*, Congressional Research Service Report for Congress RL32929 (July 26, 2007), 45 pp. www.fas.org/sgp/crs/nuke/RL32929.pdf

National Academy of Sciences (NAS) (2002) *Technical Issues Related to the Comprehensive Nuclear Test Ban Treaty*, National Academy Press, Washington, DC, 84 pp.

National Academy of Sciences (NAS) (2005) *Monitoring Nuclear Weapons and Nuclear-Explosive Materials, An Assessment of Methods and Capabilities*, National Academy Press, Washington, DC, 250 pp.

National Commission on Terrorist Attacks Upon the United States (2004) *The 9/11 Commission Report*, U.S. Government Printing Office, Washington, DC, 567 pp. www.9-11commission.gov/

D. Normile (2007) Tsunami warning system shows agility—and gaps in Indian Ocean network, *Science*, 317: 1661.

J. Rhie and B. Romanowicz (2004) Excitation of Earth's incessant free oscillations by atmosphere-ocean-seafloor coupling, *Nature* 431: 552–556.

P. G. Richards (2007) Forensic seismology and CTBT verification, *CTBTO Spectrum* 9: 1, 6 and 19. www.ctbt.org

P. G. Richards and W.-Y. Kim (2007) Seismic signature, *Nature Physics* 3: 4–5.

K. G. Sabra, P. Gerstoft, P. Roux, W. A. Kuperman and M. C. Fehler (2005) Surface wave tomography from micsoseisms in Southern California, *Geophys. Res. Lett.* 32: L14311, doi:10.1029/2005GL023155.

P. R. J. Saey, M. Bean, A. Becker, J. Coyne, R. d'Amours, L.-E. De Geer, R. Hogue, T. J. Stocki, R. K. Unger and G. Wotawa (2007a) A long distance measurement of radioxenon in Yellowknife, Canada, in late October 2006, *Geophys. Res. Lett.* 34: L20802, doi:10.1029/2007GL030611.

P. R. J. Saey, A. Becker and G. Wotawa (2007b) North Korea: A real test for the CTBT verification system? Part II: Noble gas observations, *CTBTO Spectrum* 10: 20–21. www.ctbt.org

K. Satake and B. F. Atwater (2007) Long-term perspectives on giant earthquakes and tsunamis at subduction zones, *Ann. Rev. Earth Planet. Sci.* 35: 349–347.

B. Savage and D. V. Helmberger (2001) Kursk explosion, *Bull. Seism. Soc. Am.* 91: 753–759.

J. M. Shalikashvili (2001) *Letter to the President and Report on the Findings and Recommendations Concerning the Comprehensive Nuclear Test Ban Treaty.* www.fas.org/nuke/control/ctbt/text/ctbt_report.html

N. M. Shapiro, M. Campillo, L. Stehly and M. H. Ritzwoller (2005) High-resolution surface-wave tomography from ambient seismic noise, *Science* 307: 1615–1618.

N. M. Shapiro, M. H. Ritzwoller and G. D. Benson (2006) Source location of the 26 sec microseism from cross-correlations of ambient seismic noise, *Geophys. Res. Lett.* 33: doi:10.1029/2006GL027010, L18310.

N. Suda, K. Nawa and Y. Fukao (1998) Earth's background free oscillations, *Science* 279: 2089–2091.

M. Tolstoy and D. R. Bohnenstiehl (2005) Hydroacoustic constraints on the rupture duration, length, and speed of the great Sumatra-Andaman earthquake, *Seism. Res. Lett.* 76: 419–425.

G. van der Vink, J. Park, R. Allen, T. Wallace and C. Hennet (1998) False accusations, undetected tests and implications for the CTB Treaty, *Arms Control Today*, May issue, 7–13.

S. C. Webb (1998) Broadband seismology and noise under the ocean, *Rev. Geophys.* 36: 105–142.

# 12. Regional Animosities and Nuclear Weapons Proliferation
## Jack F. Matlock Jr.

### Summary Conclusions

- Regional animosities contribute, upon occasion, to nuclear proliferation, but other considerations are usually equally or more important.
- An effective policy to prevent further proliferation will combine efforts to deal with the more general problems (such as "de-legitimizing" nuclear weapons as a source of national power) with specific moves to defuse the most dangerous aspects of regional confrontations.
- Every confrontation has unique aspects; though policy should be broadly consistent, it must be tailored to the specific situation with which it deals. In particular, policymakers must avoid the assumption that others "think like we do." Their thought processes are often quite different, which makes it important to take into account the culture and history of forces in the specific area.
- Regimes hostile to a nuclear-armed state may perceive that nuclear weapons provide the most reliable deterrence to military action aimed at removing them.
- This suggests that threats of possible military action, whether direct or implied, can be counterproductive. The historical record indicates (1) that nuclear-armed states do not use force against

other states with nuclear arms; and (2) that threats from external powers tend to unite a country in support of the existing regime.

- States that have terminated nuclear weapons programs (Brazil, South Africa, and Libya are examples) have done so—each for different reasons—when they deemed that possession of the weapons would create unacceptable dangers and that forgoing the program would actually make the ruling regime more secure.

- U.S. diplomacy in the 1980s, which led to an end of the Cold War, suggests that direct communication at the most senior levels of government is a useful—probably essential—tool to find peaceful ways to resolve disputes.

- The combination of six-power talks with bilateral negotiations seems the most appropriate approach to North Korea, despite the obvious difficulties. Steps should continue to broaden the dialogue that has begun with Iran, both bilaterally and in the context of regional fora. It might be helpful for the United States to outline the features of a *modus vivendi* with both North Korea and Iran that would permit eventually normalizing relations. Multilateral pressures on both will be an essential supplement to direct talks.

- Given Pakistan's current political instability, its nuclear arsenal constitutes a more serious immediate threat than the prospect of Iranian weapons. The current political turmoil may continue and intensify, increasing the chances that some of Pakistan's weapons could find their way into the hands of terrorists. U.S. options are severely limited, but more attention must be given to undermining the popular assumption that the United States is anti-Islam, not only in order to help stabilize conditions in Pakistan, but also to improve relations in other areas of the Islamic world.

- Should Iran resume its nuclear weapons program, it would very likely stimulate further nuclear proliferation in the Middle East. Syria is already suspected of planning a weapons program and others might well follow that pattern if the Iranian program is resumed and approaches weapons capability. Similarly, if North Korea continues to develop and improve its capability, the pressure on Japan, South Korea, and perhaps even Taiwan to follow suit would grow.

- Until there is a generally accepted settlement of the Israeli-Palestinian confrontation, Israel's possession of nuclear weapons will be used as an excuse or pretext for development of nuclear weapons in Muslim countries. Even if a settlement is possible, however, it would not, in itself, remove the allure of nukes given the high levels of tension between Islamic states.

- A new set of regional confrontations has arisen of late that have serious implications for nuclear proliferation: those of Russia with some of its neighbors, particularly with Ukraine and Georgia. A continuation and further exacerbation of these tensions could ultimately revive a desire on Ukraine's part to re-acquire a nuclear weapons capability. More immediately, these tensions, if unresolved, are likely to make Russia less willing to join the U.S. in a program to accelerate the reduction of nuclear weapons.

- This suggests that the U.S. should re-assess its attitude toward a near-term NATO membership for Ukraine (where the majority of the population is opposed to NATO membership), and for Georgia, which is confronted with unresolved disputes with the *de facto* independent enclaves it claims. U.S. policy should continue to support the independence of all the ex-Soviet states, but should encourage those governments to avoid gratuitous actions which would inevitably be viewed as provocative by Russia.

- The U.S. should also re-assess the necessity for some of its other plans, such as for missile-defense installations in Eastern Europe, if they diminish Russian willingness to cooperate on other nuclear issues. A program to develop missile defenses jointly with Russia, and perhaps China and interested NATO countries, would facilitate better overall cooperation in reducing the number of nuclear weapons and restraining further proliferation.

- To deal effectively with regional confrontations that encourage nuclear proliferation, the U.S. must avoid, whenever possible, total support for a single party to the dispute but rather cultivate a position from which it can act as an honest broker. It also must recognize, both in stated policy and in practice, that these problems cannot be solved or eliminated by unilateral U.S. action, but require multilateral cooperation, which will often require agreeing to arrangements that are less than optimum from the U.S. point of view.

Regional animosities and confrontations obviously have contributed to nuclear weapons proliferation. Israel's sense of vulnerability, combined with the open hostility of its Arab neighbors, resulted in the Israeli government's decision to "go nuclear" without publicly acknowledging the fact. India's territorial dispute with China and political animosity doubtless contributed to India's decision to develop nuclear weapons, even as it denied that it was doing so; the Indian program, in turn, practically guaranteed that Pakistan would seek its own nuclear arsenal. Therefore, it will be useful to examine the conditions under which regional animosities encourage nuclear proliferation and to consider whether there are ways the United States might reduce the risk of proliferation by dealing with such disputes.

We should bear in mind at the outset that, while regional tensions may well contribute to decisions to develop a nuclear arsenal, they rarely provide the sole motivation. Questions of prestige, the political power of incumbent governments, and relations of the country with nuclear weapons states probably contribute more to decisions to develop a nuclear capability than the specific tensions in the region where the country is located.[1] Even successful attempts to reduce regional tensions are unlikely to deter the spread of nuclear weaponry except to the degree to which to they supplement other, more general, policies. Most fundamentally, nuclear weapons must be devalued as a source of power and prestige; nuclear weapons states must renew (or—if not a party to the Non-Proliferation Treaty—undertake) the commitment to reduce their nuclear arsenals with a goal of total

---

1. Israel may be an exception in this regard, since its decision presumably resulted primarily from its feeling of vulnerability to hostile neighbors.

abolition; and all parties must be more active in strengthening an international legal framework that discourages and handicaps further proliferation.

We also need to consider the impact that American policy toward regional disputes has on the stance of other nuclear powers. In this respect, the tensions that have developed between Russia and some of the countries that were once part of the Soviet Union or members of the Warsaw Pact are relevant. To the degree that American policy is seen in Moscow as exploiting these tensions to the detriment of Russian security, the Russian government will inevitably become more resistant to cooperation with the United States in the nuclear weapons area. We also cannot exclude the possibility that, should these tensions develop into chronic confrontations, some of the ex-Soviet states might feel constrained to re-aquire some of the nuclear weapons they possessed upon the Soviet collapse, but either destroyed or transferred to Russia.[2]

This paper will first examine the reasons countries have decided to acquire nuclear weapons and why some have decided to terminate programs before they produced useable weapons. Then it will look at the salient characteristics of some regional confrontations, consider the impact that cultural differences exert on the perceptions of the main actors, and describe the impact of regional animosities on Russian nuclear policy. Finally, it will consider whether the United States can bolster its non-proliferation policy by attempting to reduce regional confrontations.

In dealing with these questions, I will refer at times to our experience in dealing with the Soviet Union during the years of Ronald Reagan's presidency. The issues we face today are in some important respects different, but in many respects similar. Where there are sim-

---

2. When the Soviet Union ceased to exist at the end of 1991, there were nuclear weapons in four of the successor states: Russia, Belarus, Ukraine, and Kazakhstan. Belarus immediately transferred the weapons on its territory to Russia; Kazakhstan and Ukraine did so subsequently, following negotiations in which the United States participated.

ilarities, we can learn from what worked in the 1980s, and in some cases lessons from that period can be usefully applied to the very different challenges of the present.

## Why Do Countries Want Nuclear Weapons?

We often hear assertions that country X or country Y provides support to terrorists and therefore terrorists are likely to obtain nuclear weapons if that country develops them. Actual experience suggests that this is unlikely: Up to now, countries with nuclear weapons that also have ties to terrorist groups have jealously guarded their weapons and kept them out of the hands of terrorists. Both the Soviet Union and China supported certain terrorist groups, but never let them come close to their nuclear weapons. Furthermore, neither supplied the weapons to third countries, however friendly, although the Soviet Union supplied some technology to China in the early stages of its program, and China supplied technology to Pakistan.

Even though the primary motivation for developing a nuclear weapons capability is unlikely to be for the benefit of terrorists, the risk that terrorists will find a way to acquire such weapons obviously increases if more and more countries develop nuclear arsenals. Therefore, every reasonable effort must be made to prevent the spread of a nuclear-weapons capability to additional states. Even so, it is equally important to make sure that terrorist groups have no access to existing stocks of nuclear weapons or their components. Both North Korea and Pakistan—for different reasons—have a record of selling nuclear materials and technology and, given the fragility of governments in both countries, they may present a greater danger than Iran would, should it acquire a nuclear weapons capability.

The reasons the five "legal" (under the NPT) nuclear powers developed their weapons are clear: the U.S. and U.K. conducted a joint program to develop a weapon to use in World War II—and to do so before their adversaries could produce such a weapon. Stalin ordered the development of nuclear weapons because he did not wish to place the USSR at a strategic disadvantage in dealing with the Western powers following World War II. Both France and China decided to develop a nuclear weapons capability to give them the basis for a foreign policy independent of the leaders of the alliances in which they participated.

Israel, India, and Pakistan refused to sign the NPT, and over time each developed an independent capability, for reasons already mentioned. North Korea was an NPT signatory but violated the Treaty by developing a weapons capability clandestinely. Brazil, South Africa, Libya, and Iraq have had active programs in the past, but have terminated their programs. Brazil became convinced that it was better served by adhering to the Treaty of Tlatelolco than by continuing with a weapons-development program which could have resulted in a nuclear arms race with Chile and Argentina. South Africa voluntarily dismantled its program when its leaders decided to end the apartheid regime and accept majority rule. Libya seems to have terminated its program when its leaders tired of trying to circumvent economic sanctions and were shaken by the U.S. invasion of Iraq. Iraq, of course, has been found to have abandoned its program in the wake of the sanctions and inspections imposed at the end of the Gulf War of 1991. However, in Iraq's case, Saddam Hussein, in calculated fashion, left the impression that he still had some WMD capability, presumably in order to enhance his leverage over neighboring states.

There are unique features of each instance cited and it would be hazardous to go far in drawing general conclusions. Nevertheless, it would seem that regimes are inclined to seek a nuclear weapons capability when they feel that nuclear weapons are necessary to deter an attack on them and/or when they seek what they perceive to be the advantage of belonging to an exclusive "club" of nuclear powers. Once started on a program to develop such weapons, these regimes seem to be deterred only if they are convinced that continuing the program will pose a greater threat to their existence than terminating it.

There is also one other clear lesson from past experience: "democratization"—even if feasible in a given instance—is no insurance against a nation's decision to develop a nuclear capability. France, Israel, and India are all countries with democratic forms of government and all decided to "go nuclear" when most of the rest of the world disapproved. Pakistan's program proceeded unimpeded when Pakistan had democratically elected governments—to attempt to terminate the program would have meant political suicide in Pakistan at the time. This suggests that, at present, even a democratically elected government in Iran might well continue the Iranian program unless the external political environment is altered.

## Huntington Light, or the Impact of Cultural Differences

In the 1990s, Harvard professor Samuel Huntington wrote a much-acclaimed article, then book, predicting a future "conflict of civilizations." Some of his conclusions seem overdrawn, particularly his definition of what constitutes a "civilization" and his predictions that most future conflicts will be between civilizations rather than within them. (Today, the violence between Shiites and Sunnis in Iraq, and between Kurds and Arabs or Turks illustrate conflicts *within* Huntington's purported "civilizations.") Nevertheless, Huntington's thesis does highlight the role of culture in conditioning nations and sub-national groups to conflict or cooperation. That factor has been given insufficient attention in most international relations theory, and is often poorly understood by policymakers.

International relations is not the interaction of undifferentiated billiard balls, as some theorists contend, but of human beings acting in what the individuals perceive as their own interest—the most important of which is to stay alive and in power. What is perceived as a threat will be determined as much by culture, history, and experience as by facts and logic. One of the most damaging assumptions that any policymaker can make is to assume that political leaders from radically different cultures think the same way we would, and tend to react to our statements and actions as we believe a "rational" person would.

## Lessons from the Cold War

The way the Cold War was ended contains many potential lessons. One of the most important was the value of establishing direct communication with the Soviet leaders even when their policies seemed diametrically opposed to U.S. interests. Some of President Reagan's advisers felt strongly that, given the nature of the Soviet regime, the Soviet record of broken promises, and the Communist ideology that aimed at the destruction of the "bourgeois West," there was no reason to deal directly with them at the highest levels. The Soviet leaders could not be persuaded to change their ways, these advisers argued, but could be defeated only by consistent military, economic, and political pressure. Proponents could find an abundance of facts to support this argument; if the Soviet Union operated the way Leninist theory dictated, they would have been right.

But President Reagan knew that ideology, important as it was, was not the whole story. The Soviet Union was an evil empire, and—unlike many of his contemporaries in the West—he was prepared to say so, but he understood that the Soviet Union was led by human beings who might be reached by reason, provided they could be persuaded that they could not win an arms race and disabused of their unfounded fear that the United States was planning a nuclear attack or was seeking military superiority to place them at a political disadvantage. Therefore, President Reagan was open to Secretary of State Shultz's ideas for engaging the Soviet leaders in a frank discussion. Communication did not mean accepting the erroneous perceptions of the Soviet leaders or compromising U.S. interests; it did mean an effort of muscular diplomacy, backed by strength, to convince the Soviet leaders that they had more to gain from abandoning their aggressive policies and ending the arms race than by engaging in a competition that they would lose.

Communication, however, would have been of limited use if the American attitude had been that cooperation with the Soviet Union would be possible only if the Communist Party relinquished power—

that is, if the object of our diplomacy had been to change the Soviet regime rather than to change the behavior of the Soviet regime. Of course we wanted the Soviet regime to change, to become more democratic and more responsive to the wishes of its people, but President Reagan knew that such changes had to come from within, and that they were unlikely to occur in a Cold War environment of threats and mutual hostility. That is why he gave explicit instructions to American officials not to question the legitimacy of the Soviet government, and also why both he and Secretary Shultz insisted on conducting our most active diplomacy to protect human rights in private, rather than in the public arena. They understood that a foreign leader does not like to be seen changing policies simply because the United States demands it.

A third lesson from the Cold War is the importance of healthy alliances. The U.S. had many disagreements with its allies on secondary issues and did not always get its way, but on the central questions of East-West relations, American policy always made sure that the Allies were on board. The most crucial test in the 1980s occurred when deployment in Europe of Pershing II ballistic missiles and Tomahawk cruise missiles was necessary to fulfill the NATO "dual-track" decision in response to the Soviet deployment of SS-20s. This was achieved despite strong public opposition, particularly in Germany, but the U.S. missiles in Europe gave Gorbachev an incentive to eliminate that class of weaponry. It also demonstrated to the Soviet leadership that they could not successfully drive a wedge between the United States and its European allies. In sum, while at times dealing with the Allies could be frustrating, as when they refused to apply effective economic sanctions on the Soviet Union following the invasion of Afghanistan and the declaration of martial law in Poland, but, by not pushing the Allies too hard on secondary issues, the U.S. succeeded in keeping the alliance solid when it came to those issues of primary concern. Multilateral diplomacy enhanced U.S. power rather than restricting it.

## Chronic Regional Disputes

Are any of these "lessons" relevant to the issues today? So far as the approach to other countries is concerned, they are. (They are much less relevant in dealing with terrorist groups.) First of all, a willingness to engage adversaries is more likely to produce the results we desire than is the use of threats without direct communication. It is possible to change or moderate a regime's behavior by muscular diplomacy, but well nigh impossible to persuade it to commit suicide if the goal is "regime change." And though the United States still possesses the military might sufficient to remove the government of any "rogue regime," the occupation of Iraq has shown that it is more difficult to produce an effective government in a foreign country than it is to conquer it.

### North Korea

Our experience in dealing with North Korea's nuclear aspirations seems to support the supposition that a combination of multilateral diplomacy and muscular direct diplomacy produces better results than isolation and threats, or multinational diplomacy alone. The situation in North Korea is still not acceptable, but the most dangerous period of nuclear development occurred when the United States refused direct talks with the North Korean regime. Creating the "group of six" was a positive step, but proved to be inadequate without the bilateral U.S.-North Korean talks. (The Chinese do not wish to have a nuclear-armed North Korea, but seem to fear the collapse of the North Korean regime more than a North Korea with some nuclear weapons.)

There is a natural aversion to providing any aid or support to a regime as tyrannical and erratic as the North Korean, or to paying a "price" for the correction of bad behavior. Nevertheless, it may be that the wisest policy in regard to North Korea is to provide enough support to reduce the sense of desperation and isolation on the part of Kim Jong-il and his cohorts. In no way does he, or his henchmen, "deserve" sympathy or support. However, our experience with East

Germany may be instructive: When Willy Brandt announced his "Ostpolitik," reversing the "Hallstein doctrine," many were shocked. How
could one deal normally with the Soviet puppets in East Germany as
if they were leaders of a normal state? If you give diplomatic recognition to the Soviet-sponsored occupation regime, you will be
consigning Germany to perpetual division, they argued. But what happened? Most countries recognized the GDR, established embassies in
East Berlin, and did not insist that the Berlin Wall come down or that
it be made easier for East Germans to leave the country. Yet, as it
turned out, legal recognition contained the seeds of destruction of the
GDR regime, not assurance of its perpetuation. More human contacts
were possible as a result of Ostpolitik, and by 1990, when the Soviet
Union was no longer willing to support the GDR regime by force, its
own people swept it out of power.

Kim Jong-il's North Korea is poorer, more tyrannical, more mil-
itarized, and more erratic than the GDR. But the sense of isolation
and of foreign hostility feeds the most dangerous features of its behavior. If these pressures are eased and foreign aid helps avert a fam-
ine and total economic collapse, an orderly change in North Korean
governance could eventually become possible. The United States
would do well to work closely with South Korea, and be willing to
consider withdrawal of U.S. military forces from the Korean Peninsula
in return for a substantial reduction of North Korean deployments.
Ultimately, a peace treaty and full diplomatic relations might be an
appropriate quid pro quo for North Korea's abandonment of its nuclear weapons facilities and ending the export of missile technology.
Diplomatic recognition would no more guarantee the perpetual division of the Korean Peninsula than recognition of the GDR guaranteed
the perpetual division of Germany.

At the moment, the prospects for freezing the North Korean nuclear program look brighter than those for inhibiting the development
of enrichment facilities in Iran. However, if current efforts fail and
the North Koreans resume an active program, testing more weapons,
pressures will rise for Japan and South Korea, and—depending on

China's reaction—Taiwan, to seek nuclear weapons. Nevertheless, at the moment the situation in East Asia seems more stable in this respect than that in the Middle East.

## Iran

If we now look at Iran, we can surmise that it has probably been a mistake to avoid any broad, official dialogue with the Iranian regime. The implicit threat by including Iran in an "axis of evil" (when there was no evidence of an "axis") and postulating "regime change" as a goal, would have increased the determination of the more nationalistic faction in the Iranian government to develop its nuclear capacity. While, according to the most recent intelligence, Iran halted its weapons program in 2003, its insistence on expanding uranium enrichment suggests that it wishes to create conditions in which it could resume weaponization at some time in the future. Given Iranian attitudes, it is not unreasonable to surmise that all factions wish to preserve a future option to "go nuclear." Iran sees itself both as the standard-bearer of Shiism within the Islamic world and as a defender of Islam as regards the world outside. One of its neighbors, Pakistan, is an Islamic state with a Sunni-dominated government and has nuclear weapons. The main perceived "enemy" of Islam in the region is Israel, also a nuclear state. The principal non-Islamic nations whose influence in the region is resented and resisted by the Iranian regime are nuclear states: the United States, the U.K., and Russia. In Iranian eyes, since the other nuclear states seem to have accepted Pakistan's nuclear status (even with its record of proliferation!), what valid motive could they have for denying Iran that capability other than a desire to make it vulnerable to military intervention, as the lack of nuclear weapons made both Serbia and Iraq vulnerable to military attacks even though they had not threatened the attackers? Such would be the rationale of the current Iranian leaders—and the likely rationale of any, more democratic, replacement regime faced with the same geopolitical configuration. One does not have to agree with the rationale (indeed, should not agree with it) to recognize that the perception is a reality that we must deal with if we are to avoid an Iran with nuclear weapons.

Nevertheless, the latest U.S. intelligence determination suggests that the international community has more time to deal with Iranian nuclear aspirations than many believed previously. Furthermore, the change of Iranian negotiators and charges against the Iranian diplomat who previously conducted negotiations on the issue suggests that nuclear policy is a matter of contention within the Iranian leadership. If that is the case, it should present opportunities for well-considered diplomacy, even though the intelligence report may make it more difficult in the immediate future to enlist international support for vigorous economic sanctions. Nevertheless, it should be possible to find ways to slow the expansion of enrichment facilities in Iran and make their activity more transparent by increasing Iranian coperation with IAEA inspectors. It will probably also be necessary for the U.S. to convince the Iranian leaders that they are not current targets for a military attack by the United States or Israel. (The most radical elements—those that support terrorism on religious grounds—would probably welcome a U.S. or Israeli air strike on Iran's nuclear facilities, since this would prove enormously helpful in recruiting terrorists and in securing nuclear technology from other countries—Pakistan, for example—on grounds of Islamic "solidarity.")

Iran's aspirations for its position and influence in the region will also have an influence on the willingness of any Iranian leadership to slow the development of its nuclear capability, or to reduce Iran's support for terrorist organizations such as Hezbollah and Hamas. For this reason, it is important to engage the Iranians, both bilaterally and multilaterally, regarding important regional issues. Not all Iranian interests conflict with those of the United States. The Iranians, for example, do not want Afghanistan to fall back into the Taliban's grip (though, paradoxically, they seem to be providing some weapons now in an obvious attempt to weaken U.S. control); they are enemies of the fanatical Wahhabism that motivates Osama bin Laden and Al Qa'eda; they probably do not want the sectarian conflict in Iraq (some of which they have encouraged) to spread and involve Arab countries such as Syria or Saudi Arabia. Such a conflict could infect the ethnic minorities in Iran itself.

Just as President Reagan was able, gradually, to find common interests with Gorbachev, and then to build on them, the U.S. should not dismiss the possibility *a priori* of finding some sort of *modus vivendi* with Iran. It will certainly not be easy or automatic, but if a concerted effort to engage the Iranians does not result in an indefinite suspension of the Iranian weapons program, that fact alone would help rally international support for vigorous sanctions—the prospect for which has improved with a change in the French position. The U.S. should also not assume that Russia is uncooperative in this respect just because Russia opposes any military action against Iran and has been reluctant to support extensive sanctions. (Essentially, the Russians have been saying what the U.S. intelligence community now reports—that there is no ongoing weaponization program in Iran.) Russia has some leverage over the Iranian program because of its provision of fuel for the Bushehr nuclear power plant. Russia, therefore, has the capacity to exert subtle, indirect pressure that, under some circumstances, may be more effective than formal sanctions. Most governments resist backing down under direct international pressure; yielding to the sort of indirect pressure Russia can exert is much easier since nobody has to admit that they backed down.

## Pakistan-India

So far as Pakistan-Indian relations are concerned, the emergence of both as nuclear powers may have diminished the temptation to direct conflict. In fact, recent efforts to de-fuse the Kashmir stand-off have shown some limited success, even though some flare-ups continue, as when Indian troops fired on demonstrators in August 2008. Therefore, it would seem that neither has an incentive to consider eliminating its nuclear arsenals, particularly since India seems on the verge of obtaining some of the privileges of an NPT-authorized nuclear power. Therefore, while settlement of the long-standing dispute over Kashmir is obviously desirable, an agreement to resolve the dispute is unlikely to diminish the desire of both countries to retain their nuclear arsenals.

The Pakistan "bomb" creates a special and serious potential problem. Whereas the Indian arsenal is presumably well secured, one cannot have the same confidence in the security of the Pakistani weapons if political conditions continue to deteriorate. Concern on this score arises not only because of the record of the Khan network of materiel and technology sales (illegal actions for which he has been pardoned), but also because the Pakistani weapons have been considered by much of the public as "Islamic" weapons, weapons for use in the service of their religion, not just for the preservation of Pakistan as a state. Furthermore, the Pakistani security organs contain elements sympathetic to radical Islam, including the Taliban (virtually created by the Pakistani intelligence service) and, by extension, Al Qa'eda. It is most troublesome that Osama bin Laden and the remnants of Al Qa'eda still apparently enjoy a refuge in the tribal areas of Pakistan. This fact alone would not necessarily give radical Islamists access to nuclear weapons or technology, but the current political turmoil in Pakistan could lead to a sharp deterioration in its government's ability to secure its nuclear assets.

The United States faces a dilemma in its dealings with Pakistan: it needs a strong, authoritative Pakistani government willing to confront the jihadists who are deeply entrenched in Pakistani society and, indeed, in some branches of the government itself. However, President Musharraf's actions in declaring martial law and making massive arrests of jurists and lawyers, as well as the assassination of former Prime Minister Benazir Bhutto, produced a grave political crisis in 2007. Elections in 2008 eased the crisis but produced a parliament dominated by parties in opposition to President Musharraf. The coalition government formed following the election seems fragile and it is not clear that it will be effective in keeping Pakistan's radical Islamists in check.

The U.S. has no practical alternative to working with the new Pakistani government, the Pakistani military, and President Musharraf to encourage effective steps to reduce the threat of Taliban and Al Qa'eda elements in the northern frontier border with Afghanistan. Nevertheless, the ability of the current government and military to deal with that threat is far from certain. Political instability in Pakistan provides another incentive to improve the dialogue with Iran. Admittedly, the idiocies perpetrated by President Ahmadinejad make this difficult indeed, but—as noted—there are common interests with Iran, and if problems should mount in Pakistan, it would be useful if we had a less emotion-charged relationship to Iran, as well as closer relations with India—which seem to be developing satisfactorily.

### Israel/Lebanon/Syria and the Palestinians

There is little this paper can add to the billions of words that have been expressed over the years regarding the Israeli-Palestinian dispute. Even if that dispute could be miraculously settled, it would not necessarily ease the potential of nuclear proliferation in the region, since—as we have seen in the case of Iran and Pakistan—many other factors are important. Nevertheless, since Israel is a nuclear power, a political settlement that resulted in peaceful relations between Israel and its Arab neighbors would diminish the importance of one reason (or pretext) some states in the region might have to acquire nuclear weapons. This argues for an active American diplomacy, and one that avoids automatic support for one side in the dispute. American influence is greatest when it can exercise some leverage over both parties.

The Israeli airstrike in September 2007 on an enrichment facility in Syria under construction with North Korean assistance may have ended, for the moment, early stages of a Syrian nuclear weapons program. However, it would seem that the myriad of tensions in the Middle East are conducive to further proliferation attempts unless rivalries and tensions in the region are tamed. Egypt, Saudi Arabia, and other states in the region have begun thinking of developing nuclear power, which could be a prelude to a weapons program. There needs to be more active diplomacy directed at settling the Golan Heights issue and some understanding regarding Syria's role and interests in

Lebanon. It is probably unrealistic to attempt to exclude Syria from any influence in Lebanon. But it may be possible to find ways to induce Syria to withdraw military support from Hezbollah in an over-all settlement including the Golan Heights, Palestinian refugees, and a sharing of power within Lebanese politics. Without such a settle-ment, it would appear that the Syrian government will have a powerful incentive to try to acquire nuclear weapons, especially if the Iranian program continues apace. If that should happen, the spread of nuclear capability is unlikely to be limited to Iran and Syria alone.

*Other Countries*

At the moment, the spread of nuclear weapons to countries in South-east Asia, Sub-Saharan Africa, and Latin America seems a remote possibility. The danger could arise rapidly, however, in any of these regions if simmering disputes should get out of hand. In most in-stances, however, it would take years to develop an in-country capac-ity. The danger would be greater if a rogue state like North Korea was able to supply the weapons for a price. Sudan and Venezuela, for example, both with oil money, might under certain circumstances seek some nuclear weapons in the belief that their presence would deter foreign (particularly U.S.) military intervention. So far as this writer is aware, however, this possibility is more theoretical than immediate.

**Russia, Its Neighborhood, and Nuclear Weapons**

The breakup of the Soviet Union has produced a new arena for re-gional disputes, this time among those newly independent states or erstwhile members of the Warsaw Pact. These disputes, whether po-tential or actual, have a direct bearing on nuclear proliferation and on the reduction of nuclear weapons since they heavily influence Russia's attitude toward its nuclear arsenal and toward its willingness to co-operate with the United States in matters of nuclear security. With a nuclear arsenal comparable to the American in size, and with abundant fissile material and technical know-how, Russian active cooperation is essential if we are to avoid further proliferation and/or leakage to criminal or terrorist organizations. (The Litvinenko murder in London is a reminder that dangerous nuclear materials can escape from Russian facilities—polonium, after all, can be used to trigger a nuclear device.)

Despite the importance of retaining active Russian cooperation on nuclear issues, American (and sometimes European) policy has, on many issues, undermined the Russian willingness to cooperate by seeming to ignore Russian national interests. In the Russian view (not balanced or necessarily accurate, but sincerely held), the United States set out to weaken Russia despite its liberation from Communism and breakup of the Soviet Union, pushing NATO eastward, even into parts of the former Soviet Union, bombing Serbia without UN Security Council approval, even though Serbia had not committed aggression against any NATO country, abrogating the ABM Treaty even when Russia was willing to amend it to permit development of defenses against ballistic missiles, eliminating on-site inspection from the latest nuclear reduction treaty (and planning to store rather than destroy the weapons subject to reduction). The complaints go on and need not be cataloged here except to observe that an absolute red line in Russian thinking was crossed when it seemed that the United States and other NATO members were scheming to bring Ukraine and Georgia into NATO.

The Russian thinking is one-sided, self-serving, and often places a sinister interpretation on innocent and reasonable acts. However, it is widely held and is not just an artifact of official propaganda, since these sentiments of wounded nationalism arose when the Russian media were free of government control. At the end of 1991, the United States was the most admired country by Russians—more than 80 percent of those polled were admirers. By 1998 and 1999, public opinion regarding the U.S. had changed, with 70 to 80 percent objecting to the U.S. use of force in the Balkans. Following the invasion of Iraq by the U.S.-led coalition, a majority of Russians have considered the United States the most "dangerous" country in the world.

Although recent polemics by President Putin have been sharp, the fact remains that U.S. and Russian security interests do not conflict at the most basic level, and in fact both countries need to cooperate if they are to improve their own security. We are not approaching a new Cold War of the sort we experienced from the late 1940s to the late 1980s, based on fundamental and profound ideological differences. The U.S.-Russian relationship can be turned into a more cooperative one in a relatively short period of time, given the right approach by the United States and the willingness of President Medvedev and Prime Minister Putin to put some of the current disputes behind us now that the Russian electoral process has run its course.

Improved U.S.-Russian relations will require concentration on those issues where our interests coincide and willingness on the part of both American and Russian authorities to place less emphasis on secondary issues that are not of critical importance to either country's security. In particular, the U.S. must stop attempting to pass judgment on Russian internal governance, so long as it does not directly threaten others. If the Russians prefer a more authoritarian government than Americans or Western Europeans would tolerate, that is their business; if it turns out to be a disadvantage—as it eventually will—it is Russians who will suffer and who will have a motive to change the situation.

The second change in U.S. policy should be to remove itself from disputes between Russia and former republics of the Soviet Union other than those now in NATO. It makes no sense to plan bringing Ukraine into NATO, particularly when the majority of Ukrainian citizens do not want to be in NATO. Ukraine's security problem is internal; some 45 percent of the population (in the east and south) want a closer relationship with Russia and around 40 to 45 percent want looser ties to Russia and closer ties to Europe. Outsiders do no one a favor becoming involved in what is essentially an internal Ukrainian issue, particularly since Russian attempts to interfere in the process normally backfire and do Russian interests more harm than good.

Ukraine is big enough and strong enough to defend its sovereignty, and all significant political factions can be expected to do so.

The majority of Georgians doubtless want to be in NATO but it would be a mistake to bring Georgia into the alliance. (I say this with reluctance since I am a great admirer of the Georgian people and of Georgian culture—I am probably the only foreign diplomat not of Georgian descent who has actually delivered speeches in the Georgian language.) The problems Georgia has with South Ossetia and Abkhazia are not unlike the problems Serbia has with Kosovo. Georgian forces attempted to subdue the non-Georgian population by force in 1991 and 1992, and as a result, the local people, with Chechen and some Russian help, expelled the Georgians and with Russian support have managed to stay independent of Georgia.

Obviously, the Russian invasion of Georgia in August 2008 will make it much more difficult to resist Georgia's desire to enter NATO. Emotions on all sides are running high, but it is incumbent on policymakers to retain a clear concept of political and security priorities, particularly in times of crisis.

The fact is that Russia reacted to an attempt by Georgia to take by force the breakaway enclave of South Ossetia. This reckless action by Georgia's government provided the pretext Moscow sought to teach the Georgians and their backers a lesson. The Russian invasion was brutal and disproportionate to Georgia's offense. However, we should resist the tendency evident in much media comment to view Russia's reaction as a "war against democracy," or an undisguised act of imperialism.

In Russian eyes, the Georgians attempted in South Ossetia what Slobodan Milošević attempted in Kosovo in the 1990s. In the latter case, the U.S. led NATO in an attack on Serbia despite Russian objections and the lack of sanction by the United Nations Security Council. Subsequently, the U.S. and some of its NATO allies recognized Kosovo's independence over Russian objections and in violation of provisions of the Helsinki Final Act. At the time, Russia warned that it would consider this as a precedent valid also for the "frozen conflicts" in former Soviet territory.

This does not excuse the Russian invation of Georgia, but it does make clear that Georgia must, at a minimum, refrain from using force to assert control over territories that were autonomous until Georgia unilaterally revoked their autonomy. (This had been Georgia's policy while Eduard Shevardnadze was president.) Most likely, Georgia will eventually have to recognize the independence of South Ossetia and Abkhazia in order to restore normal relations with Russia, just as Serbia is required to reconcile itself to the loss of Kosovo if it is to have cooperative relations with the Ruripean Union.

Russia has a practical interest in finding a way to make a reasonable peace with Georgia. If it attempts to occupy Georgian territory outside Abkhazia and South Ossetia, it risks widespread destabilization of the entire Caucasus region and a heightened risk of terrorism within Russia itself. The United States should use its influence to calm emotions on both sides and avoid being used in a futile Georgian effort to settle scores. America has too many vital interests that require Russian cooperation to involve itself in a messy local conflict, none of the parties to which have justice unequivocally on their side.

The tension between Moldova and the "Dniester Republic" is different in some respects, but also one that is remote from any discernible American security interest. Of course, the United States should continue to support the independence of all the former Soviet republics—something Russia does not challenge—but without giving Russia the impression that it is attempting to bring countries like Ukraine and Georgia into an anti-Russian military alliance. Imagine the American reaction if a European country, even a friendly one, tried to bring Mexico into a military alliance that excluded the United States! It would not consider that a friendly act, or one conducive to strategic cooperation with the perpetrator.

Other issues will of course affect Russia's willingness to return to policies leading to a nuclear-free world. The Russian government has taken strong exception to the plans to deploy missile interceptors in Poland and battle-management radars in the Czech Republic. This issue seems to have been the principal stumbling block to Russian agreement on a joint program to develop and operate missile defenses. It would seem that the necessity and timing of these deployments should be reassessed and measured against the advantages Russia can offer in developing an effective missile defense system to meet potential threats from rogue states. If Gorbachev had been willing to offer President Reagan a joint SDI program at Reykjavík, Reagan might well have accepted. He did offer Gorbachev a treaty guarantee to "share" the defenses if they proved feasible—an offer Gorbachev rejected out of hand.[3]

The Russians have important assets, both technical and geographic, and former President Putin offered the use of Russian radars in a defensive system provided the U.S. dropped plans for the installation in Poland and the Czech Republic. A joint U.S.-Russian missile defense program could defuse the political suspicions that unilateral deployments engender. They could also contribute positively to the program. We should not forget that U.S.-Soviet cooperation in manning the international space station saved the program when, after the most recent shuttle disaster, the station had to be supplied by Russian launchers. It is likely that the bureaucracies in both countries will oppose a genuinely cooperative program, so it will take strong leadership by both presidents to make it happen.

There are other aspects of U.S. and Russian nuclear policy that need careful attention and review. Some of the important arms reduction treaties will be ending soon; both governments should act promptly to insure that there is continued cooperation in the nuclear area. No other area of the relationship is as important, and other issues

---

3. Most specialists in the American bureaucracy were adamantly opposed to this offer, but Reagan was genuine in making in. In one letter to Gorbachev which I drafted for Reagan, I attempted to make a weasel-worded offer (something like "consider sharing the benefits . . .") approved by the interagency group. Reagan sent the draft back twice with the notation: "No—tell him I want to share." The third time his note read, "Damn it, Jack, it's my letter and this is what I'm going to say," followed by the sentence that offered a treaty commitment to share defenses.

should not be allowed to diminish cooperation to create a world free of the nuclear threat.

## What America Can Do to Help

It is important to the entire world for the United States to retain a strong military capacity, a healthy, productive economy, and a political system that commands widespread support. Over the long term, the United States can sustain this position only if it is willing act in concert with other powers, respects legitimate national interests of others, and seeks political solutions to disputes that arise. If we are to avoid further nuclear proliferation and the probability that terrorist groups will some day have the ability to detonate a nuclear device on U.S. territory, we must act in a comprehensive manner to *devalue* nuclear weapons as a source of political power, reduce drastically the number in existence, and create reliable control over those that remain. This will take years, probably decades, but so long as governments perceive that nuclear weapons will add to their power and prestige, or perhaps prevent a military attack on them, there will be regimes that attempt, covertly or openly, to acquire this capability.

A full discussion of the steps necessary to "devalue" nuclear weapons as a source of political influence or military deterrence is beyond the scope of this paper; they are mentioned only because they must provide a background to any successful effort to reduce the nuclear danger arising out of regional conflicts. One place to start would be to amend current strategic and nuclear doctrine to make it clear that the U.S. nuclear arsenal is intended solely for deterrence, not for the projection of force. Given the fact that U.S. "conventional" (that is, non-nuclear) forces are the most powerful in the world, it would be impossible to defend, on moral grounds, the use of nuclear weapons except for deterrence or retaliation. Their use by the United States for any other purpose would practically guarantee that someone, somewhere, would find a way to use such weapons against us.

Ever since the ill-fated Kellogg-Briand Pact, foreign policy specialists have been dubious about the value of sweeping, declaratory policies. But, when such statements represent an actual policy, they can in fact be useful under certain circumstances. A good example is the agreement Reagan and Gorbachev made in their first meeting (Geneva, 1985) that "a nuclear war cannot be won and must never be fought." Reagan had used this statement in several speeches, yet the Soviet leaders still suspected that the U.S. was possibly planning a disarming first strike. Subsequently, Soviet negotiators have stated in their memoirs that they considered Reagan's agreement to the statement an important achievement of the Geneva summit. U.S. negotiators also thought it important that Soviet negotiators would agree to a statement to that effect without mention of the ideologically loaded term "peaceful coexistence." The joint statement, therefore, provided a useful prelude to the arms reduction agreements reached subsequently. A restatement of this thought belongs in every American expression of strategic or nuclear doctrine, particularly since there is once again speculation that the United States may be "on the verge of attaining nuclear primacy" over Russia and China, combined with the capability of a disarming first strike.[4]

There is a need to reconsider the traditional American skepticism of nuclear-free zones. Although it may not be appropriate for the United States to propose nuclear-free zones for others, the U.S. should support regional efforts to create them where possible. The Treaty of Tlatelolco seems to have worked in Latin America. Nuclear-free zones in Sub-Saharan Africa and Southeast Asia might inhibit proliferation in those areas in the event current conditions change. And how about a nuclear-limited zone in Northeast Asia, with China making a commitment not to expand its nuclear weapons capability in return for zero nuclear weapons in the Koreas and Japan and a Russian commitment not to base its weapons in its territories adjacent to China, Korea, and the Bering Sea?

4. See Keir A. Lieber and Daryl G. Press, "The End of MAD? The Nuclear Dimension of U.S. Primacy," *International Security*, Spring 2006, pp. 7–44. While I find this analysis unconvincing, the arguments are those that would be used in Russia, and perhaps China, to block further cooperation with the United States to reduce the numbers of nuclear weapons.

The United States is more likely to be useful in solving regional disputes if it avoids total identification with one of the parties to a dispute. It is better to position ourselves to help in mediation by having some leverage over each of the parties. It is also not in the U.S. interest to try to do all of the "heavy lifting." We should share responsibility for keeping necessary change peaceful (more important than absolute stability, since that is impossible in an ever-changing world) with other powers in the area. As power shifts, so must responsibility, and the U.S. must be flexible in encouraging China, Japan, and India to shoulder an appropriate burden of peacekeeping in their region.

The U.S. policy of encouraging democratization has been widely misunderstood; it is probably an inappropriate slogan since each country must find its own way to create the institutions that make democracy work. A partial or (in Fareed Zakaria's words) "illiberal democracy" can be worse than the authoritarian system it replaces; as the ancient Greeks and our own founding fathers well understood, majority rule without restraining institutions can easily lead to mob rule and tyranny. The U.S. should do what it can to encourage "good government"—honest government that respects human rights and encourages economic growth—but must avoid acting as if it is the world's nanny. It can best encourage democratic government by showing how it works at home to the benefit of all Americans.

*Booneville, Tennesee*
*August 14, 2008*

# 13. Part One: A World Free of Nuclear Weapons

*Opening Remarks for*
*Reykjavik Revisited II Conference*
*October 24, 2007*

**Max M. Kampelman**

I want to thank George Shultz, Sidney Drell, and their colleagues at the Hoover Institution for elevating the deep concern about nuclear weapons into a broad national effort to revive President Reagan's serious goal of complete elimination of these weapons.

Indeed, we should keep in mind President Reagan's statement— "for the eight years I was President, I never let my dream of a nuclear free world fade from my mind"—as well as President Kennedy's remark to the nation—"the world was not meant to be a prison in which man awaits his execution."

It is encouraging to note that former Senator Sam Nunn, one of our country's most respected and experienced national defense experts and leaders, has joined his highly respected organization with this effort to restore sanity to the international community.

We obviously have challenges ahead. The drive for sanity must be an international one if it is to be effective.

I recently returned from a week in London during which I met and talked with leaders in and out of government—members of parliament and leaders of the major political parties. Sam Nunn and I both met in Washington with the then-Foreign Secretary Margaret Beckett shortly after she strongly identified herself and the government of the United Kingdom with our goal. She made clear she reviewed every word in her speech in Washington with her prime minister, and that she had been reflecting the policy of her government.

I have spent a great deal of time talking to a number of our friends in the Bush administration on this subject over the past year. And while I am not giving up hope, I think the realities of the political calendar mean that this issue will reluctantly be left for our next president.

I am encouraged that there are candidates on both sides of the political aisle who have spoken favorably of our efforts. The crucial question for our group is, What can we do to help the next president, whoever that may be, move forward with bipartisan support in our own country?

What is obviously required is leadership by the U.S. toward that goal of zero. And while U.S. leadership is a prerequisite for success, it is also true that to be successful, our leadership must be shared with, and joined by, others, including Russia.

Certainly, understanding the many technical issues associated with this task—in particular, verification—will be important. And I'm pleased to see that verification is a prominent issue for us to discuss.

But as we dive in to the many details of "getting to zero," we must keep in mind the "power of the ought"—that is, the importance of the "vision" of a world with zero nuclear weapons—in mobilizing political support in our own country, and around the world, for this effort. And we should keep in mind that over the past six decades, we have not acted—a reality that we may soon regret.

My personal fear is for the safety of my children and grandchildren. We now know that terrorists are seeking to acquire nuclear bombs and are en route to do so. There is no doubt that we are vulnerable to attack.

We know that there are countries that continue to challenge the notion that we, not they, are entitled to nuclear weapons. And we know that there are today more than 27,000 nuclear weapons in existence and that 40 countries may at some point be capable of developing nuclear bombs.

Eight years ago, Paul Nitze published an article in the *New York Times*. His dramatic suggestion was simple: "I see no compelling reason why we should not . . . get rid of our nuclear weapons. To maintain them is costly and adds nothing to our security." His recommendation to us was clear: "I know that the simplest and most direct answer to the problem of nuclear weapons has always been their complete elimination."

Paul Nitze always understood what direction we as a nation "ought" to be heading. Of course, there are still those who point to the "practical problems" as a reason for not embracing the "ought." But our own history is filled with examples of the power of the "ought."

Indeed, we in the U.S. understood the power of the "ought" at a time when our very existence as a nation was at stake. Our founders established the Declaration of Independence and our Constitution as clear goals for our nation—goals we have continually been working to achieve. And they established these "oughts" of independence, freedom, and liberty in an atmosphere of slavery, second-class citizenship for women, and property qualifications for voting.

Nevertheless, our nation has clearly and steadily overcome the original "is" of American society to achieve the "ought." The pursuit of the "ought" has made our American democracy the country it is whose principles of human dignity have earned respect by peoples all over the world. The power of the "ought" is great, warrants respect, and should not be minimized. Today, a central theme of American foreign policy must be to move the "is" of our present global nuclear peril to a more hopeful "ought" of stability and peace. We must not minimize the pursuit of the "ought." Our role must be to establish a civilized "ought" for the human race. The abolition of weapons of mass destruction now must be central to that objective.

Consistent with this development, I have respectfully urged that the president of the United States speak to the people of the world through the General Assembly of the United Nations and propose the elimination of all weapons of mass destruction, and that the Security Council work with other states to achieve this end.

The details of how we might work with leaders of other nations to make the pursuit of a world free of nuclear weapons a truly "joint enterprise" is an issue that is on our agenda for tomorrow—and we will get into more detail then. But the elimination of nuclear weapons must be our and the world's indispensable rational objective—the "ought" for the human race.

It was our President Truman who, at the creation of the United Nations, saw there is nothing more urgent confronting the people of all nations than the banning of all nuclear weapons under a foolproof system of international control. This message of leadership is particularly fitting for today.

So with Presidents Truman and Reagan as our inspiration, let us go forward the next two days in the hope that our next president will embrace the power of the "ought," and we can move forward and achieve our goal of a world free of nuclear weapons.

Thank you.

# 13. Part Two: Turning the Goal of a World without Nuclear Weapons into a Joint Enterprise
## Max M. Kampelman
## Steven P. Andreasen

### Key Judgments

- This paper focuses on two related questions pertaining to the issue of how best to work with leaders of the countries in possession of nuclear weapons to turn the goal of a world without nuclear weapons into a joint enterprise:
  - What would be the "mechanism" for getting all of the nuclear states together to agree on a program of action such as the steps listed in the *Wall Street Journal* Op-Ed article?
  - Would a new mechanism—either formal or informal—be required, or would this best be done through an existing mechanism, such as the United Nations, perhaps working with other key states?
- The review identified four central issues for analysis:
  - *Issue 1:* How can the United States government initiate the process of working with leaders of other nuclear weapon states to turn the goal of a world without nuclear weapons into a joint enterprise?
  - *Issue 2:* To what extent does this process need to be procedurally and substantively "inclusive" (i.e., involve all nuclear weapons states) from the start?

- *Issue 3:* Should the process be centered within existing structures and mechanisms or on a more *ad hoc* basis?
- *Issue 4:* How much "weight" should be given to the steps at the outset of this process?
- The review identified three options for consideration:
  - *Option 1:* A UN-centered process, whereby the UN General Assembly would first pass a resolution calling for the elimination of all weapons of mass destruction, followed by a process anchored in the Security Council.
  - *Option 2:* An *ad hoc* process with no UN involvement, whereby the U.S. would work initially with Russia (and the U.K.) on steps pertaining to U.S. and Russian nuclear forces, followed later by an *ad hoc* process involving only those states and organizations necessary for achieving further progress on specific steps.
  - *Option 3:* A "hybrid" process, which like Option 2 would focus first on bilateral steps pertaining to U.S. and Russian nuclear forces, but would then seek at an early stage to involve the UN as well as *ad hoc* assemblies, as appropriate.
- Each of the three options were evaluated against four criteria:
  - *Criterion 1:* Will the approach allow the U.S. to effectively promote and protect U.S. interests?
  - *Criterion 2:* Will the approach create early momentum behind both the vision and the steps?
  - *Criterion 3:* Will the approach be inclusive enough to prevent an "outsider dynamic" where states that are not equally involved at the outset refuse to take part at a later date?
  - *Criterion 4:* Will the approach be both flexible and sustainable over time?

*Recommendation.* The review concludes that a hybrid process—one that allows for both substantial latitude at the outset for the U.S. and Russia to lead and early involvement of other key states, including through the UN and *ad hoc* assemblies—appears most promising. Most important, a hybrid process would be most likely to generate early momentum behind the vision and steps while gaining international legitimacy and support for efforts requiring the involvement of other key states. This process will necessarily be informed by early discussions between the U.S. and Russia, . . . as well as discussions with the U.K., France, China, India, Pakistan, and Israel. This could then lead to action in the Security Council and the General Assembly. To prevent the alienation of key states at the outset of the process, care should be taken not to corner nations that may lack enthusiasm for the vision or be averse to certain steps, as their positive involvement will be required at some future date. The process will also require the direct and sustained involvement of the president and other leaders of key states; and there will need to be a calculated and sustained effort by leaders to enlist support of both domestic and international publics.

**Background**

*Wall Street Journal* Commentary

In January 2007, the *Wall Street Journal* published an op-ed titled, "A World Free of Nuclear Weapons." The essay—signed by former Secretaries of State George Shultz and Henry Kissinger, former Secretary of Defense William Perry, former Sen. Sam Nunn, and 17 others—states that we are on the precipice of a new and dangerous nuclear era, with more nuclear-armed states and a real risk of nuclear terrorism. In such a world, the authors warn that continued reliance on nuclear deterrence for maintaining international security "is becoming increasingly hazardous and decreasingly effective," and that none of the nonproliferation steps being taken now "are adequate to the danger."

A central theme of the *Wall Street Journal* commentary is that in order to deal effectively with the security challenges presented in this new era, the United States and other nations must embrace the vision of a world free of nuclear weapons and pursue a balanced program of practical measures toward achieving that goal: "Without the bold vision, the actions will not be perceived as fair or urgent. Without the actions, the vision will not be perceived as realistic or possible."

*The first "action" highlighted by the authors is the need to "work with leaders of the countries in possession of nuclear weapons to turn the goal of a world without nuclear weapons into a joint enterprise." In this context:*

- *What would be the "mechanism" for getting all of the nuclear states together to agree on a program of action such as the steps listed in the* Wall Street Journal *op-ed article?*
- *Would a new mechanism—either formal or informal—be required, or would this best be done through an existing mechanism, such as the United Nations, perhaps working with other key states?*

### Existing structures and mechanisms

*Nuclear Nonproliferation Treaty.* Elements of the existing international "order" for dealing with nuclear threats are centered in the 1970 Nuclear Nonproliferation Treaty (NPT). In Article VI of that Treaty, the parties undertake "to pursue negotiations in good faith on effective measures relating to cessation of the nuclear arms race at an early date and to nuclear disarmament, and on a Treaty on general and complete disarmament under strict and effective international control." The NPT also includes a commitment by all non-nuclear weapon states not to manufacture or acquire nuclear weapons, and the right of all signatories to nuclear energy for peaceful purposes. While Israel, India, and Pakistan have yet to sign, it is truly a global accord, with 188 signatories.

Every five years, a conference of states party to the NPT is held in order to review the operation of the Treaty to assure that its purpose and provisions are being realized. The next such conference will take place in 2010. The most recent NPT review conference in 2005 accomplished little other than to highlight tensions between the non-nuclear weapon states—which believe the existing nuclear weapon states have failed to fulfill their Article VI obligation to nuclear disarmament—and efforts on the part of the United States and other nations to deal with countries like Iran which are using the Treaty's nuclear energy provisions to develop a nuclear arms capability.

*Conference on Disarmament.* In 1979, the UN established the Conference on Disarmament (CD) as "the single multilateral disarmament negotiating forum of the international community." The CD was a result of the first Special Session on Disarmament of the UN General Assembly held in 1978. It succeeded other Geneva-based negotiating fora, which included the Ten-Nation Committee on Disarmament (1960), the Eighteen-Nation Committee on Disarmament (1962–68), and the Conference of the Committee on Disarmament (1969–78).

The terms of reference of the CD include practically all multilateral arms control and disarmament problems—including nuclear disarmament. The CD has a special relationship with the UN: it adopts its own Rules of Procedure and its own agenda, taking into account the recommendations of the General Assembly and the proposals of its members. It reports to the General Assembly annually, or more frequently, as appropriate. The Conference meets in Geneva and conducts its work by consensus. The CD and its predecessors have negotiated such major multilateral arms limitation and disarmament agreements as the NPT, the Biological Weapons Convention (BWC), the Chemical Weapons Convention (CWC), and the Comprehensive Nuclear-Test-Ban Treaty (CTBT). Currently, the CD is charged with the negotiation of the Fissile Material Cutoff Treaty (FMCT).

*Recent Developments*

*U.K. policy.* In a speech delivered in Washington in June, the United Kingdom's outgoing foreign secretary, Margaret Beckett, outlined a path forward for dealing with nuclear threats that explicitly drew on the views of the *Wall Street Journal* commentary. Beckett (who cleared her talk with the new British Prime Minister Gordon Brown) said that while the conditions for the total elimination of nuclear arms do not exist today, that does not mean we should resign ourselves to the idea that nuclear weapons can never be abolished in the future. "What we need is both a vision—a scenario for a world free of nuclear weapons—and action—progressive steps to reduce warhead numbers and to limit the role of nuclear weapons in security policy. These two strands are separate but they are mutually reinforcing. Both are necessary, but at the moment too weak."

Beckett stated that the U.K. would be a "disarmament laboratory," and would participate in an in-depth study by the International Institute for Strategic Studies on the requirements for the eventual elimination of all nuclear weapons, as well as concentrate on creating a robust, trusted, and effective system of verification that does not give away national security or proliferation-sensitive information.

On July 12 in London, Beckett (no longer Foreign Secretary) underscored to Ambassador Max Kampelman that the position outlined in her June speech was entirely reflective of the position of the whole government today, and that she was keen to use her influence with parliamentary colleagues to promote multilateral initiatives in this area. In other meetings between Ambassador Kampelman and key opinion leaders in London, there was general agreement that a nuclear weapon-free world would be desirable, if it were possible and institutions sufficiently robust to prevent breakout.

*U.S.-Russia joint statement.* On the day after the July 2007 Bush-Putin Kennebunkport meeting, Secretary Rice and Foreign Minister Lavrov issued a Joint Statement regarding strategic offensive reductions. The statement underscored that both sides are fully committed to the goals of the NPT and Article VI, and that discussions are still underway with respect to the development of a post-START arrangement.

## Issues

*Issue 1: How can the United States initiate the process of working with leaders of other nuclear weapon states to turn the goal of a world without nuclear weapons into a joint enterprise?*

*Issue 1: Discussion*

As stated in the *Wall Street Journal* Op-Ed, "U.S. leadership will be required to take the world to the next stage—to a solid consensus for reversing reliance on nuclear weapons globally as a vital contribution to preventing their proliferation into potentially dangerous hands, and ultimately ending them as a threat to the world."

Progress toward the goal of a world without nuclear weapons is not possible without early and sustained leadership by the United States—the world's leading nuclear weapon state. In the absence of U.S. leadership, there is no nation or combination of nations that can fill the leadership void and make tangible progress toward the goal.

That said, it is also true that progress will ultimately require the cooperation of every nation with nuclear weapons and every state with the capability to produce fissile material. In some instances, a heavy U.S. hand on the tiller may undercut such cooperation. This is particularly true at the beginning of the process—recognizing there are many nations looking to the U.S. to provide leadership on this issue.

There may be much to be gained—in terms of mobilizing public support both at home and abroad—from an early display of presidential leadership, for example, a speech delivered to the United Nations and / or the American people. Such a call to action by the president may be both unavoidable and indispensable; however, in order to have the maximum positive impact on establishing a "joint enterprise" among leaders, and avoid the perception of a U.S. dictate, public action by the president should be carefully preceded with consultations with key states.

At a minimum, prior consultations with our closest nuclear ally—

**Table A: Global Nuclear Inventories**

| Country | Nuclear Warheads |
| --- | --- |
| U.S. | 10,000 |
| Russia | 10,000 |
| U.K. | 200 |
| France | 350 |
| China | 200 |
| India | 40–50 |
| Pakistan | <50 |
| Israel | 75–200 |
| North Korea | <15 |

SOURCE: International Panel on Fissile Materials.

the U.K.—as well as our key nuclear interlocutor—Russia—will be required. Other nuclear-capable states—e.g., France, China, Israel, India, and Pakistan—as well as Japan and Germany (both of whom have significant stockpiles of civilian plutonium) might also be approached prior to, or soon after, a major U.S. initiative.

*Issue 2: To what extent does this process need to be procedurally and substantively "inclusive" (i.e., involve all nuclear weapons states) from the start?*

*Issue 2: Discussion*

The United States and Russia today possess nuclear stockpiles that dwarf those of all other nations, each having approximately 10,000 nuclear warheads in its inventory. Non-governmental analysts have estimated that by 2012, about 6,000 warheads will remain in the U.S. stockpile, including non-strategic and reserve warheads. The number of nuclear warheads in the Russian arsenal could also decrease by 2012 to 6,000 or fewer. The remaining nuclear weapon states today are estimated to possess a combined total on the order of 1,000 warheads (see Table A).

In this context, the U.S. and Russia could proceed bilaterally with significant reductions in their nuclear force levels before approaching the combined total of other states. That said, defining a global regime for reductions "in nuclear forces in all states that possess them"—as stated in the *Wall Street Journal* Op-Ed—as well as a world without nuclear weapons will by definition involve all nuclear weapon states, as well as those states with the ability to produce nuclear material for weapons.

Moreover, beyond the issue of reductions in nuclear forces per se, many of the "urgent steps" envisioned by the *Wall Street Journal* Op-Ed (i.e., securing entry into force of the CTBT; providing security for all stocks of weapons and materials; getting control of the uranium enrichment process; halting the production of fissile material for weapons globally; and effective measures to impede or counter any nuclear-related conduct that is potentially threatening to the security of any state or peoples) would need to involve states other than the United States and Russia in order to be effective.

Simply stated, a process that is U.S.-Russia centric at the outset might facilitate rapid progress on bilateral reductions; however, not involving other key states might hinder progress on other urgent steps as well as undermine the potential for devising a truly global prohibition on nuclear arms. Alternatively, a process that envisions the early involvement of other key states—procedurally and / or substantively—risks bogging down, undermining both the vision and steps.

*Issue 3: Should the process be centered within existing structures and mechanisms or on a more* ad hoc *basis?*

*Issue 3: Discussion*

There are existing structures and mechanisms relevant to the vision and steps. The NPT and its Article VI provides an essential foundation for the goal of a world without nuclear weapons, albeit one that does not include Israel, India, and Pakistan. That said, while the NPT's five-year review conference has at times been used to advance the vision and steps (for example, the 1995 decision to extend the NPT indefinitely), it is not a "day-to-day" mechanism suitable for centering an ongoing process.

The terms of reference for the CD—as well as its schedule of meetings (three regular sessions per year)—has made it at times a useful mechanism for achieving progress on specific steps; however, the CD's membership (65 states) and consensus rule would make it an unwieldy structure for centering this process (though it can still serve as a vehicle for accomplishing specific steps).

The UN General Assembly and the Security Council have both been engaged on nuclear issues for decades—and indeed, the Security Council is today focused on the issues surrounding Iran's nuclear program. Given the Security Council's role in international peace and security—and the fact that the five permanent members correspond with the five NPT nuclear weapon states—involvement of the Council in some fashion may be both desirable and unavoidable.

That said, the Security Council's membership does not on a routine basis include the other nuclear weapon states (Israel, India, Pakistan, North Korea), or all states that can produce fissile material. Moreover, as has been the case with Iran, the ability of any one of the P-5 to block action through the veto could be a significant procedural drag. Finally, there may be a significant constituency within the U.S. that sees any process centered in the UN as suspect.

An *ad hoc* structure might provide greater flexibility in involving key states—and come without any institutional baggage associated with existing structures and mechanisms. Initiating and sustaining an *ad hoc* process, however, could prove as complex and frustrating as centering the process within existing frameworks.

*Issue 4: How much "weight" should be given to the steps at the outset of this process?*

*Issue 4: Discussion*

The *Wall Street Journal* Op-Ed states: "Without the bold vision, the actions will not be perceived as fair or urgent. Without the actions, the vision will not be perceived as realistic or possible." This "balance" between vision and steps is underscored throughout the Op-Ed; however, consideration must be given to how much "weight" can and should be given to the steps in the context of "working with leaders of countries in possession of nuclear weapons to turn the goal of a world without nuclear weapons into a joint enterprise."

Conceptually, obtaining agreement among leaders to affirm their support for the "goal" should be straightforward—at least with respect to the five NPT nuclear weapon states, which are all committed to nuclear disarmament through the NPT's Article VI. That said, there is reason to believe that both France and Russia may be less than enthusiastic about participating in a high-profile, explicit reaffirmation of the goal, let alone a "joint enterprise" designed to achieve it. Other nuclear weapon states outside the NPT—Israel, India, Pakistan, and North Korea—may also hesitate to publicly "embrace" the goal, in particular, if they believe it will lead to early pressure on their own nuclear weapons programs.

In this context, an understanding amongst the nuclear weapon states as to what near-term "steps" might be the expected focus of the "joint enterprise"—and how those steps will impact them—might provide reassurance necessary to gain support for the goal and agreement on a process. Alternatively, the highlighting of certain steps (for example, CTBT entry into force with India) might undercut the effort.

**Options**

*Evaluative Criteria.* Each of the three options discussed below will be evaluated against the following four criteria:

- *Criterion 1:* Will the approach allow the U.S. to effectively promote and protect U.S. interests?

- *Criterion 2:* Will the approach create early momentum behind both the vision and the steps?
- *Criterion 3:* Will the approach be inclusive enough to prevent an "outsider dynamic" where states that are not equally involved at the outset refuse to take part at a later date?
- *Criterion 4:* Will the approach be both flexible and sustainable over time?

*Option 1: A UN-Centered Process*

Under this approach:

- The UN General Assembly would first pass a resolution calling for the elimination of all weapons of mass destruction—nuclear, chemical and biological weapons (see Table B).
- The UN General Assembly Resolution would also request the UN Security Council—working with other key states, in particular, other nuclear capable states such as Israel, India, and Pakistan, as well as states with the ability to produce enriched uranium and plutonium for nuclear arms—to develop effective political and technical means to achieve this goal, including stringent verification and severe penalties to prevent cheating.
- The Security Council might at an early date call a "Key States" Conference under its auspices. The objective of the conference would be to build support for the vision and identify a program of specific steps that would lay the groundwork for a world free of the nuclear threat.

*Option 1: Analysis*

- *Criterion 1: Will the approach allow the U.S. to effectively promote and protect U.S. interests?*
  - By centering the process for action in the Security Council, the United States would ensure the process took place in a

**Table B: Resolution**

*Towards a World Without Nuclear, Biological or Chemical Weapons, Draft Resolution, July 26, 2007.*

"The General Assembly,

**Expressing** its deep concern over the devastation that would ensue from even the single use of a nuclear weapon and the necessity to make every effort to prevent the proliferation of nuclear weapons and avert the danger of nuclear war,

**Underlining** the importance of the Nuclear Non-Proliferation Treaty, Biological Weapons Convention, and Chemical Weapons Convention and the need to undertake effective measures to implement, enforce, and strengthen these agreements,

**Recognizing** that the necessity now exists for all nations to conduct their affairs without nuclear, biological, or chemical weapons in accordance with the principles of the Charter of the United Nations,

**Applauding** the determination of all nations to pledge the elimination of all nuclear weapons and to place the relevant weapons-grade material under International Atomic Energy Agency safeguards until the nuclear material can be made unusable for nuclear weapons,

**Recognizing** that this commitment by all nations is reliant upon the United Nations Security Council establishing the necessary political and technical means for ensuring that all nations that have or may be developing nuclear weapons agree to implement their elimination,

1. *Calls* upon all states in possession of nuclear, biological, or chemical weapons to commit themselves unequivocally to the elimination of these weapons,

2. *Calls* upon the United Nations Security Council—working with other key states—to develop the necessary political and technical means for ensuring the elimination of nuclear, biological, and chemical weapons globally,

3. *Calls* upon the United Nations Security Council, acting under Chapter VII of the Charter of the United Nations, to ensure that any state that is: (a) not in full compliance with the Biological and Chemical Weapons Conventions, or (b) developing or that possesses weapons-grade nuclear material that has not promptly declared the material to the United Nations Security Council and placed the material in the process of elimination under International Atomic Energy Agency safeguards, shall be considered by all member states an international criminal state disqualified to engage in any relationship—security, commercial, economic, or cultural—with any member state.

forum where the U.S. has, by virtue of its veto, the power to protect U.S. interests.

- The fact that Russia, China, France, and the U.K. also possess a veto could at times complicate efforts to promote U.S. interests.

- *Criterion 2: Will the approach create early momentum behind both the vision and the steps?*
  - Adoption of a UN General Assembly resolution that embraces the "vision" and centers the process for developing concrete steps within the Security Council would be an early reaffirmation of support from the international community. A stamp of legitimacy by all nations would be firmly imprinted on the process, and the "vision" would be established as a goal in the minds of peoples of the world.
  - Failure to achieve a UN General Assembly resolution—or a Resolution that was passed without the support of key states, in particular, nuclear weapon states—might also be perceived as an early setback.
  - Once the Security Council takes up the issue, tangible progress requiring the consent of all five nuclear weapon states will be slow; moreover, efforts to involve other key states (e.g., Israel, India, and Pakistan) at an early phase may also slow progress.

- *Criterion 3: Will the approach be inclusive enough to prevent an "outsider dynamic" where states that are not equally involved at the outset refuse to take part at a later date?*
  - The combination of a UN General Assembly resolution involving all nations and a Security Council process that would include other key states from the outset has the potential to promote a great degree of "inclusiveness."
  - However, if key states oppose the Resolution or refuse to participate in a process centered in the Security Council, they will be publicly branded as "outsiders" from the outset—and

they may find it difficult to publicly change that posture at a later date.

- *Criterion 4: Will the approach be both flexible and sustainable over time?*
  - A process centered in the UN may lack flexibility and inhibit progress; lack of progress may make the approach unsustainable.

*Option 2: An* Ad Hoc *Process*

Under this approach:

- The U.S. would work first with both Russia (the other major nuclear weapon state) and the United Kingdom (whose government has embraced the framework of the *Wall Street Journal* Op-Ed) in devising a strategy for advancing both the vision and specific steps.
- Initially, the focus would be on bilateral action on steps pertaining to U.S. and Russian nuclear forces.
- The process for achieving further progress involving other nuclear states would not be centered in—or seek to involve either procedurally or substantively—the UN.
- Rather, the process would be *ad hoc*, involving only those countries—and only those organizations—necessary for achieving specific steps.

*Option 2: Analysis*

- *Criterion 1: Will the approach allow the U.S. to effectively promote and protect U.S. interests?*
  - Working initially within a framework that focuses first on bilateral steps between the U.S. and Russia is a process the U.S. has used successfully for decades to promote and protect U.S. interests.
  - Later, an *ad hoc* process that involves only those states / or-

ganizations necessary for achieving specific steps should minimize the risk that the process is used to frustrate U.S. interests.

- *Criterion 2: Will the approach create early momentum behind both the vision and the steps?*
  - This approach would give the U.S. and Russia a great deal of latitude to take early steps relating to their nuclear forces; in this way, it could best facilitate early momentum behind the vision and steps.
- *Criterion 3: Will the approach be inclusive enough to prevent an "outsider dynamic" where states that are not equally involved at the outset refuse to take part at a later date?*
  - While there are a number of steps that could be taken by the U.S. and Russia working bilaterally, a process that did not involve other key states—in particular, nuclear weapon states—at the outset may provide a rationale for those states not to participate. This could ultimately undercut achieving progress on further steps towards a world free of nuclear weapons.
- *Criterion 4: Will the approach be both flexible and sustainable over time?*
  - This approach provides maximum flexibility—both at the outset, and later into the process.
  - The key to its sustainability will be how successfully other key states can be brought in via ad-hoc arrangements; if for whatever reason that proves not to be possible, an ad-hoc approach may not be sustainable.

*Option 3: A Hybrid Process*

Under this approach:

- Like Option 2, the U.S. would work first with both Russia and the

U.K.; the initial focus would be on bilateral action on steps pertaining to U.S. and Russian nuclear forces.

- At an early stage, the U.S.—in coordination with the P-5 and other
key states—would encourage a resolution in the UN General Assembly that embraced the vision of and practical steps towards a
world free of nuclear weapons.

- The process for achieving further progress could include the Security Council, where appropriate, as well as *ad hoc* assemblies.

*Option 3: Analysis*

- *Criterion 1: Will the approach allow the U.S. to effectively promote and protect U.S. interests?*
  - Like Option 2, working initially within a framework that focuses first on bilateral steps between the U.S. and Russia is a
process the U.S. has used successfully for decades to promote
and protect U.S. interests.
  - Later, a process that involves an early UN General Assembly
resolution, the Security Council, and *ad hoc* assemblies should
prove manageable—with an emphasis on close coordination
with the P-5 and other key states.

- *Criterion 2: Will the approach create early momentum behind
both the vision and the steps?*
  - Like Option 2, this approach would give the U.S. and Russia
a great deal of latitude to take early steps relating to their
nuclear forces; in this way, it would facilitate early momentum
behind the vision and steps.
  - Later, like Option 1, the early adoption of a UN General Assembly resolution embracing the "vision" would reaffirm support from the international community, provide a stamp of
international legitimacy, and firmly enshrine the "vision" as a
goal in the minds of peoples of the world.

- *Criterion 3: Will the approach be inclusive enough to prevent an "outsider dynamic" where states that are not equally involved at the outset refuse to take part at a later date?*

- This approach—by virtue of an early UN General Assembly resolution and later involvement of both the Security Council and *ad hoc* assemblies, as appropriate—is designed to be more "inclusive" than Option 2.
- Like Option 1, however, if key states oppose the UN General Assembly resolution or refuse to participate in a future process (Security Council or *ad hoc*), they will be cast as "outsiders" and may find it difficult to publicly change that posture at a later date.

- *Criterion 4: Will the approach be both flexible and sustainable over time?*
  - Like Option 2, this approach provides a great deal of flexibility—both at the outset and later in the process.
  - The key to its sustainability will be how successfully other key states can be brought in to the process at a later date—either through the Security Council or via ad-hoc arrangements.

## Recommendations

- More likely than not, the earliest the U.S. government will be in position to start the process of working with leaders of nuclear weapons states to turn the goal of a world without nuclear weapons into a joint enterprise will be in the first half of 2009—at least 15 months from the date of the Reykjavik II conference.
- Given the number of domestic and international variables that might be in play in the first half of 2009, a determination as to the most effective "mechanism" for the U.S. to pursue with other nuclear states to advance the vision and steps identified in the *Wall Street Journal* Op-Ed will need to be made then.
- That said, a "hybrid process"—one that allows for both substantial latitude at the outset for the U.S. and Russia to lead and early involvement of other key states, including through the UN and *ad*

*hoc* assemblies—appears most promising. Most important, a hybrid process would be most likely to generate early momentum behind the vision and steps while gaining international legitimacy and support for efforts requiring the involvement of other key states.

- This process will necessarily be informed by early discussions between the U.S. and Russia, as well as discussions with the U.K., France, China, India, Pakistan, and Israel. This could then lead to action in the Security Council and the General Assembly.

- Care should be taken, however, not to "corner" those key states that may at the outset lack enthusiasm for the vision or be averse to certain steps, as their positive involvement will be required at some future date.

- To be successful, any process will require the direct and sustained involvement of the president and other leaders of key states, as the issues surrounding nuclear weapons go to the heart of national and international security. The absence of that involvement will likely doom the effort.

- Finally, there will need to be a calculated and sustained effort by leaders to enlist support of both domestic and international publics for the vision and steps—including the use of nuclear material for weapons for peaceful applications that will benefit all humankind.

# 14. Rethinking Nuclear Deterrence
## James E. Goodby
## Sidney D. Drell

### Deterrence as a Dynamic Concept

The history of the nuclear age shows that concepts of what it takes to have a sufficient nuclear weapons capability are far from immutable. Official U.S. thinking about nuclear weapons has changed many times during the 60 years since the first nuclear explosions in 1945. These changes reflected evolving assessments of what it would take to deter a well-armed adversary, the Soviet Union, from attacking the United States, its allies, or its vital interests. In turn, the reassessments resulted in changes in strategic planning, targeting, and the types and numbers of weapons in the U.S. stockpile, all of which are interrelated.

The trend until the Reagan administration was in the direction of more nuclear weapons. After that, the trend pointed downward. Now, the clarity of the bipolar U.S.-Soviet world has given way to the ambiguities and uncertainties of a world where international security is threatened by transnational terrorists, unstable and failed states, and regimes that scorn a world order based on broadly accepted principles. The dangers inherent in such a stew are magnified by easier access to nuclear technology, inadequately protected stockpiles of plutonium and highly enriched uranium, the growing availability of missiles worldwide, black market nuclear supply networks, and a trend toward acquisition of "latent" nuclear weapons capabilities through the possession of the entire nuclear fuel cycle. We are at a tipping point in history.

## The Task before Us

Now we need to rethink how, when, and whether nuclear deterrence works in present circumstances and to consider the implications for the U.S. nuclear arsenal. This is a moment in time which may be unique. The international situation changed radically through a failure to block a rapid increase in the number of nuclear weapons states. This is what a "tipping point" implies. But it is reasonable to hope for some success in preventing that outcome and to question: What is the need now for nuclear deterrence in certain situations where its effect is still thought to be of some importance? And are the unprecedented levels of destruction which could be wrought by even a few nuclear weapons a rational way of behaving in contemporary times? Examples are:

- the case of former adversaries (i.e., Russia)
- regional conflicts
- the case of potential adversaries (i.e., China)
- the case of other nuclear states
- the case of terrorist organizations.

## Russia

President Bush stated on December 13, 2001, that "the greatest threats to both our countries come not from each other, or from other big powers in the world, but from terrorists who strike without warning, or rogue states who seek weapons of mass destruction." This implies that deterrence now should be seen logically as applying to Russia's peacetime behavior, not to the existential problem of preventing a strategic nuclear attack. Dissuasion, another term that the administration has used in its nuclear planning, may be more apt in describing the current strategic problem. It should suffice to have a "responsive force" as a nuclear hedge against renewed hostility in the U.S.-Russian relationship. Ready-to-launch, operationally deployed nuclear forces should not be required between two countries that mutually declared in November 2001 that they do not regard each other as an enemy or threat.

## Regional Conflicts

Three regions where simmering disputes have boiled over into open conflict and could do so again are the Middle East, South Asia, and Northeast Asia. In the Middle East, the United States has been involved on at least three occasions in events carrying nuclear overtones. In 1973, the Nixon administration put U.S. nuclear forces on alert to send a warning signal to the Soviets that they should not intervene in the Middle Eastern war of that year. Prior to the 1991 Persian Gulf War, Secretary of State James Baker hinted at the use of nuclear weapons if Saddam Hussein used chemical or biological weapons. A stated if unsubstantiated reason for the U.S. invasion of Iraq in March 2003 was to eliminate the possibility that Iraq would build nuclear weapons. The dispute with Iran over its nuclear programs has evoked some media and even official discussion of air attacks on Iranian nuclear facilities, like the 1981 Israeli attack that destroyed Iraq's Osirak reactor.

In such a volatile region, where nuclear weapons have figured in several disputes, it is easy to conclude that U.S. nuclear weapons might exercise some deterrent effect. If a war between a still conventionally armed Iran and the United States were to occur, for example, U.S. nuclear weapons looming in the background might suggest to Tehran that the war should be limited and terminated as soon as possible. But it might also suggest to Tehran that use of terrorist proxies and the oil weapon would be the best way to continue the conflict. Asymmetrical warfare is very difficult for nuclear deterrence to deal with. In fact, nuclear deterrence would probably be less effective than other actions that the United States is capable of taking in the economic and diplomatic spheres. Under any circumstance, it is difficult to envision the need for nuclear weapons on alert status with prompt launch procedures being relevant. A responsive force with a much-reduced number of warheads relative to today's posture will be more than adequate for any conceivable circumstances.

South Asia presents even fewer scenarios where U.S. nuclear weapons would deter or dissuade a protagonist from taking actions that the United States wanted to prevent. Obviously, the U.S. nuclear arsenal did nothing to dissuade either India or Pakistan from going nuclear. The only plausible situations in which U.S. nuclear deterrence might come into play in South Asia is in the context of a radical Islamist government in Pakistan gaining control of its nuclear program or reassurance to India in the event of a serious dispute with China. These contingencies are not out of the question, but the effect of U.S. nuclear deterrence is apt to be marginal in either case. Again, economic and diplomatic actions and conventional armed force, not nuclear, are likely to be brought into play.

A crisis in Northeast Asia has some potential for erupting into a nuclear conflict. Deterrence in support of a containment strategy is essentially where things stand now. The three U.S. goals are presumably to deter North Korea from invading South Korea, to deter North Korea from launching missile attacks against Japan or South Korea, and to deter North Korea from using nuclear weapons under any circumstances. Actual U.S. use of nuclear weapons, except in retaliation for a nuclear attack, would probably be constrained by the opinions of all of North Korea's neighbors. In the event, North Korea may turn out to be more of a "virtual" or a "latent" nuclear weapons state than one that deploys an array of nuclear strike forces.

### China

A conflict with China over Taiwan cannot be ruled out, but U.S. use of nuclear weapons would not be the first step in an attempt to convince China to stop military action and, most likely, nuclear weapons would not enter the picture at all except in the form of mutual deterrence. A credible U.S. deterrent against the current threat of China in the straits can be managed with a reserve force and many fewer warheads than the current levels.

Japan has set great store by the U.S. "nuclear umbrella." The presence of that umbrella has made it easier for Japan (and other allies) to continue to renounce the building of nuclear weapons and has thwarted a nuclear arms race between China and Japan. This effect does not require operationally deployed U.S. nuclear warheads. A responsive force should suffice, particularly in circumstances where China's nuclear forces remain at relatively low levels.

## Other Nuclear States

For the foreseeable future, there are no "big powers" that U.S. nuclear forces need to deter, dissuade, or defeat. France, Israel, India, Pakistan, and the United Kingdom have nuclear weapons but are not our current adversaries, and their nuclear forces are much smaller than those of the United States. None of these countries are adversaries of the other nuclear superpower, Russia, which like the United States can meet potential security needs exclusively with a much smaller reserve force.

## Terrorist Organizations

The administration and independent experts acknowledge that nuclear deterrence has little effect on suicidal, fanatical terrorists. There are Islamic fundamentalists who welcome martyrdom. Otherwise, no role for U.S. nuclear weapons in any mode is very likely in the case of terrorists. The best way of blocking nuclear-armed terrorism is to prevent nuclear weapons or materials from escaping the control of responsible governments. It is not nuclear deterrence but activities such as the Cooperative Threat Reduction program that are key to preventing nuclear terrorism.

## Ballistic Missile Defense

Current discussions about U.S.-Russian missile defense cooperation should be encouraged and given sustained high-level support leading to developing cooperative multilateral ballistic missile defense and early warning systems. This is what Presidents Bush and Putin proposed at their 2002 summit meeting in Moscow. In an environment where total global numbers of warheads deployed on ballistic missiles are heading downward toward zero, it would make sense to have such joint defensive systems among cooperating states. It would help to stabilize their own strategic nuclear relationships with each other and would link them in an effort to thwart the ambitions of noncooperating states and would-be cheaters.

# 15. Diplomacy for the Future
## George P. Shultz
## Henry S. Rowen

Ronald Reagan often said, "We have arms because we have tensions, not the other way around." Of course, arms—and particularly nuclear arms—do create tensions. Nevertheless, President Reagan has a good point. So part of the effort to find our way to a world free of nuclear weapons must be an effort to construct a world where hope and achievement relieve tension and where diplomatic engagement resolves problems. Even virtually perennial disputes such as those in Kashmir or the multiple tensions in the Middle East can be better managed when the diplomatic atmosphere is positive. What can be done to achieve this result? Let us start by setting out the main challenges.

A truly outstanding feature of the world today is the strength of the economy on a global scale. Expansion is taking place in most countries and all regions of the world. A world once split by the cold war now operates as a global economy, able to raise standards of living by a broader application of the law of comparative advantage. Low-income-per-capita countries, as in the case of China, India, Brazil, now Indonesia, and others, are experiencing rapid economic advances. New middle classes are emerging. Poverty, while still a huge problem, is going down. Of course, there are problems. Some people's incomes are rising faster than others'—as is always true—but relatively few people are absolutely worse off than before. In many respects, you could say the world has never been at such a propitious moment. In this respect, a golden age is upon us. Of course, there are problems. [Right now the world economy is slowing down—as happens from time to time. But one should not doubt the determination—and the know-how—of these people to develop.] Some people's incomes are rising faster than others'—as is always true—but relatively few people are absolutely worse off than before. In many respects, a golden age is upon us.

At the same time, there is more tension than ever in the world as destructive weapons, even nuclear weapons, appear in more hands, as the international system for limiting their spread erodes, and as loosely structured arrays of Islamic extremists, some supported by Iran, use the weapon of terror. The nation-state, the historic way of organizing civilized life and governmental activity, is under attack, and all too many parts of the world are barely governed. Such places, used by terrorists for training and launching attacks, are a grave danger to the civilized world.

The diplomatic task for the future, then, might be called "protecting the golden age" from assaults by radicals who want to change the system and who use violence indiscriminately—the weapon of terror—as a primary means of persuasion. How is this task to be accomplished?

First of all, we should be careful not to undermine the conditions that have helped make the world economy flourish. But today in the United States, and also more widely, there is a growing sentiment that would put sand in the gears of trade with the aim of trying to protect specific jobs. The failure of the Daha round of trade negotiations is discouraging and if this sentiment is translated into legislation, much damage will be done—including harm to American workers, let alone workers elsewhere. We and other countries have been there before, notably between the two world wars, and we should know better than to return to those grim times. This means being careful about booby traps. For instance, you can be strong supporters of improving the environment on a global, let alone national scale, while being skeptical about imposing environmental requirements on openness to trade. Protectionism painted green is still protectionism.

A second objective in the economic area is to encourage further development. Many Muslims, especially Arabs, see themselves—correctly—as missing out on the last several centuries of industrial development. Arguably a necessary condition for their politics to change for the better is for them to catch up economically. For perspective, it is useful to remember that, not very long ago, both China and India were widely seen as mired in poverty and stuck there with hopeless politics. Among Islamic countries, the Arab states have been especially held back by the appeal of destructive socialism and authoritarianism, and, for some of them, by the well-known "oil curse." The latter are now flush with money but the record shows that this situation might not endure. They need better economic policies, and they now have more examples to look at than just the already wealthy countries. This implies moving away from policies that are often ostensibly populist but that actually protect their elites. So they need to produce goods and services (other than oil-related ones) and the ways to do this are now on display around the world. We can help ourselves by using less oil and thereby reducing our vulnerability. At the same time, a lower oil price would induce producers to turn to different work. Economic development based on human effort, not just the exploitation of oil wealth, can lead to more open political systems. We must encourage that kind of development in Islamic lands and communities.

But for this to work there must be a demand for their products (other than oil), so sustained world growth and open trading arrangements are needed for them to grow.

Next, looking at the problem from a diplomatic perspective, we have to recognize that today's world is more fractured than in recent times. A sense of potential chaos is combined with a dependence on oil that has a long history. That dependence is now resulting in huge uncertainties because the areas where the oil is located are in many cases highly unstable. The uncertainty is also propelling vigorous work in scientific, venture capital, and other areas in a search for ways to use oil more efficiently and to find alternatives to oil.

In addition, the sense of drift and potential chaos is fed by the inability of established institutions to function effectively. The UN Security Council, even when a strong statement is issued, typically fails to follow through with tough action. This, of course, is usually because the members in fact don't agree and this, in turn, leads to a search for other—non-Security Council—ways to deal with urgent, indeed potentially life-threatening, matters.

The structure for dealing with current issues is loose and elusive. The cold war was a period of serious tension, with a palpable danger of massive nuclear destruction, so we said good riddance to it. However, its structure was easy to understand with two superpowers, some additional important countries, and many smaller ones. They tended to be aligned with one side or the other. Even the non-aligned movement was, in many ways, subject to the disciplines of the cold war standoff. In a sense, you could say that it was a period when there were relatively few known variables and two big and clear constants.

The current period is different in that the simplicity and discipline of the cold war have eroded drastically. Now we see a world with more variables and with constants that are not as strong, becoming semi-variables themselves. The result is that the world is harder to understand and therefore more uneasy, even though the tension of the cold war has been relieved. One especially important reason is the widespread erosion of sovereign authority. Walter Wriston, in his classic, *The Twilight of Sovereignty*, sets out how the emerging information age means that borders constrain less and less the flow of ideas, information, and even money and people. At the same time, the creation of the European Union, with all its merits from economic and political viewpoints, nevertheless means that the sovereign powers of ancient nation-states of traditional importance are deliberately and seriously eroded.

So all this means that we in the United States and in other countries as well face a radically changed world with rising powers, compromised sovereignty, ungoverned territories, radical Islamists, and immensely powerful weapons spreading around. This situation requires a much larger and invigorated commitment to the tasks of diplomacy, conducted on a global scale. On the U.S. side, fortunately, Colin Powell, in his time as Secretary, strengthened the Department of State to meet this challenge. He reinvigorated the recruitment process, improved the resource base and technological capability, and raised the spirits of the foreign service. But much more needs to be done. The size of the foreign service needs to match global needs, the means need to be developed to retain access to the services of senior people, and more political appointees of high quality need to be brought on board.

This added capability can enable a vigorous program of gardening: developing relationships around the world by working hard with people in ordinary times. The idea is to get out the weeds when they are small in order to develop an agenda of work that will be helpful to both parties. When you work with people at times when nothing critical is at stake, you lay the groundwork for collaborative efforts with them when extraordinary demands are made.

The amount of contact between U.S. officials and people in many other countries is extensive. The military-to-military contacts are widespread and are fundamentally constructive. Admiral Crowe as Commander-in-Chief, Pacific (CINCPAC) saw to it that, when his ships moved around the islands, they always carried Seabees on them. The idea was that when they made port, the Seabees would get in contact with local officials and put their services to good use. Seabees can fix anything, and they made lots of friends.

We also need to emphasize the importance of exchange visits between the citizens of the United States and those of other countries. Exchange programs have been languishing, but we need to encourage their growth, just as we need to make our libraries as accessible as possible to people around the world.

What ideas can underlie the diplomatic effort? Here are several that have proven useful in earlier times:

- Change toward freedom and openness is possible but requires patience.
- Political openness usually proceeds in tandem with economic development, not ahead of it.
- Strength of purpose and capability are essential.
- Strength and diplomacy are intertwined and are mutually reinforcing.
- A deep and continuing consultative process among like-minded people is needed to create understanding necessary to make hard choices.
- A successful strategy must be based on realism and sustainability.

But, when all is said and done, some problems go on and on. One way to classify problems is to put them in two piles: problems you can solve and problems that seem insoluble. In the construction business, for example, if someone asks you to build a bridge from A to nearby B, you can solve the problem. If someone asks you to create a construction site free of accidents, you can put up guardrails and other safety devices, but the minute you think that the problem is solved, you've lost. The issue is all about attitudes. You have to realize that the problem is not soluble but needs constant attention and work. In that way, you minimize or maybe even eliminate accidents.

Some of the most intractable international issues are like the second class of problems. Palestinians and Israelis claim the same land and so play a zero-sum game. Anyone can write down a solution on paper, but the answer goes deeper. You have to work at the problem all the time and be willing to take on possibilities, not just probabilities. Constant attention can keep the situation from deteriorating and, eventually, an accommodation might emerge, as in Northern Ireland. We should ask, when considering our work on any problem: Are these ideas being applied and, if not, why not? To paraphrase Teddy Roosevelt, even if you have a big stick, speak softly, firmly, and in a manner that will be sustained by the evolution of facts. Remember that tricks can be played by asymmetric warfare, so look out for surprises.

A guiding idea in the struggle against terrorism is the notion of prevention. If we can help prevent the spread of hateful ideology, then we have taken the first essential step. There are antidotes to terrorism in all Islamic societies, not least because terrorists are killing large numbers of Muslims. Indonesia and Malaysia, countries with large numbers of Muslims, show that governments can strengthen these antibodies by mobilizing public support against the terrorists and by avoiding indiscriminate suppression of dissent. Outsiders can help, but only in a low-key way.

And remember that the strategy of prevention is consistent with the idea that change is possible if prevention can be sustained. So look at Algeria today, where, as reported by the *New York Times*, 60 percent of the enrollment in colleges is by women. They are filling an increasing array of jobs, making up 70 percent of Algeria's lawyers and 60 percent of its judges. This is hardly consistent with stereotypes of what is possible in a predominantly Muslim society.

Strength is always a key: economic and ideological strength, and also military capability, willpower, and the self-confidence to act when necessary. A special challenge is created by the potentially devastating consequences of a terrorist attack: huge numbers of lives lost, in addition to destruction of property and economic damage and dislocation. The need for sharply improved intelligence capability is obvious. Knowledge about attacks before they take place makes a huge difference. If we get it, then we have an uncomfortable decision to make, especially when the culprit group or individuals are in a country where terrorists are tolerated or even assisted. But the decision is always difficult: intelligence is hardly ever clear-cut, targets can be elusive and may be embedded in civilian surroundings, consequences may be hard to predict. Nevertheless, the failure to use preventive force in circumstances when one has credible evidence of impending terrorist actions can have terrible consequences. And they are not limited to the immediate damage. The precedent of inability to act carries implications for the future.

Perhaps we can also gain some momentum for this agenda of strength, cooperation, prevention, and diplomacy from the pursuit of two big ideas on a global scale. Each one is drawn from the Ronald Reagan playbook.

First, can we find our way to a global structure that allows us to attack the issues of global warming? The Kyoto Protocol could not work because the concept behind it had no chance of global acceptance. No one should expect that countries such as China or India can accept an agreement that amounts to a cap on their economic growth. The Montreal Protocol, which was developed during the Reagan period, was an international agreement to phase out the production of materials that were depleting the ozone layer of the atmosphere. When the agreement was completed, Ronald Reagan called it a "magnificent achievement." Work remains to be done on this problem. Nevertheless, the Protocol has been implemented with such wide support that former UN Secretary-General Kofi Annan called it "perhaps the most successful international agreement to date." The Protocol worked in part because every state knew it would feel the problem and so took part in the solution. The effort was and is action oriented. The only feasible way to move ahead with global warming is to act together, but often in ways that differ from country to country, to do what can be done—now. The key is to remember that one size does not fit all. In this respect, Montreal has a lot to teach post-Kyoto. We can put ideas that work into play once again.

Second, can we find our way to a world free of nuclear weapons? We take a cue from development of that idea at the Reykjavik meeting between President Reagan and General Secretary Gorbachev. Many steps need to be taken and with great care. Each one presents difficulties and requires hard work and, in some cases, skillful diplomacy.

That is the work of this conference. Success here would almost surely have desirable after-effects.

The use of nuclear weapons has never made sense. Now, as they spread, the likelihood that they will be used rather than merely relied upon for their deterrent value grows, with potentially disastrous consequences. The steps identified as the subject of this conference, steps essential for progress to a world free of nuclear weapons, are desirable in and of themselves.

In some cases, the steps interact with other objectives, as in the effort to deal with global warming. For this goal, more use of nuclear power is desirable since electricity is produced without greenhouse gases. But that cannot go forward comfortably under present circumstances. A basic fact of technology complicates the ability to limit access to nuclear weapons: readily fissionable material usable in bombs is present in either the fuel going into nuclear power stations or in the spent fuel. This implies that the possessor of such power stations is technically within a short distance of being able to make explosives. The prospect for building more nuclear power plants implies the wider distribution of potential bomb material. So the goal of international control of the nuclear fuel cycle takes on added urgency. Both technical advances and political ones are needed.

The new system would be a return to a version of the earlier Acheson-Lilienthal plan in which nuclear power would have been controlled by an international agency. That plan foundered on the rock of the cold war, leaving us today with a weak and crumbling bulwark against widespread access to bomb materials.

The goal of a world free of nuclear weapons and success in taking the steps necessary to achieve it call for a vigorous diplomatic effort on a multinational scale. The dangers growing in the Middle East suggest a concentrated focus on that region. Although the difficulties of achieving it would be great, the alternative to a nuclear-weapon-free zone in the Middle East is fearsome to contemplate.

Some positive developments have occurred: there have been important successes in tracking critical materials moving around the world. Some countries have given them up and the total number of nuclear weapons in the world is going down.

So the present situation is precarious. On the one hand, there might be a rapid expansion in the number of countries trying to get these weapons; on the other, past successes and prospective dangers are creating new opportunities for diplomacy. The essential need is to persuade governments that their countries will be worse off with these weapons than in a world without them.

The pursuit of big ideas on a world scale might well generate just the sense of cohesion that would help like-minded nations face down other problems that threaten our peace and our prosperity. At the same time, a little cold war history reminds us that unpleasant realities can change if we confront them with strength, cohesion, and sustained diplomatic effort.

APPENDIX ONE:

# Conference Agenda

Reykjavik Revisited:
Steps Toward a World Free of Nuclear Weapons
October 24–25, 2007
Hoover Institution
Stanford University

**Wednesday, October 24**

8:00 a.m.    Continental Breakfast

8:30 a.m.    Welcome and Opening Remarks
             John Raisian, Sam Nunn, Sergio Duarte,
             Max Kampelman, and George Shultz

9:30 a.m.    Session I: Force Reductions and Redeployment
             James Goodby, David Holloway, Bruce Blair,
             Rose Gottemoeller
             • Further Reductions in Nuclear Forces
             • De-alerting Strategic Forces
             • Eliminating Short-Range Nuclear Weapons
               Designed to be Forward-Deployed

1:00 p.m.    Lunch

2:00 p.m.      Session II: Controls on Nuclear Weapons and Fuel
               James Timbie, Robert Einhorn, Matthew Bunn
               • Preventing the Spread of Enrichment
                 and Reprocessing
               • Controlling Fissile Materials Worldwide:
                 A Fissile Material Cutoff Treaty and Beyond
               • Securing Nuclear Stockpiles Worldwide
5:00 p.m.      Meeting Adjourns
6:00 p.m.      Reception & Dinner

**Thursday, October 25**

8:00 a.m.      Continental Breakfast
8:30 a.m.      Session III: Test Restraints and Verification
               Raymond Jeanloz, Raymond Juzaitis
               • Comprehensive Nuclear Test Ban Treaty
                 and U.S. Security
               • Challenges of Verification and Compliance
                 within a State of Universal Latency
11:30 a.m.     Session IV: Regional Confrontations and
               Nuclear Weapons Proliferation
               Jack Matlock
12:30 p.m.     Lunch
1:30 p.m.      Session V: Turning the Goal of a World without
               Nuclear Weapons into a Joint Enterprise
               Max Kampelman
               • Intensive Work with Leaders of Countries
                 Possessing Nuclear Weapons
2:30 p.m.      Session VI: Getting to Zero
               All participants
5:00 p.m.      Meeting Adjourns

APPENDIX TWO:
# Reykjavik Revisited
# Conference Participants

1. General John Abizaid
   Distinguished Visiting Fellow
   Hoover Institution
   Stanford University

2. Richard Allen
   Senior Fellow
   Hoover Institution
   Stanford University

3. Graham Allison
   Director of the Belfer Center for Science and International Affairs
   Douglas Dillon Professor of Government
   Kennedy School of Government
   Harvard University

4. Brooke Anderson
   Vice President for Communications
   Nuclear Threat Initiative (NTI)

5. Prof. Martin C. Anderson
   Keith and Jan Hurlbut Fellow
   Hoover Institution
   Stanford University

6. Mr. Steven Andreasen
   Herbert H. Humphrey Institute of Public Affairs

7. Michael H. Armacost
   Distinguished Sorenstein Fellow at the Asia Pacific Research Center
   Freeman Spogli Institute for International Studies
   Visiting Fellow
   Hoover Institution
   Stanford University

8. Bruce G. Blair
   President
   World Security Institute

9. Dr. Matthew Bunn
   Senior Research Associate
   Belfer Center for Science and International Affairs
   Harvard University

10. Prof. Ashton Carter
    Chair of the International and Global Affairs
    Kennedy School of Government
    Harvard University

11. Dr. Sidney D. Drell
    Senior Fellow, Hoover Institution
    Professor Emeritus
    Stanford Linear Accelerator Center

12. Sergio Duarte
    High Representative for Disarmament Affairs
    United Nations Headquarters

13. General Vladimir Dvorkin
    Center for International Security
    Institute for World Economy and International Relations
    of the Russian Academy of Sciences
    Moscow, Russia

14. Robert Einhorn
    Senior Adviser, International Security Program
    Center for Strategic and International Studies

15. Mark Fitzpatrick
Senior Fellow for Non-Proliferation
International Institute for Strategic Studies

16. James E. Goodby
Research Fellow
Hoover Institution

17. Rose Gottemoeller
Director, Moscow Center
Carnegie Endowment for International Peace

18. Mr. Tom Graham
Former Special Representative of the President for Arms Control,
Non-proliferation, and Disarmament

19. Dr. David Hamburg
President Emeritus
Carnegie Corporation of New York

20. Prof. Siegfried Hecker
Co-Director, CISAC
Stanford University

21. Prof. Tom Henriksen
Senior Fellow
Hoover Institution
Stanford University

22. Prof. David Holloway
Senior Fellow
Freeman Spogli Institute for International Studies
Stanford University

23. Prof. Raymond Jeanloz
Department of Astronomy
University of California, Berkeley

24. Josef Joffe
Marc and Anita Abramowitz Fellow in International Relations
Hoover Institution
Stanford University

25. Prof. Raymond Juzaitis
    Department of Nuclear Engineering
    Texas A&M University

26. Max M. Kampelman
    Fried, Frank, Harris, Shriver & Jacobson

27. Henry A. Kissinger (Dr.)
    Kissinger Associates, Inc.

28. Jack Matlock, Jr.
    Kennan Professor Emeritus
    Princeton University

29. Robert McFarlane (Bud)
    McFarlane Associates Inc.

30. Michael A. McFaul
    Senior Fellow
    Hoover Institution
    Stanford University

31. John E. McLaughlin
    Senior Fellow
    Merrill Center for Strategic Studies
    Paul H. Nitze School of Advanced International Studies
    The Johns Hopkins University

32. Senator Sam Nunn
    Co-Chairman and Chief Executive Officer
    Nuclear Threat Initiative (NTI)

33. Mr. Don Oberdorfer
    Distinguished Journalist in Residence
    Adjunct Professor of International Relations
    Nitze School of Advanced International Studies
    Johns Hopkins University

34. Mr. Richard Perle
    Resident Fellow
    American Enterprise Institute for Public Policy Research

35. William J. Perry
   Michael & Barbara Berberian Professor and Senior Fellow
   Freeman Spogli Institute for International Studies
   Stanford University

36. Dr. Pavel Podvig
   Researcher
   Center for International Security and Cooperation
   Stanford University

37. Dr. William C. Potter
   Director
   James Martin Center for Nonproliferation Studies and
   Sam Nunn and Richard Lugar Professor of Nonproliferation Studies
   Monterey Institute of International Studies

38. Richard Rhodes
   Pulitzer Prize winning author

39. Mr. Peter Robinson
   Research Fellow
   Hoover Institution
   Stanford University

40. Joan Rohlfing
   Senior Vice President
   Nuclear Threat Initiative (NTI)

41. Prof. Henry S. Rowen
   Senior Fellow
   Hoover Institution
   Professor of Public Policy and Management Emeritus
   Graduate School of Business
   Member Stanford University's Asia/Pacific Research Center
   Senior Fellow
   Freeman Spogli Institute for International Studies
   Stanford University

42. Scott Sagan
   Professor of Political Science
   Co-Director of Center for International Security and Cooperation
   Stanford University

43. **Prof. Roald Z. Sagdeev**
Distinguished Professor of Physics
University of Maryland

44. **George P. Shultz**
Thomas W. and Susan B. Ford Distinguished Fellow
Hoover Institution
Stanford University

45. **Abraham Sofaer**
Senior Fellow
Hoover Institution

46. **Mr. Richard Solomon**
President
United States Institute of Peace

47. **Dr. James P. Timbie**
Adviser to the Under Secretary for Arms Control and International Security
U.S. Department of State

48. **Prof. Philip D. Zelikow**
White Burkett Miller Professor of History
University of Virginia

APPENDIX THREE:

# A World Free of Nuclear Weapons

## George P. Shultz, William J. Perry, Henry A. Kissinger, Sam Nunn

[*Wall Street Journal*, January 4, 2007]

Nuclear weapons today present tremendous dangers, but also an historic opportunity. U.S. leadership will be required to take the world to the next stage—to a solid consensus for reversing reliance on nuclear weapons globally as a vital contribution to preventing their proliferation into potentially dangerous hands, and ultimately ending them as a threat to the world.

Nuclear weapons were essential to maintaining international security during the Cold War because they were a means of deterrence. The end of the Cold War made the doctrine of mutual Soviet-American deterrence obsolete. Deterrence continues to be a relevant consideration for many states with regard to threats from other states. But reliance on nuclear weapons for this purpose is becoming increasingly hazardous and decreasingly effective.

North Korea's recent nuclear test and Iran's refusal to stop its program to enrich uranium—potentially to weapons grade—highlight the fact that the world is now on the precipice of a new and dangerous nuclear era. Most alarmingly, the likelihood that non-state terrorists will get their hands on nuclear weaponry is increasing. In today's war waged on world order by terrorists, nuclear weapons are the ultimate means of mass devastation. And non-state terrorist groups with nuclear weapons are conceptually outside the bounds of a deterrent strategy and present difficult new security challenges.

Apart from the terrorist threat, unless urgent new actions are taken, the U.S. soon will be compelled to enter a new nuclear era that will be more precarious, psychologically disorienting, and economically even more costly than was Cold War deterrence. It is far from certain that we can successfully replicate the old Soviet-American "mutually assured destruction" with an increasing number of potential nuclear enemies worldwide without dramatically increasing the risk that nuclear weapons will be used. New nuclear states do not have the benefit of years of step-by-step safeguards put in effect during the Cold War to prevent nuclear accidents, misjudgments, or unauthorized launches. The United States and the Soviet Union learned from mistakes that were less than fatal. Both countries were diligent to ensure that no nuclear weapon was used during the Cold War by design or by accident. Will new nuclear nations and the world be as fortunate in the next 50 years as we were during the Cold War?

* * *

Leaders addressed this issue in earlier times. In his "Atoms for Peace" address to the United Nations in 1953, Dwight D. Eisenhower pledged America's "determination to help solve the fearful atomic dilemma— to devote its entire heart and mind to find the way by which the miraculous inventiveness of man shall not be dedicated to his death, but consecrated to his life." John F. Kennedy, seeking to break the logjam on nuclear disarmament, said, "The world was not meant to be a prison in which man awaits his execution."

Rajiv Gandhi, addressing the U.N. General Assembly on June 9, 1988, appealed, "Nuclear war will not mean the death of a hundred million people. Or even a thousand million. It will mean the extinction of four thousand million: the end of life as we know it on our planet earth. We come to the United Nations to seek your support. We seek your support to put a stop to this madness."

Ronald Reagan called for the abolishment of "all nuclear weapons," which he considered to be "totally irrational, totally inhumane, good for nothing but killing, possibly destructive of life on earth and civilization." Mikhail Gorbachev shared this vision, which had also been expressed by previous American presidents.

Although Reagan and Mr. Gorbachev failed at Reykjavik to achieve the goal of an agreement to get rid of all nuclear weapons, they did succeed in turning the arms race on its head. They initiated steps leading to significant reductions in deployed long- and intermediate-range nuclear forces, including the elimination of an entire class of threatening missiles.

What will it take to rekindle the vision shared by Reagan and Mr. Gorbachev? Can a worldwide consensus be forged that defines a series of practical steps leading to major reductions in the nuclear danger? There is an urgent need to address the challenge posed by these two questions.

The Non-Proliferation Treaty (NPT) envisioned the end of all nuclear weapons. It provides (a) that states that did not possess nuclear weapons as of 1967 agree not to obtain them, and (b) that states that do possess them agree to divest themselves of these weapons over time. Every president of both parties since Richard Nixon has reaffirmed these treaty obligations, but non-nuclear weapon states have grown increasingly skeptical of the sincerity of the nuclear powers.

Strong non-proliferation efforts are under way. The Cooperative Threat Reduction program, the Global Threat Reduction Initiative, the Proliferation Security Initiative and the Additional Protocols are innovative approaches that provide powerful new tools for detecting activities that violate the NPT and endanger world security. They deserve full implementation. The negotiations on proliferation of nuclear weapons by North Korea and Iran, involving all the permanent members of the Security Council plus Germany and Japan, are crucially important. They must be energetically pursued.

But by themselves, none of these steps are adequate to the danger.

Reagan and General Secretary Gorbachev aspired to accomplish more at their meeting in Reykjavik 20 years ago—the elimination of nuclear weapons altogether. Their vision shocked experts in the doctrine of nuclear deterrence, but galvanized the hopes of people around the world. The leaders of the two countries with the largest arsenals of nuclear weapons discussed the abolition of their most powerful weapons.

* * *

What should be done? Can the promise of the NPT and the possibilities envisioned at Reykjavik be brought to fruition? We believe that a major effort should be launched by the United States to produce a positive answer through concrete stages.

First and foremost is intensive work with leaders of the countries in possession of nuclear weapons to turn the goal of a world without nuclear weapons into a joint enterprise. Such a joint enterprise, by involving changes in the disposition of the states possessing nuclear weapons, would lend additional weight to efforts already under way to avoid the emergence of a nuclear-armed North Korea and Iran.

The program on which agreements should be sought would constitute a series of agreed and urgent steps that would lay the groundwork for a world free of the nuclear threat. Steps would include:

- Changing the Cold War posture of deployed nuclear weapons to increase warning time and thereby reduce the danger of an accidental or unauthorized use of a nuclear weapon.
- Continuing to reduce substantially the size of nuclear forces in all states that possess them.
- Eliminating short-range nuclear weapons designed to be forward-deployed.
- Initiating a bipartisan process with the Senate, including understandings to increase confidence and provide for periodic review, to achieve ratification of the Comprehensive Test Ban Treaty, taking advantage of recent technical advances, and working to secure ratification by other key states.

- Providing the highest possible standards of security for all stocks of weapons, weapons-usable plutonium, and highly enriched uranium everywhere in the world.
- Getting control of the uranium enrichment process, combined with the guarantee that uranium for nuclear power reactors could be obtained at a reasonable price, first from the Nuclear Suppliers Group and then from the International Atomic Energy Agency (IAEA) or other controlled international reserves. It will also be necessary to deal with proliferation issues presented by spent fuel from reactors producing electricity.
- Halting the production of fissile material for weapons globally; phasing out the use of highly enriched uranium in civil commerce and removing weapons-usable uranium from research facilities around the world and rendering the materials safe.
- Redoubling our efforts to resolve regional confrontations and conflicts that give rise to new nuclear powers.

Achieving the goal of a world free of nuclear weapons will also require effective measures to impede or counter any nuclear-related conduct that is potentially threatening to the security of any state or peoples.

Reassertion of the vision of a world free of nuclear weapons and practical measures toward achieving that goal would be, and would be perceived as, a bold initiative consistent with America's moral heritage. The effort could have a profoundly positive impact on the security of future generations. Without the bold vision, the actions will not be perceived as fair or urgent. Without the actions, the vision will not be perceived as realistic or possible.

We endorse setting the goal of a world free of nuclear weapons and working energetically on the actions required to achieve that goal, beginning with the measures outlined above.

*Mr. Shultz, a distinguished fellow at the Hoover Institution at Stanford, was secretary of state from 1982 to 1989. Mr. Perry was secretary of defense from 1994 to 1997. Mr. Kissinger, chairman of Kissinger Associates, was secretary of state from 1973 to 1977. Mr. Nunn is former chairman of the Senate Armed Services Committee.*

*A conference organized by Mr. Shultz and Sidney D. Drell was held at Hoover to reconsider the vision that Reagan and Mr. Gorbachev brought to Reykjavik. In addition to Messrs. Shultz and Drell, the following participants also endorse the view in this statement: Martin Anderson, Steve Andreasen, Michael Armacost, William Crowe, James Goodby, Thomas Graham Jr., Thomas Henriksen, David Holloway, Max Kampelman, Jack Matlock, John McLaughlin, Don Oberdorfer, Rozanne Ridgway, Henry Rowen, Roald Sagdeev and Abraham Sofaer.*

*URL for this article:*
http://online.wsj.com/article/SB116787515251566636.html

APPENDIX FOUR:
# Toward a
# Nuclear-Free
# World

## George P. Shultz, William J. Perry,
## Henry A. Kissinger, Sam Nunn

[*Wall Street Journal*, January 15, 2008]

The accelerating spread of nuclear weapons, nuclear know-how and nuclear material has brought us to a nuclear tipping point. We face a very real possibility that the deadliest weapons ever invented could fall into dangerous hands.

The steps we are taking now to address these threats are not adequate to the danger. With nuclear weapons more widely available, deterrence is decreasingly effective and increasingly hazardous.

One year ago, in an essay in this paper, we called for a global effort to reduce reliance on nuclear weapons, to prevent their spread into potentially dangerous hands, and ultimately to end them as a threat to the world. The interest, momentum and growing political space that has been created to address these issues over the past year has been extraordinary, with strong positive responses from people all over the world.

Mikhail Gorbachev wrote in January 2007 that, as someone who signed the first treaties on real reductions in nuclear weapons, he thought it his duty to support our call for urgent action: "It is becoming clearer that nuclear weapons are no longer a means of achieving security; in fact, with every passing year they make our security more precarious."

In June, the United Kingdom's foreign secretary, Margaret Beckett, signaled her government's support, stating: "What we need is both a vision—a scenario for a world free of nuclear weapons—and action—progressive steps to reduce warhead numbers and to limit the role of nuclear weapons in security policy. These two strands are separate but they are mutually reinforcing. Both are necessary, but at the moment too weak."

We have also been encouraged by additional indications of general support for this project from other former U.S. officials with extensive experience as secretaries of state and defense and national security advisors. These include: Madeleine Albright, Richard V. Allen, James A. Baker III, Samuel R. Berger, Zbigniew Brzezinski, Frank Carlucci, Warren Christopher, William Cohen, Lawrence Eagleburger, Melvin Laird, Anthony Lake, Robert McFarlane, Robert McNamara and Colin Powell.

Inspired by this reaction, in October 2007, we convened veterans of the past six administrations, along with a number of other experts on nuclear issues, for a conference at Stanford University's Hoover Institution. There was general agreement about the importance of the vision of a world free of nuclear weapons as a guide to our thinking about nuclear policies, and about the importance of a series of steps that will pull us back from the nuclear precipice.

The U.S. and Russia, which possess close to 95 percent of the world's nuclear warheads, have a special responsibility, obligation and experience to demonstrate leadership, but other nations must join.

Some steps are already in progress, such as the ongoing reductions in the number of nuclear warheads deployed on long-range, or strategic, bombers and missiles. Other near-term steps that the U.S. and

Russia could take, beginning in 2008, can in and of themselves dramatically reduce nuclear dangers. They include:

- *Extend key provisions of the Strategic Arms Reduction Treaty of 1991.* Much has been learned about the vital task of verification from the application of these provisions. The treaty is scheduled to expire on Dec. 5, 2009. The key provisions of this treaty, including their essential monitoring and verification requirements, should be extended, and the further reductions agreed upon in the 2002 Moscow Treaty on Strategic Offensive Reductions should be completed as soon as possible.
- *Take steps to increase the warning and decision times for the launch of all nuclear-armed ballistic missiles, thereby reducing risks of accidental or unauthorized attacks.* Reliance on launch procedures that deny command authorities sufficient time to make careful and prudent decisions is unnecessary and dangerous in today's environment. Furthermore, developments in cyber-warfare pose new threats that could have disastrous consequences if the command-and-control systems of any nuclear-weapons state were compromised by mischievous or hostile hackers. Further steps could be implemented in time, as trust grows in the U.S.-Russian relationship, by introducing mutually agreed and verified physical barriers in the command-and-control sequence.
- *Discard any existing operational plans for massive attacks that still remain from the Cold War days.* Interpreting deterrence as requiring mutual assured destruction (MAD) is an obsolete policy in today's world, with the U.S. and Russia formally having declared that they are allied against terrorism and no longer perceive each other as enemies.
- *Undertake negotiations toward developing cooperative multilateral ballistic-missile defense and early warning systems, as proposed by Presidents Bush and Putin at their 2002 Moscow summit meeting.* This should include agreement on plans for countering

missile threats to Europe, Russia and the U.S. from the Middle East, along with completion of work to establish the Joint Data Exchange Center in Moscow. Reducing tensions over missile defense will enhance the possibility of progress on the broader range of nuclear issues so essential to our security. Failure to do so will make broader nuclear cooperation much more difficult.

- *Dramatically accelerate work to provide the highest possible standards of security for nuclear weapons, as well as for nuclear materials everywhere in the world, to prevent terrorists from acquiring a nuclear bomb.* There are nuclear weapons materials in more than forty countries around the world, and there are recent reports of alleged attempts to smuggle nuclear material in Eastern Europe and the Caucasus. The U.S., Russia and other nations that have worked with the Nunn-Lugar programs, in cooperation with the International Atomic Energy Agency (IAEA), should play a key role in helping to implement United Nations Security Council Resolution 1540 relating to improving nuclear security—by offering teams to assist jointly any nation in meeting its obligations under this resolution to provide for appropriate, effective security of these materials.

As Gov. Arnold Schwarzenegger put it in his address at our October conference, "Mistakes are made in every other human endeavor. Why should nuclear weapons be exempt?" To underline the governor's point, on Aug. 29–30, 2007, six cruise missiles armed with nuclear warheads were loaded on a U.S. Air Force plane, flown across the country and unloaded. For 36 hours, no one knew where the warheads were, or even that they were missing.

- *Start a dialogue, including within NATO and with Russia, on consolidating the nuclear weapons designed for forward deployment to enhance their security, and as a first step toward careful accounting for them and their eventual elimination.* These smaller and more portable nuclear weapons are, given their characteristics, inviting acquisition targets for terrorist groups.

- *Strengthen the means of monitoring compliance with the nuclear Non-Proliferation Treaty (NPT) as a counter to the global spread of advanced technologies.* More progress in this direction is urgent, and could be achieved through requiring the application of monitoring provisions (Additional Protocols) designed by the IAEA to all signatories of the NPT.

- *Adopt a process for bringing the Comprehensive Test Ban Treaty (CTBT) into effect, which would strengthen the NPT and aid international monitoring of nuclear activities.* This calls for a bipartisan review, first, to examine improvements over the past decade of the international monitoring system to identify and locate explosive underground nuclear tests in violation of the CTBT; and, second, to assess the technical progress made over the past decade in maintaining high confidence in the reliability, safety and effectiveness of the nation's nuclear arsenal under a test ban. The Comprehensive Test Ban Treaty Organization is putting in place new monitoring stations to detect nuclear tests—an effort the U.S should urgently support even prior to ratification.

In parallel with these steps by the U.S. and Russia, the dialogue must broaden on an international scale, including non-nuclear as well as nuclear nations.

Key subjects include turning the goal of a world without nuclear weapons into a practical enterprise among nations, by applying the necessary political will to build an international consensus on priorities. The government of Norway will sponsor a conference in February that will contribute to this process.

Another subject: Developing an international system to manage the risks of the nuclear fuel cycle. With the growing global interest in developing nuclear energy and the potential proliferation of nuclear enrichment capabilities, an international program should be created by advanced nuclear countries and a strengthened IAEA. The purpose should be to provide for reliable supplies of nuclear fuel, reserves of enriched uranium, infrastructure assistance, financing, and spent fuel management—to ensure that the means to make nuclear weapons materials isn't spread around the globe.

There should also be an agreement to undertake further substantial reductions in U.S. and Russian nuclear forces beyond those recorded in the U.S.-Russia Strategic Offensive Reductions Treaty. As the reductions proceed, other nuclear nations would become involved.

President Reagan's maxim of "trust but verify" should be reaffirmed. Completing a verifiable treaty to prevent nations from producing nuclear materials for weapons would contribute to a more rigorous system of accounting and security for nuclear materials.

We should also build an international consensus on ways to deter or, when required, to respond to, secret attempts by countries to break out of agreements.

Progress must be facilitated by a clear statement of our ultimate goal. Indeed, this is the only way to build the kind of international trust and broad cooperation that will be required to effectively address today's threats. Without the vision of moving toward zero, we will not find the essential cooperation required to stop our downward spiral.

In some respects, the goal of a world free of nuclear weapons is like the top of a very tall mountain. From the vantage point of our troubled world today, we can't even see the top of the mountain, and it is tempting and easy to say we can't get there from here. But the risks from continuing to go down the mountain or standing pat are too real to ignore. We must chart a course to higher ground where the mountaintop becomes more visible.

*Mr. Shultz was secretary of state from 1982 to 1989. Mr. Perry was secretary of defense from 1994 to 1997. Mr. Kissinger was secretary of state from 1973 to 1977. Mr. Nunn is former chairman of the Senate Armed Services Committee.*

*The following participants in the Hoover-NTI conference also endorse the view in this statement: General John Abizaid, Graham Allison, Brooke Anderson, Martin Anderson, Steve Andreasen, Mike Armacost, Bruce Blair, Matt Bunn, Ashton Carter, Sidney Drell, General Vladimir Dvorkin, Bob Einhorn, Mark Fitzpatrick, James Goodby, Rose Gottemoeller, Tom Graham, David Hamburg, Siegfried Hecker, Tom Henriksen, David Holloway, Raymond Jeanloz, Ray Juzaitis, Max Kampelman, Jack Matlock, Michael McFaul, John McLaughlin, Don Oberdorfer, Pavel Podvig, William Potter, Richard Rhodes, Joan Rohlfing, Scott Sagan, Roald Sagdeev, Abe Sofaer, Richard Solomon, and Philip Zelikow.*

# About the Authors

**Steven P. Andreasen** served as Director of Defense Policy and Arms Control on the National Security Council during the Clinton administration and in the Department of State during the George H. W. Bush and Reagan administrations. He is a national security consultant and lectures at the Hubert H. Humphrey Institute of Public Affairs.

**Bruce G. Blair** is the founding president of the World Security Institute and the executive producer of the weekly PBS series *Foreign Exchange*. He was a Senior Fellow at the Brookings Institution (1987–2000), project director at the Congressional Office of Technology Assessment (1982–1985), and a Minuteman ICBM launch control officer (1970–1974). He has taught at Yale and Princeton and has testified frequently before Congress. He received a MacArthur Fellowship for his work and leadership on de-alerting nuclear forces. He holds a Ph.D. in operations research from Yale.

**Matthew Bunn** is a Senior Research Associate for the Project on Managing the Atom at the Belfer Center for Science and International Affairs, Kennedy School of Government, Harvard University. He is a former adviser for the White House Office of Science and Technology Policy and a former study director for the National Academy of Sciences. Dr. Bunn is a former editor of *Arms Control Today*.

**Sidney D. Drell** is a professor of physics, emeritus, at the Stanford Linear Accelerator Center. He is also a Senior Fellow at Stanford University's Hoover Institution. He has been an adviser to the U.S.

government on technical national security and arms control issues, most recently as a member of the President's Foreign Intelligence Advisory Board. He currently serves on the Boards of Governors that manage the Lawrence Livermore National Laboratory and the Los Alamos National Laboratory, and he is an active member of JASON, a group of academic scientists who work on issues of national importance for the U.S. government.

**Robert Einhorn** is a Senior Adviser at the Center for Strategic and International Studies. He served for 29 years in the U.S. Department of State, including as Assistant Secretary for Nonproliferation from 1999 to 2001.

**James E. Goodby** is Research Fellow at the Hoover Institution where he works with former Secretary of State George P. Shultz and Dr. Sidney Drell on the project which is the theme of this book. During his Foreign Service career he was involved as a negotiator or as a policy adviser in the creation of the International Atomic Energy Agency, the negotiation of the limited nuclear test ban treaty, START, the Conference on Disarmament in Europe, and cooperative threat reduction (the Nunn-Lugar program). He was Ambassador to Finland in 1980–1981. He has taught at Stanford, Syracuse, and Georgetown Universities and is a Distinguished Service Professor Emeritus at Carnegie Mellon University. He is a nonresident Senior Fellow at the Brookings Institution.

**Rose Gottemoeller** has been Director of the Carnegie Moscow Center since January 2006. Prior to that time, she was a Senior Associate at the Carnegie Endowment in Washington. From 1997 to 2000, she served in the Department of Energy as Assistant Secretary for Nonproliferation and National Security, and later as Deputy Undersecretary. From 1993 to 1994, she served on the National Security Council as a director responsible for denuclearization in Ukraine, Kazakhstan, and Belarus.

**David Holloway** is the Raymond A. Spruance Professor in International History, a professor of history and political science, and a Senior Fellow at the Freeman Spogli Institute for International Studies at Stanford University.

**Edward Ifft**, a retired member of the Senior Executive Service, has a Ph.D. in physics and is currently adjunct professor in the Security Studies Program at Georgetown University. His primary career was at the Department of State, where he served on the U.S. delegations that negotiated the SALT, START, and CTB treaties. He was also Deputy Director of the On-Site Inspection Agency and Senior Adviser to the Defense Threat Reduction Agency.

**Raymond Jeanloz** is a professor of geophysics at the University of California at Berkeley and chairs the U.S. National Academy of Sciences' Committee on International Security and Arms Control. He has been an adviser to the U.S. government and the University of California in areas related to national and international security as well as on issues concerning earth and environmental sciences and resources.

**Raymond J. Juzaitis** is currently head of the Department of Nuclear Engineering at Texas A&M University. In his earlier 28-year career at the DOE/NNSA National Laboratories, he served as Associate Director for Weapons Physics at Los Alamos National Laboratory and Associate Director for Nonproliferation, Homeland, and International Security at Lawrence Livermore National Laboratory. He holds a BSE in chemical engineering from Princeton University and a Ph.D. in nuclear engineering from the University of Virginia.

**Max M. Kampelman** was head of the U.S. delegation to the Conference on Security and Cooperation in Europe from 1980 to 1983 and Ambassador and Head of the U.S. delegation to the negotiations with the Soviet Union on nuclear and space arms in Geneva from 1985 to 1989. He served as Counselor to the Department of State from 1987 to 1989.

**Jack F. Matlock Jr.**, a retired diplomat, has held academic posts since 1991 at Columbia University (1991–1996 and 2007), the Institute for Advanced Study (1996–2001), Princeton University (2001–2004), Hamilton College (2006), and Mount Holyoke College (2007). He served as Ambassador to the Soviet Union, Special Assistant to the President, and Ambassador to Czechoslovakia. He is the author of *Reagan and Gorbachev: How the Cold War Ended* (2004); *Autopsy on an Empire* (1995); and a handbook to Stalin's *Collected Words* (1955, second edition, 1971).

**John E. McLaughlin** is a Senior Fellow at the Johns Hopkins School of Advanced International Studies. He served as Deputy Director and subsequently as Acting Director of the Central Intelligence Agency from 2000 to 2004.

**Henry S. Rowen**, a Senior Fellow at the Hoover Institution, is a professor of public policy and management emeritus at Stanford University's Graduate School of Business. He is also a member of the Asia/Pacific Research Center and is a Senior Fellow at the Freeman Spogli Institute for International Studies, both at Stanford. He was Assistant Secretary of Defense for International Security Affairs in the U.S. Department of Defense from 1989 to 1991, and was chairman of the National Intelligence Council from 1981 to 1983. From 2001–2004 he served on the Secretary of Defense Policy Advisory Board. In 2004–2005, he served on the Presidential Commission on the Intelligence of the United States Regarding Weapons of Mass Destruction.

**George P. Shultz** served as a senior staff economist on President Eisenhower's Council of Economic Advisers. He taught at MIT and the University of Chicago, where he served as dean of the Graduate School of Business. He resumed public service under President Nixon as Secretary of Labor, Director of the Office of Management and Budget, and Secretary of the Treasury. Mr. Shultz left government service in 1974 to become president and director of Bechtel Group,

Inc. and a part-time professor at Stanford University. Mr. Shultz held two key positions in President Reagan's administration: Chairman of the President's Economic Policy Advisory Board (1981–1982) and Secretary of State (1982–1989). His many awards include the Medal of Freedom, the nation's highest civilian honor, and the Seoul Peace Prize. He is the Thomas W. and Susan B. Ford Distinguished Fellow at the Hoover Institution, Stanford University.

**James Timbie** has been the Senior Adviser to the Under Secretary for Arms Control and International Security for the Department of State since 1983. From 1971 to 1983, he served as Senior Official of the Arms Control and Disarmament Agency. Mr. Timbie was a graduate student in physics at Stanford University from 1966 to 1971.

# Index

Abizaid, John (general), 467, 485
Abkhazia, 419
abolition, moving toward, 44–45
Acheson-Lilienthal plan, 338, 339, 344–45, 346, 463
"Achieving the Vision of a World Free of Nuclear Weapons" (ElBaradei), 344
Afghanistan, 247
Akram, Munir, 291n12
Albright, D., 384
Albright, Madeleine, 480
Algeria, 461
Allen, Richard, 467, 480
Allison, Graham, 467, 485
Anderson, Brooke, 467, 485
Anderson, Martin C., 467, 478
Andreasen, Steven P., ix, xv, 1, 47, 429, 467, 478, 485, 487
Andrews, Anthony, 356n16
Angarsk, 317–18
Annan, Kofi, 12, 254, 462
annual assessments; deterrents and, 371–72; stockpile weapons and, 372
Apartheid, 405
Arabs, 456, 457
Arbatov, Aleksei, 19, 20, 43, 113n1, 157t
Arbman, Gunnar, 113n1, 114n2, 123n11, 145n22, 156t, 157t
Areva, 355n15, 363
Argentina, 36, 322, 350; uranium enrichment facilities in, 349n9
Arguello, Irma, 350n10
Armacost, Michael H., 468, 478, 485
Arms Control and Disarmament Agency, 491

*Arms Control Today,* 487
Asia; northeast, 451; nuclear fuel cycle and, 362–64. *See also* China; India; North Korea; South Asia
"Atoms for Peace" (Eisenhower), 474
Aum Shinrikyo, 243, 254
*Autopsy on an Empire* (Matlock), 490

Bailey, Kathleen, 377n2
Baker, James A. III, 451, 480
ballistic missile defense, 161; Bush, George W., and, 199, 454; Putin and, 454
Baruch, Bernard, 345, 392
Baruch Plan, 194
Baruch-Lillienthal Plan, 392
baseline posture; Britain's, 67n19; China's, 67n19; de-alerting strategic forces and, 56–69; drills, 58; France's, 67n19; real threats aligning with, 62–69; wartime aims of nuclear, 59–62
Basrur, Rajesh, 25n29
Beckett, Margaret, xvi, 235, 425, 433, 434
Belarus, 150, 403n2, 488
Belgium, 156t; MOX fuel and, 352n12
Bell, Robert, 118
Berberian, Barbara, 471
Berberian, Michael, 471
Berger, Samuel R., 480
Bilateral Implementation Commission, 6n8
bin Laden, Osama, 247, 250, 413
Biological Weapons Convention (BWC), 433
black box, 325

Blaire, Bruce G., 1, 18, 41, 64n15,
157t, 465, 468, 485, 487; de-alerting
strategic forces and, 47–105
Bodman, Samuel, 287, 288, 288n9
Brandt, Willy, 410
Brannan, P., 384
Braun, Chaim, 333, 356n16
Brazil, 36, 322, 350, 455; uranium
enrichment facilities in, 349n9
Brewer, Garry D., 64n15
Britain, xvii, 37, 453; baseline posture,
67n19; nuclear warheads in, 3;
reduction of nuclear stockpiles since
Cold War by, 32, 33, 34
Bukharin, Oleg, 213n8
*Bulletin of the Atomic Scientists,* 3n2
Bunn, George, 43n39
Bunn, Matthew, 205, 214n9, 243, 246,
247n2, 253n10, 308n22, 466, 468,
485, 487
Bush, George H. W., 43, 68, 111, 129,
487
Bush, George W., 295, 344n6, 482;
ballistic missile defense, 199, 454;
effective global nuclear security
standards and, 265; joint statement
from Putin and, 8, 30n30; Moscow
Treaty and, 4, 6n8, 172; National
Security Strategy (Sept. 2002) and,
10; nuclear terrorism and, 261–62,
273; SORT and, 4; START and, 6,
27; two-tier system and, 341
Butler, George Lee (general), 47, 68
BWC. *See* Biological Weapons
Convention

Caldicott, Helen, 340n1
Canada, 291, 343n4
Carlucci, Frank, 480
Carter, Ashton, 253n11, 468, 485
Cartwright, James E., 152
CD. *See* Conference on Disarmament
Center for Strategic and International
Studies, 488
*At the Center of the Storm: My Years at
the CIA* (Tenet), 247n3
Central Intelligence Agency (CIA), 490

certification, pit production and, 373
CFE. *See* Conventional Forces in
Europe
Chalmers, Malcolm, 1
changes; diplomatic, 456–57, 459–60;
strategic concepts, 117–18
Chayes, Abram, 351n11, 352n13
Chemical Weapons Convention (CWC),
433
Chernobyl, 266, 341
China, xvii, 35, 283, 455, 456; baseline
posture, 67n19; nuclear deterrence
and, 452–53; nuclear stockpiles in,
32, 33n32; nuclear warheads in, 3;
uranium enrichment facilities in,
349n9; world nuclear weapon
stockpiles and, 209t
Christopher, Warren, 480
CIA. *See* Central Intelligence Agency
Clinton, Bill, 68, 143, 213, 224n20, 487
Cochran, Thomas B., 276
Cohen, William, 480
Cold War, 33, 34, 37, 458, 473; end of,
8; fissile materials in, 292; lessening
threats since, 10, 11; present political
context different from, 13–14;
reduction of nuclear stockpiles since,
32; regional animosities and, 407–9
*Collected Words* (Matlock), 490
Comprehensive Nuclear-Test-Ban Treaty
(CTBT), xxi, 433, 476, 483;
conclusion, 391–94; IMS and, 377;
international norms, 388–90;
introduction, 370–71; laboratory
privatization and, 390–91; objections
to ratification, 370t; objectives and
limitations, 385–87; periodic review
and, 390–91; role of, 385–92;
security benefits, 387–88; security-
enhancing actions and, 393t; stockpile
stewardship accomplishments and,
371t; summary, 369; sustaining U.S.
deterrent and, 371–76; U.S. security
and, 369–98; verification and, 369,
377–85
Conference on Disarmament (CD), 281,
282, 433

conflicts, regional, 451–52
Congressional Office of Technology
    Assessment, 487
consensus, international, 161–62
*Controlling Nuclear Warheads and
    Materials* (Bunn, M., Wier, Holdren),
    253n10
Convention on the Physical Protection
    of Nuclear Material, 306
Conventional Forces in Europe (CFE),
    120
Cooperative Threat Reduction program,
    230, 453, 475
costs, 325
counting rules; nuclear warhead, 7;
    START, 7
countries; advanced nuclear, 313;
    Islamic, 457; with nuclear weapons,
    32–33, 453; nuclear weapons and
    regional animosities in, 404–6;
    regional animosities in other, 416–17;
    verifying, 177
Crowe, William (admiral), 459, 478
CTBT. *See* Comprehensive Nuclear-
    Test-Ban Treaty
CTR. *See* Cooperative Threat Reduction
    program
CWC. *See* Chemical Weapons
    Convention

DARHT. *See* Dual-Axis Radiographic
    Hydrodynamic Test Facility
data exchange; center for joint, 482;
    monitoring and verification, 28;
    negotiating new, 127–28; nuclear
    terrorism and, 264; reductions and,
    126–28; verification strategies and
    encryption, 177–79
*The Day After: Action in the 24 Hours
    Following a Nuclear Blast in an
    American City* (Carter, May, Perry),
    253n11
de-alerting options; bomber warheads
    relocated, 94–95; dropping massive
    attack options from strategic war
    plans, 73; dropping prompt launch
    from EWO, 72–73; fostering nuclear-

free world, 71, 77–78, 86–87, 92,
    100; illustrative Russian and U.S.
    measures, 93–94; illustrative Russian
    measures, 80–81; illustrative U.S.
    measures and, 78–80; implications
    and concluding thoughts, 101–5;
    keeping submarines out of range of
    targets, 73–76; land-based missile
    force (U.S.), 78–79; land-based
    rocket weapons de-mating (U.S.), 93–
    94; minuteman missiles, 88–89;
    physical modifications, 78–101;
    procedural modifications, 72–78;
    responsive warhead force in warhead
    storage depots, 93–95; responsive
    warhead force with on-site de-mating,
    87; risk of accidental/unauthorized/
    theft, 71–72, 78, 87, 92–93, 101;
    road-mobile missiles (Russia), 80–81;
    silo-based missiles (Russia), 80;
    strategic forces and evaluation criteria
    for, 69–72, 77; strategic stability, 70–
    71, 77, 83–85, 90–91, 96–98;
    submarine missiles (Russia), 81;
    submarine warheads to storage
    depots, 94; summary
    recommendation, 98–99; time to re-
    alert, 70, 76, 82–83, 89–90, 95–96;
    transparency and verifiability, 71, 77,
    85–86, 91–92, 99–100; trident
    submarine force (U.S.), 79–80
Declaration on Nuclear Energy and
    Nonproliferation, 331
declarations, 168
Defense Threat Reduction Agency, 489
deproliferation, 347n7
deterrents; annual assessment, 371–72;
    core capabilities, 374–76; future
    planning, 376; LEPs, 372–73;
    nuclear, 449–50, 451, 452–53, 454;
    pit production and certification, 373;
    sustaining U.S., 371–76
Dillon, Douglas, 467
diplomacy; Acheson-Lilienthal plan and,
    463; change and, 456–57, 459–60;
    economic and ideological strength
    with, 461; eradication of hateful

ideology and, 461; future, 455–64; Kyoto Protocol, 462; monitoring, verification and, 160; Montreal Protocol and, 462; muscular, 408; oil dependency and, 457; Seebees and, 459

"dirty bomb" attacks, 246

dismantlement; background, 206–8; best balance with transparency, secrecy and, 224; capacity, 209–11; confirming, 217–21; fissile materials and, 221–23; issues, 215–21; key judgments, 205–6; nuclear weapons and transparent/irreversible, 205–27; number of nuclear weapons, 208–9; recommendations, 226–27; related measures and verified, 211–15; strategic and tactical warheads with, 223; warhead and fissile material reductions and, 225–26; world nuclear weapon stockpiles, 209t

DNDO. See Domestic Nuclear Detection Office

Domestic Nuclear Detection Office (DNDO), 166

Drell, Sidney D., ix, 1, 11, 19, 20, 21, 22, 47, 333, 345, 425, 449, 468, 478, 485, 487, 488

drills, 58

Dual-Axis Radiographic Hydrodynamic Test Facility (DARHT), 375

Duarte, Sergio, 465, 468

Dvorkin, Vladimir (general), 9n17, 19, 20, 43, 468, 485

Eagleburger, Lawrence, 480

earthquakes, 385

economic strength, 461

Egypt, 291

Einhorn, Robert, 1, 29, 134n18, 194, 279, 466, 468, 485, 488

Eisenhower, Dwight D., 338, 474

ElBaradei, Mohamed (general), 314, 344, 365, 365n25

Emergency War Orders (EWO), dropping prompt launch from, 72–73

encryption, 177–79

enrichment; appropriate reactors and, 328; assurances of reliable supply of fuel with, 328; background, 314–21; conditions/rights/beneficiary commitments and, 322–24; elements of solution for, 327–31; facilities, 296, 350; financing and, 330; fissile material and, 313; fuel cycle's back end and, 325–27; fuel supply assurances and, 315–16; GNEP and, 316; IAEA director general's report and, 319–20; incompatibility with existing, partially privatized industry and, 325; infrastructure assistance and, 330; international uranium enrichment center at Angarsk, 317–18; issues, 321–31; key judgments, 313–14; multinational facilities and, 324–25; NTI proposed reserve and, 318; nuclear energy expansion and, 321–22; preventing spread of reprocessing and, xxii, 313–31; spent fuel management and, 314, 330; U.S.-Russia declaration on nuclear energy and nonproliferation with, 320–21; WNA proposal and, 319

Etzioni, Amitai, 333, 347n7

EU. See European Union

European Union (EU), 458

EWO. See Emergency War Orders

expansion, 455

expiration dates; SORT Treaty, 6 START Treaty, 6, 26, 159, 234

facilities; Dual-Axis Radiographic Hydrodynamic Test, 375; Mayak Fissile Material Storage, 215; National Ignition, 375; Rokkasho reprocessing, 286; sole operational U.S. (dis)assembly, 210, 211

false alarms, 58n4

Feiveson, Harold, 157t

Fetter, Steve, 276

Financial Times, 147n23

financing, 330

Finland, 488

Fischer, Joschka, 152

Fissile Material Control Initiative (FMCI), 193–97, 280; civil plutonium and HEU, 307–8; declarations, 305–6; disposition, 308–9; excess material and safeguards, 306–7; existing fissile material and, 304–9; physical protection, 306

*Fissile Material Cut-Off Treaty,* 194

Fissile Material Cutoff Treaty (FMCT), xx, xxi, 241; addressing existing stocks and, 302–9; broader scope and, 290–91; CD and, 281, 282; civil HEU, 289; civil plutonium, 286; comprehensive approach, 300; comprehensive *vs.* focused verification, 299–301; controlling fissile materials worldwide and, 279–311; entry into force requirement, 301–2; excess weapons material, 286–88; focused approach, 299–300; frustrating record with, 280–83; international verification provisions with, 295–97; issues not covered and, 285–89; key issues in pursuing, 293–302; naval reactor fuel, 288–89; nuclear terrorism and, 292; outlook for negotiations about, 309–10; scope, 283–85; scope of prohibition, 293–95; Shannon mandate and, 281; today's strategic, 291–93; verification measures negotiated separately or subsequently, 297–99; toward world without nuclear weapons and, 310–11

fissile materials; addressing existing stocks of, 302–9; broader scope with, 290–91; Cold War storage of, 292; controlling, 279–311; enrichment and reprocessing prevention and, 313; existing, 304–9; FMCT in today's strategic, 291–93; FMCT scope and, 283–85; frustrating record with, 280–83; issues not covered with, 285–89; key issues in pursuing FMCT and, 293–302; limits of verification and, 274–77; outlook for negotiations about, 309–10; toward world without

nuclear weapons and, 310–11. *See also* Fissile Material Cutoff Treaty

Fitzpatrick, Mark, 333, 469, 485

FMCI. *See* Fissile Material Control Initiative

FMCT. *See* Fissile Material Cutoff Treaty

Ford, Christopher, 284n2

Forden, Geoffrey, 201, 202, 333, 360, 361, 364

*Foreign Affairs,* 9n17

*Foreign Exchange,* 487

Forsberg, Charles, 333, 341n2, 348n8, 352n13, 357n17

France, xvii, 37, 453; baseline posture, 67n19; civil plutonium reprocessing in, 281; nuclear warheads in, 3; reduction of nuclear stockpiles since Cold War by, 32, 33, 34; uranium enrichment facilities in, 349n9; world nuclear weapon stockpiles and, 209t

Friedman, Joshua, 247n2

fuel; cycle, 314, 325–27, 333–68, 450; cycle facilities, 292; enrichment and reliable supply of, 328; management, 314, 330; MOX, 300, 352n12, 352n13; naval reactor, 288–89; supply assurances, 315–16. *See also* nuclear fuel cycle

future, diplomatic changes for, 455–64

G-8 moratorium, 343n4

Gandhi, Rajiv, 474

General Electric, 363

Georgia, 120, 419

Germany, 156t, 475; uranium enrichment facilities in, 349n9

Ghoshroy, Subrata, 333, 363

global cleanout; expanded set of material and, 270–71; expanded set of reactors and, 270; incentives, 269; nuclear stockpiles and, 268–71; shutdown as policy tool with, 269–70

global expansion, 455

Global Initiative to Combat Nuclear Terrorism, 195, 257, 261–62

Global Nuclear Energy Partnership

(GNEP), 316; nuclear fuel cycle and, 335, 357–58

Global Positioning System (GPS), 383

Global Strike concept, 108, 152

Global Threat Reduction Initiative, 195, 289, 308, 475

Global Threat Reduction Initiative (GTRI), 256

GNEP. *See* Global Nuclear Energy Partnership

Golan Heights, 416

Goldschmidt, Pierre, 333, 357n18, 365n25

Goodby, James E., ix, 1, 11, 19, 20, 21, 22, 41, 47, 212n7, 333, 449, 465, 469, 478, 485, 488

Gorbachev, Mikhail, ix, xv, xvi, 43, 68, 111, 129, 345, 413, 420, 422, 462, 475, 476, 478, 480; rejection of shared defenses, 420n3

Gottemoeller, Rose, 31, 107, 465, 469, 485, 488

GPS. *See* Global Positioning System

Graham, Thomas Jr., 469, 478, 485

Greece, 156t

GTRI. *See* Global Threat Reduction Initiative

Guhin, Michael, 297n16

Guidelines for the Management of Plutonium, 309

Gulf War, 405

Hamas, 413

Hamburg, David, 469, 485

Hannah, Barry, 373

Hecker, Siegfried, 469, 485

Helsinki; framework, 229, 230, 241; summit, 143, 213

Henriksen, Tom, 469, 478, 485

HEU. *See* Highly Enriched Uranium

HEU Purchase Agreement, 308

Heuser, Beatrice, 40n36

Hezbollah, 413, 416

Highly Enriched Uranium (HEU), xx, xxi, 213, 224n20, 243, 283n1; civil, 289; excess, 286–89; research

reactors, 250; significant quantities, 385n3; stolen and recovered, 250

Hiroshima, 338

Holdren, John, 253n10

Holgate, Laura, 333, 355n15

Holloway, David, 1, 43n39, 47, 111, 130, 465, 469, 478, 485, 489

Holt, Mark, 356n16

Hoover Institution, xv, 465

human intelligence (HUMINT), 168, 169

HUMINT. *See* human intelligence

Huntington, Samuel, 406

Hussein, Saddam, 343, 405, 451

hydro-acoustics, monitoring sensitivity with, 379–81

IAEA. *See* International Atomic Energy Agency

IC. *See* Intelligence Community

ICBM force, 5

ideology, strong and hateful, 461

Ifft, Edward, 1, 14n23, 229, 489

IMS. *See* International Monitoring System

incompatibility, with existing, partially privatized enrichment industry, 325

India, xvii, xxi, 25n29, 283, 452, 455, 456; civil plutonium reprocessing in, 281; nuclear policies, 35; nuclear stockpiles in, 33, 34; nuclear warheads in, 3; refusal to sign NPT, 405; regional animosities in, 414–15; uranium enrichment facilities in, 349n9

Indonesia, 455, 461

INF. *See* Intermediate-Range Nuclear Forces treaty

infrasound; documentation of, 381–82; GPS and, 383; low-frequency acoustic waves of, 381; monitoring sensitivity with, 381–83; Tunguska explosion and, 382

infrastructure assistance, 330

INMM. *See* Institute for Nuclear Materials Management

inspections, on site, 179

Institute for Nuclear Materials Management (INMM), 266
Intelligence Community (IC), 167
intelligence monitoring; NTM and, 167–68; OSI, 168
Intermediate-Range Nuclear Forces treaty (INF), 229
International Atomic Energy Agency (IAEA), xxi, 15, 216, 224n20, 314, 322, 349, 350, 477, 483, 488; black box and, 325; director general, 319–20
international community, moving toward nuclear-weapons-free world, 292–93
International Monitoring System (IMS), 377
International Nuclear Fuel Cycle Evaluation project, 314
International Uranium Enrichment Center at Angarsk, 317–18, 322
Iran, 341n2, 348, 350, 455, 475, 476; nuclear disarmament and, 361; nuclear fuel cycle and, 360–62; proposal on nuclear issue, 361n21; regional animosities in, 411–14; religious nature, 411; uranium enrichment facilities in, 349n9
Iraq, 341n2; voluntary dismantlement of nuclear program, 405
Ireland, northern, 460
Islam, 411, 457, 458
Israel, xvii, 402n1, 453; nuclear capabilities, 299n18; nuclear stockpiles in, 33; nuclear warheads in, 3; refusal to sign NPT, 405; regional animosities in, 415–16; world nuclear weapon stockpiles and, 209t
Israelis, 460
Italy, 156t
Ivanov, Sergei, 147n23

Japan, 452, 453, 475; civil plutonium reprocessing in, 281; MOX fuel and, 352n12; nuclear fuel cycle and, 363; Rokkasho reprocessing facility in, 286; uranium enrichment facilities in, 349n9
Japan Nuclear Fuel Limited (JNFL), 363
JASON, 488
Jeanloz, Raymond, 369, 466, 469, 485, 489
JNFL. See Japan Nuclear Fuel Limited
Joffe, Josef, 469
John Wilson, Lewis, 34n33
Joint Data Exchange Center, 482
Joint Nuclear Energy Action Plan, 362
Joseph, Robert, 144n21
Juzaitis, Ray, 14, 28, 159, 466, 470, 485, 489

Kampelman, Max M., 425, 429, 434, 465, 466, 470, 478, 485, 489
Kargil crisis, 25n29
Kashmir, 35, 455
Kazakhstan, 150, 318, 403n2, 488
Kellogg-Briand Pact, 422
Kennedy, John F., 163, 425, 474
Khan, A. Q., 348, 359
Khrushchev, Nikita, 114
Kim, Jong-il, 410
Kimball, Daryl, 333
Kissinger, Henry A., xv, 31n31, 235, 346, 347, 431, 470, 473, 478, 479, 485
Klingenberger, Kurt J., 144n21
Korea. See North Korea; South Korea
Kosovo, 419
Kristensen, Hans M., 3n2, 7, 113n1, 152, 156t
Krypton-85, 296
Kuwait, 341n2
Kyoto Protocol, 462

laboratory, privatization, 390–91
Laird, Melvin, 480
Lake, Anthony, 480
Larson, Jeffrey A., 144n21
Lavrov, Sergey, 4, 4n3, 6, 27, 434
Lawrence Livermore, 194, 374, 390
leadership, 244

Lebanon, 416; regional animosities in, 415–16
Lee, Rensselaer, 253n9
LEPs. *See* Life-Extension Programs
LEU. *See* Non-Weapons-Usable Low-Enriched Uranium
Lewis, Bennett W., 351n11, 352n13
Lewis, Jeffrey, 33n33
Libya, voluntary dismantlement of nuclear program, 405
Lieber, Keir A., 423n4
Life-Extension Programs (LEPs); deterrents and, 372–73; stewardship and, 372; W76, 373, 373n1
lightning problems, 123n11
Lithuania, 148
Los Alamos, 374, 390
Lugar, Richard, 254, 471

Malaysia, 461
martyrdom, 453
Material Consolidation and Conversion Program, 308
*Materials Protection, Control and Accountability,* 195
Mathews, Jessica, 366–67
Matlock, Jack F. Jr., 399, 466, 470, 478, 485, 490
May, Michael M., 253n11
Mayak Fissile Material Storage Facility, 215
McFarlane, Robert (Bud), 470, 480
McFaul, Michael A., 470, 485
McGoldrick, Fred, 333
McLaughlin, John E., 14, 28, 159, 470, 478, 485, 490
McNamara, Robert, 480
Medvedev, Dmitry, 418
Middle East, 34, 455, 463; conflict resolution before elimination of nuclear weapons in, 35; regional conflicts, 451
Mikhailov, Victor, 206
Military Doctrine of the Russian Federation (2000), 9
Miller, Marvin, 333
minuteman missiles, 88–89

missile(s); defense, xviii–xix, 29–31, 454; road-mobile, 80–81; silo-based, 80; submarine, 81
missile defense; cooperation, 30–31; early warning and, xviii–xix; further reductions in nuclear forces and, 29–31; nuclear deterrence and ballistic, 454
Missile Technology Control Regime (MTCR), 199
Mitsubishi, 363
Mixed Oxide (MOX), 222; fuel, 300, 352n12, 352n13
Molander, Roger, 166
Moldova, 120, 420
monitoring and verification; cheating and consequences with, 21; continuing reductions of deployed weapons with, 159–60; criteria for assessing reductions and, 14–15; data exchange/notifications, 28; diplomacy and, 160; further reductions in nuclear forces and, 27–29; handheld/fixed nuclear detection devices, 28; international consensus and, 161–62; Moscow Treaty and, 27; non-deployed warheads and difficulty with, 15; NTM, 28; nuclear explosive material and, 161; on-site inspection, 28; perimeter and portal continuous, 28; remote monitoring techniques, 28; stage 1, 20–21; stage 2, 22; stage 3, 24–25; START Treaty and, 2, 27–28; tools, 28
Monnet, Jean, 346, 347
Montreal Protocol, 462
Moscow, 454, 482
Moscow Nuclear Safety and Security Summit Declaration, 306
Moscow Treaty, xvii, 1, 18, 31, 37; Bilateral Implementation Commission and, 6n8; Bush, George W., and, 4, 6n8, 172; monitoring and verification with, 27; Putin and, 6n8, 172; reduction plans, 4, 5, 7–8, 21; warheads and, 5–6
MOX. *See* Mixed Oxide

MTCR. *See* Missile Technology Control Regime
multinational facilities, 324–25
Musharraf, Pervez, 415
Muslims, 456, 461
mutually assured destruction, 474

Nagasaki, 338
National Academy of Sciences (NAS), 162, 370, 487
National Ignition Facility (NIF), 375
National Intelligence Council, 490
National Security Strategy (Sept. 2002), 10
National Technical Means (NTM), 28, 167, 231–32
NATO. *See* North Atlantic Treaty Organization
The Netherlands, 152, 156t; uranium enrichment facilities in, 349n9
Nevada Test Site, 373
New Mexico, 325
*New York Times,* 427, 461
NIF. *See* National Ignition Facility
Nikitin, Mary Beth, 356n16
9/11, 165, 213; nuclear, 257; post, 247, 292
Nitze, Paul, 427
Nixon, Richard, 451, 475
NNWS. *See* Non-Nuclear Weapon States
Non-Nuclear Weapon States (NNWS), 187–92
Non-Proliferation Treaty (NPT), xxi, 160, 171, 314, 315, 322, 432, 475, 483
non-strategic nuclear weapons, 156t
Non-Weapons-Usable Low-Enriched Uranium (LEU), 256, 289
NORAD, 120
Norris, Robert S., 3n2, 7
North Atlantic Treaty Organization (NATO), xix; eliminating short-range nuclear weapons and, 117–20, 121–42, 143, 151; strategic concept changes, 117–18
North Korea, xvii, 32, 251, 272,

301n19; nuclear capabilities, 299n18, 452, 473, 475, 476; nuclear warheads in, 3; regional animosities in, 409–11; seismology test and, 379; tyrannical/erratic regime of, 410; violation of NPT, 405; world nuclear weapon stockpiles and, 209t
Northern Ireland, 460
NPT. *See* Non-Proliferation Treaty
NSG. *See* Nuclear Suppliers Group
NSP. *See* Nuclear Security Plan
NTI. *See* Nuclear Threat Initiative
NTM. *See* National Technical Means
nuclear attacks, 253–54
*Nuclear Black Markets: Pakistan, A. Q. Khan and the Rise of Proliferation Networks: A Net Assessment,* 250n8
nuclear deterrence; ballistic missile defense and, 454; China and, 452–53; CTR and, 453; dynamic concept of, 449–50; nuclear umbrella and, 453; Osirak reactor and, 451; other nuclear states and, 453; regional conflicts and, 451–52; rethinking, 449–54; Russia and, 450–51; task of, 450; terrorist organizations and, 450, 451, 453; tipping point and, 450
nuclear energy, expansion of, 321–22
nuclear explosive material, 161
nuclear forces; contribution to elimination and assessing reductions in, 15–18; criteria for assessing reductions in, 1, 12–18; current plans for reductions in, 4–8; feasible reductions in, 18–23; further reductions in, 1–45; going to zero deployed warheads and, 23–27; introduction, 2–3; making deep reductions in, 38–43; missile defenses and, 29–31; monitoring/verification and assessing reductions in, 1, 14–15; moving to abolition in, 44–45; number of warheads per state and, 38–40; other nuclear powers and, 2–3, 31–38; political/doctrinal context for substantial force reductions in, 8–12; strategic stability and assessing

reductions in, 1, 12–14; summary, 1–2; verification/monitoring and, 27–29; zero warheads operationally deployed and, 38–40

nuclear fuel cycle, 450; Asia and, 362–64; back-end, 315–16, 325–27, 350–53; complementary policies and, 356–57; conclusions and recommendations, 334–38; dilemmas, 338–40; enforcement, 364–67; first priority to front end of, 348–50; GNEP and, 335, 357–58; implications for U.S. policy and, 353–56; internationalizing, 333–68; Iran and, 360–62; Japan and, 363; key issues, 334; as major weakness of nonproliferation regime, 314; multinational enrichment facilities and, 358–60; nuclear renaissance and, 340–41; rejection of two-tier world and, 341–50; summary, 333–34; world without nuclear weapons and, 367–68

nuclear material; convention on physical protection of, 306; verification limits, stockpiles and accounting for, 274–77. *See also* fissile material

Nuclear Nonproliferation Treaty, 26

Nuclear Posture Review, 4, 5n5, 8–9, 10, 11

*Nuclear Power is Not the Answer* (Caldicott), 340n1

nuclear security; beyond, 271–72; deterrence and, 272; disrupt and, 271; interdict and, 271–72; prevent and, 272

Nuclear Security Plan (NSP), 195

nuclear states, deterrence and other, 453

nuclear stockpiles; at-risk, 248–49; background, 246–57; beyond nuclear security and, 271–72; building sustainability and strong security cultures, 266–68; China's, 32, 33n32; dismantlement and world, 209t; following through with job of, 272–74; global cleanout and, 268–71; global nuclear security standards and,

265–66; issues, 257–61; key judgments, 243–46; nuclear terrorism and, 243; obstacles to securing, 244; recommendations, 261–64; reduction since Cold War, 32; reductions, 171–77; securing worldwide, xx–xxi, 243–77; setting nuclear security standards with, 245–46, 371t; stewardship accomplishments, 371t; sustained leadership and, 244; theft prevention of, 243; threat urgency with, 244–45; transparent accounting of, 243; unacceptable risks with, 243–44; upgrading security with, 244; U.S.-funded programs to secure, 257f; verification limits, nuclear-material accounting and, 274–77; weapons, 372

Nuclear Suppliers Group (NSG), 333, 342, 343, 343n4, 477

nuclear terrorism, 391; adapting Nunn-Lugar and, 262–63; beyond nuclear security and, 271–72; building sense of urgency about, 263–64; Bush, G. W., 261–62, 273; data exchange and, 264; deterrence and, 450, 451, 453; fast-paced security reviews, 264; FMCT and, 292; global campaign to prevent, 261–64; global initiative to combat, 195, 257, 261–62; joint threat briefings, 263–64; nuclear stockpiles and, 243; Pakistan and, 250; prevention agenda, 251; Putin and, 262; realistic testing of security performance with, 264; shared databases of threats and incidents with, 264; terrorists and, 246n1, 456, 461; war games and exercises to combat, 264

nuclear theft, 222; difficulty stopping, 252–54; highest risk of, 249; ongoing reality of, 250–51; prevention, 243; recovered HEU and, 250; risk of accidental/unauthorized, 71–72, 78, 87, 92–93, 101; threat of, 248–49

Nuclear Threat Initiative (NTI), ix, xvi, 196, 266, 329

*Nuclear Threat Initiative Research Library: Securing the Bomb,* 247n2
nuclear umbrella, 453
nuclear warheads; Britain's, 3; China's, 3; counting rules and, 7; de-alerting options and relocating, 94–95; definition of, 1n1; deployed, 14; inventories, 173–77; monitoring, 229–42; monitoring deployed, 231–35; monitoring disassembly/dismantlement of, 241–42; monitoring non-deployed, 235–38; monitoring virtual, 238–41; on-site de-mating of, 87; reduction numbers of, 1–2, 19; responsive force and storage depots for, 93–95; verification and latency graduation life-cycle of, 175f; verification/monitoring of non-deployed, 15
Nuclear Weapon States (NWS), 170
nuclear weapons; background, 206–8, 431–34; chronic regional disputes and, 409–17; Cold War lessons and, 407–9; contribution to elimination of, 15–18, 21–27; countries with, 32–33, 453; criteria for assessing reductions and contribution to elimination of, 15–18; cultural differences and impact with, 406–7; dismantlement capacity of, 209–11; eliminating short-range, xix, 107–57; fissile-materials waste management and, 221–23; further reductions in, xvii; global nuclear inventories and, 436t; issues, 215–21, 435–39; joint enterprise for eradication of, 429–47; key judgments, 205–6, 429–31; non-strategic, 156t; number of, 208–9; options, 439–46; past discussions of verified dismantlement and related measures, 211–15; recommendations, 226–27, 446–47; regional animosities and proliferation of, 399–424; regional confrontations and proliferation of, xxiii–xxiv; resolution with, 441t; Russia, neighborhood and, 417–21; stage 1, contribution to

elimination of, 21–22; stage 2, contribution to elimination of, 22–23; stage 3, contribution to elimination of, 25–27; strategic and tactical warhead distinctions and, 223; summary conclusions, 399–404; transparency and secrecy balance and, 224; transparent and irreversible dismantlement of, 205–27; U.S. help with, 421–24; warhead and fissile-material reduction initiatives and, 225–26; why countries want war and, 404–6; world free of, 425–28; world stockpiles, 209t
the Nuclear Notebook, 3n2
numbers; of all nuclear warheads, 3; Moscow Treaty and current target, 1–2; nuclear weapons, 164f, 172, 208–9; reducing operationally deployed strategic nuclear warhead, 1–2, 19, 22; Russian short-range nuclear weapons, 157t; U.S. short-range nuclear weapons in Europe, 156t; world nuclear weapon stockpiles, 209t; world's nuclear warheads and peak, 2–3. *See also* counting rules; nuclear warheads
Nunn, Sam, ix, xv, xxiv, 235, 254, 346, 347, 425, 465, 470, 471, 473, 478, 479, 485
Nurgaliev, Rashid, 248
NWS. *See* Nuclear Weapon States

Oberdorfer, Don, 470, 478, 485
oil; cost per barrel, 341n2; dependency, 457; money, 416; primary five exporters of, 341n2; weapon, 451
On Site Inspections (OSI), 168, 231, 489
operationally deployed nuclear forces; responsive *vs.,* 4; U.S.'s definition of, 5
OSI. *See* On Site Inspections
Osirak reactor, 451
Oslo Conference, 344, 350n10
Ostpolitik, 410

Paine, Christopher, 276
Pakistan, xvii, xxi, 25n29, 256, 283,
  452, 453; nuclear policies, 35;
  nuclear stockpiles in, 33, 34; nuclear
  terrorists and, 250; nuclear threat risk
  and, 249; nuclear warheads in, 3;
  refusal to sign NPT, 405; regional
  animosities in, 414–15; secrecy with
  nuclear security cooperation and, 256;
  uranium enrichment facilities in,
  349n9; world nuclear weapon
  stockpiles and, 209t
Palestinians, 460; regional animosities
  in, 415–16
Panofsky, W.K.H., 1
Parillo, Jill Marie, 356n16
Perimeter and Portal Continuous
  Monitoring (PPCM), 231
periodic review, 390–91
Perle, Richard, 470
Perry, William J., xv, 235, 253n11, 346,
  347, 431, 471, 473, 478, 479, 485
Persian Gulf War, 451
physical modifications; bomber
  warheads relocated, 94–95; de-
  alerting modifications and, 78–101;
  fostering nuclear-free world, 86–87,
  92, 100; illustrative Russian
  measures, 80–81; illustrative U.S.
  measures and, 78–80; land-based
  missile force (U.S.), 78–79;
  minuteman missiles, 88–89;
  responsive warhead force in warhead
  storage depots, 87, 93–95; risk of
  accidental/unauthorized/theft, 87, 92–
  93, 101; silo-based missiles (Russia),
  80–81; strategic stability, 83–85, 90–
  91, 96–98; submarine missiles
  (Russia), 81; submarine warheads to
  storage depots, 94; summary
  recommendation, 98–99; time to re-
  alert, 82–83, 89–90, 95–96;
  transparency and verifiability, 85–86,
  91–92, 99–100; trident submarine
  force (U.S.), 79–80
pit production, certification and, 373
pit-stuffing, 217, 219

Platte, James, 214n9
plutonium, 222, 242, 283n1, 314, 315;
  civil, 281, 286, 306, 307–8, 308n22;
  guidelines for the management of,
  309; reactor-grade, 286; separated,
  243. See also fissile material
Plutonium Management and Disposition
  Agreement, 308
PNI. See Presidential Nuclear Initiatives
Podvig, Pavel, 333, 471, 485
Poland, 148, 409
Postol, Theodore, 31n31
Potter, William C., 471, 485
Power, Colin, 5, 6, 458, 480; counting
  rules of START outlined by, 7
PPCM. See Perimeter and Portal
  Continuous Monitoring
Predictive Knowledge Systems, 191
Presidential Nuclear Initiatives (PNI),
  110, 141
Press, Daryl G., 423n4
procedural modifications; de-alerting
  options and, 72–78; dropping massive
  attack from strategic war plans, 73;
  dropping prompt launch from EWO,
  72–73; foster nuclear-free world, 77–
  78; impact on strategic stability, 77;
  keeping submarines out of reach, 73–
  76; risk of accidental/unauthorized/
  theft, 78; time to re-alert, 76;
  transparency and verifiability, 77
Proliferation Security Initiative, 475
Pu. See plutonium
Putin, Vladimir, 120, 418, 482; ballistic
  missile defense and, 454; joint
  statement from Bush, George W.,
  and, 8, 30n30; Moscow Treaty and,
  6n8, 172; nuclear terrorism and, 262;
  SORT and, 4'

al-Qaeda, xx, 162, 243, 247, 250, 254,
  413, 414

radiation detectors, 252
radionuclides, 377; monitoring
  sensitivity with, 383–84;

xenonisotopic anomaly predictions and, 383

Raisian, John, 465

ratification, 370t

reactors; appropriate, 328; Osirak, 451

*Reagan and Gorbachev: How the Cold War Ended* (Matlock), 490

Reagan, Nancy, 479

Reagan, Ronald, ix, xv, xix, xxiii, 345, 392, 413, 420, 422, 425, 428, 455, 462, 475, 476, 478, 479, 484, 491; administration, 449, 487; global verification regime and, 369; muscular diplomacy and, 408; offer to Gorbachev for shared defenses, 420n3

reductions; ban on short-range nuclear weapons for, 129–32; close-out activities and, 124; complicating factors, 134–37; confidence-building for, 123–26; contributions to elimination of nuclear weapons and, 15–18; cooperation on nuclear weapon safety and, 123–24; data exchange, 126–28; declassification/ unilateral declarations and, 126–27; European complication and, 132–34; history of problem, 143–45; making PNIs legally binding and, 129; momentum of new strategy and deployments with, 149–54; monitoring and verification, 14–15; negotiating new data exchange agreements and, 127–28; new unilateral steps with, 128–29; observation of personnel training, 125–26; past constraints, 146–49; renewing PNIs and, 127; short-range nuclear weapons, 122–37; site visits and, 124–25; strategic stability, 12–14; ways to do arms control and, 128–32

regional animosities; chronic disputes and, 409–17; Cold War and, 407–9; cultural differences influence on, 406–7; Iran, 411–14; Israel, 415–16; Lebanon, 415–16; North Korea, 409–11; nuclear weapons proliferation and, 399–424; other countries and, 416–17; Pakistan-India, 414–15; Palestine, 415–16; Russia, surrounding areas, nuclear weapons and, 417–21; summary conclusions, 399–404; Syria, 415–16; U.S. help with, 421–24; why countries want nuclear weapons, 404–6

regional conflicts, 451–52

Reliable Replacement Warhead program, 376

"Report of the Commission of Eminent Persons on the Future of Agency," 365n25

reprocessing, xxi; appropriate reactors and, 328; assurances of reliable supply of fuel with, 328; background and, 314–21; conditions/rights/ beneficiary commitments and, 322–24; elements of solution for, 327–31; financing and, 330; fissile material and, 313; fuel cycle's back end and, 315–16; GNEP and, 316; IAEA director general's report and, 319–20; infrastructure assistance and, 330; international uranium enrichment center at Angarsk, 317–18; issues, 321–31; key judgments, 313–14; multinational facilities and, 324–25; NITI proposed reserve and, 318; nuclear energy expansion and, 321–22; preventing spread of enrichment and, 313–31; spent fuel management and, 330; U.S.-Russia declaration on nuclear energy and nonproliferation with, 320–21; WNA proposal and, 319

responsive nuclear forces, operationally deployed *vs.,* 4

Reykjavik Revisited II Conference, xv, 2, 200; conference agenda, 465–66; conference participants, 466–72; opening remarks, 425–28; Reagan and Gorbachev at, 475, 476; "World Free of Nuclear Weapons," 473–78;

"World Free of Nuclear Weapons: What to Do Now," 479–86
Rhodes, Richard, 471, 485
Rice, Condoleezza, 4, 4n3, 6, 27, 434
Richter, Burton, 333, 352n13
Ridgway, Rozanne, 478
road-mobile missiles, 80
Robinson, Peter, 471
Rocca, Christina, 282
Rocky Flats Plant, 373
Rohlfing, Joan, 1, 47, 471, 485
Rokkasho reprocessing facility, 286
Roosevelt, Theodore, 460
Rosatom, 255
Rothwell, Geoffrey, 333, 343n5, 344n6
Rowen, Henry S., 47, 333, 341n3, 455, 471, 478, 485, 490
Rumsfeld, Donald, 147n23
Russia, xvii, xix, 350, 403n2, 483; boycott of Georgian goods, 419; civil plutonium in, 308n22; civil plutonium reprocessing in, 281; controlling fissile materials worldwide and, 279–311; criteria for assessing reductions with U.S. and, 12–18; current plans for reduction, 4–8; de-altering strategic forces, 47–105; eliminating short-range nuclear weapons designed to be forward deployed and, 107–57; further reductions in nuclear forces between U.S. and, 1–45; illustrative measures and de-alerting options in, 80–81, 93–94; internationalizing nuclear fuel cycle and, 333–68; monitoring nuclear warheads and, 229–42; "mutual understanding" between US and, 287; nuclear deterrence and, 450–51; nuclear security in, 249; nuclear threat risk and, 249; nuclear warheads in, 3; nuclear warheads in U.S. and, 1, 2; nuclear weapons and neighborhood around, 417–21; numbers of nuclear weapons in, 208; political/doctrinal context for substantial force reductions for U.S. and, 8–12; preventing spread of enrichment/reprocessing and, 313–31; regional animosities, nuclear weapons proliferation and, 399–424; road-mobile missiles and, 80–81; securing nuclear stockpiles worldwide and, 243–77; short-range nuclear weapons and, 120–22, 157t; silo-based missiles and, 80; starting with feasible reductions, 18–23; submarine missiles and, 81; submarines, 379; transparent/irreversible dismantlement of nuclear weapons in, 205–27; two operational (dis)assembly facilities in, 210, 211; uranium enrichment facilities in, 349n9; world nuclear weapon stockpiles and, 209t
"Russia's Tactical Nuclear Weapons," 156t
Ryabev, Lev, 206

Saakashvili, Mikheil, 419
"Safeguarding Reprocessing Facilities: The Impact of Multinationalization," 352n13
Safeguards, Transparency, and Irreversibility (STI), 212
Sagan, Scott, 471, 485
Sagdeev, Roald Z., 472, 478, 485
SALT. See Strategic Arms Limitations Treaty
Samson, Victoria, 157t
San Onofre Nuclear Generating Station, 194
Sandia National Laboratory, 194
satellites, 57, 382; Kara Sea earthquake and, 385; monitoring sensitivity with imagery from, 384–85
Saudi Arabia, 341n2
Scheinman, Larry, 333, 344n6, 352n13
Schell, Jonathan, 44n40
Schwarzenegger, Arnold, 482
Seabees, 459
secrecy, 244; enrichment facilities, 296; networks operating under, 348; nuclear security/cooperation with Pakistan shrouded in, 256; transparency, dismantlement and, 224

*Securing the Bomb* (Bunn, M.), 246n1
security; actions enhancing, 393t; benefits, 387–88; nuclear, 271–72; standards, 265–66; upgrading, 244 U.S., 369–98
seismology, 377; monitoring sensitivity with, 379–81; North Korean test, 379; tests on land and in water, 379–80
Semmel, Andy, 333
September 11, 2001. *See* 9/11
Serbia, 419
Sevastopulo, Demetri, 147n23
Shalikashvili, John (general), 370, 371, 390
Shannon, Gerald, 281
Shlyapuzhnikov, Sergey (general), 249
short-range nuclear weapons; arms control and reductions with, 128–29; background materials, 143–54; ban on, 129–30; close-out activities and, 124; complicating factors and, 134–37; concluding recommendations, 137–43; confidence-building and, 123–26; cooperation on safety with, 123–24; data exchange and, 126–28; declassification/unilateral declarations and, 126–27; toward eliminating, 117–22; eliminating forward-deployed designed, 107–57; European complication with, 132–34; history of problem, 143–45; introduction, 113–17; make PNIs legally binding and, 129; momentum of new strategy and deployments with, 149–54; NATO and, 117–20; negotiating new data exchange agreement and, 127–28; observation of personnel training and, 125–26; options for controls and reductions with, 122–37; past constraints, 146–49; renew PNIs and, 127; returning to reduction agenda with, 115–17; road to eliminating, 137–43; Russia and, 120–22; Russian, 157t; site visits and, 124–25; summary of conclusions, 107–13; U.S. weapons in Europe, 156t

Shultz, George P., ix, xv, 47, 235, 333, 345, 346, 347, 408, 425, 431, 455, 465, 472, 473, 477, 478, 479, 485, 488, 490–91
Siemens, 355n15
silo-based missiles, 80
Simpson, John, 131n16
Six Party Talks, 301n19
SLBMs, 5
Sofaer, Abraham, 472, 478, 485
Solomon, Richard, 472, 485
SORT. *See* Strategic Offensive Reductions Treaty
South Africa, 322, 385; voluntary dismantlement of nuclear program, 405
South Asia; conflict resolution before elimination of nuclear weapons in, 35; regional conflicts, 451, 452
South Korea, 209n3, 452
South Ossetia, 419
Spanel, Margaret R., 47
specialized sensors, 168
Squassoni, Sharon, 356n16
stage 1, nuclear reduction, 1; contribution to elimination, 21–22; monitoring and verification, 20–21; strategic stability, 20
stage 2, nuclear reduction, 2; contribution to elimination, 22–23; monitoring and verification, 22; strategic stability, 22
stage 3, going to zero deployed warhead; contribution to elimination, 25–27; monitoring and verification, 24–25; strategic stability, 23–24
stage 4, bringing in other nuclear powers, further reductions in nuclear forces, 31–38
stage 4, variant 1, further reductions in nuclear forces, 38–40
Stalin, Joseph, 490
START Treaty. *See* Strategic Arms Reduction Treaty
Steinbruner, John, 47
stewardship, 372

STI. *See* Safeguards, Transparency, and
Irreversibility
stockpiles. *See* nuclear stockpiles
Strategic Arms Limitations Treaty
(SALT), 229
Strategic Arms Reduction Treaty
(START), 2, 31, 213, 232, 488; Bush
and, 6, 27; counting rules, Powell
and, 7; deployed warheads and, 14;
expiration date, 6, 26, 159, 234;
monitoring and verification with, 27–
28, 143; possible arrangement for
post, 6; reduction plans, 5, 6–7, 21
strategic forces, xvii–xviii; baseline
posture and, 56–69; de-alerting, 47–
105; de-alerting options and
evaluation criteria, 69–101;
evaluation criteria and, 69–101;
implications and concluding thoughts,
101–5; introduction, 53–55; key
findings and judgments, 47–53
Strategic Offensive Reductions Treaty
(SORT); Bush and, 4; current plans,
4, 6, 234; expiration date, 6; Putin
and, 4
strategic stability; balance and, 13;
criteria for assessing reductions and,
12–14; political context of, 13–14;
stage 1, 20; stage 2, 22; stage 3, 23–
24
strategies; momentum of new
deployments and, 149; verification's
framework and, 165–200
strength, 461
submarine missiles, 81
submarines, 57, 379; de-alerting options
and, 73–76, 79–80; missiles, 81;
trident force, 79–80; warheads to
storage depots, 94
"Suggestions for Progressing the Fissile
Material Cutoff Treaty," 298n17
supplier states, 323–24
Syria, regional animosities in, 415–16

tactical nuclear weapons, 156t
Taiwan, 452
Taliban, 258n15, 413, 415

technology security, 325
Tehran, 451
template approach, 219
Tenet, George, 247, 247n3
tensions, 455; nuclear weapons and,
455–56
terrorists, 246n1, 456, 461; Aum
Shinrikyo, 243, 254; global effects of
nuclear attacks by, 253–54; global
initiative to combat nuclear, 257;
martyrdom and, 453; non-state, 473,
474; nuclear, xx, 52, 162, 243,
246n1, 247, 248, 249, 250, 251, 253–
54, 257, 258n15, 261–62, 273, 413,
414, 450, 451, 453, 456, 461, 473,
474; nuclear deterrence and, 450,
451, 453; organizations, 450, 451,
453; al-Qaeda, xx, 162, 243, 247,
250, 254, 413, 414; reconnaissance of
nuclear storage sites by, 249; state
transfers to, 251–52; Taliban, 258n15,
414, 415. *See also* nuclear terrorism
Thomson, John, 360, 361, 364
Thornton, Charles, 113n1, 114n2,
123n11, 145n22, 156t, 157t
Timbie, James, 131n14, 313, 466, 472,
491
tipping point, 348, 450
Toshiba, 363
transparency; de-alerting options and,
71, 77, 85–86, 91–92, 99–100;
dismantlement, secrecy and, 224
Treaty of Almelo, 359
Treaty of Tlatelolco, 405
Trezza, Carlo, 293
Trilaterial Initiative (1996), 15, 230,
307
Truman, Harry S., 428
tsunamis, 382
Tunguska explosion, 382
Turkey, 152, 156t
*The Twilight of Sovereignty* (Wriston),
458
two-tier system, 367; Bush, George W.,
and, 341; rejection of, 341–50

Ukraine, 150, 403n2, 488

UN Security Council, 457, 458
UNGA. *See* United National General
Assembly
United Kingdom, 156t; civil plutonium
reprocessing in, 281; policy and
recent developments, 433–34;
uranium enrichment facilities in,
349n9; world nuclear weapon
stockpiles and, 209t. *See also* Britain
United National General Assembly
(UNGA), 280
United Nations Monitoring, Verification
and Inspection Commission
(UNMOVIC), 28, 229
United Nations Security Council
Resolution 1540, xxi, 265, 482
United Nations Special Commission
(UNSCOM), 28, 229
United States, xvii; civil plutonium in,
308n22; comprehensive nuclear-test-
ban treaty and security in, 369–98;
controlling fissile materials worldwide
and, 279–311; criteria for assessing
reductions with Russia and, 12–18;
current plans for reduction, 4–8; de-
alerting strategic forces, 47–105;
deterrent sustaining in, 371–76;
diplomacy for future, 455–64;
dismantlement rates, 210; further
reductions in nuclear forces between
Russia and, 1–45; illustrative
measures, 78–80, 93–94;
internationalizing nuclear fuel cycle
and, 333–68; monitoring nuclear
warheads and, 229–42; Moscow
Treaty and, 5; "mutual
understanding" between Russia and,
287; nuclear warheads in, 1, 2, 3;
nuclear warheads in Russia and, 1, 2;
nuclear weapons and help from, 421–
24; numbers of nuclear weapons in,
208–9; political/doctrinal context for
substantial force reductions for Russia
and, 8–12; preventing spread of
enrichment/reprocessing and, 313–31;
regional animosities, nuclear weapons
proliferation and, 399–424; rethinking

nuclear deterrence and, 449–54;
securing nuclear stockpiles worldwide
and, 243–77; short-range nuclear
weapons in Europe, 156t; sole
operational (dis)assembly facility in,
210, 211; starting with feasible
reductions, 18–23; transparent/
irreversible dismantlement of nuclear
weapons in, 205–27; uranium
enrichment facilities in, 349n9; world
nuclear weapon stockpiles and, 209t
universal latency, verification and
compliance with, 159–203
UNMOVIC. *See* United Nations
Monitoring, Verification and
Inspection Commission
UNSCOM. *See* United Nations Special
Commission
uranium, 313, 314, 315; centrifuge
technology for enriching, 340;
enrichment facilities worldwide,
347n7, 349n9. *See also* fissile
material
Urenco, 359

Venezuela, 341n2
verification; compliance and, xix–xx;
compliance with universal latency
and challenges of, 159–203;
comprehensive framework and
strategies for, 165–200; countries
and, 177; CTBT and, 369, 377–85;
de-alerting options and, 71, 77, 85–
86, 91–92, 99–100; executive
summary, 159–63; fissile material and
limits of, 274–77; infrasound, 381–
83; introduction, 163–65; latency
graduation life-cycle of nuclear
warhead, 175f; monitoring sensitivity
and, 379–85; monitoring with low-
yield threshold, 378–79; radionuclide
method, 377; radionuclides and, 383–
84; satellite imagery, 384–85; seismo-
acoustic method, 377; seismology,
hydro-acoustics and, 379–81; space
and, 200–202; Wiesner Curve and,

164f. *See also* monitoring and
  verification
verification strategies; chain of custody,
  181–82; comprehensive framework
  for, 165–200; credible response
  capabilities and, 197–200; data
  exchange and encryption, 177–79;
  FMCI and, 193–97; latency
  graduation, 175f; new arms control
  *vs.* traditional notions, 165–71;
  NNWS and, 187–92; perimeter-portal
  continuous monitoring, 182–85;
  return to protocol, 172–73; on site
  inspections, 179–80; stockpile
  reductions and, 171–77; virtual
  stockpiles, 185–87; warhead
  inventories and, 173–77
Verkhovtsev, Vladimir (general), 133
Virtual Abolition of Nuclear Arsenals,
  166
Von Hippel, Frank, 47, 333

W76, 373, 373n1
*Wall Street Journal,* ix, xv, xvi, xvii,
  235, 345, 347, 433; commentary,
  431–32, 436, 437, 438
Waller, Douglas C., 56n1
war games, 264
Warhead Safety and Security
  Agreement (WSSX), 109, 123–24,
  127, 139
warheads. *See* nuclear warheads
Warsaw Pact, 403, 417
weapons; biological, 450; chemical,

450; of mass destruction, 248, 450;
  oil, 451; stockpile, 372
Westinghouse, 363
Wetsel, Hubert, 147n23
White Paper; British, 25n29; Chinese
  2006, 33n32
Wier, Anthony, 247n2, 253n10
Wiesner Curve, verification and, 164f
Wiesner, Jerome, 163, 164f
Wilson, Peter A., 166
WINS. *See* World Institute of Nuclear
  Security
WNA. *See* World Nuclear Association
women, 461
World Association of Nuclear
  Operators, 161, 266
World Institute of Nuclear Security
  (WINS), 196, 266
World Nuclear Association (WNA),
  319, 352n12
World Security Institute, 487
World Trade Organization, 347n7, 419
Wriston, Walter, 458
WSSX. *See* Warhead Safety and
  Security Agreement

Xue, Litai, 34n33

Yeltsin, Boris, 68, 143, 213

Zelikow, Philip D., 472, 485
zero; deployed warheads, 23–27, 31–32,
  37, 38–40; operation, 163, 165, 426;
  option, 41, 172, 199